Building and Sustaining Meaningful and Effective Relationships as a Supervisor and Mentor

Linda A. LeBlanc, Ph.D., BCBA-D
LeBlanc Behavioral Consulting

Tyra P. Sellers, Ph.D., BCBA-D
Behavior Analysis Certification Board

Shahla Ala'i, Ph.D., BCBA-D
University of North Texas

2020
Sloan Publishing
Cornwall on Hudson, NY 12520

Library of Congress Control Number: 2020942156

Cover photo: ID 108373514 @ Denis Churin Dreamstime.com

© 2020 by Sloan Publishing, LLC

Sloan Publishing, LLC
220 Maple Road
Cornwall-on-Hudson, NY 12520

All rights reserved. No portion of this book may be reproduced, in any form or by any means, without permission in writing from the Publisher.

Printed in the United States of America

10 9 8 7 6 5 4 3

ISBN 13: 978-1-59738-120-8 pbk
ISBN 13: 978-1-59738-123-9 cb

Praise from Reviewers…

Having worked as a professional in the fields of education and behavior analysis for over 20 years, I've learned the value of effective supervision and mentorship. The methods for achieving competency in these areas are all in this book—bi-directionality, centrality of relationships, self-reflection and more. The information presented in this work is relevant and necessary, and a must-read for anyone seeking to improve upon their repertoire of mentorship and supervisory capabilities in the field of behavior analysis and related disciplines.
—Nasiah Cirincione-Ulezi, Ed.D., BCBA

In their book, Drs. LeBlanc, Sellers, and Ala'i masterfully combine personal stories, best-practices informed by existing research, and practical tools for supervisors. They provide a model for compassionate supervision every behavior analyst should strive to incorporate in their practice. The activities and resources offered at the end of each chapter are aimed at developing a thoughtful and effective supervisory practice. These can be especially useful for behavior analysts beginning their journey as supervisors and mentors. This book provides many ready-to-use tools that can be easily incorporated into supervisory practice and in graduate training to ensure future behavior analysts are well equipped to embark on this important role. Although there are many gems throughout the book, I particularly enjoyed the chapter exploring the impact of culture, which includes activities for identifying the supervisor's place of privilege and perspective—an area often overlooked in our field. This is an aspirational read that allows the reader to set clear, attainable goals as they strive to become the supervisors these authors model in their own work. May we all embody a bit of Linda, Tyra, and Shahla in our own role as supervisors!
—Corina Jimenez-Gomez, Ph.D., BCBA-D, LBA

This book is a must-have purchase for any professional engaged in behavior-analytic supervision. It summarizes relevant content for a competency-based approach to supervision, which is necessary for a book on this topic. What impressed me most was the emphasis on cultural awareness and responsiveness supplemented by immediately actionable steps readers can adopt to build their cultural repertoires. In addition, the book tackles critical areas, such as interpersonal and problem-solving skills, which are not discussed enough in the behavior-analytic literature. This book should be required reading for supervisors and mentors, supervisors in training, BCBA aspirants, and graduate students.
—Florence D. DiGennaro Reed, Ph.D., BCBA-D

LeBlanc, Sellers, and Ala'i provide an invaluable resource for those who aspire to supervise and mentor in our field. With an emphasis placed on the importance of establishing and sustaining strong relationships, the authors' approach toward effective supervision and mentorship is based on their collective experiences and conceptually sound training and supervision practices. This thoughtful and compassionate approach not only prepares behavior analysts for effective supervision and mentorship in their early years, but also encourages ongoing professional growth so that one may continue to develop as a supervisor and mentor throughout their career. My graduate students and I found the content easily consumable and we thoroughly enjoyed the reflection activities and the group discussions they generated. I am confident that this resource will positively influence the nature of supervision delivery in our practice and, as a result, will have a meaningful impact on our field and those it aims to serve.
—Adam M. Briggs, PhD, BCBA-D, LBA

Contents

Preface   vii
Acknowledgements   ix
About the Authors   x

Section 1: Developing a Positive Approach to Supervising and Mentoring   1

1. An Introduction to Supervision and Mentoring as Relationships   3
   Definitions and Roles   5
   Evolving Relationships   8
       Activity 1: Identifying Your Supervisory Relationships   12
       Activity 2: Current and Past Roles   13

2. Starting Strong in a Collaborative Supervisory Relationship   14
   Strategies for Starting Strong   16
       Activity: Exploring Collaboration Topics   24
       Appendix: How to Talk About Feedback   26

3. Understanding Past and Current Supervisory and Mentored Relationships   28
   Reflection and Values Determination   31
   The Mentor Tree Activity   33
   Examples from the Authors   34
   Planning for Continued Development   36
   Summary   37
       Activity 1: The Mentor Tree   40
       Activity 2: Planning for Continued Development   42

iii

4. The Impact of Culture on Supervisory Relationships   42
   Collaboration as a Supervisory Strategy   43
   Behavior Analysis and Culture   44
   Opportunities for Learning   47
   Pathways to Cultural Responsiveness   54
       Activity 1: Cultural Awareness Interviews   58
       Activity 2: Exploring Your Place of Privilege   60
       Activity 3: Exploring Your Perspective   61
       Activity 4: Community of Practice Assessment   62
       Activity 5: Cultural Satisfaction Survey for Employees and Supervisees   64

Section 2: Teaching Meaningful Repertoires   67

5. Using a Competency-Based Approach to Supervision   69
   Considerations for a Competency-Based Curriculum   70
   Determining Scope of Content and Skills   71
   Addressing Ethics   74
   Job Models and Curriculum   75
   Determining Mastery Criteria   78
   Considerations for Assessing Performance   81
   On-Going Assessments   82
   Considerations for Teaching Content   83
       Appendix A: Tracking Competencies   91
       Appendix B: Examples for Assessing Competency   92
       Appendix C: Script for Explaining Feedback and Responding to Feedback   94

6. The Benefits of Learning from Experts and Self-Managing Development   96
   Considerations for Identifying an Expert   98
   Considerations for Teaching Effective Observing   101
   Considerations for Teaching Effective Self-Observation and Reflection   103
   Teaching Self-Management for Long-Term Success   107
   Considering Communities of Practice as Long-Term Supports   111
       Appendix A: Observational Learning Self-Checklist   113
       Appendix B: Self-Management Planning   114

7. Structured Problem Solving Skills   116
   Definitions: Problems and Problem-Solving   117
   A Structured Approach to Problem-Solving   120
   Problem Solving in the Supervisory Process   133

Appendix A: Problem Solving Worksheet   134
Appendix B: Assessing Common Difficulties with Problem Solving   136

8. Organizational and Time Management Skills   140
   OTM Skills   142
   Appendix A: Sample Task Plan for Completing an Assessment Report   155
   Appendix B: Agenda for Initial Supervision Session   158
   Appendix C: Sample Agenda for Client Session   159
   Appendix D: Assessing Organization and Time Management Issues   161

9. Interpersonal and Therapeutic Relationship Skills   164
   Core Interpersonal Skills   166
   Communication Skills   166
   Noticing and Self-Reflection Skills   170
   Perspective-Taking Skills   171
   Compromising and Harmonizing Skills   173
   Integrity   175
   Applying the Core Skills in Different Contexts   176
   Peer Workplace Relationships   177
   Multi-Disciplinary Collaboration   178
   Therapeutic Relationships with Clients and Families   180
   Appendix A: Therapeutic Relationship Self-Evaluation   186
   Appendix B: Assessing Difficulties with Interpersonal Skills and Therapeutic Relationships   193

Section 3: Evaluating Supervision and Building Career Resilience   195

10. Evaluating the Effects of Supervision   197
    Evaluating Effects Using Data from the Client   199
    Evaluating the Effects Using Data from the Supervisee   201
    Evaluating the Effects Using Data from Caregivers and Others   205
    Evaluating the Effects Using Data from the Supervisor   206
    Appendix A: General "Check-In" Questions   207
    Appendix B: Supervision Monitoring and Evaluation Form   209

11. Identifying and Resolving Problems in the Supervisory Relationship   212
    Detecting Issues: Looking for Smoke   214
    Detecting Indicators in the Supervisee's Behavior   214
    Detecting Indicators of Problems in the Supervisory Relationship in Your Own Behavior   216

Evaluating and Addressing Contributors to the Issue   217
Supervisor Self-Evaluation   219
Addressing Issues   221
    Case Example 1—Multitasking while Supervising   222
    Case Example 2—A Supervisor's Harsh Feedback   223
    Case Example 3—A Supervisee's Immaturity   224
Ending the Supervisory Relationship   226
Conclusion   227
    Appendix A: Looking for Smoke: Detecting Indicators of Issues in the Supervisory Relationship   228
    Appendix B: Considerations to Determine Scope and Focus of the Issue   230
    Appendix C: Self-Reflection on Supervisory Practices   231
    Appendix D: Self Reflection on Personal History and Biases   232

12. Planning for a Sustained Career and Lifelong Growth   234
Transitioning into Your Career   235
Know Your Values and Reinforcers and Maintain Access to Them   237
Preventing and Addressing Burnout   241
Summary and Recommended Strategies for Sustained Career Engagement and Enjoyment   245
    Appendix: Recommended Practices for Career Resilience and Enjoyment   246
    Activity A: Identifying Your Preferred Work Activities   248
    Activity B: Identifying Your Personal Reinforcers   249

13. Failures and Successes Are Teachers   251
Conclusion   258

References   261
Appendix I: BACB 5th Edition Task List   273
Appendix II: BACB Supervisory Training Outline 2.0   281
Appendix III: BACB 5th Edition Task List Self-Assessment   295
Appendix IV: Additional Resources   301
Name Index   317
Subject Index   325

Preface

The field of behavior analysis is growing rapidly in response to the demand for services. The Behavior Analyst Certification Board® (BACB®) reported the demand for behavior analysts in the US from 2010 to 2017 increased by 800 percent (BACB, 2018a). From 1999 to 2019, the number of board certified behavior analysts (i.e., BCaBA®, BCBA®, BCBA-D®) grew from 28 to just over 34,000. The number of Registered Behavioral Technicians™ (RBT™) grew from 328 in 2014 to over 60,000 in 2019 (BACB, 2019). This rapid growth increases the need for effective and efficient supervisory practices. Many behavior analysts receive little to no explicit instruction and mentoring in supervision practices during their training. Those behavior analysts then go on to provide supervision for others soon after graduation and certification, creating vulnerability for the field. A recent report from the Behavior Analyst Certification Board (BACB) indicates that the most common actionable ethical violation against BACB certificants is improper or inadequate supervision or delegation of responsibilities (BACB, 2018b).

In response to the growing need for qualified supervisors, the BACB added an explicit requirement for training in supervision practices (i.e., the eight-hour training) following certification, but before supervising others pursuing certification. The BACB provides guidelines covering the timing, documentation, content, and structure of the supervision. In 2019, the BACB instituted a one year delay requirement before new BCBAs can supervise others pursuing the BCaBA or BCBA credential or practicing BCaBAs unless they are supervised by a qualified supervisor (BACB, *March 2018 Newsletter*). Finally, as of 2022, the coursework requirements will include 30 hours of instruction in "personnel supervision and management" (BACB, *January 2017 Newsletter*). However, these requirements and guidelines represent only a starting point for the form and structure of supervision, rather than a full exploration of the functional components that are likely to produce well-trained young professional behavior analysts (LeBlanc & Luiselli, 2016). A supervisor could meet each entry requirement and follow each guideline but still be perceived as a disengaged, disorganized, or harsh supervisor. Much like a contagious virus, those who have been supervised by a poor supervisor often become poor supervisors themselves. The negative pay-forward may occur due to imitation of the previous supervisor's actions or lack of other skills, even if the prior supervisor's actions are recognized as a non-exemplar.

This book covers entry-level and advanced functional components of supervision. Those functional components include strategies for initiating and maintaining professional relationships, higher-order skills that should be targeted in supervision, and strategies for teaching critical practice and supervision repertoires and managing ongoing supervisee performance. The book focuses on effectively including and celebrating people from diverse cultural backgrounds and life experiences (e.g., race, ethnicity, gender identity). Our goal is to provide a conceptually sound set of supervision practices that can guide the actions of those who aspire to effect lifelong positive change in those they are supervising or mentoring.

The book is intended for those who are in graduate training (i.e., are being supervised) and are likely to supervise others (e.g., RBTs, aspiring BCBAs) in the near future. The material in this book may help them develop a greater understanding of their ongoing supervision experience and decide which aspects of their supervision experiences they want to integrate into their future professional selves and which parts they want to discard. This book is also intended for those who are already supervising and mentoring others, perhaps for a few months or even for many years. The material in this book may help them reflect on the strategies that they have been using and how those actions were shaped by their prior experiences. Hopefully, it will give seasoned supervisors some additional perspective or new ideas, and reinforce their already strong repertoires.

A supervisor may find it beneficial to revisit this resource in its entirety many times throughout their career. The new supervisor may take away different key points than an experienced supervisor, but each should find something useful that helps them anchor or re-anchor their supervisory practices to their ultimate goals of professional growth and contribution to the field. Similarly, the same person may take away different nuanced messages each time the material is revisited. A supervisor may reread the whole book, or might go back to a specific section because that information is relevant to what is happening in the supervisory relationship at that point. Being an effective supervisor and mentor to young professionals is akin to yoga or a martial art, in that you never achieve perfect balance, perfect mastery, or perfect supervision. Any supervisor can have a bad day, but a good supervisor will quickly recognize that fact and take specific action to minimize any negative effects for the supervisee. The joy and fulfillment provided by guiding and teaching others comes from the fact that the experience changes you and helps you grow. We have selected the artwork throughout the book to reflect the themes of nature, growth, and nurturing. As authors, we have learned and grown from the experience of writing this book and we hope others will learn and grow from the experiences of reading it or using it as a tool to teach others.

ACKNOWLEDGEMENTS

We would like to acknowledge Katelyn Rindlisbaker for her drawings of the Mentor Tree, Codey Carr and Jim Carr for their assistance with the author index, Cooper Sellers for creating social media marketing materials, April Linden and Sarah Sommers for their assistance with the references, subject index, and additional resources, and Dr. Heather McGee (Western Michigan University), Dr. Ellie Kazemi (California State University, Northridge), and Dr. Ben N. Witts (St. Cloud State University) for their helpful reviews of the manuscript as it was being prepared.

We would also like to acknowledge the following scholars who generously gave permission for us to reprint their wonderful work: Bridget Taylor, Melissa Nosik, Keith Allen, Shannon Biagi, Becca Tagg, Laura Turner, Aaron Fischer, and Jim Luiselli.

About the Authors

Linda A. LeBlanc, Ph.D., BCBA-D, Licensed Psychologist is the President of LeBlanc Behavioral Consulting. Her 25-year career has included academic positions at Claremont McKenna College, Western Michigan University, and Auburn University as well leadership positions in human services organizations. She established LeBlanc Behavioral Consulting in 2017 and consults to technology companies, universities, and behavior analytic human service organizations. Her research interests include behavioral treatment of autism, technology-based behavioral interventions, supervision and mentorship, leadership, and systems development in human services.

Tyra P. Sellers, J.D., Ph.D., BCBA-D is the Director of Ethics at the Behavior Analyst Certification Board. During her career she has held leadership positions in clinical service agencies, owned her own consulting company, and worked as an Assistant Professor at Utah State University. Her professional and research interests focus on professional ethics, training, supervision and mentoring, assessment and treatment of severe problem behavior, and variability.

Shahla Alai, Ph.D., BCBA-D, LBA is an Associate Professor in the Department of Behavior Analysis at the University of North Texas. Her teaching and research activities focus on community and interdisciplinary collaborations to support the needs of under resourced children and families. Shahla teaches courses in technology transfer, ethics, autism intervention, parent training, behavioral systems, applied research methods, behavior change techniques, and assessment. She serves on several community and disciplinary boards and committees, all dedicated to improving inclusive and culturally responsive practice and supervision in behavior analysis.

Linda LeBlanc dedicates this book to:
Jim and Codey Carr for their support and love;
Her mentors for teaching her about the important things and how to do them;
Her undergraduate and graduate students for teaching her how to supervise;
and
The Trumpet Behavioral Health team for teaching her how to lead.

Tyra Sellers dedicates this book to:
Adam, Maxwell, and Cooper Sellers for their continued support and patience;
Her mentors and co-authors for their never-ending kindness and instruction;
and
Every supervisee or trainee who was brave enough to take
the supervision journey with her.

Shahla Ala'i dedicates this book to:
Nadia, Emiliano and Penelope;
Nemat-jon, for setting a standard of supervision excellence and integrity;
and
Baha'u'llah, for illuminating the purpose of life and the importance of education.

Section One

Developing a Positive Approach to Supervising and Mentoring

The four chapters in this section focus on how to approach supervision and mentoring in a positive and constructive way.

Chapter 1 encourages behavior analysts to think about the supervisory process in the context of a relationship. This relationship is perhaps one of the most important and influential professional relationships that will ever exist for the supervisee. The terms *supervision, mentoring* and *sponsorship* are explored. Finally, the chapter explores the benefits of supervision activities for both the supervisor and supervisee and the evolution of healthy supervisory relationships.

Chapter 2 describes practical strategies for starting strong, collaborative supervisory relationships. The supervisory relationship should be predicated on clear expectations, effective communication, and appropriate positive contingencies to support the supervisee's skill development. The goal should be for the supervisee to view the supervisor as a resource for information and guidance, a provider of positive reinforcement, and a role model for professional behavior of all kinds.

Chapter 3 focuses on how past experiences can influence the current supervisory experience. The chapter guides the reader through reflection and goal-setting activities designed to assist the current supervisor or future supervisor in constructing their own purposeful and positive approach to supervising and mentoring others. The chapter discusses the importance of describing the beneficial and concerning influences on one's own learning history to increase the likelihood that positive supervisory strategies are imitated, while coercive ones are avoided whenever possible.

Finally, Chapter 4 addresses cultural issues in supervisory relationships. This chapter focuses on the benefits of cultural awareness and strategies for facilitating competence when a supervisor is supervising a trainee from a different cultural background.

Chapter 1

An Introduction to Supervision and Mentoring as Relationships

The supervision experience, at least for me... has sometimes involved sharing the best and the worst of times. So, if I was to summarize the supervision experience in one phrase, it would be 'a shared journey of discovery.'
—Dermot Barnes-Holmes (2018, p. 176)

Effective supervision is critical to the overall development of our field. It facilitates delivery of high-quality behavioral services and the professional development of both the supervisor and supervisee (LeBlanc & Luiselli, 2016). A Board Certified Behavior Analyst (BCBA) typically provides supervision for Registered Behavior Technicians (RBTs) and Board Certified Assistant Behavior Analysts (BCaBAs) who assist with the delivery of behavioral services for clients. BCBAs also supervise those who aspire to become BCBAs who may or may not already have the RBT or BCaBA credential, referred to as *trainees* by the BACB. We use the term "supervisee" throughout the book.

The Behavior Analyst Certification Board (BACB) specifies that there are several key purposes of supervision (BACB, 2020). First, the supervisor guides the actions of the less experienced supervisee and increases the quality of services and client outcomes. Second, supervision improves and maintains the skills of the supervisees in areas relevant to the field of practice. These two goals indicate that the supervisor should be engaged in direct training and performance management of the supervisee's current performance (Reid, Parsons, & Green, 2012). Third, supervision should develop the behavior-analytic, professional, and ethical repertoires of the trainee. Fourth, supervision should guide behavioral case conceptualization, problem solving, decision making, and assistance seeking of the supervisee. In other words, the supervisor is teaching the supervisee how to think about cases and how to design interventions. Finally, supervision serves as a critical opportunity to model effective supervision practices for the supervisee who will undoubtedly soon be supervising others. These last three goals are most critical when the supervisee is pursuing the BCBA credential, as the supervisor is training the individual for their professional responsibilities as an independent, practicing behavior analyst.

> **Key Purposes of Supervision**
> 1. Guiding actions to ensure high-quality services and desired client outcomes
> 2. Improving and maintaining clinical skills
> 3. Developing behavior-analytic, professional, and ethical repertoires
> 4. Building behavioral case conceptualization, problem solving, decision making, and assistance seeking repertoires
> 5. Modeling high quality supervisory practices

The multiple purposes of supervision illustrate the gravity of the supervisory role and the opportunity afforded by that role. The supervisor is responsible for the current performance of the supervisee (e.g., RBTs) and may also be responsible for the development of all aspects of the supervisee's professional development. This includes the conceptual repertoire, assessment and treatment skills sets, ethical skill sets, overall values and professional behavior, and interpersonal and communication skills (Sellers, Valentino & LeBlanc, 2016). The supervisor has an opportunity to shape the repertoires of successful behavior analysts who produce meaningful and important behavior change for clients and who become representatives of the profession. The supervisor also serves the role of establishing professional values, coaching interpersonal skills, and shaping organizational and time management skills to facilitate future success after training. Once credentialed, a behavior analyst still benefits from supervision and mentoring from more experienced professionals. That supervisor can oversee their work and the quality of the supervision that they provide to others, helping them to continue to develop as a professional.

Once a supervisor fully recognizes the importance of their role, they will likely never again think of supervision as "the meeting I have on Tuesday morning." Effective supervision is far more than a meeting to address the basic requirements established by our credentialing body. Instead, supervision should be viewed as the opportunity to establish and maintain a meaningful, rewarding, sustained relationship that enhances the professional growth of both parties. When supervision is approached as a meaningful relationship, the *supervisor* often becomes viewed as a *mentor* either during or after the formal supervisory period is over. To understand the differences between supervisors and mentors, let's explore the definitions of each.

> *Supervision should be viewed as the opportunity to establish and maintain a meaningful, rewarding, sustained relationship that enhances the professional growth of both parties.*

Definitions and Roles

The dictionary defines *supervision* as the "act of overseeing, inspection" (http://www.merriam-webster.com/dictionary/citation). The terms "supervisor" and "supervision" have different meanings in different contexts and professions. In the business world, a supervisor is typically concerned with directing the performance of employees. That type of supervisor focuses on communicating what needs to be done and monitoring the "doing." That type of supervisor might never engage in direct training of employees, as they likely rely on a specialized trainer to fill that role. The term supervisor in the vernacular of business and industry is typically the person who provides feedback, evaluates the supervisee's performance and makes employment and compensation decisions (Clark, et al., 1985; Reid, et al., 2012). In human service employment settings, the supervisor has immediate oversight over the training, work activities, and performance monitoring of an employee (Reid et al., 2012). For the purposes of this book, supervisory activities include the following: 1) designing and delivering training; 2) monitoring and evaluating the supervisee's performance (and client outcomes); 3) providing guidance or direction on work processes such as goal setting and making data-based clinical decisions; and 4) evaluating the effects of the supervision.

Behavior analysts supervising those accruing supervised field-work experience or providing clinical services are responsible for "all facets of the undertaking" (Code 5.0, BACB, 2014). That is, the supervisor is ultimately responsible for the client outcomes as well as the supervisee's professional growth. In the field of ABA, BCBAs have many job responsibilities (e.g., managing a clinical caseload, conducting professional training, teaching courses, conducting research) in addition to supervising others. Some individuals may not feel prepared to provide supervision or may not find supervision activities enjoyable. We hope that readers will find strategies and approaches to increase their skills and, in doing so, find enjoyment in providing supervision.

> *Behavior analysts supervising those accruing supervised field-work experience or providing clinical services are responsible for "all facets of the undertaking" (Code 5.0, BACB, 2014).*

The dictionary defines a *mentor* as "a trusted counselor or guide" or "a coach"(http://www.merriam-webster.com/dictionary/citation). The term originated from a character in Homer's *Odyssey* named Mentor. Mentor served as the educator, counselor and guide to Telemachus, the son of his dear friend Odysseus. Later, the goddess Athena appears in the form of Mentor to guide Telemachus on his journey to find his father (Schwiebert, Deck, Bradshaw, Scott, & Harper, 1999). In modern terms, mentor refers to someone who is a positive, guiding influence in another person's life. The mentor typically has accrued life and professional experience that informs the guidance they provide throughout the course of their relationship with the mentee. Although every behavior analyst will have at least one supervisor and potentially additional faculty advisors and employment supervisors, not every aspiring professional has someone who fills the role of mentor.

These terms (i.e., *supervisor, mentor, manager*) seem to convey greater clarity and role distinction than is often evident in everyday experiences. Professions tend to approach these role distinctions somewhat differently (Salter & Gannon, 2015). Some suggest that a mentor should not be in the role of supervisor, allowing the mentor greater distance from the everyday workplace concerns of the supervisee and eliminating the direct responsibility for the supervisee's work performance (i.e., the management aspects). Some have distinguished between the roles of a *mentor* (i.e., offers advice and guidance to a mentee) and a *sponsor* (i.e., advocates for and facilitates opportunities and advancement for the protege) (Salter & Gannon, 2015).

We suggest that these terms and definitions are useful for enhancing our understanding of the important roles that people might play in our lives; however, these roles do not necessarily need to be filled by different people. The supervisor and supervisee may end the relationship after the direct oversight responsibilities are completed. Alternatively, a supervisor with a strong relationship with their supervisee may be a mentor as well as a supervisor. Their advice may be sought long after direct oversight ends. A person may have a trusted mentor who eventually assumes the role of supervisor *and* mentor in a new professional role. A sponsor is often a current or former supervisor or mentor. A person may be more likely to sponsor someone with whom they have a relationship that

> *A supervisor with a strong relationship with their supervisee may be a mentor, as well as a supervisor. Their advice may be sought long after direct oversight ends.*

Check Your Knowledge

Question 1: Which of the following has direct oversight responsibility for performance and training experiences: a) supervisor, b) mentor, c) sponsor.

Question 2: Which of the following terms implies an ongoing and valued relationship: a) mentor, b) sponsor.

Question 3: Which of the following terms refers to endorsing someone for an advancement opportunity: a) supervisor, b) mentor, c) sponsor.

Question 4: Do the roles of supervisor, mentor, and sponsor always have to be served by different people. a) True, b) False

Answers: 1) a, 2) a, 3) c, 4) b

has produced confidence about future performance and accountability, so mentorship and/or supervision likely precedes sponsorship (Mentor Loop, 2018).

We provide two activities to help you identify and analyze your relationships with prior and current supervisors and mentors. Everyone (i.e., those being supervised, and those who are supervising others) should complete *Activity 1* at the end of this chapter to identify important professionals in your graduate training. You will identify these people and the basic roles they have played in your professional life (Part 1). Later, Chapters 3 and 12 expand the analysis of the roles these professionals have played and the influences they have had on your professional repertoires and approach to supervision. Those who are already supervisors and/or mentors should also complete *Activity 2* to identify the roles that you serve in for others.

Evolving Relationships

LeBlanc (2015) described her mentors from her psychology graduate training, internship, and post-doctoral fellowship as having a lasting influence on her career through their advice and their examples as models for personal and professional life. Several of these *mentors* previously served as direct *supervisors* and some of them *sponsored* her for critical advancement opportunities in her career. Other supervisors who once held oversight responsibility for her work were never considered mentors. The critical distinction is the purpose, strength, and nature of the relationship. The term *mentor* implies an ongoing and valued relationship with a lasting impact on both the mentor and mentee. We suggest that the supervisor who thinks of themselves as having a bi-directional relationship with the supervisee is more likely to have a lasting positive influence on the supervisee and may be perceived as a mentor. Conversely, there are times when the purpose of supervision involves a restricted set of interactions for a narrowly circumscribed set of skills. In those cases, supervision is less likely to develop into an ongoing mutually productive mentoring relationship.

The supervisor who thinks of supervision as a relationship is likely to behave differently than a supervisor who thinks about supervision as a task or burden (i.e., "the meeting I have on Tuesday morning"). A supervisor who thinks of the supervisee as a person with whom they are in a relationship is likely to care more about the long-term effects of their supervision than if they view the supervisee as one of many job tasks. Healthy relationships lead us to a) be responsive to the other person's needs; b) think about how our actions impact the other person and the relationship; and c) convey how much we care.

> *A supervisor who thinks of the supervisee as a person with whom they are in a relationship is likely to care more about the long-term effects of their supervision than if they view the supervisee as one of many job tasks.*

A supervisor who views the supervisee as a Tuesday morning 9:00 a.m. task may approach supervision in a transactional and directive way (e.g., ensure the meeting lasts long enough, sign documentation materials). They may pay less attention to interpersonal dynamics (e.g., noting the supervisee's demeanor, assessing the quality of the supervisee's interactions with the client or family, observing for indicators that the supervisee has not experienced feedback as overly harsh). They may also be more likely to focus on immediate behaviors and immediate effects by providing answers and solutions (e.g., supervisee shows graphs and supervisor makes decisions to improve programming as opposed to guiding the supervisee to make an improvement). This approach may stunt the development of long-term repertoires such as responding to critical data and using systematic decision-making skills.

Regardless of whether the supervisor thinks of supervision as a relationship or a meeting, there will still be a meeting and it will still be documented. However, the nature of the interactions in that meeting are likely to change if supervision is viewed as a relationship instead of a task. Even when a supervisor thinks of supervision as a relationship, time and workload constraints and other work contingencies may produce negative effects. They may tip the scales toward transactional, short-term oriented supervision, particularly if supervising someone is an assigned job duty rather than the opportunity to positively impact another human being. The entire experience will likely be improved for both parties if the supervisor focuses on building a healthy relationship and developing a plan for comprehensive and effective supervision. The later chapters in this book will help you develop that plan with a goal of helping you be a better supervisor in the limited amount of time available to supervise.

Relationships are evolving and dynamic and they include at least two individuals. Those relationships can develop into positive and productive collaborations, into dysfunctional and aversive interactions, or almost anything in between. A relationship is unlikely to develop into a positive and productive collaboration unless both parties are aware that they are in a relationship and share some commitment to making the relationship a positive one. The purpose of this book is to assist supervisors and supervisees in creating healthy supervisory relationships.

> *A relationship is unlikely to develop into a positive and productive collaboration unless both parties are aware that they are in a relationship and share some commitment to making the relationship a positive one.*

Each party must experience benefits from the relationship if the relationship is to evolve in a positive, constructive way. The most immediate and clear benefits are for the supervisee. The benefits to the supervisee include: a) a competent model of technical skills; b) answers to their questions; c) assistance with difficult decisions; d) learning opportunities; and e) a safety net associated with having a more experienced person with accountability for the quality of their programming. High quality supervision provides the additional benefits of: a) an effective model for how to approach professional situations; b) a high rate of reinforcement for initial performance approximations; c) clear explanations of why something may have gone wrong; d) resources for how to perform their duties more efficiently and effectively; and e) opportunities for expanded growth beyond the minimum requirements of the context. Early in the relationship, the supervisee is the dominant beneficiary and the supervisor explicitly takes the role of teacher or coach while the supervisee learns from the direct teaching and from the model that the teacher provides for all aspects of the professional role. Over time, the supervisee should develop greater independence, competence, confidence, and higher-order skills (e.g., problem-solving, self-awareness) and the supervisor should monitor for these changes so that they can allow greater independence and provide more challenging opportunities.

Check Your Knowledge

Question 1: Which of the following supervisor statements might be best characterized as transactional and directive?
a) "Please bring graphs of this client's problem behavior data to supervision next week"
b) "Can you think of a reason why this family might be cancelling sessions frequently?"

Question 2: Which of the following supervisor statements implies an ongoing and valued relationship:
a) "Tell me something that I could do differently to help you feel confident in your growing skills."
b) "I think you need to conduct an experimental functional analysis."

Answers: 1) b, 2) a

The supervisor also benefits from being in a supervisory relationship. Happy, committed supervisors understand that the relationship is, or will eventually be, beneficial to them. The benefits to the supervisor include: a) learning new skills, growing professionally, and contributing to the field; b) developing more flexible ways of communicating knowledge to others; and c) developing a deeper understanding of concepts, principles, procedures, and the literature. Additional benefits include: a) renewing enthusiasm and passion for the discipline; and b) developing meaningful, human relationships that make our professional lives fuller and richer.

The greatest long-term benefit of healthy supervisory relationships to the supervisor may be that they allow for a positive, lasting impact on the profession. You can do good in the world by directly serving clients *and* you can do good in the world by teaching others to do that same good. By teaching others, you exponentially increase the impact you have (i.e., you might teach five people well who then each teach five others well who each then teach five others well, and so on).

As the three authors reflected on the benefits encountered in careers of supervising others, each noted that the goal of supervision should never be "making more just like me." The supervisee may learn the specific knowledge and skills that the supervisor has, but hopefully will not be a duplicate of the supervisor. The knowledge and skills learned from the supervisor will become outdated over time. The supervisor should focus on teaching how to learn, reflect, solve problems, and make data-based decisions informed by the literature. Doing so facilitates the supervisee becoming the best they can be given their unique life experiences and their future practice context. Rather than a replica, the supervisee should enter the field with their own strong contributions to make in their own style.

> *Rather than a replica, the supervisee should enter the field with their own strong contributions to make in their own style.*

As previously stated, the primary purpose of this book is to provide guidance on how to establish and maintain healthy, positive supervisory and mentoring relationships. However, any relationship can hit a rough patch or even evolve in a negative or dysfunctional direction. In fact, everyone can probably identify at least one non-optimal supervisory relationship. The supervisee is likely to think about this as their "bad supervisor," but the problem could also be contextualized as a broken or damaged relationship. Thus, a second purpose of the book is to provide guidance on how to quickly identify stressors, strains, and cracks in the relationship and how to repair them.

In summary, we propose that supervision can be approached as a relationship that creates valuable learning opportunities for both the supervisor and the supervisee. The likelihood of the supervisee's future success in their own supervisory role may increase if they participated in a supervisory relationship designed to teach behavior analytic skills and to model a thoughtful and structured approach to supervision. Viewing the relationship as an evolving dynamic may lead the supervisor to behave in ways that strengthen the connection with the supervisee and avoid some of the common concerns that arise in supervision. When a supervisory relationship flourishes, the supervisor is often also viewed as a mentor and the relationship continues past the point of requirement. Once the requirements are past, both individuals can freely choose to access and provide supports to each other. The past supervisee moves into more independent practice, but with the counsel of a wise mentor who understands them and has developed a trusting and healthy relationship. The past supervisor has the satisfaction of continuing to participate in the career of an increasingly stronger professional. In the best cases, they will become life-long colleagues who collaborate with one another on all kinds of interesting and important projects along the way.

Activity 1 for Supervisees and Supervisors: Identifying your Supervisory Relationships

1. List the people who have served as a supervisor for your professional training activities.

2. Did/do you have an explicitly-stated relationship with each of these people?

3. Do you have a mentor (i.e., wise counselor) or mentors? If so, was this person ever your direct supervisor or did the mentoring relationship develop through some other connection?

4. Have you ever been sponsored for some professional advancement opportunity? If so, do you consider the person who sponsored you a mentor as well as a sponsor?

You will explore these supervisor, mentor, and sponsor relationships in more detail in a Chapter 3 Activity.

Activity 2 for Supervisors and Mentors Only: Current and Past Roles

1. List the people for whom you have served as a supervisor for professional training activities (past and current).

2. Did/do you have an explicitly-stated relationship with each of these people?

3. Do you have a mentor or mentors as described in this chapter? If so, was this person ever your direct supervisor or did the mentoring relationship develop through some other connection?

4. Have you ever been sponsored for some professional advancement opportunity? If so, do you consider the person who sponsored you a mentor as well as a sponsor?

5. In thinking about your supervisors and mentors, how strong was each of these relationships? What strengthened or weakened each relationship?

6. Do you think there is someone out there who considers you their current or past mentor? In what areas have you advised or counseled that person?

Chapter 2

Starting Strong in a Collaborative Supervisory Relationship

Without a solid foundation you'll have trouble creating anything of value.
—Erika Oppenheimer

Effective supervisory relationships require a strong foundation built on collaborative effort on the part of the supervisor and the supervisee. That is, both parties should contribute to the supervision goals, activities, and outcomes, though the contributions of each party do not have to be equal or identical. The contributions will change throughout the relationship, with stronger influence on goal-setting by the supervisor initially and greater influence by the supervisee over time. The critical part of the collaborative effort is that each party communicates respectfully and honestly and feels as though his or her input, ideas, and efforts are valued and acknowledged (Mohtady, Könings & van Merriënboer, 2016). There is also some indication that taking a participatory approach enhances outcomes and satisfaction (Peck, Killen, & Baumgart, 1989; Dunst, Trivette, & Hamby, 2010). There are serious risks associated with supervision that is solely directed by the supervisor, rather than collaboratively directed in a participatory approach (Clark et al., 1985). For example, if there was no collaboration in establishing goals, the supervisee may value the supervision experience less because the supervision is not helping them reach their unstated goals. If the supervisee and supervisor do not collaboratively evaluate the outcomes being produced by the supervision, each may become frustrated by a perceived lack of progress and blame the other for the ineffectiveness of the supervision.

> *There are serious risks associated with supervision that is solely directed by the supervisor, rather than collaboratively directed in a participatory approach (Clark et al., 1985).*

Collaboration in supervisory relationships may focus on skill development, prioritization of goals in supervision, and maintaining the health of the supervisory relationship. The supervisor and supervisee collaborate to produce many new repertoires for the supervisee (e.g., therapeutic procedures, clinical decision-making, organizational and professional skills). Skill development is likely to proceed more smoothly and swiftly if both parties feel engaged in the process and responsible for the outcomes. The focus of supervision is likely to change frequently as new skills are mastered, new areas of need are discovered, and more complex problems are tackled. If both people have input into the prioritization of the focus of supervision, they may identify multiple, complimentary goals, such as confidence with respect to programing for clients and application of concepts learned in courses. Then, the supervisee may be more likely to generate agenda items related to their challenges with clients. In addition, the supervisor may be more likely to present open-ended questions that link specific problems to concepts such as stimulus control or avoidance behavior. If either individual provided the sole guidance for supervision meetings, there is a risk that one or the other of these areas might be missed.

As in any relationship, the supervisee and supervisor should each feel partial responsibility for the health of the supervisory relationship. A participatory or collaborative supervisory relationship typically involves periodic bi-directional feedback and open discussion about the supervisory interaction. For example, in some instances, the supervisor may be over-supporting, resulting in a feeling of stifled indepen-

> *A participatory or collaborative supervisory relationship typically involves periodic bi-directional feedback and open discussion about the supervisory interaction.*

dence. In other cases, the supervisee may not be changing their behavior in response to feedback. When the supervisor and supervisee collaborate throughout the relationship, many barriers may never arise (e.g., frustration with the focus of supervision). Those that do arise can be resolved more quickly and positively, generally resulting in better progress for the supervisee and better outcomes for clients.

Activity 1 at the end of this chapter can be given to the supervisee after the first supervision meeting, completed, and then reviewed at the beginning of the second meeting. In doing so, you provide a specific, assigned task and an expectation for a timeline for completion. Beginning supervision with this kind of framework may establish collaboration, expectations, and communication as valued aspects of supervision at the outset. The activity also teaches the supervisee how to examine their own professional goals and interests in greater detail. It may help the supervisee if you provide context for this task as a way to get to know each other's backgrounds and preferences as part of building a strong, open communicative supervisory relationship. This may result in the supervisee viewing the activity as a meaningful opportunity rather than another item on the "to do" list.

The supervisory relationship should be built on a strong foundation and a clear commitment to the ultimate outcomes of the relationship. That foundation is based on a shared understanding of the importance of the relationship and the need to focus on skill development, communication, and clarity of expectations. If the relationship is not established with clear guidelines, mutual agreement, and mutual respect, dysfunction may develop in the relationship. For example, if the supervisor has not clearly described the expectation for mutual timeliness for all meetings, tardiness may result in annoyance and inadequate time for discussing complex issues. However, if the supervisor sets clear expectations and adheres to the same expectations, this potential issue will be avoided rather than managed after the fact.

> *If the relationship is not established with clear guidelines, mutual agreement, and mutual respect, dysfunction may develop in the relationship.*

Strategies for Starting Strong

The next sections explore two core components to starting strong that will increase the chances of finishing strong. Both are related to establishing clear lines of communication and processes for identifying needs and resolving difficulties. The first core component is a shared understanding of the supervision expectations and conditions. The second core component is a committed and positive relationship.

Conditions and Basic Expectations of Supervision. The first step in establishing an effective supervisor-supervisee relationship is to ensure that both parties understand their roles, the process, and the scope of the supervision. The specific expectations will depend on the supervision conditions. Typically, some of the areas in which the supervisor might want to set expectations include: 1) interpersonal interactions and professionalism; 2) timeliness in correspondence and meetings; 3) meeting assignment deadlines with a high quality of product; and 4) responsiveness to feedback. For each area, the supervisor should state the expectation (i.e., what behaviors or patterns they would like to see) and provide examples of behavior that would meet the criterion. For example, the supervisor might state that timeliness is important, and that they would like to have the meeting agenda sent to them 24 hours in advance of the meeting or that they expect a response to email correspondence within 24 hours. Additional examples of these types of expectations are covered in detail in subsequent chapters.

> *The first step in establishing an effective supervisor-supervisee relationship is to ensure that both parties understand their roles, the process, and the scope of the supervision.*

If the supervisee is pursuing a credential from the BACB, other requirements covered in the eight-hour supervisor training become pertinent (e.g., a contract, restriction of activities to those that are behavior analytic, percentage of time supervised). For example, the BACB requires a contract clarifying expectations and responsibilities at the onset of the supervisory relationship (BACB, 2020). The supervisor can use the sample contract provided on the BACB website (https://www.bacb.com/supervision-and-training/#Training_Resources_and_Documents) or create their own contract that meets the same specifications. Even if the supervisory relationship does not fall within the purview of the BACB, it is still wise to have clear expectations. The advantage of a contract is that it provides the opportunity to formally describe the terms of the relationship. If there is a supervision contract, the supervisor should have a conversation with the supervisee to review the expectations that are delineated in a written contract, in detail, and answer any questions. That is, the process of reviewing and signing the contact should be viewed as analogous to the informed consent process for research or assessment and treatment services (i.e., clear understanding and no remaining questions before anyone signs). At the same time, the supervisee should be learning about expectations and preparing to engage in the supervision process as a professional. This can be facilitated by assigning the supervisee handbook developed by Kazemi, Rice, and Adzhyan (2018). This handbook provides an excellent guide for the supervisee on expectations, requirements, and various aspects of professional behavior (e.g., self-reflection, responding effectively to feedback). The chances of success increase if both the supervisor and the supervisee are prepared and clear about relationship expectations.

Once the supervisor's basic conditions and expectations are clarified, the supervisor can guide the supervisee to explore their own goals and expectations for supervision. The supervisee may not have well-formulated expectations beyond "I have to complete this experience requirement" or "you are my boss and I want to please you." Thus, the supervisor should teach the supervisee strategies for thinking in greater depth about their goals and expectations for the supervision experience (e.g., make a list of personal and professional goals, reflect on other supervisory relationships, identify preferences for components of supervision). The supervisor can use the collaboration exercise (*Activity 1*) at the end of the chapter to assist the supervisee with reflection and goal development repertoires.

Logistically, the first and second meetings present the perfect opportunity to set expectations for interpersonal interactions, and for critical professional skills such as organization and timeliness (Bailey & Burch, 2010). Many supervisees may be relatively new to the realm of professional relationships (as opposed to personal relationships). They may not understand the etiquette and the specific ethical guidelines around establishing therapeutic relationships and supervisory relationships. For example, the supervisor should state how they prefer being addressed (e.g., "Please call me Linda." "Feel free to call me Linda or Dr. LeBlanc, whichever you prefer"). In turn, the supervisor might ask the supervisee how they prefer to be addressed in supervision (e.g., "Do you have a nickname you prefer?" "What are your pronouns?"). The supervisor might also prompt the supervisee to think about how they should be addressed by clients (e.g., "Gently correct them if they call you doctor and offer them a few other options of things to call you such as Ms. Smith or Janet", "Choose options that are comfortable for you and the culture of the setting. If 'Sir' and 'Ma'am' are terms of respect and a gender-neutral term is more appropriate, perhaps 'Teacher' would work").

Finally, the supervisor should make it clear that the supervisee is now in a professional role with all that this entails. This role includes professional expectations for dress code, punctuality, interpersonal interactions, and professional behavior in meetings (Kazemi, et al., 2018). Although specific details may not be provided for every situation, the supervisee should discriminate their new professional role from their prior personal ones. They should also be prepared to ask if they do not know. The supervisor can facilitate this by setting these expectations (e.g., "Professional relationships, contexts, and meetings may be new for you, so be sure to ask if there's something about which you are unsure"). Finally, the supervisor might provide texts, such as, *25 Essential Skills and Strategies for the Professional Behavior Analyst* (Bailey & Burch, 2010) as additional resources for developing professional behavior. Equally important, the supervisor should clarify that once training commences, the Professional and Ethical Compliance Code for Behavior Analysts (BACB, 2014) applies to all actions. Supervisees may mistakenly think that they are only bound to the Code once they are fully certified. Chapter 8 will cover practical strategies for teaching organization and professional skills in greater detail and will provide resources for teaching the supervisee how to prepare to make the most of their time in supervision.

Creating a Committed and Positive Relationship. In addition to establishing and reviewing the conditions and expectations of supervision, the supervisor should convey a strong commitment to creating a positive learning context. A committed and healthy learning context involves several components. It includes acknowledgement of the learning process, attentiveness, welcoming perspectives and diversity, and, perhaps most important, ongoing communication and feedback. Each of these are addressed in detail in the coming chapters. The importance here is that both the supervisor and supervisee acknowledge and start with an understanding and basis for these foundational relationship components.

Committed and Healthy Learning Context

1. Acknowledgement of the learning process
2. Attentiveness
3. Welcoming perspectives and diversity
4. Ongoing communication and feedback

Under the best learning conditions, the supervisee is expected to flourish and also make some mistakes. The supervisor can explicitly convey this commitment by expressing their interest in the supervisee and their eagerness to start the relationship. A more experienced supervisor might say, "I am excited to start supervision with you, and I think we are going to each learn a lot from this process!" A newer or young supervisor might modify the statement to say, "I am excited to supervise you and I want you to feel comfortable bringing me successes, questions, and struggles." In all cases, accomplishments and learning opportunities should be mutually noticed and discussed between the supervisor and supervisee.

The supervisor also conveys commitment to the relationship by being attentive during supervision (e.g., eliminate distractions, ask follow-up questions, explain in detail). Being pleasant and caring (e.g., getting to know the supervisee, smiling, praising successes and accomplishments) and being respectful and professional (e.g., arriving on time, responding to requests for assistance) also convey commitment. These actions provide an important model for the supervisee's own behavior and communicate that the supervisor values the supervisee and the supervisory role (Sellers, Valentino, et al., 2016). In addition, these efforts to build rapport may result in increased trust and comfort, leading to greater productivity and discretionary effort on the part of the supervisee (Curry, Gravina, Sleiman, & Richard, 2019).

The supervisor can also ask about the supervisee's perspective and feelings about their commitment to the relationship. This is important in any relationship, but becomes critical the more diverse the supervisor and supervisee's life experiences. Chapter 4 provides guidance on how to ask questions and listen to answers when supervisees differ from the supervisor in cultural identity or life experiences. In general, certain actions might convey a lack of commitment or valuing of the relationship. For example, in many cases, rushed interactions in which the supervisor talks at the supervisee without allowing questions could be off-putting. In addition, being distracted during supervision (e.g., looking at devices), frequently canceling meetings, or being emotionally unresponsive can be just as damaging as providing harsh feedback.

When the supervisor and supervisee have chosen each other, both are likely to be eager participants in discussions about goals and expectations. In optimal circumstances, a positive relationship may develop between the supervisor and supervisee with seemingly little effort. However, not all circumstances are optimal. When the supervisee is assigned to the supervisor, the situation may not produce the same excitement and eagerness to begin the relationship. In this circumstance, it is more important than ever to follow a structured process for the supervisor to learn about the supervisee's perspectives and goals. Without a structured process or activity to support rapport building and goal identification, the supervisor may never learn things about the supervisee that might have increased their motivation to help this person pursue a meaningful career.

The overarching goal of the supervisor should be to develop and foster a relationship where feedback and guidance are valued by the supervisee. The supervisee should want to be an active participant in supervision meetings, and the entire process of supervision should result in skill development. Supervisors can foster the supervisee's interest and commitment by providing frequent, specific praise and feedback (Sellers, Valentino, et al., 2016). It should be noted, however, that many people have learning histories that establish feedback as an aversive experience (e.g., someone telling you that you screwed up). The supervisor should assume that there are some of these experiences in the past of any new supervisee and use the

Activity at the end of this chapter to initiate discussion about preferences for supervision, especially with feedback as it is the primary means of communication about expectations and performance.

In terms of the specific recommendations for providing feedback, Chapter 5 covers specifics related to performance feedback during instruction and Chapter 11 provides guidance on having difficult conversations in the context of issues with the supervisor relationship itself. However, given the important role that feedback plays in shaping performance, let's review some guidance on providing feedback to help start the process on a healthy track. Definitely avoid the use of the "feedback sandwich" (i.e., positive statement, corrective feedback, positive statement), even though it is commonly recommended in management resources (Daniels & Bailey, 2014; Henley & DiGennaro Reed, 2015; Sundberg, 2015). Use of this strategy often leads to discounting of the positive statements. Some prefer to hear the corrective feedback before the praise of accurate performance (Henley & DiGennaro Reed, 2015). The feedback itself should be frequent and specific (Park, Johnson, Moon, & Lee, 2019). We recommend providing frequent, specific feedback for desired behavior, as well as for behavior that needs to be corrected. That is, do not make the common mistake of providing general praise statements and reserving detailed feedback for areas of improvement. Describe all of the things the supervisee is doing well and the effects of the correct performance (e.g., increased client outcome, safety, collaborative relationships with caregivers).

Another common recommendation is to deliver feedback following a performance opportunity. However, one study (Aljadeff-Abergel, Peterson, Wiskirchen, Hagen, & Cole, 2017) found that feedback delivered immediately prior to a teaching session produced more improvements than feedback delivered following a teaching session. In contrast, Wine, et al. (2019) found no difference in terms of feedback delivered before or after the performance. These findings highlight the importance of different aspects of feedback (e.g., when it is delivered, how it is delivered). Feedback delivery should be based on individual's preference and learning history, as well as the effects of the feedback whenever possible. In other words, a one-size-fits-all approach to feedback in supervision is unlikely to be successful for all supervisees. A skilled supervisor adjusts the relevant dimensions of feedback for each supervisee, monitors the effects of the feedback, and makes changes to the feedback when needed.

The supervisor can acknowledge that the expectation is that the supervisee is learning, and that performance will not be perfect. The role of the supervisor is to provide feedback that helps the supervisee improve over time through copious amounts of feedback and reinforcement. Though receiving corrective feedback can be difficult, if both parties understand

> *A skilled supervisor adjusts the relevant dimensions of feedback for each supervisee, monitors the effects of the feedback, and makes changes to the feedback when needed.*

the importance of the feedback and agree to be professional and respectful, the process should be positive (Sellers, Valentino, et al., 2016). The supervisor should also explain the role of feedback and that feedback includes information about aspects of the supervisee's performance that met expectations, as well as those that did not and what actions the supervisee should take to remediate deficits (Reid, et al., 2012).

One might argue that giving and receiving feedback are the most important skills that you teach your supervisee, as they should be used every day in professional activities as a trainee, a clinician, and as a future supervisor. *Activity 2* at the end of this chapter provides examples for discussions a supervisor might have with a supervisee about feedback. The purpose of the activity is to help the supervisor create their own personal scripts for the same topics. In doing so, supervisors in training should practice talking about these sometimes uncomfortable topics to increase their comfort and fluency. Setting the expectation for both positive and constructive feedback will probably redefine feedback for the supervisee (e.g., it isn't just the mistakes—feedback is a collaborative effort designed to improve skills). These expectations also prepare the supervisee for feedback sessions and model for the supervisee how to give feedback in the current relationship. This is critical because supervisees in collaborative supervisory relationships should give their supervisor feedback (!), as well as in their future supervision of others.

In summary, to create a positive, healthy supervisory relationship, the supervisor should focus on setting clear expectations, ensuring shared understanding of the conditions of supervision, and creating a committed and positive relationship based on open communication and feedback. These conversations should take place during the first few supervision sessions and this focus should continue to be reflected throughout the supervisory experience. Direct, supportive discussions guided by the scripts and activities included in this chapter can help new supervisors broach subjects such as feedback, fears, and goals to ensure that supervision is a collaborative effort. As we mentioned in Chapter 1, framing the supervisory relationship

> *To create a positive, healthy supervisory relationship, the supervisor should focus on setting clear expectations, ensuring shared understanding of the conditions of supervision, and creating a committed and positive relationship based on open communication and feedback.*

as one of bi-directional learning opportunities sets the stage for success. Implementing the strategies in this chapter allows the supervisor to actively cultivate a meaningful relationship that both parties value. These strategies also allow the supervisor to avoid many of the pitfalls that come from failing to identify shared goals and clarify shared expectations.

Next, Chapter 3 will help you examine your own supervisory experiences and provides additional coverage of strategies for identifying features of past relationships and how they might be affecting current relationships. Although the past cannot be erased, the supervisor should initiate an honest and empathetic reflection about past experiences and how future relationships will be similar or how they will differ. That is, Chapter 3 provides you with an opportunity to decide how to establish expectations and develop your supervisory relationships.

Activity: Exploring Collaboration Topics

Complete the following questions prior to your next supervision session. These questions will help you reflect on your past experiences to help your supervisor understand how these might impact the relationship the two of you have. These questions will also help you refine your thoughts about what you hope to get out of the supervisory relationship.

1. What does the word "feedback" mean to you? Have you had experiences with feedback in the past that make you nervous about receiving feedback from me?

2. How do you prefer to receive feedback? (Circle any that apply, add your own thoughts, and we will discuss it.)

    a. Live in person
    b. Written
    c. Privately
    d. All kinds are great
    e. I need help figuring this out

    Other thoughts on feedback: _____
    _____
    _____
    _____
    _____

3. How would you like to give me feedback about how supervision is going and things I might be able to do to help you learn?

   a. Let's have a monthly agenda item to discuss this live

   b. I can send you an email or bring it up as needed

   c. I will probably be nervous to do this, so I need help coming up with ideas

4. List a few things that you are most excited to learn from this supervision experience:

   a.

   b.

   c.

5. What professional skills (e.g., talking with parents, talking with other professionals, conducting research, making public presentations) do you hope to learn or improve as a result of our supervision?

   a.

   b.

   c.

6. What are you excited to show me that you can already do pretty well?

   a.

   b.

   c.

Appendix: How to Talk About Feedback

Below are examples of how to talk directly about feedback with your supervisee. These are examples of how to give rationales and descriptive statements during communication. There are many different ways to say things, depending on the purpose and the interaction partners. Read each of the statements below and think about how you would talk with your supervisee. Compose similar statements to help rehearse clear, kind, and constructive ways of communicating with your supervisee about the feedback process.

Describing Importance of Feedback
- "You know, the most powerful tool for shaping behavior is feedback. What I mean is that telling you, in detail, all of the things that you are doing well *and* all of the things we still need to work on gives us our best chance at making sure that you maintain your skills and acquire new ones."

- "The research tells us that performance feedback is most impactful when it is delivered frequently and in detail. Given that it is critical to design supervision using evidence-based practices, that means that we will rely heavily on a rich feedback schedule."

- "As a supervisee, it is your job to engage in a lot of responding, some of which will be spot on, and some won't. That's your job, to get some stuff right, and to make mistakes. Those mistakes provide us both with learning opportunities: you will have the chance to improve your specific performance, and I will have the chance to improve my ability to teach the specific skill."

- "Remember that feedback is a 2-way street. Not only will I provide frequent, specific feedback to you, but I need you to do the same for me. I won't increase my skills as supervisor if I don't hear from you what is and what is not working."

Describing Commitment to Feedback
- "You have provided me really great information about your preferences related to receiving feedback. I will do my best to provide you feedback (insert specifics here)."

- "Because feedback is so critical to both of our growth, let's both make a commitment to creating a feedback-rich environment. What are some things that we can do to ensure we are upholding our commitment?"

How to Accept Feedback
- "Remember that feedback is bi-directional—how it is received is as important as how it is given. We have outlined some specifics around how feedback should be given, so now let's pivot to talking about how it should be received."

- "One thing that will be important to me is that you understand the feedback I have given to you and that you find it useful. What are some of the ways that you indicate understanding? What are some of the ways that you indicate that information is helpful or not helpful?"

- "Feedback is important for both of us. I will give you feedback on technical, ethical and professional issues as your supervisor. You will give me feedback on the supervision process, the degree to which you are supported, and about additional steps I can take to support you. I am excited that I will also have the opportunity to receive feedback from you. When you are providing me with feedback, I will likely take some notes and I may also ask you for some examples or ideas on how to respond to your feedback, okay?"

Chapter 3

Understanding Past and Current Supervisory and Mentored Relationships

Life can only be understood backwards; but it must be lived forwards.
—Søren Kierkegaard

Each person is a product of their own complex history of influencers. We use the term "influencer" to refer to people who exert a strong influence on behavior and beliefs (dictionary.com). The resulting influences begin early and continue throughout life, in both personal and professional contexts. Some of these influencers may have had their impact in early school experiences (e.g., coach, teacher), in work settings (e.g., first manager, practicum supervisor), or as friends and family members who served as role models. Some of these influencers were consciously chosen (e.g., choosing swimming over basketball because you like the coach better) and some were not (e.g., families, teachers). Chosen or not, people from our past can exert great influence on current behavior by inspiring and encouraging us, serving as models, establishing rules and values that guide our behavior, and teaching us specific lessons (Eby, Rhodes, & Allen, 2007).

Just as people from our childhood (e.g., family, coaches, teachers) influence us, supervisors can exert powerful influence on our training practices, professional values and ethics, interpersonal skills, and organizational skills. A great supervisor can serve as a model for future great supervisors and, unfortunately, an ineffective supervisor can serve as a model for future ineffective supervisors.

We do not have to be consciously aware of specific influences for them to have an effect. However, there are several potential advantages to reflecting on our history and the people who have had important and lasting impacts on our lives. First, reflecting on the people and events that have influenced us allows us to be an active participant in our own learning, rather than simply having our behavior shaped by others. Reflection allows us to purposefully integrate our past influences into our current supervisory activities. For example, reflection may allow us to identify important rules and lessons learned from each person in a way that can more directly guide our future decisions (see examples from the authors below). Additionally, identification of non-optimal strategies used by a prior supervisor may be just as useful as identifying the optimal ones. Doing so may help us avoid imitating the wrong examples or repeating mistakes from our past. Finally, it can help us be more purposeful in choosing our future mentoring opportunities (see examples from the authors below). There is evidence that strong mentorship increases high-level performance and expertise (Eby, et al., 2007).

Benefits of Reflecting on Past Relationships

1. Active participation in your own learning
2. Increased gratitude for your "influencers"
3. Increased understanding of the models you've observed
4. Identification of examples and non-examples
5. Identification of professional development needs and new areas of interest

The purpose of this chapter is to assist the supervisor in identifying the core values surrounding their unique approach to supervision. Each supervisor can examine their own key influencers and select lessons and past influences to integrate into future activities as a supervisor or mentor. As we think about prior influences, it is worth thinking about the conditions under which those people developed their skills sets. We may discover those conditions in the answers to several questions. First, how did that person become a supervisor? Second, did they have prerequisite behaviors that made learning to be a supervisor easier? Third, were they hired or promoted because they were already well-qualified for the job? Fourth, did they receive any specific training on how to be an effective supervisor? Finally, what were their supervisors or mentors like? Considering these questions and their answers might reveal why a supervisor or mentor behaved the way they did.

Each of our past experiences offers guidance for our potential future actions, though some of the reflections on those experiences will be less enjoyable than others. We tend to either avoid thinking about prior aversive experiences or ruminate on them and demonize the individuals involved in those experiences. The less pleasant experiences in life (e.g., failure in a past endeavor, harsh feedback) can still spark growth. However, this requires experiencing a little discomfort as we reflect, describe, and contextualize the lessons learned from those experiences. Reflection on less enjoyable past experiences must focus on understanding why the prior person behaved as they did (e.g., stress, life distractions, inexperience, our own performance). It is this understanding of the variables controlling the person's behavior that allows us to avoid behaving the same way under similar circumstances.

Reflecting on the influences of those from our past and present affords the additional advantage of revealing ongoing professional development needs. For example, one might identify that they have never had experience with someone who fits the bill of a "great supervisor." This might lead the person to identify several supervisory strategies that they want to avoid (e.g., harsh feedback, inattentiveness, unclear instructions, appearing disinterested). The person may also identify that they have not seen effective implementation of better strategies (e.g., positive reinforcement, constructive feedback, modeling, conceptualizing and problem solving). This revelation might lead the person to seek a mentor to provide guidance and shaping for their own supervisory activities.

Additionally, reflection on past experiences in conjunction with future planning might lead to identification of a new area of interest or a new skill set to develop. Let's consider the example of a behavior analyst who has previously worked only in the area of autism and intellectual disabilities.

If they decide to begin serving individuals with dementia, they will need additional training and supervision (LeBlanc, Heinicke, & Baker, 2012). They might reach out to prior supervisors and valued peers for suggestions about how to explore that new area and make connections to others who already have that expertise. In this way, the networks of all of our prior supervisors and mentors, and those of our peers, potentially become part of our own networks.

> *Reflection on past experiences in conjunction with future planning might lead to identification of a new area of interest or a new skill set to develop.*

Reflection and Values Determination

We developed the concept of the Mentor Tree and a corresponding activity for supervisors. The idea of the Mentor Tree facilitates reflection on past and present influences of all types, including family, peers, teachers, supervisors, and mentors. In many ways, the people (e.g., mom, grandfather) or groups of people (e.g., my 11th grade track team, first job supervisors) represented on the tree helped to make you who you are today. With each entry to the tree, you should be able to describe the contributions these people made to your growth and development and the specific ways that they influenced you. For some entries, the contributions and influences will be too numerous to list, but note general categories (e.g., work ethic) and strategies (e.g., accountability for chores and contributions to the family well-being). There does not need to be a strong distinction between professional influences and personal ones because core values exert pervasive influence. LeBlanc (2015) describes her mentors from her professional training as having a lasting influence on her as models for different aspects of both personal and professional life.

The Mentor Tree is divided into three parts that each represent a different part of the supervisor's learning journey: roots, trunk, and branches. The roots represent those critical formative mentors who influenced your primary values, rules, and core repertoires early in life (e.g., parents, siblings, teachers, coaches). Some of these people may have inspired your later career pursuit or shaped the things you value (e.g., diversity and travel, volunteerism, education). The trunk represents those who influenced your basic professional repertoires. This portion of the tree will likely be populated by professors, practicum or fieldwork supervisors, and peers. The branches at the top of the Mentor Tree represent the different influences that continue to occur throughout your career even when your primary training is complete. If you take a continuous learning approach, you are likely to encounter new people who spark growth or to learn new things from those who are already on the tree. The branches will continue to expand and

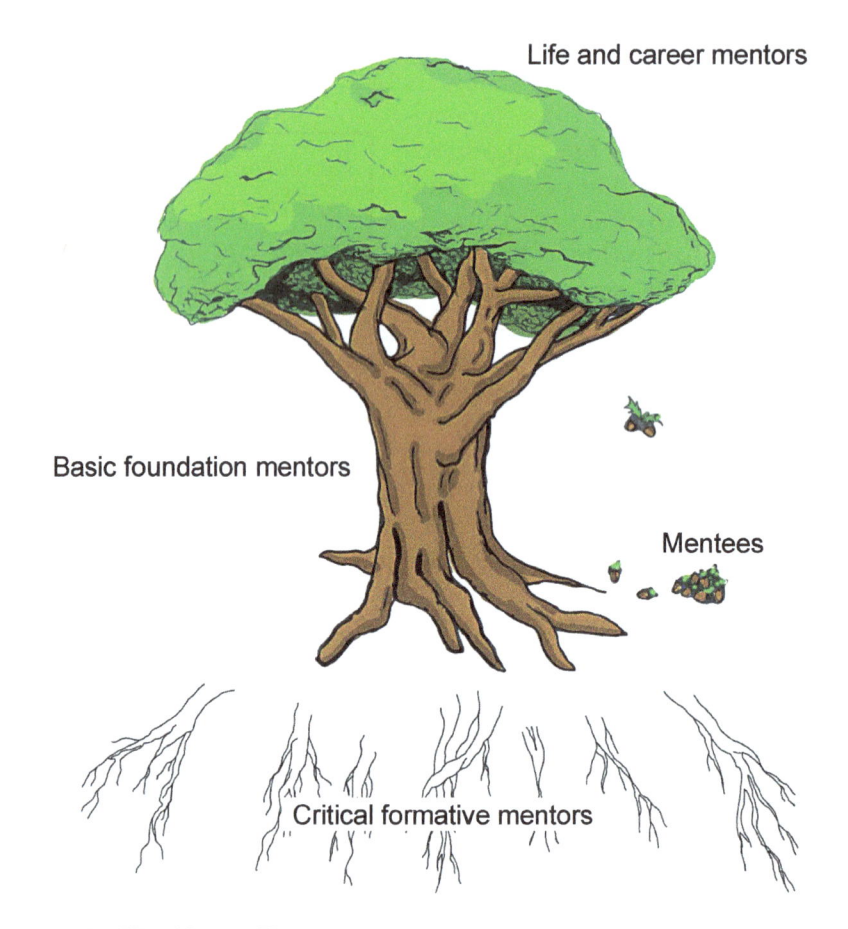

Figure 3.1 The Mentor Tree

diversify throughout your professional career if you actively pursue professional development experiences that facilitate your continued growth.

With career progress, peer mentors begin to exert more influence. Peer mentors do not have direct control over relevant work contingencies, but do have strengths and expertise to share. For example, you may have a colleague who is unflappable during difficult conversations, whereas you struggle to keep your composure. Observing the colleague in difficult situations and discussing their preparatory strategies and private events during a critical interaction could provide valuable learning opportunities. Peer mentors may help to continue to shape and refine interpersonal skills (e.g., negotiation, advocacy), writing skills (e.g., training manuals, grant proposals), practical and technical skills (e.g., literature searches and graphing), or more advanced or specialized clinical skills (e.g., interventions when multiple risk factors are present).

There is one other component to the Mentor Tree: the acorns that represent the next generation. Each supervisor will be responsible for creating future professionals. The tree represents those who have influenced the supervisor, while the acorns represent those influenced by the supervisor (i.e., the supervisees). The Mentor Tree concept and activity help you to understand your past influences to identify and develop your core values for supervising others.

The Mentor Tree Activity

Let's begin *Activity 1, Create your Mentor Tree,* with your roots. Who were your critical, formative influencers? What impact did each have on your personal and professional development? Fill in the area around the roots identifying people and their impact (e.g., main lessons learned from these people). Alternatively, you can start by identifying known characteristics and impacts and reflecting on the likely sources of those impacts.

Next come the trunk and branches. In Chapter 1, you completed *Activity 1* to identify important supervisors, mentors, and sponsors. Expand the analysis to the specific influences these professionals have had on your professional repertoires, approach to supervision, and career opportunities. Try to avoid the "rosy glow" effect and the "demonizing" effect. That is, almost everyone on your tree has probably done some things well, and some things not so well. It is not disloyal to describe the latter as illustrating how even a great supervisor can have a bad day or an area in which they could improve. Learning can occur in effective as well as ineffective mentoring relationships (Eby, et al., 2007). No supervisor has ever known all of the answers or been perfect in their execution of supervision. It is often how the supervisor or mentor responds to their own mistakes, and to the mistakes of others, that influences your impression of them.

Use the names from the Chapter 1 activity, you can start to fill in the trunk and branches. For each name, try to specify the influence this person has had on you, the lessons you have learned, and the specific behaviors you want to imitate or that you want to avoid imitating. As you summarize the central influences, reflect on each person's likely motivations, individual and cultural learning histories, and the person's specific actions you hope to emulate. If you are still in a relationship with these people, you might consider asking them some of these questions directly. Identify important branches in your career path and the people who helped you to pursue those professional accomplishments. Specify what you learned from them and how you became connected to them (e.g., met at a conference, introduced by a mutual colleague). If you are recently graduated or about to graduate, you might leave the branches unmarked for now as you reflect on your desired career trajectory. You will spend more time on future planning in *Activity 2: Planning for Continued Development*.

It is likely that you are either supervising others already, or you are soon to become a supervisor. In the section labeled "mentees," acorns represent the opportunity to influence others who are just beginning in their careers. Think about how you want to influence your supervisees and mentees (i.e., the acorns) and the strategies you want to use to achieve that influence. For example, you could be a supervisor who focuses on providing interpersonal support to build rapport (e.g., expressing interest in the relationship, anchoring the supervision experience to the overarching values of the field). You could focus on teaching how to communicate information to multiple audiences using modeling and role playing. You could also focus on teaching independent problem-solving by using a structured problem solving model rather than providing direct answers that only apply to one situation. Describe your aspirational goals for yourself as a supervisor and the strategies that you want to use during supervision.

Each person will have their own variation of the Mentor Tree based on their different origins and experiences. That will lead to developing your own supervision approach, which does not have to be identical to another person's for it to be supportive and effective. We provide the following descriptions of each of our Mentor Trees and supervision styles to give you examples of how to engage in this activity to identify your own core values. You are not likely to adopt these specific approaches as your own, but we hope they illustrate the value of reflection on your past experiences.

Examples from the Authors

In Linda LeBlanc's tree, she identified several core early influencers (i.e., the roots of the tree). The majority of these individuals were her family members (e.g., mother and father) who taught her to be self-reliant and to always put forth her best effort. The less rosy part about these influences was a lifelong pattern of guilt over letting people down and difficulty accepting help and compliments. The roots also contain people who sparked her early career interests by providing volunteer opportunities throughout high school to explore psychology. The trunk of the tree includes professors and supervisors who taught, mentored, and sponsored her in some capacity. Their efforts in shaping her professional repertoires and client-centered values were invaluable, but sometimes focused more on negative reinforcement than positive reinforcement. The branches include personal and professional role models, including fellow faculty members, the co-authors of this book and several editors of the *Journal of Applied Behavior Analysis*. These people helped her learn how to publish and serve as an editor and how to succeed in an academic environment.

LeBlanc (2015) described her aspirational approach to supervising and managing as incorporating "copious amounts of praise and direct, supportive feedback." This is a skill she developed later in her career after valued mentors pointed out that her feedback was often too harsh and demoralizing to others. She had inadvertently imitated models from personal and professional life. In addition, she frames corrective feedback as "an opportunity to see them do even better" at some particular skill. While that is her general approach to supervision, it does not mean that she always provides as much praise as a given supervisee might like to have. She also endeavors to set a high bar for being organized and efficient by providing clear expectations. Although she aspires to always create clear expectations, she sometimes falls short and relies on honest discussion and feedback to facilitate change when her actions as a supervisor are not fully consistent with her desired supervision style.

On Shahla Ala'i's tree, the roots include extended family going back several generations. These influencing themes included education, sacrifice for the well-being of others, and the power of the collective in deciding the best courses of action. Her great grandparents sacrificed so that her grandmother could attend the first girls' school in Tehran in the 1920s. Her mother spent weekends visiting the elderly who had no family. Even when her father was dying of cancer, he called everyone to his bed to discuss his end of life decisions. The less rosy part is learning to understand to what degree one should feel responsible for others and who should be involved in decision making. The trunk of her tree includes her high school mentor, Ms. Juliet Whittaker, an educator, artist, and community activist. From her, Ala'i learned the value of seeing across disciplines and boundaries for the greater good and to search for beauty in life. From her professors, the lessons involved the power of science and her ethical responsibility for the well-being of the children and families served. As she has progressed through her career, mentors have included colleagues across many applied disciplines including anthropology and public health. Here the lessons have focused on the struggles involved in helping staff bring humanity to difficult and complicated problems, such as children with autism living in poverty or the prevention of human trafficking. They also involved a lot of discomfort and conflict in the process of learning to listen when the languages and perspectives are different.

Shahla Ala'i's aspirational goals for mentoring and supervision relate to creating a strong, shared mission, and creating communities of practice where groups of people can mentor one another in serving that mission. She sees her supervisory position as creating conditions that make organizational goals clear and transparent and having ongoing conversations about how skill advancement is related to the mission. In most cases, the community, or group of people, under her mentorship have aligned goals and helped one another, but at times have had miscommunications about expectations, roles, or directions. She sees these moments as opportunities for everyone, including herself, to learn to reflect, reset, and continue learning.

The roots of Tyra Sellers' tree are made up of her parents and siblings, who taught her to appreciate the small things in life, to be kind, but to also take care of business. Due to some unhealthy dynamics, she also learned to heavily value the role of caretaker, resulting in an overly developed sense of responsibility for others, including things that she cannot control. Her childhood drama teacher cultivated the idea that it is all right to make mistakes and that fear and growth are bedfellows. Also present in the roots are a few key elementary school teachers who strengthened her love of helping others by providing opportunities to tutor peers. The trunk is comprised of her spouse and some early supervisors who were critical in facilitating the development of critical repertoires, supporting her intellectual curiosity, and bringing her career path into focus. Her tree is rich with branches of impactful friends, mentors, and colleagues who all have, in various ways, pushed her to continue to grow and refine skills by challenging her with collaborative opportunities and thoughtful feedback. This includes some broken branches that represent difficult relationships with peers and colleagues that provided learning opportunities around setting limits and clarifying values.

Tyra Sellers approaches supervision as a continual journey of learning; meaning that each supervisory relationship functions to positively shape both peoples' repertoires. Supervision and training provide both parties opportunities to learn by doing and telling, and to expand repertoires and perspectives. She endeavors to create a space wherein the supervisee feels comfortable engaging in a lot of behavior that can then be shaped by direct feedback. In other words, it is the supervisee's job to try and to fail, and to persist in continuing to try again with support and guidance. Likewise, her supervisee is likely to see her try and fail, which provides an opportunity for modeling self-observation and reflection and soliciting feedback from the supervisee. Other supervisors may have success with a more directive approach; however, taking a shared-learning approach has been effective for her throughout her career.

Planning for Continued Development

Once graduate training is complete, behavior analysts often do not have a supervisor specifically tasked with fostering professional growth of their supervisees or mentees. Instead, a manager is tasked with making sure that all assigned tasks are accomplished in a timely and complete manner.

The wise behavior analyst will determine for themselves which skills in their behavior analytic or supervisory skill set still need refining. An independent practicing professional needs to be active in seeking out personal and professional development opportunities and arranging situations in which the right people provide influence. The right person might be a peer or might be someone more senior than you. He or she might be part of your work environment or they might be a person of stature in the field or in your community. First, focus on the area of desired learning and growth, then identify people who are more competent and fluent in that area than you so that you can approach them about providing mentorship.

The purpose of *Activity 2: Planning for Continued Development* is to help you begin to articulate your next goals and mentorship needs. This will allow you to seek the appropriate influencers to help you achieve those goals. Begin this activity in the left column by identifying the next accomplishments that you hope to achieve. If you are still in graduate school, this column might include things like "find a fulfilling job" along with a list of characteristics of a fulfilling job (e.g., access to an experienced supervisor). Next, move to the middle column where you specify what actions you need to take to achieve that goal (e.g., finish your degree, study and prepare for the exam, become certified, apply for jobs). In the final column, identify people who might offer you advice, resources, or support in your actions (e.g., your professors, former students who passed the exam, the position posting boards of professional organizations).

If you have been practicing and supervising for a while, you might focus on other goals such as staying engaged with the literature or enhancing skills for compassionate care and therapeutic relationships. For these goals, the middle column might include articles that can guide your efforts (e.g., Carr & Briggs, 2010; Taylor, LeBlanc, & Nosik, 2019) or actions that you might pursue (e.g., attending a workshop, seeking a senior supervisor with the target skills, subscribing to a journal, setting up automatic alerts for new issues of journals). The link between the first two columns and the third column (e.g., people who might guide you) may not be immediately apparent until you start taking the actions in the middle column. Those actions might put you in contact with people who could mentor you on the new skills that you are trying to develop. Regardless of whether you have a name to put in the right column, you will now know what opportunities you are looking for and where to begin looking.

Summary

This chapter provided an opportunity to reflect on your core values related to supervision. The process of exploring your core values on this topic should include spending time thinking about the individuals and situations that have effectively shaped your perceptions about and approaches to providing supervision. We have pointed out that there is value in thinking about the key influencers throughout your life, and in critically evaluating what you have learned from these individuals with respect to supervision. Such reflections and exercises allow you to take an active approach to assessing and purposefully building key repertoires. You have learned about the concept of the Mentor Tree and read examples of the three co-authors' key influencers that make up their Mentor Trees. In the activities you used some of the strategies and approaches discussed to create your own Mentor Tree and to craft an action plan to direct your continued professional or personal development. These activities can be revisited many times throughout a career to anchor or re-anchor supervisory practices to ongoing goals of professional growth and contribution to the field.

Activity 1: The Mentor Tree

This Mentor Tree will facilitate reflection on past and present influences of all types, including family, peers, teachers, supervisors, and mentors, among others. Begin with your roots (i.e., critical, formative influencers) and the impact each one had on your personal and professional development. Fill in the area around the roots by identifying people and their impact. Next, fill in the trunk using the names from the Chapter 1 activity where you identified your prior supervisors. For each name, try to specify the influence this person has had on you, the lessons you have learned, and the specific behaviors you want to imitate or that you want to avoid imitating. As you summarize the central influences, reflect on each person's likely motivations, individual and cultural learning histories, and the person's specific actions you hope to emulate. For the branches, decide whether to take a retrospective, prospective or both approaches to further growth. Identify the influences of many life and career influencers that are not represented elsewhere on your tree and consider where you want to focus your next career steps and the people you might want to recruit as mentors. In the section of mentees, the acorns represent the opportunity to influence others who are just beginning in their careers. List some of the core values you want to influence in your supervisees and mentees.

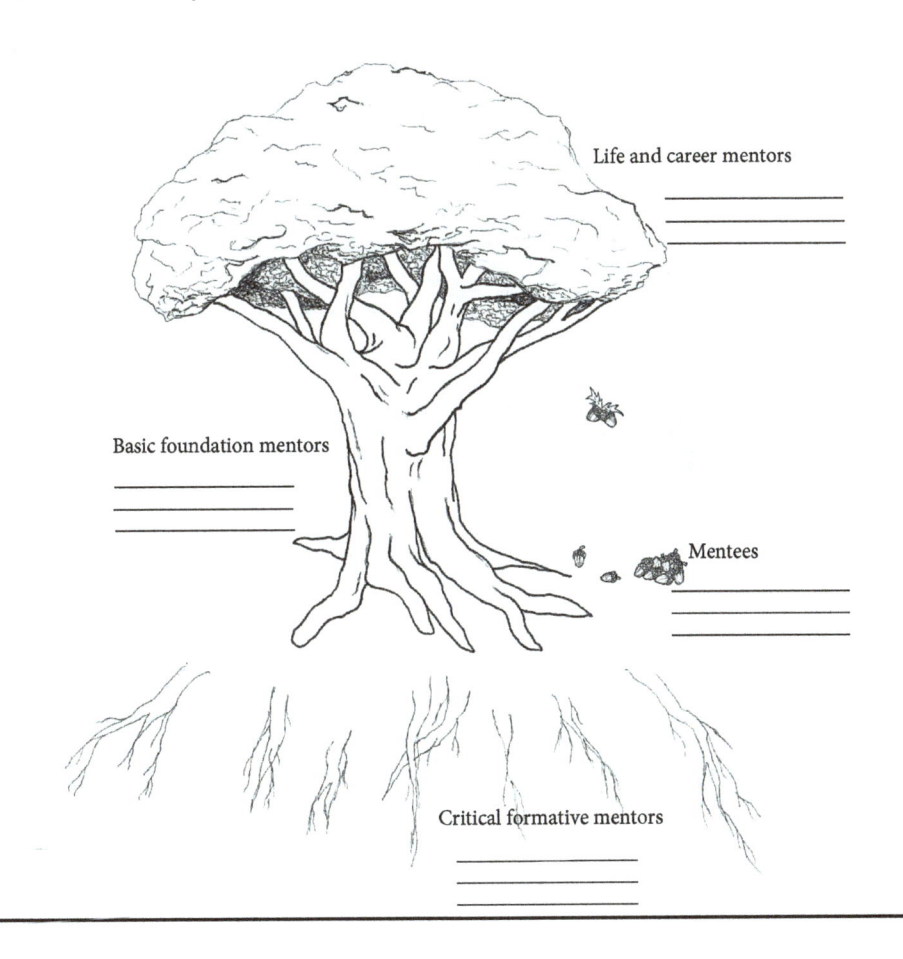

Life and career mentors
_____
_____

Basic foundation mentors
_____
_____

Mentees
_____
_____

Critical formative mentors
_____
_____

Activity 2: Planning for Continued Development

The purpose of this activity is to guide your efforts in identifying areas in which you would like to enhance your personal or professional development. In the "Goal" column, note personal or professional goals for yourself that you or a supervisor or mentor identified. Use the "Actions" column to list the specific actions that you will need to take to meet the goal. You will likely have several actions or tasks for each goal. In the "People & Resources" column, list resources or individuals who can help you carry out the actions to meet the goal. If you do not have items for the final column yet, add them as you get started with your actions. You might create a separate chart for different areas (e.g., self-care, research and writing, advanced clinical and supervision skills).

Goal	Actions	Possible People & Resources

Goal	Actions	Possible People & Resources

Chapter 4

The Impact of Culture on Supervisory Relationships

Instead of denying these differences, she accepts and explores them: she opens herself to the lives of these others, allows herself to imaginatively feel their conflicts and pain, and uses this empathy and openness as pathways to explore possible points of connection.

—AnaLouise Keating (2002, p. 520)

Our changing world reflects real and meaningful differences among humans in what we value and how we behave. At a physical level, global migration is occurring more rapidly than ever before (World Bank Group, 2016). At a social level, people now have access to previously unavailable arenas of life. In 2008, for the first time in United States history, an African American man became president. In 2018, the first indigenous woman became a member of congress and the first openly gay governor was elected. The diversity of the human experience is becoming more apparent.

These changes are happening globally and in our field (Miller, Re Cruz, & Ala'i-Rosales, 2019). Over the span of your career you will likely see increasing diversity among members of your personal and professional communities. Sometimes people respond to change with fear, anger, bewilderment, or estrangement (e.g., political isolationist and segregationist activities of supremist groups). Sometimes we respond by building understanding and creating harmony between diverse groups of people (e.g., people of color, people of different ethnic, racial, and religious backgrounds, people who identify as LGBTQ+).

While sometimes uncomfortable, diversity brings opportunities for learning, connection, and progress. As an inclusive profession dedicated to meaningful change, behavior analysis is well-positioned to engage in socially valid and culturally responsive practices (Miller, et al., 2019), including supervisory practices. Cultural differences impact supervision whether the supervisor and supervisee are aware of it or not. As behavior analysts, we have a mandate to competently perform all of our behavior analytic activities, including supervision, in diverse environments (BACB, 2014).

> *While sometimes uncomfortable, diversity brings opportunities for learning, connection, and progress.*

This chapter provides a framework for supervising in culturally diverse environments. We introduce and define concepts related to cultural responsiveness, describe common difficulties related to differences, and offer guidance for inclusive supervision. These rationales and suggested strategies are designed to assist supervisors in adhering to the BACB's ethics standards regarding non-discriminatory practices within the supervisory relationship (BACB, 2014).

The chapter does not refer to specific cultures or provide rules for responding to people of certain cultures. This omission is an intentional attempt to avoid incorrect characterizations of cultures as static or defined by a few overarching features. Instead, we focus on ways to increase understanding, connection, and learning. Throughout this book we emphasize developing healthy supervisory relationships that consider cultural history.

Collaboration as a Supervisory Strategy

As discussed in Chapter 2, strong supervisory relationships involve collaborative and participatory interactions, with the supervisee eventually taking full responsibility for their own development. The parties work together toward common goals of increasing supervisee skills and producing favorable client outcomes. Supervisory relationships have a hierarchy;

> A healthy supervisory relationship should not involve the domination of one person by another, nor should it be heavily directive.

however, that hierarchy should be based on experience and skill rather than race, gender, age, religion, sexual orientation, economics, or ethnicity. A healthy supervisory relationship should not involve the domination of one person by another, nor should it be heavily directive.

When supervisees and supervisors have very different life experiences and cultural identities, the collaborative process may become more challenging. Ultimately, the supervisor bears the responsibility to manage the quality of the supervisory process, even when the task is challenging. Nothing will be gained by ignoring meaningful differences in experiences and cultural identity. The first key to success is understanding the general concepts surrounding culture.

Behavior Analysis and Culture

One dictionary defines culture as "the customary beliefs, social forms, and material traits of a racial, religious or social group; also: the characteristic features of everyday existence shared by a people in place or time" (Merriam-Webster, 2018). Behavior analysts have provided a description of culture that emphasizes the contingency and its component parts:

> *The extent to which a group of individuals engage in overt and verbal behavior reflecting shared behavioral learning histories, serving to differentiate the group from other groups, and predicting how individuals within the group act in specific setting conditions. That is, "culture" reflects a collection of common verbal and overt behaviors that are learned and maintained by a set of similar social and environmental contingencies (i.e., learning history), and are occasioned (or not) by actions and objects (i.e., stimuli) that define a given setting or context.* (Sugai, O'Keeffe, & Fallon, p. 200, 2012)

Describing culture this way helps us understand that learning histories are shared by groups of people, resulting in similar patterns of behavior exhibited by those in the group. These differences require additional effort and collaboration to facilitate effective supervision.

The discipline of behavior analysis is not particularly diverse (see Beene, 2019; Beaulieu, Addington, & Almeida, 2019; Conners, Johnson, Duarte, Murriky, & Marks, 2019) although there are increased efforts to appreciate and increase diversity. Journal initiatives have focused on understanding cultural issues and responding constructively. For example, *Behavior Analysis in Practice* and *Perspectives on Behavior Science* both published special issues on culture in 2019 (Cihon & Mattaini, 2019; Zarcone, Brodhead & Tarbox, 2019*)*. Additionally, professional conferences and special interest groups devoted to the advancement of underrepresented groups and empowering women now exist in our field (e.g., Fong & Tanaka, 2013, ABAI Multicultural Alliance; Sundberg, Zoder-Martell, & Cox, 2019, Women in Behavior Analysis).

The BACB has articulated a firm position regarding responsibility in this area. In section 1.0 of the Code (BACB, 2014), there are three very specific sets of directives related to professional relationships. Here, we apply them to supervision and mentoring. First, behavior analyst supervisors do not harass or demean supervisees (1.05e). Second, behavior analyst supervisors do not engage in discriminatory behavior against supervisees (1.05d). Third, behavior analysts must be competent to supervise people who are of a different "age, gender, race, culture, ethnicity, national origin, religion, sexual orientation, disability, language, or socioeconomic status (BACB Code, section 1.05c, 2014)." If a behavior analyst is not competent, they must seek guidance or refer to someone who is competent to supervise their practice in this regard.

Straight From the Code

1. Behavior analysts do not harass or demean supervisees (1.05e).
2. Behavior analysts do not engage in discriminatory behavior against supervisees (1.05d).
3. Behavior analysts must be competent to supervise people who are different than they are (1.05c).

Helping profession disciplines such as education, medicine, social work, and behavior analysis have debated a variety of approaches, terminology, and actions reflecting their efforts to be inclusive and respectful of human diversity (Danso, 2018). This chapter uses the term "cultural responsiveness" to refer to practices that are consistent with appreciation and respect for diversity. Culturally responsive approaches share several core features with other approaches to diversity (see, for example, Betancourt, Green, & Carrillo, 2002; Cross, 1989; Fong & Tanaka, 2013; Fong, Catagnus, Brodhead, Quigley, & Fields, 2016; Fong, Ficklin, & Lee, 2017; Kornack, Cernius, & Persike, 2019; Wang, Kang, Ramirez, & Tarbox, 2019). First, they emphasize the importance of assessing and understanding one's own cultural experience. Second, they focus on the importance of learning from and appreciating the cultural experiences of others. Third, they recommend tailoring systems to honor and meet the social, cultural, and linguistic needs of people of diverse backgrounds. At the same time, culturally responsive practices also focus on addressing inequities related to identity

> **Supervisors Who Are Culturally Responsive:**
>
> - Assess and understand their own culture
> - Learn from and appreciate the culture of others
> - Tailor systems to meet the unique cultural and linguistic needs of diverse people in their organizations
> - Acknowledge and respond to inequities related to identity
> - Work towards educational justice
> - Embrace diversity and inclusion as an organizational strength
> - Understand that cultural responsiveness is a lifelong endeavor
> - Are humble

(Riehl, 2000). They also include a professional obligation to champion educational justice and inclusion for all members of a community (Bassey, 2016; Wlodkowski & Ginsberg, 1995). For example, if a supervisee experiences workplace discrimination related to gender identity, the supervisor will play a role in addressing the situation. If a supervisee is excluded from learning activities due to religious ordinances, the supervisor will address the issues so that the supervisee does not miss important opportunities.

More recent discussions across fields have also included the concept of "cultural humility" (Wright, 2019). Cultural humility places an emphasis on understanding the power differentials that exist in most professional relationships and the benefits of being humble with regard to cultural knowledge (Fisher-Bourne, Cain, & Martin, 2015; Hook, Davis, Owen, Worthington, & Utsey, 2013). Humility allows supervisors to admit what they do not know and to actively pursue understanding and learning. Cultural differences between a supervisor and supervisee provide valuable opportunities for learning about personal differences and their effects on supervisory relationships. We explore these learning opportunities below.

Check Your Knowledge

Question 1: The BACB Professional and Ethical Compliance code mandates that we do not discriminate and that we obtain training to increase our competence with people of diverse backgrounds. a) true, b) false

Question 2: Which of the following are cultural factors to consider: a) race, b) ethnicity, c) religion, d) gender, e) sexual orientation, f) nationality, g) all of the above

Question 3: A culturally responsive supervisor considers and addresses power imbalances between themself and their supervisee. a) true, b) false

Answers: 1) a, 2) g, 3) a

Opportunities for Learning

In Chapter 1, we reflected on the many benefits the supervisor may experience from the supervisory relationship (e.g., growth, continued professional development). These benefits are perhaps most evident when a supervisor has the opportunity to supervise people from cultures different than their own. Differences require constant evaluation and adjustment of skills and strategies used in supervisory interactions. Here, we discuss some of the most common supervisory "hot spots" that provide opportunities for cultural learning.

Learning Hot Spot 1: People have different preferences and values. Behavior analysis is based on a fundamental tenet that people are motivated by different things under different conditions, as determined by the individual learning history. In particular, reinforcers derive meaning from a person's learning history and should be assessed on an individual basis. This includes seemingly superficial things (e.g., preferred smells and colors) as well as profound things (e.g., patterns of accepted authority, priorities for family and professional events). Supervisors and supervisees will sometimes be very different in the way they respond to the world.

We often make assumptions about an individual's reinforcers and values that are framed by our own culture and our field. Often this comports with an acronym describing the behavioral sciences, "WEIRD" (i.e., westernized, educated, industrialized, rich, and democratic; Henrich, Heine, & Norenzayan, 2010). While initially referring to researchers and participants, this characterization is also reflected in practice. The WEIRDness of the dominant culture is not wrong, but does need to be contextualized and recognized as a source of potential bias toward particular ways of behaving. For this reason, multi-layered strategies for reinforcer and value assessment become a central part of culturally responsive supervision. The process of reinforcer and value assessments for adults begins with conducting interviews. *Activity 1, Culture Awareness Interview*, at the end of this chapter is aimed at developing cultural interviewing and conversation skills. This activity prepares you to have similar discussions with your supervisees. The best way to understand is to ask and listen. This activity should help with that process.

Activity 1 may also encourage you to expand the diversity of your network of associates. Cross (1989) recommends developing relationships with people from many cultures. Having diverse friends and colleagues allows several beneficial outcomes. First, you learn more about how to interact with people of different backgrounds and life experiences. Second, you develop fluency in responding to the kinds of problems that may arise (e.g., misunderstandings about directions, opposing opinions related to procedural implementation). If you live in a seemingly homogeneous area it may feel difficult to find diversity. Some differences are readily apparent to us and others require a deeper search, keeping in mind that diversity includes "age, gender, race, culture, ethnicity, national origin, religion, sexual orientation, disability, language, or socioeconomic status" (BACB Code, section 1.05c, 2014). For example, many rural areas have migrant populations, people of differing ages, and people of different educational and economic background.

Sometimes cultural differences are subtle and can lead to discomfort during the supervisory process. Groups that have different histories with the same stimuli, or cues, may respond very differently to them. For example, in some cultures an individual might express keen interest and respect by looking down when an esteemed person is talking. In other cultures, this same behavior of looking down may convey disinterest or disrespect. A period of silence might indicate lack of response or disapproval, but alternatively it might convey respect for the statement. If two people in an interaction interpret these behaviors differently due to differing cultural backgrounds, one or both may feel uncomfortable and might not understand why. The supervisor bears the responsibility to detect or respond to expressions of discomfort and to learn the supervisee's unique responses to particular events when culture is not shared. The first step to detect and alleviate discomfort is to ask about the supervisee's experiences using forthright questions that are kind and open ended. The second step is to listen thoughtfully to the response and ask for elaboration and examples. A supervisor's observation and communication skills are especially important in this area. The third step is to develop a plan of action. The problem solving and resolution process are described in Chapters 7 and 11.

Tips for Alleviating Discomfort

1. Ask kind, open-ended, forthright questions
2. Listen thoughtfully
3. Develop a plan of action

In summary, supervisors are best prepared to consider differences in preferences and values when they have learned to directly discuss preferences and values and are attentive to any discomforts. Supervisory discomforts and tensions are often related to differences regarding power, mistaken assumptions, authority, communication, time, affective displays, and moral practices.

Learning Hot Spot 2: There are power differences between people. Another important lesson is that power differences exist between people and can be magnified by differences in culture and identity. Contemporary scholars have studied the complex societal relationships that occur when some groups are afforded privilege and others are in positions of disadvantage (DiAngelo, 2011). "Privilege" in this context means that some people are afforded different and better chances, opportunities, and benefits based on being members of certain groups. Group membership often determines differences in power within a given interaction or situation. The relevant group memberships may include gender, race, ethnicity, religion, education, wealth, language, ability, sexual preferences, and nationality, among others (Kim & Whitehead, 2009). For example, in behavior analysis, white men have played a more powerful role in the development of the field than white women, and white women a more dominant role than women of color (Sundberg, et al., 2019).

When the supervisee and supervisor have different backgrounds, the dynamics can impact the supervisory relationship. One group may be seen as having more authority or opinions that take precedence over the opinions of others. These unspoken rules about power may lead to some supervisees feeling uncomfortable or as if they do not have access to the same learning opportunities as others. In *Activity 2: Exploring Your Place of Privilege*, we adapted a diagram of privilege based on Augilar (2020) and Kim and Whitehead (2009). In this activity we ask you to locate your group identities and then to think about how your supervisee or colleagues identify and differ from you.

When there are power differentials, supervisors can develop plans for addressing the resulting difficulties. This is done, in large part, by directly talking about privilege and disadvantage with the supervisee and determining specific areas to address. Chapter 11 offers ways to navigate the problem-solving process and methods to develop solutions to insure the supervisee learns skills and feels comfortable in their training setting.

Learning Hot Spot 3: Often we assume incorrectly. Making assumptions can lead a supervisor into cultural danger zones full of tension, conflict, and avoidance. There are at least three dangerous assumptions that a supervisor might make. One is assuming that the supervisee has bad intentions (e.g., disregard, disrespect, deceit). In general, it is better to assume good intentions and operate on the premise that most supervisees are seeking supervision because they value the supervisor's ability to help them learn. If there is continuing doubt based on the supervisee's behavior, it is best to have an open discussion.

Dangerous Assumptions

1. Bad intentions
2. Similar values and preferences
3. Behavior is attributable to cultural identity

The second dangerous assumption is that another person has the same values and preferences as you. For example, this is often apparent when there are conflicting values about clients. One supervisee may feel that one parent should not make decisions for the whole family and another supervisee may feel this is appropriate. In another example, one supervisee may feel comfortable with a family's same sex marriage and another supervisee may not. We can be bothered when we view their behavior from the perspective of our own values and preferences—unless we actively prompt ourselves to engage in perspective taking. Accordingly, perspective taking is considered a critical skill for cultural responsiveness (Barrera & Kramer, 2009). This involves trying to see issues from another person's point of view. We do this by placing ourselves in their context. *Activity 3: Exploring Your Perspective*, is designed to prompt supervisors to try and see things from their supervisees' point of view.

The third dangerous assumption is that any given behavior occurs because of a person's cultural identity, which can lead to stereotyping that hinders the supervisory relationship. It is our tendency as humans to identify patterns and classify events and people, but the dangers of these assumptions (e.g., classifying wrongly, engaging in prejudice) outweighs the benefits. Cultures are in constant states of change and action upon one another, and static assumptions are bound to be incorrect. Anytime we say a person is "doing that" because of a certain identity (e.g., woman, African-American, Latino, Native American, Muslim, gay, veteran, elderly, physically disabled), we should pause and examine our potential bias. Supervisors who want to facilitate the development of a responsive supervisor relationship should instead endeavor to create an environment where the supervisor and the supervisee can learn about one another's particular values, conditions and histories. At this point, look over your responses to Activity 3 and determine if they are reflective of stereotyping in any way.

Learning Hot Spot 4: People respond differently to authority. Different cultural groups have different ways of organizing themselves, accomplishing activities, responding to authority, and adhering to rules (Lynch & Hanson, 2011). These differences can produce tensions regarding supervisory and mentoring expectations and authority in the supervisory relationship. For example, some supervisees may feel they cannot act without explicit instruction and approval from their supervisor. Others may feel that the supervisor's recommendations should be followed loosely, depending on the situation. One supervisee may feel devastated and shamed by corrective feedback and another may feel annoyed that the supervisor is not providing more corrective feedback. Discussing these issues and setting clear expectations at the onset of the supervisory relationship (see Chapter 2) will help to minimize misunderstandings surrounding cultural differences related to authority.

Learning Hot Spot 5: People communicate in different ways. Effective communication is more likely if the supervisor is informed about different communication preferences and styles. Cultures are sometimes viewed along a continuum of "high" and "low" context communication structures (Hall & Hall, 1959; Lewis, 2010; Lynch & Hanson, 2011). Cultures that are considered "low context" often rely on: a) explicit and direct verbal instructions; b) equal control of conversational exchanges by communication partners; and c) privacy and respect for personal space. Cultures that are considered "high context" rely on: a) contextual cues and stories to direct behavior; b) voice tone, facial expressions, and other physical cues as implicit communication; c) differential importance and time allotted to communication partners; and d) communal space. It is important to reflect on where your culture and background falls on the high- to low-context continuum and to explore where the supervisee's falls as well.

Communication differences can create misunderstandings or, alternatively, they can complement one another and increase productivity (see Lewis, 2010; Lynch & Hanson, 2011). Recommended techniques such as "skilled dialogues" can help communication when problems arise between cultures (Barrera & Kramer, 2009). Skilled dialogue involves six steps. The first step, *welcoming,* conveys a recognition of the person's dignity and receptivity to interacting. The second step, *sense-making,* helps to take perspective and see the person's behavior in context. The third step, *appreciation,* involves communicating feelings of gratitude for what the person adds to the relationship and the setting. The fourth step, *allowing,* involves recognizing the validity of each person's perspective. The fifth step, *joining,* involves articulating how different perspectives fit with one another. The final step, *harmonizing,* involves developing third perspectives that incorporate the viewpoints of each and transcend both cultures (Barrera & Kramer, 2009). Strategies such as these can be incorporated into supervisory interactions and are compatible with the suggestions in Chapter 9 on developing interpersonal communication skills.

Learning Hot Spot 6: There are different notions of time. Responses to time and time-related activities vary widely across cultures, which can cause friction in cross-cultural interactions (Pant, Chamorro-Premuzic, Molinsky, Hahn, & Hinds, 2016; White, Valk, & Dialmy, 2011). Time is important in all cultures, but it is valued in different ways. For example, one group may view time as a commodity controlled by the individual and exchanged or spent on others. Another may view time as shared by a group and prioritized

> *Time is important in all cultures, but it is valued in different ways.*

according to relationships. Pant, et al., (2016) described consulting with groups from two different cultures. One group arrived together at precisely one minute before training. They were interested in how the new equipment would improve time efficiency. The others arrived in small groups up to 15 minutes after the announced start time, laughing and talking, with one another. They had questions about the ability of the new equipment to create team synergy. The time etiquette of the two groups and the priorities (i.e., efficiency, collaboration) differ and each offer something of value to a diverse work setting. However, even within a particular culture, responses to time are situational and related to the purpose of the events and the hierarchy of event participants (White, et al., 2011).

If the supervisor notices that a supervisee seems to have cultural values for time that are inconsistent with those of the supervisor or clients, the supervisor can point this out and provide strategies to prevent possible negative impacts. For example, if a school principal starts meetings promptly at 4 p.m., the supervisee should employ strategies for arriving at 3:55 p.m.. If the supervisee spends time building relationships with families and is subsequently late to the next appointment, the supervisee can be coached to plan more time for parent training sessions to ensure a prompt arrival at the next event. Similarly, a supervisor may have meetings scheduled back-to-back with different supervisees, one of whom consistently arrives late. The supervisor should clarify the expectation for timeliness (see Chapter 2) and contextualize the expectation as ensuring that all supervisees get sufficient time for learning and improving their client services. Alternatively, the supervisor should make it clear that training time will be extended if needed and that all supervisees should bring extra work and allow up to 30 minutes of flexibility in scheduling.

Finally, it is important to note that while culture can play a significant role in variable responses to time, other factors can affect timeliness or tardiness. For example, survey respondents have indicated that, separate from culture, issues related to caregiving of young children and organizational commitment affect timeliness and tardiness (Dishon-Berkovits & Koslowsky, 2002).

Learning Hot Spot 7: People have different ways of expressing emotions. People respond emotionally to situations in different ways, and some emotions are not easily understood from one culture to another. Usually those emotions have a specific word (e.g., in Portuguese, "saudade" is a certain kind of nostalgia for something that will never happen). It may be challenging, but we can learn to observe and understand how different people show their feelings about what is happening during the supervision process. For example, supervisees can be guided through video samples of interactions between people of differing cultures to identify and discuss emotions conveyed in individualized ways (Garden, 2016). It is particularly helpful to do this during group supervision with people of diverse backgrounds so that supervisees see and hear different perspectives about what people might be feeling in different situations.

Emotional responses that differ from our own (e.g., crying, freezing, kowtowing) may confuse us or hold different significance or meaning. For example, there are cultures that cry often (e.g., touching moments, when someone is hurt, when sad or angry) in contrast with cultures that seldom cry or show overt emotions. In both cases, strong feelings may exist even though the overt responses differ. Understanding that emotions may be culturally anchored may help us to be more sensitive to the feelings of our supervisees, thereby strengthening our supervisory relationships.

> *Understanding that emotions may be culturally anchored may help us to be more sensitive to the feelings of our supervisees, thereby strengthening our supervisory relationships.*

Learning Hot Spot 8: Religious and moral practices have a wide range of expression. This subtitle, and all it evokes (e.g., belief in God(s), rules about sexuality, body art, and marriage) is at the core of our cultural differences, but are often mistakenly compartmentalized as "outside of the workplace." For example, immigrants to the United States have reported feeling that they have to suppress spiritual expressions in work settings (Mitroff & Denton, 1999). At the same time, according to Pew Research Center (2016), a majority of Americans pray daily. Whether an expression of belief is appropriate is often defined by the dominant group. As society becomes more inclusive and diverse, the visibility and participation of groups with varied backgrounds and preferences increases. Since the 1990s, there has been a growing conversation about the entry of these issues into the workplace as diversification has increased (Blank & Slipp, 1994).

Approaching supervision as a relationship to be fostered and strengthened helps in navigating some of the issues associated with religious and moral practice differences. A supervisor and supervisee in a healthy relationship can create the expectation of positive intent, pay careful attention to actions and reactions, and initiate conversations before an issue becomes hurtful or damaging to the relationship. Consider, for example, a supervisee might like to have a 15-minute break at noon to say an obligatory prayer. She carefully mentions her religion to her supervisor and instead of ignoring the topic the supervisor leans in and says, "Tell me more about that." After her supervisor showed interest and not rejection, she felt more comfortable initiating a request to change her break time. These challenging topics also present a chance for personal growth and alliance for the supervisor to learn about different views and advocate for those in less privileged positions. Issues such as finding a quite space and time for a supervisee to say their daily prayers, advocating for benefits for same sex partners at your mentee's organization, formalizing organizational policy to include gender responsive pronouns, or establishing "stop the clock" policies for supervisees starting families are examples of advocacy.

> *Challenging topics also present a chance for personal growth and alliance as the supervisor comes to understand different views and becomes and advocates for those in less privileged positions.*

Pathways to Cultural Responsiveness

There are no shortcuts or one-size-fits-all approaches to cultural responsiveness, so we rely on continuous observation and adaptive practice to build competence throughout the process (Pant, et al., 2016). Our suggestions come from several sources and are meant to be progressive approaches that lead to continual and socially meaningful changes (Miller, et al., 2019; Sugai, et al., 2012; Fong, et al., 2016).

Create environments dedicated to responsive and caring practices. People allocate time to things that are important to them. If diversity and inclusion are important to you, your time will need to be spent learning about the cultures of your supervisees and clients and to learn strategies using resources beyond the scope of this chapter (e.g., other books, trainings, working with a mentor). Set aside time to contemplate these issues and to develop strategies that are effective and comfortable. Yes, we mean go to your calendar and schedule time to learn and reflect. The greater the cultural differences between supervisors and supervisee, the more time that must be built into schedules to ensure success.

Devoting supervisory time to learning about other cultures, relationship development, and problem solving can be difficult in an environment where time is scarce and billable hours are carefully monitored. Time and resources must be allocated to training and collaboration. It may be possible to yoke the activities with other goals. For example, cultural issues can be covered in initial orientation, weekly meetings, and satisfaction surveys. However, learning how to be more culturally responsive also requires specifically dedicated time for educational experiences.

Seek new experiences to learn about other cultures. It is helpful to enroll in cultural competency and responsiveness trainings as a way to step outside of your comfort zone and understand the issues related to culture and leadership. There are intercultural webinars and conferences as part of business leadership training and opportunities in health services, due to the growing recognition that some groups receive grossly unfair and prejudicial health treatment (e.g., people of color, women; Hardeman, Medina, & Kozhimannil, 2016; Hoffman & Tarzian, 2001). Behavior analysts are also increasing their own efforts in this regard and formal training opportunities focused on culturally responsive leadership are increasing. Indicators of quality training include recommendations from trusted colleagues and seeking opportunities that involve discussion, practice, feedback, and follow-up.

Next, begin to make friends outside of your own cultural circles by pursuing activities that put you into contact with people who are different than yourself. Remember that diversity includes a wide range of the human experience and look for different kinds of diversity (e.g., age, religion, gender, race, ethnicity, economic, and social experiences). There are also opportunities via teleconferencing to connect to people engaged in work across diverse communities. For example, the *Global Autism Project Skills Corp* (2020) offers service opportunities for behavior analysts to travel and build cultural understanding.

The desire to increase engagement with individuals from different backgrounds and cultures should come from a place of honest curiosity and compassion. Relationships are meant to build connections and to help both members of the relationship grow and develop. Referring back to your responses from *Activity 1: Cultural Awareness Interview*, will help you to reflect about the cultural diversity in your personal and professional relationships.

As you develop new personal and professional relationships, you will engage in dialogues with people who differ from you in many ways, perhaps by age, gender, race, ethnicity, religion, sexual orientation, and/or nationality. As discussed in Chapters 1, 2 and 3, these relationships will require you to reflect on your own behavior during interactions, understand sources of influence, and learn communication skills. Asking open-ended questions allows sharing in ways that close-ended questions do not (Westby, Burda, & Mehta, 2003; Barrera & Kramer, 2009). Some of these communication skills are addressed in Chapter 9. By engaging in meaningful conversations, one begins to learn about a person's identity, what it means to them, and how it influences their responses in the workplace. *Activities 1 and 3* provided you with opportunities for asking open-ended questions.

Nurture communities of practice dedicated to inclusion and fairness. Communities of practice are groups of individuals who share a common mission and a commitment to learning to advance that mission (Wenger & Snyder, 2000). Supervisors and supervisees can seek organizations that that support diversity and inclusion through clear mission statements focusing on a commitment to cultural responsiveness, as well as increasing the diversity of clients, staff membership, leadership, advisory boards, and consultants. It is difficult to ask people to change behavior, to disagree with people, and to challenge people unless the community has a lofty and shared goal. These communities have to develop methods of articulating values and create mechanisms for ensuring that values are integrated into the organization (Binder, 2016). Values such as cultural humility will often form the core of organizations wishing to increase cultural responsiveness (Hook, et al., 2013). A supervisor cannot create a community of practice alone, but he or she can advocate for their creation or choose employment settings with diversity missions. *Activity 4: Community of Practice Assessment*, includes a tool for evaluating a community of practice built around culture. If there is not such a community, the supervisor can start on a smaller scale with something as simple as hosting a weekly reading club devoted to discussing issues of diversity. For example, if the supervisee is employed in a setting that serves families who speak multiple languages, the reading group may select articles on non-discriminatory language use (e.g., Kornack, et al., 2019). If there are staff that identify as LGBTQ+, the reading group may start with reading the work of Leland and Stockwell (2019). Any of these represent a great first step in building a community of practice to provide ongoing support for culturally responsive behaviors.

> *Communities of practice are groups of individuals that share a common mission and a commitment to learning to advance that mission (Wenger & Snyder, 2000).*

Reflect and evaluate progress. The science of applied behavior analysis is built on a continuous interplay between formal and objective analysis and consideration of social importance (Baer, Wolf, & Risley, 1968; 1987; Wolf, 1978). Deciding what to measure, how to collect baseline data, and how to design behavior change programs is an area where behavior analysts have made important contributions. Doing so for cultural repertoires will be a new frontier. This final pathway involves observing our own behavior related to culture, evaluating failures and successes, and revising our strategies. This process begins with assessing one's own behavior and then progresses to assessing aspects of the environment in your organization.

Activity 4: Communities of Practice Assessment, focuses on organizational questions and *Activity 5: Cultural Satisfaction Survey for Employees and Supervisees*, focuses on questions for supervisees. With these two tools, individuals and agencies can begin to shape the cultural measures and outcomes they value and are willing to work toward.

In conclusion, the BACB ethics standards most relevant to this chapter are related to non-discriminatory practices in scientific and professional relationships (1.05 and all of 5.0; BACB, 2014). These standards make it clear that, in the absence of cultural competence, supervisors require training and mentoring to supervise people from differing backgrounds or who work within diverse workplace settings. In all instances, the supervision process should accomplish the supervision goals, but in no way should it demean, disregard, or discriminate against a person because they are a member of a particular group. Optimally, culturally responsive supervision should enhance the skills and growth of all individuals and the settings wherein they provide services. Our hope is that this chapter and these activities will help you begin to develop culturally responsive supervisory strategies.

Activity 1: Cultural Awareness Interviews

We all belong to many cultures which are formed by our histories, circumstances, and choices. The first step in learning about culture is to humbly ask questions and listen. The purpose of this activity is to explore cultural conditions and how they relate to some supervisory issues. We ask you to start with yourself and people with whom you are familiar so you can get comfortable asking the questions and really listening to the responses. Next, using the table on the next page, we ask you to interview a supervisee or a professional colleague. Try to pick at least two people that are different from you in some way (e.g., race, ethnicity, gender, nationality, religion). How WEIRD were your responses and the responses of others? How do you think most professionals in your discipline would answer these questions? Reflect and discuss.

These questions and discussion items are based on the scholarship of several groups (e.g., Ala'i-Rosales, Ferris, & Fabrizio, 2014; Miller, Re Cruz & Ala'i-Rosales, 2019; Lewis, 2006; Lynch & Hanson, 2011; Mirsky, 2013; Roysircar, 2004).

Question/Discussion Item	You	Friend from a Similar Culture	Friend from a Different Culture	Supervisee or colleague from a Different Culture
Tell a story or two about your life and/or the life of one of your family members.				
Describe your culture(s). Identifiers? Heritage? Geography? Race? Ethnicity? Religion? Social class? Gender identity? Gender preferences? Education? Socioeconomic level?				
What are some of the most important things that have happened to you in your life?				
Make a list of your top five priorities in life. Make a pie chart of your week. How much time do you spend in different activities? How much of that relates to your life priorities?				

Question/Discussion Item	You	Friend from a Similar Culture	Friend from a Different Culture	Supervisee or colleague from a Different Culture
Discuss specific beliefs and values related to work performance and importance.				
Discuss specific beliefs and values related to family composition and importance.				
Discuss specific beliefs and values related to authority, equality, hierarchy & respect.				
Discuss specific beliefs and values related to time and scheduling.				
Discuss specific beliefs and values related to skill performance and ethics.				
Discuss specific beliefs and values related to diversity. How many friends do you have with distinct cultural identities different than your own? How important do you think this is?				

Activity 2: Exploring Your Place of Privilege

There are different types of power relationships in society. Research suggests that certain groups have more privilege and others have less privilege. Having privilege means that you have sources of advantage that other people do not have. The purpose of this activity is to help you consider your positions of privilege in relation to your supervisee. In the first grid, mark the groups to which you belong and in the second grid, mark those of your supervisee. Reflect on the results. Do you have an equal relationship? If not, think about things you can do to create additional ways for your supervisee to feel safe and included in the same way as other supervisees who are more privileged.

You might also have your supervisee do the same activity for the two of you and compare the results. If you do this, take extra precaution that, in fact, you will be able to insure the safety for your supervisee. This is particularly true for privlege factors that are not physically apparent but result in discrimination and disadvantage, such as gender, religion and mental illness.

If you are not in a supervisory relationship you can reference and discuss with a colleague, preferably one that is in different groups than you.

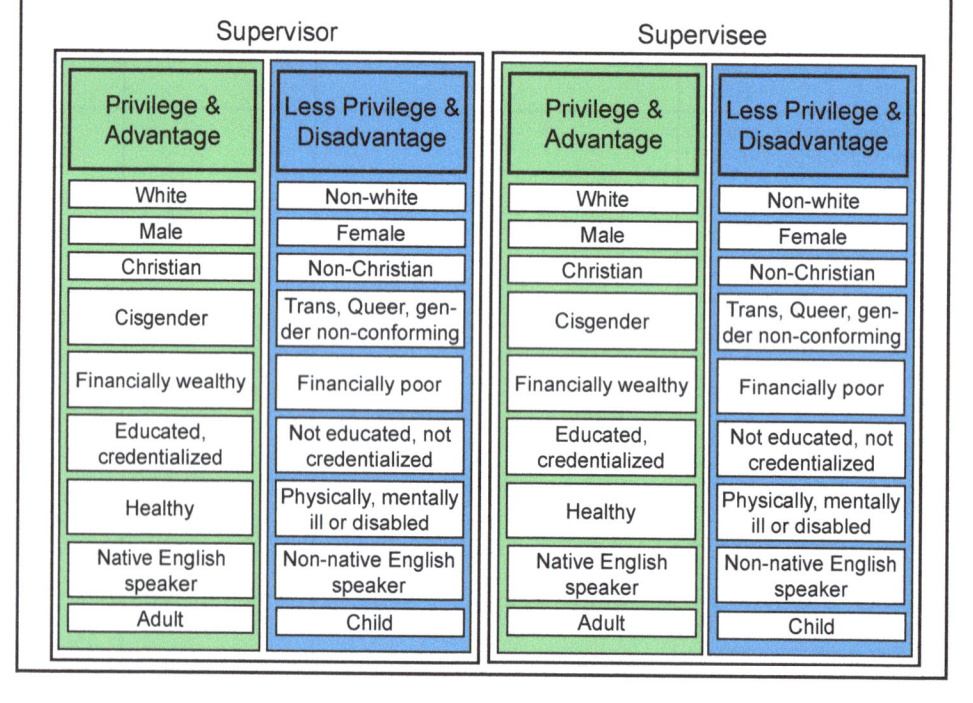

Supervisor

Privilege & Advantage	Less Privilege & Disadvantage
White	Non-white
Male	Female
Christian	Non-Christian
Cisgender	Trans, Queer, gender non-conforming
Financially wealthy	Financially poor
Educated, credentialized	Not educated, not credentialized
Healthy	Physically, mentally ill or disabled
Native English speaker	Non-native English speaker
Adult	Child

Supervisee

Privilege & Advantage	Less Privilege & Disadvantage
White	Non-white
Male	Female
Christian	Non-Christian
Cisgender	Trans, Queer, gender non-conforming
Financially wealthy	Financially poor
Educated, credentialized	Not educated, not credentialized
Healthy	Physically, mentally ill or disabled
Native English speaker	Non-native English speaker
Adult	Child

Activity 3: Exploring Your Perspective

Perspective taking is an important skill for supervisors. This activity is designed to help you see things from the vantage pint of another person's values and preferences. Pick a person that is very different from you and try to answer these questions. After you have answered them, interview that person and consider how your responses are the same or different. In some cases, you will understand why you viewed things differently, in other cases you may only know by asking them, which is part of the point of the activity. We can sometimes see another person's perspective and we sometimes have to be told or shown.

Questions	Your Response	Their Response
What do you value most in life?		
What qualities are important to you in a teacher, supervisor or mentor?		
What have been your happiest work situations? Why do you think they were so satisfying?		
What do you think are the most important skills and perspectives you bring to your work?		
What do you worry about the most in professional situations?		
Are there situations that make you feel unsafe or uncomfortable in work situations?		
What do you think are the most important things to consider for your clients?		

Activity 4: Community of Practice Assessment

A group of people dedicated to learning to serve a mission is called a community of practice. There are organizations that have communities of practice surrounding cultural responsiveness. We have applied the logic of several tools and adapted them to culturally responsive supervisory practices (Bertone et al 2013; Verburg & Andriessen, 2006). Responses to these questions can be used to identify organizations that have a community of practice surrounding culture, to help develop culturally responsive practices, and to create metrics for assessing progress overtime.

Who are the members of your Community of Practice?
This can include people in the organization providing supervision, your supervisees, colleagues, consultants; anyone is included that shares dedication and effort to learning and advance the mission of culturally responsive supervision.

Do you have a clear mission statement related to culturally responsive supervision?
For example, "The Mission of Blue Star Consulting is to train the best behavior analysts in the most culturally responsive ways."

Is there a breakdown of what the mission means to different individuals in the group?
For example, for the CEO of an agency, it might mean increasing the number of trained behavior analysts who are from different cultural and linguistic backgrounds and that they report high job satisfaction with their supervision and their work environment. For an RBT receiving training it might mean that she can talk about her experiences regarding approaches to child interactions and how they are the same or different as the families she works with. For a BCBA it might mean an environment that allows for discussions about such things as ways to respond when families ask about their gender identity, how to arrange schedules to accommodate

prayer periods for supervisees, how to communicate effectively with a person from a different cultural background than themselves, etc.

How is knowledge related to culturally responsive supervision shared within a group?
This can include a variety of activities, such as conversations, attending formal informational speakers and seminars, article sharing, formal training (with modeling, practice and feedback opportunities).

What resources are allocated to increasing culturally responsive supervision?
Do people in leadership positions share the mission? Are resources provided for expert training and consultation? Is time allocated for activities to increase knowledge and skills? Are time and compensation provided for reflection and group feedback and discussion? Are time and compensation provided for program and policy development and revision? Are there technological resources dedicated to provide easy access to information and exchange between members of the community?

Are there measures in place to formally evaluate the success of the CoP?
This can include demographic information (diversity of supervisors and supervisees), satisfaction surveys regarding signs of health (sense of inclusion, trust, ability to talk honestly and openly) and signs of discomfort (a sense of "otherness", distrust, feelings of being excluded, discounted, devalued, demeaned or harassed, submissive to an uncomfortable way of being). This may also include activity frequency counts, participation counts, activity complexity changes, and policy inclusion changes. Finally, it will include criteria for organization outcomes and the ways those outcomes relate to cultural values.

Activity 5: Cultural Satisfaction Survey for Employees and Supervisees

There are several reasons to directly ask people about your supervisory practices in relation to cultural diversity. First, you get an idea of what supervisees and employees think about efforts. Second, you are fostering cultural responsiveness by asking at frequent and regular intervals how people feel about the environment. Finally, if done within a consistent framework, the responses can be used as measures for evaluating progress over time.

These questions can be asked individually through anonymous surveys, discussed individually, or discussed in focus groups. It might be helpful to use an anonymous survey initially, at which point you can ask how supervisees would like to respond in the future. If you have one person say that they would feel most comfortable with anonymous responses, it is probably best to consider why and address the overall climate (see Chapter 6 on Structured Problem Solving).

Do you feel your organization values diversity? Describe examples of how diversity is valued or how it is not valued.

What does your supervisor know about your culture? How do you think they know this?

Circle all the words that best describe your feelings during supervision: Excluded, demeaned, harassed, discriminated against, devalued, bullied, respected, included, valued, treated fairly, cherished. Give examples that illustrate the two strongest feelings you have about supervision.

In what ways does the physical environment reflect all members of your community? Give two examples.

In what ways are meeting and activity schedules arranged to support the needs of all cultural groups in your community? Give two examples.

Circle the identity categories that represent differences between you and your supervisor: age, gender, race, culture, ethnicity, national origin, religion, sexual orientation, disability, language, or socioeconomic status.

Circle the identity categories that you feel create tension between you and your supervisor: age, gender, race, culture, ethnicity, national origin, religion, sexual orientation, disability, language, or socioeconomic status.

What ideas do you have for improving cultural responsivity?

Is there anything else you would like to discuss?

Section Two

Teaching Meaningful Repertoires

The five chapters in this section focus on teaching new and complex repertoires that are critical for success as a practicing behavior analyst and as a supervisor. Chapter 5 focuses on strategies for teaching the core content for behavior analysis. This content is what most supervisors think of as the primary task of fieldwork experience for aspiring behavior analysts. Chapters 6 through 9 focus on teaching pivotal professional repertoires that enhance overall effectiveness in supervision and the practice of behavior analysis. These skills, often referred to as "soft skills," are considered critical for success in life and almost any profession (Wentz, 2013) from technology (Muzio, Fisher, Thomas & Peters, 2007) to human service professions (Bailey & Birch, 2010).

Each chapter focuses on the pivotal behavioral skills and behavioral strategies for teaching a particular repertoire. Chapter 6 focuses on strategies for learning from experts and engaging in self-observation, reflection, and management. Chapter 7 focuses on using a structured problem-solving approach across multiple contexts (e.g., clinical problems, organizational problems). Chapter 8 focuses on enhancing organization and time management skills in order to experience productivity and success without undue stress. Finally, Chapter 9 focuses on interpersonal skills for professional success with a specific emphasis on therapeutic relationship skills that enhance one's ability to work with clients.

In summary, Section Two provides a framework for teaching the core content of behavior analysis and critical supplemental repertoires for professional effectiveness. Each of these skill sets represents an opportunity to approach another aspect of your own professional repertoire within a behavior analytic framework. Finally, each chapter provides tools for assessment for the skills addressed in that chapter. These tools can be used for self-assessment or as a supervisee assessment.

Chapter 5

Using a Competency-Based Approach to Supervision

I have always looked at my competencies before accepting any responsibilities.
—N. R. Narayana Murthy

The purpose of training and supervision is to ensure that an individual acquires the content knowledge and skills needed to perform requisite tasks related to client success and organizational progress. This process is supported by implementing competency-based instruction. Specifically, competency-based instruction focuses on teaching identified outcomes with workplace relevance to a pre-determined competence, using assessments or evaluations as the measure of competence. More simply put, it is performance in relation to a pre-set criterion (Reid, Parsons, & Green, 2012). The best way to determine the critical skills and tasks and acceptable levels of performance competence in a profession is to seek information directly from that field. In behavior analysis, the content knowledge and skills included in the BACB Task List (BACB 2017, hereinafter referred to as the "task list") provide the starting point by indicating what an entry-level individual should know and be able to do (the task list is provided at the end of this book as a resource). The BACB task list was developed by workgroups of subject matter experts and informed by surveying behavior analysts who indicated what knowledge and skills practitioners must be able to perform. This process began in 1998 with validation and revision processes occurring every few years (Johnston & Shook, 2001; Johnston, Mellichamp, Shook, & Carr, 2014). The focus of this chapter is to explore *how* a supervisor should go about developing these competencies for their supervisees. We discuss considerations for developing an effective competency-based curriculum, as well as strategies for assessing and teaching the content knowledge and skills.

The BACB task list includes the foundational and applied knowledge and skills that are critical for entry-level behavior analysts to master (Johnston, et al., 2014); therefore, it makes sense to start here when developing the content to be covered in training (Garza, McGee, Schenk, & Wiskirchen, 2018; Sellers, Valentino, et al., 2016). An early approach to competency-based supervision involved creating a competency for each BACB task list item and then evaluating mastery (Johnston, 2016). That approach was later refined by LeBlanc and colleagues by grouping task items and considering the applied function of those items to determine how mastery would best be determined. For example, simply providing a correct definition of extinction was determined to be an insufficient indication of mastery. They must be able to describe extinction to someone using plain language and to identify conditions under which it would be safe and appropriate to implement extinction. Then they must be able to use and evaluate extinction procedures safely, ethically, and under the conditions of best fit for a particular client. Finally, a competent master's-level behavior analyst would also be able to teach someone how to implement extinction procedures and to determine the appropriateness, fidelity, and effectiveness of that implementation. That curriculum was later adopted by a large human service agency where the competencies were further developed in terms of clinical relevance and tied to critical skills required for client progress and promotion opportunities.

We recommend taking a similar competency-based approach that considers the applied function of the content (i.e., how is the knowledge or skill actually applied in clinical work), and to the degree possible, the context within which the training is provided, similar to the approach outlined by Garza, et al. (2018). This chapter provides guidance for developing a structured competency-based curriculum.

Considerations for a Competency-Based Curriculum

The first step in developing a competency-based curriculum is to determine what will be included. A supervisor should be familiar with and incorporate the most recent version of the BACB task list. For example, the 5th edition task list is split into two sections. The first section covers content knowledge related to basic underlying principles and basic skills. The second section includes content and skills that have a more practice focus (BACB, 2017). It is noteworthy that the 5th edition task list is the first version to include specific content related to the knowledge and skills necessary for personnel supervision and management. A supervisor should look

> **Competency-Based Approach to Supervision**
> 1. Use a competency-based curriculum (scope and content)
> 2. Assess performance (initial and ongoing)
> 3. Teach content (use BST)
> 4. Monitor performance

to the BACB's *BCBA Fieldwork Requirements* (BACB, 2020). The document provides a description of other applied skills and activities that should be incorporated, including things like case-conceptualization and planning (see Chapter 6 for a discussion of related skills). A supervisor should also review and incorporate information from the BACBs *Supervision Training Curriculum Outline 2.0* (BACB, 2018c) for specific content related to providing effective supervision (the *BACB Supervisor Training Curriculum Outline 2.0* is provided at the end of this book as a resource). Furthermore, if a supervisor is providing supervision outside of the context of the individual's formal coursework, the supervisor should consider asking for copies of syllabi from all completed courses, and each course that the supervisee takes during the supervisory relationship. Knowing what has been, or is being, covered may help the supervisor map out a more meaningful supervision content sequence. With this information the supervisor can help the supervisee link the concepts and evidence base from classes to applied activities in clinical practice. Finally, there will be competencies, or extensions to the BACB task list competencies, that are specific to the clinical needs of the clients the supervisee serves and the values and desired accomplishments of the relevant organization.

Ethics are intertwined with all aspects of our knowledge and skills; therefore, it is crucial to incorporate instruction and discussion around ethical behavior and the BACB's *Professional and Ethical Compliance Code for Behavior Analysts* (the "Code", 2014) into each topic and skill set, and to review the RBT Ethics Code (BACB, 2018d).

Determining Scope of Content and Skills

A supervisor may feel responsible for addressing every single item on the task list. In fact, it may be the case that supervision encompasses the entire task list, as a supervisor may be providing the full scope of an individual's training and supervision through work or university-based practicum courses. Furthermore, if a supervisee is receiving training in the context of an ongoing work position, the skills required for ethical work performance for their caseload are a primary consideration in the design of a training program. In either case, it may be helpful to take a sequential approach, grouping knowledge and skills together and then prioritizing the content within those groups. For example, a supervisor may group activities and Code sections relative to conducting a skills-based assessment separate from those related to functional behavior assessments, skill acquisition programming, and behavior reduction programming. Within the skills-based assessment group, the supervisor might then prioritize related concepts and principles (e.g., operational definitions, stimulus control, reinforcer control, verbal operants) that must be mastered before tackling more applied skills, such as conducting assessments to evaluate a client's strengths and areas of need.

In his book *Making Instruction Work: Skillbloomers*, Mager (1997) describes a helpful process for designing instruction that may be helpful for new supervisors. Several chapters focus on strategies for determining the desired outcomes of instruction, which is particularly relevant for designing the curriculum and instruction to be used during supervision. The first step is to determine the specific objectives of the instruction, or as Mager calls them, the "blueprints" (p.73). Objectives describe the desired terminal performance. In other words, the objectives describe what the performer will be able to do, under what conditions, and by what criterion mastery will be measured. Having clear objectives allows the supervisor to evaluate the supervisee's performance and evaluate their own ability to effectively teach the concepts and skills.

The next step Mager lays out is development of skill hierarchies. Identifying skill hierarchies involves reviewing the skills and determining the relationships among and between them to determine if certain content is enhanced by teaching in a specific order, simultaneously in pairs or groups, or can be taught alone. Mager suggests reviewing the identified skills to group items that can be taught together. Next, Mager recommends listing the items, pairs, or groups in order, from bottom to top, that must be mastered before moving on to others. For example, it may be beneficial to teach schedules of reinforcement together, but it may be important to teach continuous measurement before moving on to discontinuous. In this way, the supervisor can streamline instruction and ensure that strong foundational skills are mastered before moving on to related skills.

In the chapter on sequencing (p. 197), Mager provides recommendations for ordering content in a way to maximize the learners motivation to engage with the material. Specifically, he recommends the following points: 1) start with a topic of high interest to the supervisee (which can be obtained in those first few supervision meetings that focus on rapport building and goal identification); 2) "sprinkle" items that are of particular interest to the supervisee throughout; 3) move from the big picture to smaller details (overarching concepts to specific skills); and 4) provide the supervisee with some control over which topics to work on during supervision (have the supervisee nominate items to be addressed every meeting, or every other meeting.

Taking a comprehensive approach where the supervisor attempts to cover all items on the task list might appear daunting, particularly if a supervisor does not have the capacity or resources for such an undertaking. At the same time, approaching supervision in a haphazard or unstructured manner may result in no more than cursory treatment of some or all of the critical content knowledge and skills needed to be an effective behavior analyst. This approach, in turn, may produce superficial and/or deficient skills sets for the supervisee. Furthermore, attending only to the items on the task list (out of context and not in relation to one another or the particular needs of a client) may mean that the supervisor does not address skills such as effective communication, problem solving, time-management, and organization, all of which are necessary to be an effective behavior analyst.

Therefore, it may be helpful to consider the scope of task list items for which the supervisor will take responsibility. The supervisor should include a clear description of the specific scope in the contract and carefully review that document with the individual at the first meeting. In making this consideration, the supervisor should consider: 1) their own areas of competence; 2) the clinical setting in which the supervisee works; and 3) the supervisee's professional goals. Garza, et al. (2018) make the excellent point that it is best to focus on knowledge and skills for which there are naturally-occurring practice opportunities in the given setting. For example, if a supervisee is working exclusively with very young children with autism in a clinic setting and has identified that they only want to work with that population in the future, the supervisor might work to ensure that a greater focus is placed on developing robust repertoires related to the skills necessary for success in that clinical context (e.g., skill acquisition strategies such as discrete trial instruction, natural environment training, and verbal behavior training). While it is critical that the supervisee master the basics of functional behavior assessments, it may not be as relevant for them to be proficient in designing and implementing functional analyses (FA) and interpreting complex data from functional analyses. In this example, there are likely to be more naturally-occurring opportunities to teach and refine basic functional behavioral assessment (FBA) processes and likely few, if any, opportunities to address FA technology with very young children. If FA technologies are to be included in the scope of competencies, the supervisor may have to create or find opportunities to expose the supervisee to FA technology and processes, a task that will require thoughtful planning and coordination.

Addressing Ethics

Regardless of whether the supervisor focuses on a subset of tasks or the whole task list, it is important that they address ethics throughout the supervisory relationship and in relation to all aspects of behavior analytic work. A supervisor should not assume that instruction regarding ethics in a class will produce a sufficient understanding for the supervisee to readily apply the principles to their daily work and to successfully identify and address ethical dilemmas. Supervisors should begin by ensuring that supervisees have a working understanding of the core principles that guide a behavior analyst's responding in professional contexts. These include principles such as beneficence, do not harm, autonomy, justice, compassion, and according dignity (Bailey & Burch, 2016). It is also important that the supervisor provide a review of our field's history in relation to ethics in research and clinical practices. In doing so, the supervisor provides a context for understanding rationales and principles as they apply to the development of our discipline.

Next, the supervisor should review the relevant professional codes of ethics by discussing: 1) the rationale for each code element; 2) the related overarching principle or principles; 3) the benefits of ethical responding; 4) the risks associated with violating the code; 5) common indicators of a potential violation and scenarios; 6) antecedent strategies to minimize violations; and 7) some potential solutions. As the supervisor moves through the curriculum, they should embed the relevant codes into each specific task area with applied examples and address those seven discussion points. Supervisors may wish to review Sellers, Ala'i-Rosales, and MacDonald (2016) which used a similar approach to reviewing code 5.0 related to supervision.

The supervisor can discuss ethics relative to each BACB task list item and indicate the relevant related code elements. For example, 5th edition task list items B-6, G-16, and H5 (BACB, 2017) are all related to punishment, as is Code 4.08 of the Professional and Ethical Compliance Code for Behavior Analysts (BACB, 2014). A savvy supervisor will be sure to link the elements of Code 4.08 surrounding considerations for using punishment procedures any time they are addressing the related task list items. A less obvious example might be the link between all of the task list (1.15) items in section B *Concepts and Principles* to a variety of Code elements, including 1.01 *Reliance on Scientific Knowledge* and 1.05(b) requiring behavior analysts to use language that is easily and completely understood by the recipient. A full discussion of task list items B-1 through 15 will include talking about the need to understand the concepts and principles well enough to determine if a practice is grounded on behavior analytic principles, and therefore based on scientific knowledge. This affords consumer protections by ensuring that consumers are not inadvertently exposed to non-scientific or pseudo-scientific procedures. In addition, Code 1.05b indicates that mastery of the basic concepts and principles requires that the supervisee not only be able to explain them in behavior analytic terminology, but also in lay terms that a consumer of their services (e.g., a parent, caregiver, teacher) could completely understand. This protects consumers by facilitating informed consent, as individuals cannot consent to something they do not fully understand. Whereas there are many more interactions between ethics and the task list items, we hope that the considerations provided here demonstrate the process of linking ethics requirements to each of the task list items in a meaningful way for supervisees.

The responsible supervisor will also include explicit instruction on taking a systematic approach to identifying and solving ethical dilemmas, accompanied by ample practice with case examples and scenarios. For strategies on how to teach a structured approach to addressing ethical problems, supervisors can refer to Chapter 7 on structured problem solving, as well as the process outlined in *Ethics for Behavior Analysts* (Bailey & Burch, 2016). Rosenberg and Schwartz (2019) provide a helpful decision-making process with specific steps and considerations (i.e., what caught your attention, brainstorming solutions, evaluating the solutions, implementing the selected solution, and reflecting on decisions), including a discussion on when code elements are or seem or to be contradictory. Finally, it is important for the supervisor to cover the procedures for ethical responding when an individual violates a code or suspects someone else of violating an ethics requirement. To achieve this, the supervisor should schedule time to review relevant reporting requirements and process of appropriate professional organizations (e.g., BACB) and governmental agencies (e.g., specific state licensure boards) typically found on the applicable websites.

Job Models and Curriculum

Once the supervisor identifies specific content and tasks to address, they may find it useful to create job models to streamline and highlight critical skills. A job model is a list of the work responsibilities for a specific job, which can then be expanded to include a variety of relevant elements, such as the component tasks required to accomplish the responsibilities, measures of mastery and performance, and desired outcomes (Rummler & Brache, 2012). As mentioned at the start of this chapter, this approach was taken by LeBlanc and colleagues when refining the competencies for a large human service agency. Garza, et al. (2018) provide a description of how to create a job model informed by the task list where specific task items are grouped by relevance to clinical work tasks, as well as examples of job models. Then, task clarification can be used to create task analyses that specify the targeted behaviors involved in the skill, the order in which the behaviors must occur (if appropriate), and any requirements around relevant dimensions of how the task must be completed (e.g., how quickly, in what format; Anderson, Crowell, Hantula, & Siroky, 1988).

As mentioned, supervisors need a curriculum to support taking a structured approach to covering the critical content. By "curriculum" we mean a planned sequence of topics to meet specific learning goals. There are a few books that that include curriculum that a supervisor can use in part, or in their entirety (Britton & Cicoria, 2019; Theisen, Bird, & Zeigler, 2015). If a decision is made to create a curriculum, this might involve a concerted effort to consider, arrange, and develop the curriculum before beginning any formal training or supervisory activities. Of course, this requires having the time, resources, and piloting capacity to do so. Alternatively, for a supervisor who does not have the time and resources to create a comprehensive curriculum before beginning to provide supervision, it may be more feasible to build a framework that allows for the development of discrete competency-based tasks and evaluations as they arise with supervisees. In either scenario, the supervisor must identify the specific concept or skill and the conditions under which the individual must be able to successfully demonstrate the knowledge or skill to be considered mastered (Mager, 1997). In addition, the supervisor should consider including information about when the content was introduced, feedback or additional training provided, mastery date, and maintenance dates and performance (if relevant). This might be housed in a Word document or an Excel spreadsheet (see Appendix A for an example). Taking a systematic approach like this ensures that the scope of the training is clearly identified, skills are trained to competency, and the relevant information is tracked. This is useful for both the supervisee and the supervisor.

Regardless of whether a supervisor uses prepared materials or creates their own, it is imperative that they are thoughtful in including representation from, considerations about, and training for effective services to diverse populations. Conners, Johnson, Duarte, Murriky, and Marks (2019) presented survey results indicating that individuals certified at the BCaBA, BCBA, and BCBA-D levels generally felt that they did not receive sufficient training in their courses, practica, and fieldwork supervision experiences related to training and application of skills to individuals from different racial, ethnic, and religious backgrounds, as well as different sexual orientations. There are different ways to refer to the process of welcoming, honoring and embracing diversity (Miller, Re Cruz, & Alai'i-Rosales, 2019). Here we rely on the notion of "cultural responsiveness" as opposed to "competence." In fact, it has become increasingly apparent that there is no point of competence when it relates to cultural responsiveness. The idea of "cultural humility" must be acknowledged and ever-present. Behavior analysts should make an ongoing commitment to continually increase their understanding of other cultures and individuals who are different from them (Wright, 2019). This active approach stands in opposition to attempting to acquire some measurable competency that can be met (Wright, 2019). Supervisors play a critical and necessary role in developing an understanding of the process of moving toward cultural humility for their supervisees. Supervisors might review Chapters 1, 2, 3, 4, and 9, paying close attention to Chapter 4, in building the skills needed to navigate these topics with supervisees.

We encourage supervisors to incorporate Wright's *Individual and Organizational Questions to Assess Cultural Humility* into supervisory practice, as well as the case studies presented in the article (Wright, 2019). Conners, et al. (2019) provide useful recommendations for supervisors to ensure that supervisees are receiving experiences that move them toward cultural humility, such as engaging in self-evaluation and reflection surrounding views and practices related to culture and diversity. This is particularly true when looking at training materials and curricula. It would be useful for supervisors as they are developing curricula to include formal review by diverse groups of people who can provide feedback on the extent to which the materials are inclusive and not exclusionary with respect to gender, sexual orientation, race, ethnicity, religion, and socio-economic status. Conners, et al. (2019) also recommend that supervisors require supervisees to contact examples, cases, and clients from diverse populations and to support systematic examination of how culture impacts considerations around designing and providing services. In addition to using tools and strategies from articles, supervisors can assign research and recommed articles in the area of multiculturalism and diversity to supervisees and then engage in critical discussion during supervisory meetings as to how these apply to the specific areas of competency under consideration (Fong, Catagnus, Brodhead, Quigley, & Fields, 2016; Conners, et al., 2019, Wright, 2019). For example, Angell, Frank, and Solomon (2016) interviewed Latino parents and found cultural incongruence with some of the ways procedures were implemented with their children. The supervisor and the supervisee could discuss this within the context of the competency areas related to consent and assessment strategies that are more likely to result in procedures that are effective and valued by the family culture.

Determining Mastery Criteria

Once the specific content and skills to be covered have been determined, the supervisor should set about identifying the mastery criteria for the content (i.e., the observable evidence that the individual has acquired the relevant concept or skill). According to Skinner (1953), knowledge "…is our behavior with respect to the world" (p.140). Therefore, to determine if someone *knows* something, we must measure that in relation to the relevant stimulus conditions. Therefore, it is important that the mastery criterion not be arbitrarily selected or used just because "that's what has always been used" (e.g., using 80 percent mastery for everything) Instead, the mastery criterion should be purposefully selected based on the specific skill or content knowledge and conditions under which the information or skill will be used. Some methods for determining the meaningful mastery criterion include surveying experts, observing expert performers, and testing the skill in real world or analog contexts (Cooper, Heron, & Heward, 2020). If competence involves a client, competence in the context of that client's well-being should be the priority. Deciding on the specific mastery criterion for a concept or skill can be informed by many variables; therefore, what follows is not meant to be an exhaustive discussion.

> *If competence involves a client, competence in the context of that client's well-being should be the priority.*

Initially, it may be useful to determine if the content of the training is related to verbal or performance skills. Verbal skills are those that result in an individual being able to accurately describe or answer questions about a topic or skill, whereas performance skills are related to accurately carrying out a task or skill. There may be some areas where an individual, as an entry-level behavior analyst, will only need to be able to accurately define or describe a concept. For example, having a solid understanding of the concepts of conditioned punishers and conditioned reinforcers is probably sufficient for an entry-level behavior analyst. In that instance, the mastery criteria likely involve providing accurate definitions, based on some rubric, and potentially providing a few correct examples and non-examples. On the other hand, many concepts and skills will require not only mastery of verbal skills, but competent implementation, which will require an evaluation of the performance of a procedure. For example, it is critical that behavior analysts are able to describe and answer questions about stimulus-preference assessments, perform them with accuracy, and select the type

> ### Teach Them to Know What They Don't Know
>
> Supervision often focuses on teaching concepts and knowledge to supervisees, which is a worthy endeavor. However, just as critical (perhaps even more critical in some contexts), is teaching a supervisee to critically and honestly evaluate the boundaries of their knowledge and skills. It is also important to teach a supervisee how to solicit support by way of training and supervision, or to professionally decline work that would force them to practice outside of their scope of competence.

of preference assessment needed for client programming. Therefore, determining if a content area is a verbal skill, performance skill, or some combination, will help decide how mastery will be described, demonstrated, and evaluated.

For both verbal and performance skills, it is important to identify the depth of understanding or doing required for mastery. Continuing with the stimulus-preference assessment example, behavior analysts likely have to discriminate which type of assessment is appropriate based on client characteristics and the therapeutic goals (i.e., advanced verbal skills), and may have to carry out modifications to the procedures based on a client's performance (i.e., advanced performance skills). It is also likely that they will need to teach others how to implement the procedures, which means they will also need to identify correct and incorrect performance responses and provide effective feedback. For example, Mager (1997) describes three specific types of feedback that are important to effective instruction: 1) adequacy feedback that lets the performer know if the performance was correct or not; 2) diagnostic feedback that lets the performer know specifically what was incorrect; and 3) corrective feedback that lets the performer know what needs to be corrected and how it can be corrected. These are important considerations in determining the mastery criteria to avoid developing insufficient repertoires by indicating a skill as mastered without a full evaluation. Similarly, most concepts and skills require fluency, as they are so essential to a behavior analyst's practice (e.g., operational definitions, functional relations, schedules of reinforcement, stimulus-preference assessments, mand training); whereas others might be less relevant and not require training to fluency for all supervisees (e.g., punishment procedures, autoclitics).

Clearly, relevance is related to the context in which the supervisee works and should be considered on an individual-by-individual basis. For content that is highly relevant, foundational, and frequently used, the mastery criteria should reflect that (e.g., demonstration of fluency and mastery over time). For content or skills that might be implemented much less frequently, an initial demonstration of mastery may be enough and should be supported by a demonstration that the individual knows where to access high quality support when the skill does need to be implemented. For example, if the supervisee is not likely to work with individuals requiring an FA, a demonstration of basic verbal competency may be appropriate. It is also critical for the individual to understand that if the need to implement FA technology arises in the future, they should not proceed independently. Instead, they will need guidance from someone who is competent in the safe and effective design and implementation of the FA, as well as in the interpretation of the resulting data. In other words, it is essential that supervisees learn to evaluate the scope of their skills, such that they can effectively identify what they do not know. Supervisors can use strategies from Chapters 6 and 7 to facilitate focusing on teaching supervisees to develop these critical skills.

The likelihood and potential risk of errors should be considered when setting the mastery criteria. Some concepts and skills are simple and frequently used, which may minimize the chances that errors will occur, provided they were trained to accuracy and fluency in the first place. Others are complex or involve many steps or components (e.g., designing simple to conditional discrimination programs), which likely increases the risk of errors. When content is more complex, the supervisor should consider if the content requires a demonstration of accuracy over more opportunities (for sufficient exemplars) and/or longer periods of time (for stable performance) than simpler content. Likewise, content that involves more potential errors and subsequent substantial risk of harm to the client or others (e.g., feeding programming, FAs, or treatment of severe aggression, SIB, or other unsafe behavior) should have more strict mastery criteria under more heavily-guided conditions.

Finally, consideration should be given to the conditions under which the skills will be used in the natural clinical environment. Many concepts and skills must be applied in contexts with significant distractors and disruptors (Mager, 1997). Consider learning to implement discrete trial teaching, mand-training, or play skills for young children with autism spectrum disorder. If the skills are taught and mastered in the relatively controlled university or clinic-based setting, there is no guarantee that the individual will implement the skills with same level of integrity in a more complex home-based or community setting. Similarly, if those same skills are mastered only in optimal role-play situations, it does not follow that the individual will successfully implement the skills in a session with a client for whom the procedure is ineffective or who exhibits problem behavior or other idiosyncratic responding (e.g., side bias, ritualistic behavior). A supervisor should consider if mastery in analog conditions (e.g., office

> **Strategies for Addressing Generalization**
> (Stokes & Osnes, 2016)
>
> - Contacting and recruiting natural consequences
> - Modifying maladaptive consequences
> - Reinforcing occurrences of generalization
> - Using sufficient stimulus and response exemplars
> - Making antecedents and consequences less discriminable
> - Incorporating common salient physical and social stimuli
> - Incorporating self-mediated physical, verbal, and covert stimuli

role-play, highly controlled clinics) is enough, or if mastery should include a demonstration of the content in contexts relevant to the intended practice setting (e.g., in home, in the community). A supervisor might consider reviewing the areas related to generalization as offered by Stokes and Osnes (2016; see box at top of next page). See Appendix B for an example of how a supervisor might take a structured approach to programming for meaningful generalization of skills.

Considerations for Assessing Performance

Once a supervisor has a plan for the scope of what they will cover in supervision, they need to determine when and how they will assess the acquisition of knowledge and skills. The work a supervisor puts into clearly defining the content knowledge and making task analyses of the focus skills can then be translated into checklists and data sheets for conducting assessments (Ala'i-Rosales, Weinkauf, & Zeug, 2011; Garza, et al., 2018). It is recommended that a supervisor obtain a baseline measure of the supervisee's knowledge and skills before beginning formal instruction on a specific topic or task (Turner, Fischer, & Luiselli, 2016; Garza, et al. 2018). Baseline measures allow a supervisor to assess acquisition and mastery, as well as to evaluate the effectiveness of the supervision itself, as is required by 5.07 of the Code (BACB, 2014). Initial assessments provide a supervisor with the information needed to prioritize areas of focus and set goals with the supervisee (Garza, et al., 2018).

Initial Assessment. A supervisor may elect to conduct a comprehensive assessment at the outset of supervision. Doing so allows the supervisor to establish knowledge and performance levels prior to any supervision, as well as to identify areas of existing competency and areas of need which may result in a more streamlined supervision plan. However, the drawback to this approach is that it requires the time to conduct initial assessments across a large number of knowledge and skill areas. An alternative approach is to simply assess knowledge and skills in the sequential order they are to be addressed. Turner, et al. (2016) suggest including several activities in the initial assessment such as observations, interviews and discussions, and reviews of permanent products. Other methods include self-assessments and performing role-plays (Sellers, Valentino, et al., 2016).

Garza, et al. (2018) recommend a clever approach, which is to have the supervisee complete an initial comprehensive self-assessment wherein the individual self-reports their level of experience and comfort across the identified knowledge and skills areas. Supervisors can refer to the self-assessment by Tagg and Biagi (2020) that is provided at the end of this book as a resource. The supervisor should follow up by carrying out targeted validation activities to assess the accuracy of the individual's self-report. This systematic approach allows the supervisor to assess items and to detect disconnects between verbal competence and performance competence for a given skill area (i.e., the supervisee can define a discriminative stimulus but cannot accurately present one during discrimination training, the supervisee cannot identify the different types of social validity but consistently selects meaningful targets, acceptable interventions, and implements intervention until meaningful outcomes are achieved). Another benefit to this approach is that it provides the supervisor with a means to evaluate the supervisee's ability to accurately engage in self-observation and self-detect competencies and deficiencies (i.e., "knowing what they don't know"), which are critical skills for continued professional development and growth. A final benefit of this approach is that through the self-observation and reporting process, the supervisor has the opportunity to observe, discuss, and reflect on the supervisee's cultural context, how they communicate, and where they place emphasis and priority. For this reason, self-observations serve not only to help in the assessment and training process, but also in the cultural responsiveness and relationship development that are the foundation of the supervision process.

In determining how to evaluate skill development, it is recommended that the supervisor consider if the item is primarily knowledge-based (a verbal skill), performance-based, or a combination (Sellers, Valentino, et al., 2016). Knowledge-based skills lend themselves to assessment through discussion and the provision or identification of examples and non-examples. Performance-based skills, on the other hand, need to be assessed *in vivo*, via video reviews or in role-play situations.

On-Going Assessments

In addition to conducting an initial assessment, either at the start of the supervisory relationship, or before addressing each item, a supervisor should schedule regular assessments. Once skills are mastered, a supervisor might elect to conduct periodic informal (observing or discussing) and formal performance monitoring and assessments to ensure that the supervisee is maintaining the knowledge and skills at the required level. Doing so allows the supervisor to provide continued praise and to identify areas that need remediation before poor habits are established. The assessments could also be arranged to systematically evaluate generalization of skills (e.g., carrying out tasks with novel materials, clients, and in untrained contexts). The supervisor should systematically track the supervisee's performance on informal and formal assessments to evaluate overall performance and the effectiveness of the supervision provided.

Because it is our opinion that high-quality supervision includes much more than the task list items, a supervisor should systematically assess other skills that are critical to success for a clinician, often classified as "professionalism." For example, no matter the technical skill level of a clinician, if an individual cannot prioritize and organize tasks, they are likely to experience difficulties in carrying out required tasks. If the individual cannot effectively build rapport and communicate with others, or effectively solve problems when they arise, they are not likely to experience success. In fact, these skills are so crucial in developing a well-rounded repertoire, and are well within the supervisor's ability to shape, that we have devoted entire subsequent chapters to them (see Chapter 7 for a discussion of taking a structured approach to problem identification and solving, Chapter 8 for organization and time management skills, and Chapter 9 for interpersonal and therapeutic relationship skills).

Considerations for Teaching Content

Through the language in the Code (BACB, 2014) and in the *Supervisor Training Curriculum Outline 2.0* (BACB, 2020), the BACB directs supervisors to implement effective training and supervision. Behavioral skills training (BST) is considered an effective and evidence-based training strategy (Parsons, Rollyson, & Reid, 2012). BST is a competency-based training method that includes several components: 1) providing a description of the skill (including the rationale); 2) giving a written/visual description (including the rationale); 3) demonstrat-

> **BST STEPS**
> **(Parsons, et al., 2012)**
>
> 1. Discuss rationale and describe skill
> 2. Give written/visual description and rationale
> 3. Demonstrate skill (model)
> 4. Provide practice opportunities
> 5. Deliver feedback
> 6. Repeat Steps 1 through 5 to mastery

ing the skill; 4) providing the supervisee with sufficient opportunities to practice the skill; 5) delivering feedback to the supervisee regarding their performance; and 6) repeating Steps 1 through 5 until a predetermined mastery is demonstrated (Parsons, et al., 2012). Researchers have demonstrated the success of BST as an effective method for training across a variety of populations (Belisle, Rowsey, & Dixon, 2016; Gianoumis, Seiverling, & Sturmey, 2012; Gilligan, Luiselli, & Pace, 2007; Hall, Grundon, Pope, & Romero, 2010; Miles & Wilder, 2009; Nigro-Bruzzi & Sturmey, 2010; Parsons, et al., 2012; Roscoe & Fisher, 2008; Sarokoff & Sturmey, 2004) and in a wide range of settings (Hall, et al., 2010; Nigro-Bruzzi & Sturmey, 2010; Jerome, Kaplan, & Sturmey, 2014).

The instruction and BST procedures for each knowledge area and skill should be well planned ahead of time. Though a supervisor should also capture in-the-moment teaching opportunities as they arise, the bulk of the training activities should be pre-designed. One approach is to create training storyboards (Garza, et al., 2018). The process of creating a training storyboard functions as a series of prompts to ensure that the supervisor does not miss any of the critical steps in planning to use BST (Garza, et al., 2018). Garza and colleagues provide a useful training storyboard template (Garza, et al., 2018). Whether a supervisor uses a training storyboard or not, when implementing the steps of BST, there are some critical considerations for each step.

Steps 1 and 2: Descriptions and Rationales. First and foremost is pre-planning by determining the specific content and mastery criteria, as well as gathering the needed materials ahead of time. In describing the skill to the supervisee, the supervisor should not only provide a clear explanation of the skill, but also discuss why the knowledge or skill is important. The rationale allows the supervisor to clearly describe how the supervisee and client will benefit from the supervisee accurately performing the skill, as well as what potential risks of harm are avoided. The rationale also provides an opportunity to incorporate content related to ethics, cultural responsiveness, evidence-based practice, safety, and the development of therapeutic relationships. For example, when describing the common side effects of extinction procedures, the rationale for the importance of knowing the side effects might include that failing to consider the likely side effects could result in ethics violations (e.g., client's rights, focus on reinforcement-based procedures), safety issues (e.g., increases in problem behavior could lead to injury), and damaging the therapeutic relationship (e.g., increases in emotional responding may be unpleasant for the caregiver to witness).

The vocal and written training descriptions should be clear and concise. Despite the value of vocal explanations during training, many supervisors and trainers often provide overly complicated written documents (e.g., lengthy intervention and teaching protocols) or fail to provide supporting written explanations at all (Parsons, et al. 2012). Job aids are concise written descriptions of a task that include things like checklists, summary sheets, flow charts, and visuals that can be accessed by the supervisee during and after training (Parnell, Lorah, Karnes, & Schaefer-Whitby, 2017; Sasson, Alvero, & Austin, 2006). The supervisee can also use job aids during their practice, eventual independent performance, and during self-assessment, if it is likely that these job aids will be allowed in the terminal job setting. If job aids will not be allowed, the supervisor must work to systematically fade the presence of such supports before checking for skill mastery.

Steps 3 and 4: Demonstration and Rehearsal. The supervisor should plan and practice skill demonstrations to ensure that the demonstrations are competent models of the desired skill (McGimsey, Greene, & Lutzker, 1995). It is critical to resist the urge to take a play-it-by-ear approach to modeling and practicing the skills, as this increases the likelihood of several possible issues. Consistently demonstrating and practicing off the cuff means that each supervisee is getting a slightly different experience and, therefore, slightly different skill development. It could also mean that the model does not capture critical elements of the performance or the critical features of the circumstances in which the skill must be implemented. This approach is also less time efficient than having pre-planned procedures and scripts at the ready. Parsons and colleagues recommend planning out the role-play and practice opportunities and considering things such as: the specific model; whether non-examples will be demonstrated; the role-play partner (e.g., if the supervisee plays a role the supervisor must provide clear instructions); and the specific "pause points" for detailed explanations or opportunities for the supervisee to ask questions (Parsons, et al., 2012). A supervisor should begin by demonstrating the simplest version of the skill. Subsequently, the supervisor can systematically increase the complexity of the skill by adding more complex components to the demonstrations (for example: prompting, data collection, and blocking procedures). Throughout and after the demonstration, the supervisor should encourage supervisees to ask questions. As an alternative to live role-plays, a supervisor may choose to implement video-models to provide consistent examples and free up the trainer to provide enhanced explanations, point out exemplars or errors, and to pause or rewind.

> *A supervisor should begin by demonstrating the simplest version of the skill. Subsequently, the supervisor can systematically increase the complexity of the skill by adding in the demonstrations.*

Researchers have demonstrated that the rehearsal or practice component is critical for the supervisee to successfully acquire the target skill (Nigro-Bruzzi & Sturmey, 2010; Rosales, Stone, & Rehfeldt, 2009) and a supervisor should not skip this step. If the training activities occur over several days, it might be helpful to plan the rehearsal activities to occur immediately after the modeling component to increase the likelihood that the supervisees will respond based on the model that was just observed. As with the demonstration activities, a supervisor should develop the practice activities ahead of time and include clear instructions for the supervisees to ensure systematic implementation and effective use of time. As discussed above, the practice activities should also proceed from simple to more complex, progressing through the levels once mastery is demonstrated. In this way the supervisee can master the basic skills to fluency before the supervisor introduces distractors and disruptors (e.g., prompting, collecting data, addressing problem behavior).

Step 5 and 6: Feedback and Repeat to Mastery. The feedback component of BST deserves extra attention, as feedback is the critical element for improving future performance (Ward-Horner & Sturmey, 2012). In referring to feedback, we mean information provided to the supervisee about some specific aspect of their performance that is meant to either support similar performance in the future (in the case of optimal or desired behavior), or that is meant to change some aspect of that performance (Daniels & Bailey, 2014). Section 5.06(a) and (b) of the Code specify that we provide feedback that is specifically designed to improve performance, is delivered in a timely manner, is documented, and is provided consistently over time (BACB, 2014). Provision of feedback is not constrained to structured BST activities. In a recent review of the organizational behavior management literature, researchers identified feedback as the second most common evidence-based intervention used to affect performance change in human-service settings (Gravina, et al., 2018).

Feedback is one of the most powerful tools we have for shaping and maintaining a supervisee's performance; therefore, a supervisor should actively implement high-quality feedback as frequently as possible with a supervisee. The idea is to create a feedback-rich environment. The supervisor should deliver frequent high-quality feedback about what is going right, along with well-timed corrective feedback that a supervisor delivers in a professional and compassionate manner (see Chapters 2, 6, and 11 for more specific information on feedback). If the only time

> *Obviously, a supervisee is most likely to look forward to and seek out feedback opportunities if the feedback is helpful, meaningful, specific, and delivered in a culturally responsive, kind, and professional manner.*

the supervisor provides feedback is following an incorrect performance, the supervisee may come to dread receiving feedback. Obviously, a supervisee is most likely to look forward and seek out feedback opportunities if the feedback is helpful, meaningful, specific, and delivered in a culturally responsive, kind, and professional manner. In their book *Fieldwork and Supervision for Behavior Analysts, A Handbook*, Kazemi, Rice, and Adzhayn (2018) include a discussion of feedback from the perspective of the supervisee in Chapter 6, "Gaining the Most from Your Supervision Experience" (p. 56–65). Specifically, they define feedback and outline its importance in shaping behavior, describe strategies that a supervisee can employ when receiving feedback (accept, restate, clarify, thank), and provide recommendations for how a supervisee can solicit feedback and give feedback. Supervisors may find it helpful to review the information that Kazemi and colleagues provide, as approaching feedback from the supervisee's perspective may increase the likelihood that supervisors will provide compassionate and effective feedback. It may also be a helpful exercise to review the recommendations and vignettes provided by those authors together with supervisees, as a proactive and structured way to discuss feedback.

As mentioned, there are three main types of performance feedback: adequacy (what was done well), diagnostic (what was done incorrectly), and corrective (what to fix and how) (Mager, 1997). Regardless of the type of feedback delivered, it is important that it is specific and prescriptive. That is, effective performance feedback includes: specifying the relevant behavior; delivering frequent and immediate feedback; and providing the feedback in a manner that is understandable and meaningful to the supervisee. Parsons, et al. (2012) describe supportive feedback as telling the individual exactly what was done correctly, to which we might add ini-

Instead of this…	Try saying this…
- Don't do it like that. - No, you are doing that wrong. - That's not how to do X. - Ok, what you are doing wrong is X. - The mistake you are making is Y. - You are forgetting to do X.	- I think doing it like Y will make a big difference. - Let's see what happens when you try X. - I'd love for you to X, instead of Y. - Hey, what do you think will happen if you do it like X? Let's give it a try and see! - You know what works for me is to do Y. Why don't you give it a try? - It's easy to overlook, but remember to X.

tially explaining why it was correct and why it is important (i.e., what the positive outcomes will be related to performing the skill correctly). Corrective feedback is described as clearly indicating what was done incorrectly and how to correct the error (i.e., what to do instead) (Garza, et al., 2018; Parsons, et al., 2012; Sellers, Valentino, et al., 2016); which might include modeling the correct implementation (Sellers, LeBlanc, & Valentino, 2016). A great approach is to frame the feedback in "do" statements that instructs the individual what they should be doing. See the table below for specific examples.

During the practice portion of BST, a supervisor can deliver unobtrusive supportive feedback (e.g., thumbs up, smiling, nodding) during the performance. According to Parsons, et al. (2012), the supervisor should deliver more detailed descriptive supportive feedback and corrective feedback at the conclusion of the practice or role-play. However, if based on interactions with the supervisee, the supervisor finds that the supervisee prefers "in the moment" feedback most helpful, and it is appropriate to do so (i.e., providing the feedback will not be overly disruptive), the supervisor may pause the practice to deliver feedback. Practice opportunities and feedback should be provided until the individual meets the pre-determined mastery criteria. It may be the case that there are two levels of mastery; an initial criterion during training that allows the supervisee the opportunity to implement the skill with clients, and a more advanced criterion for mastery that requires demonstration in a variety of applied contexts over time. For some skills, a third mastery level might be identified in which the individual must demonstrate the ability to train others and correct performance errors.

In addition to the supervisor being mindful about the frequency and content of the feedback delivered, it will be helpful to provide the supervisee with some guidance and expectations regarding how to respond to the feedback that will provided. It may be the case that the supervisee has not received much corrective feedback in the past, has a history of feedback being unpleasant, or simply does not know how to effectively respond to receiving corrective feedback.

Early in the supervisory relationship, the supervisor can begin having conversations about the importance of feedback and how feedback will occur. Refer to Chapter 2 for guidance on facilitating a discussion about feedback and other critical topics. The supervisor can then ask the supervisee about their preferred and non-preferred forms of feedback and might describe specific behaviors for receiving feedback (e.g., smiling, nodding, taking notes, paraphrasing back to the supervisor, asking for clarification, examples, models, or opportunities to practice, asking for a break if they are getting upset) (Algiraigri, 2014; Kruse, 2014; Sellers, Valentino, et al.,

2016). If a supervisor has not had this type of discussion with a supervisee before, they might find the script in Appendix C helpful. Ehrlich and colleagues (2020) describe eight skills related to effectively receiving corrective feedback that included: 1) preparation; 2) eye contact; 3) appropriate follow-up questions; 4) acknowledging the mistake; 5) active listening; 6) committing to the behavior change; 7) making an appreciative statement; and 8) overall demeanor, as well as rationales and operational definitions of the target behaviors (Ehrlich, Nosik, Carr, & Wine, 2020). As previously mentioned, Kazemi and colleagues also provide excellent suggestions directed at supervisees on how to receive feedback in their book (Kazemi, et al. 2018).

On-Going Performance Management. A supervisor's work is hardly done when a supervisee masters a skill in the training context. Once the supervisee masters a skill, a supervisor must employ ongoing performance management to ensure that the skills maintain over time via performance feedback (Parsons, et al., 2012). Performance management also provides the opportunity for continued development of the supervisee's skills through coaching (Gravina & Siers, 2011). Upon completion of training, a supervisor can engage in ongoing performance management by conducting informal and formal observations and assessments, providing a means for evaluating maintenance and generalization of the skill (Garza, et al., 2018). The results of those observations and assessments can provide data for the development of more advanced goals for the supervisee as they move through the competency-based curriculum.

A supervisor should address performance issues as soon as they detect them by determining the barriers to correct performance and providing supportive corrective feedback and function-matched interventions to address the performance deficit. For example, the supervisor can use the *Performance Diagnostic Checklist—Human Services* (PDC–HS; Carr, Wilder, Majdalany, Mathisen, & Strain, 2013) to systematically evaluate and identify the environmental variables contributing the performance issues and develop a well-matched intervention. In addition, refer back to the strategies covered in this chapter and in Chapters 6, 10, and 11 for ideas on how to evaluate the barriers associated with the performance issue. If it appears that the performance issue is instead related to deficits or excesses typically described as "professionalism," see Chapters 7, 8, or 9 as applicable.

Given the complexity of teaching the skills required to identify and address potential or actual ethical dilemmas, it is worth providing some additional guidance for the supervisor who identifies persistent issues related to unethical behavior. The supervisor should evaluate the supervisee's understanding of the general ethics principles and the specific ethics requirements of the field, as well as the supervisee's ability to identify the risks associated with violating general principles and specific ethics requirements. Following that, two important questions to ask are 1) does the supervisee seem to view right and wrong as absolutes (e.g., rigid black and white judgements); and 2) does the supervisee seem to have difficulty distinguishing between personal and professional ethics? These considerations may be indicative of learning histories resulting in inflexible application of rules and or difficulty seeing multiple sides to a given situation. It may be the case that the supervisee simply needs more instruction and exemplars in these areas, as supervisees are likely to have limited experience with identifying and addressing ethical dilemmas. In addressing deficits related to ethical behavior, we encourage supervisors to review Chapter 4 on how culture impacts the supervisory relationship. There are a multitude of potential contributing factors to deficits in this area and discussing them all is beyond the scope of this book. Supervisors are, therefore, directed to the strategies in specific books devoted to the topic of ethics for further consideration (Bailey & Burch, 2016; Brodhead, Cox, & Quigley, 2018).

> *The full scope of skills that a supervisor might teach is too large to leave unplanned.*

In summary, the full scope of skills that a supervisor might teach is too large to leave unplanned. Although the currently required number of supervised experience hours seems large, it can be difficult and perhaps impossible to target all of the critical repertoires for a practicing behavior analyst in that time frame unless the supervisor has a clearly organized plan. That plan should describe the scope and order of the targeted skills and the strategies that will be employed to change the supervisee's repertoires so that he or she can make important changes in people's lives, as well as a plan for incorporating ethics into each topic. This chapter focused on developing competencies in the core skills in the BACB task list and the Code. Future chapters focus on other repertoires that are critical for success in independent practice, including skills for learning from experts, problem solving and case conceptualization skills, organization and time management skills, and interpersonal and therapeutic relationship skills.

Appendix A: Tracking Competencies

Supervisee: _____   Primary Supervisor: _____

Date Contract Signed: _____

Knowledge/ Skill	Intro Date	Mastery Date	Demo Context	Gen Context	Maint Period	Notes

Demonstration Context Codes

Def = Defines
DefPL = Defines in plain language
Ex = Gives at least 3 examples
NonEx = Gives at least 2 non-examples
TransNonEx = Identifies why something is a non-example and transforms a non-example into an example
RP = Demos in role-play (with supervisor or other confederate)
W/C = Demos with client
W/P = Demos with a parent or other relevant individual to case
Train = Demos in training delivery to other/s

Generalization Context Codes

NTC = Demos in a non-training context
Unfam = Demos in an unfamiliar context
W/NTIndiv = Demos with a non-training context individual
W/NTMatrl = Demos with non-training material

Maintenance Periods

1w = 1 week
2w = 2 weeks
1m = 1 month
3m = 3 months

Appendix B: Examples for Assessing Competency

Skill: Functions of Behavior

☐ Define using behavior analytic terms measured against an acceptable definition

☐ Define using plain language for at least 3 different target listeners
  ☐ parent
  ☐ therapist with little behavior analytic training
  ☐ non-ABA service provider
  ☐ other:

☐ Give 3 examples across each function
  ☐ auto-negative   ☐ auto-negative   ☐ auto-negative
  ☐ auto-positive   ☐ auto-positive   ☐ auto-positive
  ☐ social-negative ☐ social-negative ☐ social-negative
  ☐ social-positive ☐ social-positive ☐ social-positive

☐ Give 1 example for each function for at least 3 different target listeners
  ☐ auto-negative: ☐ parent of preschooler ☐ social worker serving adults ☐ 10th grade SPED teacher. ☐ other:
  ☐ auto-negative: ☐ parent of preschooler ☐ social worker serving adults ☐ 10th grade SPED teacher. ☐ other:
  ☐ auto-negative: ☐ parent of preschooler ☐ social worker serving adults ☐ 10th grade SPED teacher. ☐ other:
  ☐ auto-negative: ☐ parent of preschooler ☐ social worker serving adults ☐ 10th grade SPED teacher. ☐ other:
  ☐ auto-negative: ☐ parent of preschooler ☐ social worker serving adults ☐ 10th grade SPED teacher. ☐ other:

☐ Identify 2 non-examples from options that include examples for each function, state why they are non-examples, and offer an appropriate function-matched explanation of the maintaining contingencies
  ☐ Non-example 1: ☐ identifies   ☐ states why   ☐ provides function-matched explanation
  ☐ Non-example 2: ☐ identifies   ☐ states why   ☐ provides function-matched explanation

Skill: Stimulus Preference Assessments (SPA): for each of the main SPA methods

☐ Name: ☐ Free Operant (FO) ☐ Paired Stimulus (PS) ☐ Multiple Stimulus without Replacement (MSWO)
☐ Describe in behavior analytic terms in writing and vocally
  ☐ FO: ☐ describe, written   ☐ describe, vocally
  ☐ PS: ☐ describe, written   ☐ describe, vocally
  ☐ MSWO: ☐ describe, written   ☐ describe, vocally

- ☐ Describe in plain language (intended audience is parent or other non-behavior analytic professional) in writing and vocally
    - ☐ FO: ☐ describe, written ☐ describe, vocally
    - ☐ PS: ☐ describe, written ☐ describe, vocally
    - ☐ MSWO: ☐ describe, written ☐ describe, vocally
- ☐ Name the SPA method from an example (vocally described or depicted in a live-model or video): ☐ FO ☐ PS ☐ MSWO
- ☐ Describe the pros and cons
    - ☐ FO: ☐ pros ☐ cons
    - ☐ PS: ☐ pros ☐ cons
    - ☐ MSWO: ☐ pros ☐ cons
- ☐ Pick the best matched SPA method for at least 3 case examples or clients
    - ☐ Example 1
    - ☐ Example 2
    - ☐ Example 3
        - ☐ Accurately implement in role-play, including collecting data
    - ☐ FO: ☐ implement ☐ collect data
    - ☐ PS: ☐ implement ☐ collect data
    - ☐ MSWO: ☐ implement ☐ collect data
- ☐ Accurately score and describe appropriate use of results in programming for specific cases examples or clients
    - ☐FO: ☐ score ☐ use of results
    - ☐PS: ☐ score ☐ use of results
    - ☐MSWO: ☐ score ☐ use of results
- ☐ Accurately conduct procedural integrity checks
    - ☐ FO
    - ☐ PS
    - ☐ MSWO
- ☐ Accurately train another person to implement using BST
    - ☐ FO
    - ☐ PS
    - ☐ MSWO

Appendix C: Script for Explaining Feedback and Responding to Feedback

A supervisor can use this script to get some ideas about how to: a) explain the positive purposes of feedback; b) anchor the feedback experience with respect to the intent of the supervisor; and c) discuss any past negative experiences with feedback and how to succeed despite them.

Supervisor: "Thank you for adding this topic to the agenda. I think it is one of the most important discussions we will have. I want to take a few minutes to talk about feedback. Feedback is something that many people view as a negative thing because in the past it has meant that you are in trouble. Have you had any experiences like that?"

Pause: Give the supervisee a chance to nod, agree, tell a story, or nothing at all. It is not critical that the supervisee reveal any personal stories yet. It is important that the supervisor express sympathy and understanding about how the past can change how we respond to the present.

Supervisor: "I see feedback in a specific way and I hope that you will, too, as we progress through supervision. To me, feedback is the greatest gift I can give you. To give you feedback, I have to pay attention to what you are already doing well, what things you could do a little differently, and I have to figure out exactly how to tell and show you the approach that might make you more successful in the future. So that means describing the things you do really well IS FEEDBACK—not just the things you could do better. For my part, I will try my best to spend as much, or more time on doing that as I do on showing you how to do new things. For your part, try your best to listen to the praise, acknowledge it, and remember that this is also feedback about what you should keep doing. Do you ever have trouble hearing compliments or are you more the 'keep it coming' type?"

Pause: Give the supervisee a chance to nod, agree, tell a story or nothing at all.

Supervisor: "Part of my job is to teach you how to do things that you don't know how to do yet. This means that I don't expect you to be perfect—if you were, you wouldn't need me. But people who are achievers and strivers often have a bit of the perfectionist in them which can lead to feeling defensive. If you ever have thoughts or responses like that, remember that you shouldn't ever feel bad about making a mistake or having a question because I am here to help with those things. You will make mistakes or do things mostly right and I will be explaining why and how you might do it differently.

For my part, I will try to remember to be as specific as I can about what you might try in the future and I will try to be as direct, supportive, and kind as I can

> *with my feedback. For your part, remember that my intent is always to help and to teach, monitor whether you are having an emotional reaction to the feedback, and try to respond in ways that let me now that you heard the feedback and plan to try your best. For example, even if it doesn't feel great to hear that something wasn't quite right, remind yourself that this is a good opportunity to learn and that I love helping you learn. Please show me that you acknowledge the feedback and say something along the lines of 'Oh, I see,' 'Ok, that makes sense,' 'Does that mean (follow up question),' or even a simple 'Thank you, I will try that.' Don't forget that I also want you to provide me with feedback about how things are going and what I can do better to support you."*

Chapter 6

The Benefits of Learning from Experts and Self-Managing Development

Learning how to learn is life's most important skill.

—Tony Buzan

Effective behavior change can make important differences in the lives of the people we serve. Continued learning and professional development will help to maintain skills and increase effectiveness. The technologies behavior analysts use are regularly evaluated and refined through research and careful clinical application, and effective outcomes require that we are aware of these advancements and advance our skills accordingly. Additionally, clients' needs often require a behavior analyst to advance their own existing skills or develop new skills to best serve that client. This is especially true in the case of clients who have markedly different life experiences or cultures from their clinician's (e.g. gender, race, ethnicity, sexual orientation, religion). The BACB's *Professional and Ethical Compliance Code for Behavior Analysts* requires that we ensure that our knowledge and skills in our specific area of practice (including supervision) remain up to date (Code 1.03, BACB, 2014).

Upon entering the field, most behavior analysts have learned the basic skills in their graduate training program and supervised fieldwork to effectively teach and correct performance issues using evidence-based, behavior-analytic strategies such as those outlined in Chapter 5. However, behavior analysts wishing to maintain effectiveness and achieve greater levels of expertise need to actively develop more robust repertoires and seek environments that support those repertoires. This generally involves at least three components: 1) advanced observation and discrimination skills; 2) self-management skills; and 3) membership in a skilled community of practice to ensure access to high-quality peers for skill maintenance and development. Working in orchestration, these three components can facilitate continued professional development.

Once in the field, many behavior analysts find that structured professional development opportunities are infrequent. One way to engage in professional development is to observe someone else's performance. To maximize growing professional skills through observation, we will outline four critical components: 1) discriminating high-quality performers from those who are merely competent performers and from those whose performance is deficient; 2) attending to the performance; 3) intentionally imitating the critical correct responses modeled; and 4) accurately self-evaluating one's own performance and adjusting as needed. These four steps allow ongoing learning that can continue throughout one's career.

The process just described can be described as observational learning. Observational learning is a way of acquiring skills after watching someone else demonstrate the skill and observing the contingencies related to that performance (Catania, 1998). However, we should not assume that just because we observe something, we are then able to do it, let alone do it well. Learning through observing, without also engaging in careful discrimination and self-evaluation, could lead to defective repertoires and ineffective practice. In other words, it is not enough to observe responses and replicate them in a similar context.

> *Learning through observing, without also engaging in careful discrimination and self-evaluation, could lead to defective repertoires and ineffective practice.*

In addition to teaching supervisees to effectively and efficiently learn from experts through observation, careful discrimination, imitation, and self-evaluation, the supervisor should spend some time teaching the supervisee how to engage in self-management for long-term success when they no longer have access to frequent support from a supervisor. In this chapter we outline how a supervisor can teach a supervisee how to effectively learn from experts and engage in self-monitoring. We discuss some strategies for identifying experts and teaching supervisees how to effectively observe, describe, and discriminate when watching them. We then describe the critical steps for teaching effective self-observing, self-evaluation, and soliciting feedback. Finally, we provide suggestions for how a supervisor can help a supervisee develop effective self-management skills for longer-term success.

Considerations for Identifying an Expert

Before we address how to teach supervisees to carefully and effectively observe expert performers, let's review how to identify an expert worth observing. Merriam-Webster defines *expert* as "one with the special skill or knowledge representing mastery of a particular subject" and "having, involving, or displaying special skill or knowledge derived from training or experience" (http://www.merriam-webster.com/dictionary/citation). There are various models of expertise levels, but in every case, there is consensus that distinct levels exist. For example, Dreyfus and Dreyfus studied chess players, pilots, tank drivers and commanders in the context of experience, situations and performance (Dreyfus & Dreyfus, 1980; Dreyfus, 2004). Based on extensive observations, they identified five categories of expertise: novice, advanced beginner, competent, proficient, and expert. In general, the novice, or new learner, tends to respond to situations in a rule-based, decontextualized fashion. As expertise develops, decision making becomes more situational, contextual, and guiding principles and goals direct the expert's behavior. Once proficient, the expert is highly mission-based, analytical, and so fluent that their behavior appears "intuitive." A final and important hallmark of an expert is the ability to identify the boundaries of their skill set. Generally, the more expertise a person has, the more they can identify things that they are *not* skilled to perform (Kruger & Dunning, 1999). Experts can identify and are willing to admit when they are unsure, do not know something, or make a mistake. In addition, they take action to find answers and fix their mistakes.

We might say that an expert in our field is someone who consistently engages in contextually appropriate responding consistent with behavior-analytic strategies and technologies that reliably produces valued outcomes. An expert also conceptualizes and narrates within a behavior analytic framework. Finally, it should be noted that expertise is situational (i.e., certain situations will serve as a great match for the exceptional skills of the expert and some will not). At different points in a person's education and training, they will need mentors and models with different kinds of expertise. In behavior analysis, areas of expertise include diverse content areas

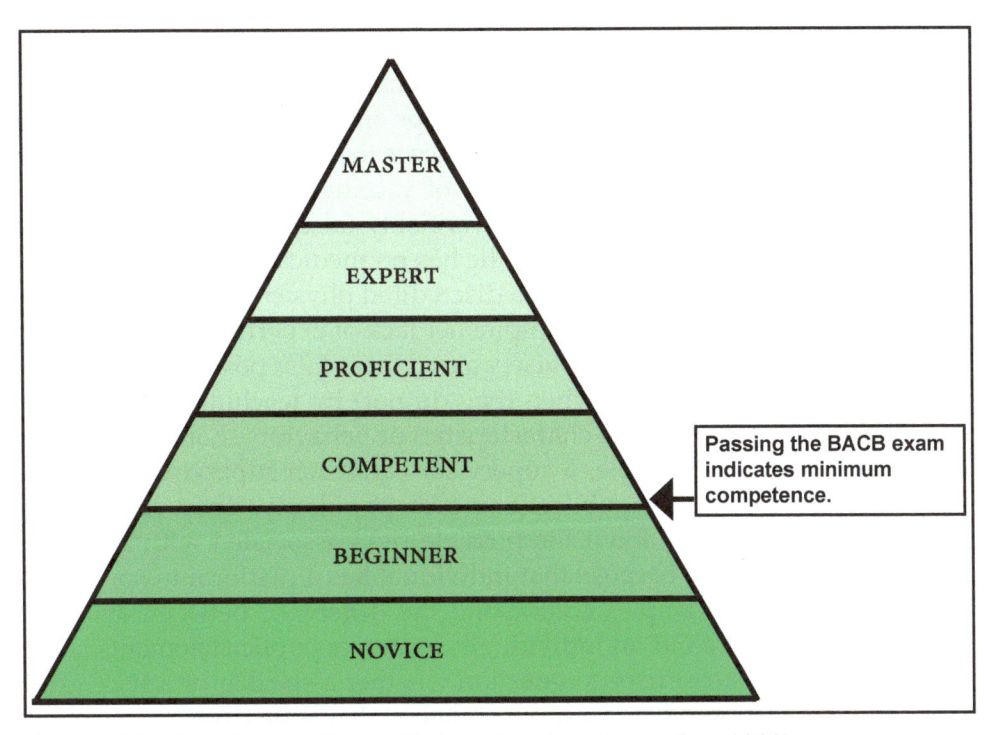

Figure 6.1 The Dreyfus Pyramid (from Dreyfus & Dreyfus, 1980)

Pyramid levels from top to bottom: MASTER, EXPERT, PROFICIENT, COMPETENT, BEGINNER, NOVICE. Arrow pointing to COMPETENT level: "Passing the BACB exam indicates minimum competence."

such as early intervention, assessment and treatment of severe problem behavior, and organizational behavior management, or process areas such as research, leadership, cultural practices, and values. In all cases, the greater the level of expertise, the greater the opportunity to learn more complex skills and have a greater effect on the success of our clients and the organizations that serve them.

> *An expert in our field is someone who consistently engages in responding that reliably produces valued outcomes, in contextually appropriate ways, that are consistent with behavior-analytic strategies and technologies. An expert also conceptualizes and narrates within a behavior analytic framework.*

Expertise is defined by exceptionally skilled performance in some area, but some characteristics typically associated with competence can also be present in non-experts. For example, someone who is only somewhat knowledgeable about an area may speak with such authority and confidence (i.e., characteristics also associated with expertise) that others are convinced by their inaccurate statements. In this instance, certain aspects of the speaker's repertoire have led listeners to assume that the speaker has expert-level knowledge. In addition, popularity on a social-media platform or fame from another discipline (e.g., acting) can lend credibility to statements simply because the name or face is familiar even though the individual does not have expert-level skill. Perhaps one of the most disheartening examples of this kind of negative influence is the role that Jenny McCarthy has played in increasing families' fear of vaccinating children due to her frequent, confidently-asserted—but verifiably false—claims that vaccines cause autism, despite the fact that she has no medical training. Her advocacy of the falsified research from a discredited physician has had and continues to have wide influence, despite her lack of expertise.

A supervisor can help supervisees avoid these false positives (i.e., thinking someone has expertise when they do not) by teaching them how to identify an expert and what characteristics or behaviors should be viewed as "red flags." For example, a supervisor can teach supervisees to value peer-reviewed scientific publications over popularity. They can do this by having discussions about the possible risks associated with believing an individual simply because that individual has a platform to speak and providing a few examples contrasting the difference between available published research and an individual's incorrect public statements. They can also teach a supervisee to question whether a speaker or advice giver has any publication record to support their status as an expert by teaching how to find and review resources such as published bios, CVs, published articles, professional presentations. Although having peer-reviewed publications does not automatically make the author an expert, it is at least an indication that the authors are knowledgeable about the literature base for that topic. A supervisor can also point out individuals whom they believe to be experts to their supervisees, and clearly describe why (e.g., number of years in successful practice, client outcomes and accomplishments, production of high-quality research, time spent training with other experts).

Supervisors should describe common high-quality indicators of experts, such as adjusting practice as the science advances and articulating an evidence-based rationale for a given clinical practice. Conversely, statements such as "Well, that's how I was trained." or "That's just how I have always done it" might spark concern about the expertise of the speaker. Supervisors can also teach supervisees to ask and answer critical self-reflection questions like "Why do I think X is an expert?" and "What makes me trust this person's opinion?" If the supervisee answers by citing that others think the person is an expert, or because they have seen many social media posts from the person or naming the person, the supervisor can support a critical analysis of the differences between indicators of expertise and popularity. Supervisors should consider reviewing and incorporating the information laid out by Daniels and Bailey (2014) in their book section titled "Common Sense is Not Science and Will Not Consistently Improve Behavior" (pp.12–

14). The authors discuss the difference between common sense and scientific knowing and describe four common ways of knowing. Supervisors can review the four ways of knowing (i.e., authority, agreement, personal experience, science) to support taking a systematic approach to evaluating the degree to which what an "expert" is saying involves scientific knowledge, or one of the other three types.

Considerations for Teaching Effective Observing

Assuming that an individual can select someone worth carefully observing, let's consider the skills necessary to be an effective observational learner. The basic components of observational learning involve watching a performance and discriminating the effects of the performance. A supervisor can do several things to teach the supervisee to take an active role in observing expert performers to maximize the utility of observation. First, let's examine what is involved in active observing and discriminating, then we will cover some specific strategies and activities for how a supervisor can shape this repertoire in a supervisee.

One of the most critical components of effective observing is to carefully and precisely describe what is being observed (i.e., a tact in Skinner's taxonomy). In the same way that it is critical for behavior analysts to develop an operational definition of a target behavior in a client's program, it is equally critical to clearly describe the responses being observed. Before observing, the individual should decide on the purpose of the observation and consider the level of detail needed to describe the performance. The required level of detail depends on how familiar the observer is with the skills being performed. If the skills are novel, the purpose may be basic familiarity with the procedure and the level of detail will be relatively minimal such that the general responses are broadly described. However, if the observer is very familiar with the skills and is primarily concerned with learning more about a particular aspect of the performance, then they may describe only the relevant portion of the performance, and in a very detailed and precise manner.

In addition to describing what the observer sees, it is equally important to describe what they are not seeing. In other words, for a full discrimination of the optimal performance, the observer must consider and describe the alternative responses that could have occurred. By describing the actual performance and the likely alternative responses that could have occurred under the same conditions, the observer is positioned to begin to ask critical questions that may assist in identifying under what conditions they should engage in a given response to obtain a desired outcome. This is similar to creating a task analysis or a detailed job aid (described in Chapter 5).

For example, when observing an expert conduct a parent interview, an observer might note that the expert asked: "Tell me a little bit about your bedtime routine." while leaning in and smiling. It might be equally important for the observer to note that they did not ask: "Does your child brush their own teeth?" or "Does your child sleep in their own bed all night?" In addition to identifying these different potential responses, the observer must consider under what conditions a response is more appropriate or desirable. Comparing the first question with the second and third might assist in enhancing the observer's understanding that the expert framed their questions in general and non-judgmental ways. Additionally, a thoughtful comparison of the posed question against those that were not posed reveals that open-ended questions are more likely to evoke narrative responses from the parent, whereas other questions likely produce a yes or no answer. Furthermore, this approach to exploring the family context allows a greater degree of cultural responsiveness. For example, the mother might say that her wife takes care of the bedtime routines. If the expert had asked "Does your husband help with bedtime?" an implicit prejudice may have been implied and felt by the parent. Upon reflection on these observations and discussions with the supervisor, the supervisee will see the expert's question might make the parent feel more comfortable and valued, resulting in a stronger therapeutic relationship (see Chapter 9 for a thorough discussion of therapeutic relationships). A behavior analyst may have been lucky enough to have a supervisor who explicitly taught effective interviewing skills. However, it is likely that no matter the quality of supervision, there will remain skills for behavior analysts to acquire post-supervision. Therefore, this example serves to illustrate how critical careful observing is and that it may functional as a pivotal behavior, allowing supervisees to continue to learn without being expressly taught.

Check Your Knowledge

- What are some of the risks associated with failing to identify an expert?
- What are the two basic components of observational learning?

Up to this point, we have discussed some of the things a supervisor will want their supervisee to do and consider when observing an expert (see Appendix A for a checklist the supervisee can use when observing). Now let's turn our focus to some strategies and activities that a supervisor can use to help teach these critical skills to their supervisee. The process for teaching the supervisee to implement the observational learning sequence involves BST (describe, model, practice with feedback) and providing ample opportunities to practice with less and less support from the supervisor. Observing someone else's performance can be enhanced if we have a structured approach to observing that helps guide the process. For example, a job aid or a procedural fidelity checklist to use and score during an observation may increase attention to the critical aspects of the performance. Therefore, the supervisor may wish to begin teaching effective observation skills to the supervisee by focusing on familiar skills and allowing the supervisee to use a job aid or fidelity checklist during the observation.

Initially, the supervisor models the components of effective observing for the supervisee. This can be done by arranging opportunities for the supervisor and supervisee to observe an expert's performance together. The observation should allow the supervisor and supervisee to talk out loud during the observation; therefore, video examples may work best. During initial observations the supervisor should describe what they did and did not observe, what the effects of the responses were, and the conditions under which those different responses would and would not be appropriate based on the goals and likely outcomes. The supervisor should also describe any errors or sub-standard performance they observed, the risks associated with continued errors, and appropriate corrective actions that may have improved the performance.

Over time and subsequent opportunities, the supervisor should systematically reduce the supportive narratives provided so that the supervisee can initiate the sequence independently. This might begin by prompting the supervisee to vocally tact the performance ("What did you see there?" "What did the person not do?" "What might be an alternative to that?"), decision points ("At that point they could have done X, why do you think they did Y instead?" "What do you think led them to A instead of B?"). Finally, the supervisee should perform an entire observation independently, followed by a debriefing with a discussion, feedback, and suggestions. At this point, the supervisor can praise successes and address any errors or missed opportunities.

Considerations for Teaching Effective Self-Observation and Reflection

It is not enough to teach a supervisee how to do things—a highly effective supervisor must also be able to teach the supervisee to engage in effective self-observing and self-reflection. Self-observing requires the performer to attend to: (a) their own behavior (Bandura, 1997), some of which cannot be readily observed (e.g., facial expressions); (b) their own private events (e.g., thoughts and feelings); and (c) external stimuli that are correlates of the

> *It is not enough to teach a supervisee how to do things, a highly effective supervisor must also be able to teach the supervisee to engage in effective self-observing and self-reflection.*

individual's own behavior (e.g., others' facial expressions, body language, and vocal responses). Self-reflection involves observing and evaluating the performer's own behavior against some standard and using that information to determine whether or not their behavior needs to change (Bandura, 1997). This includes precisely and effectively describing what needs improvement, why it needs improvement (i.e., what is the risk of the continued error), how to fix it, and how to know when it is fixed. This process involves teaching the supervisee how to simultaneously serve as speaker and listener for themselves and how to simultaneously behave and evaluate their own behavior. From that vantage point, they learn to discriminate what they do and do not know, what they have and have not mastered, how to do things differently, and how to identify if they achieved the desired result.

Check Your Knowledge	
Match the term with the definition	
Self-observing	observing and evaluating one's own behavior and determining if it is sufficient or it is needs improvement
Self-reflection	observing one's own behavior and external stimuli related to one's own behavior

Supervisees can be guided to the realization that it is not just about imitating behavior exactly, but also about discriminating the responses that produced a particular outcome and how to engage in the same or similar responses to produce the same outcome in similar situations even if the topography (i.e., the specific behavior) differs. The behaviors that work well to produce a certain outcome for someone else might not work for you, but you can adapt the response to your style and cultural context if you are aware of the function of the response. For example, you might observe that an accomplished speaker uses jokes to engage the audience. If you are not particularly good at telling jokes, you might instead decide to tell an endearing story to produce the same effect (i.e., engage the audience).

Adapting observed behaviors becomes more relevant, and often more complicated, when we consider cultural differences and meaning. Observed behaviors may have a different meaning for the person being observed than for the person engaging in observational learning. For example, Nina, a supervisee, observes Shelby, her supervisor, watching Jack run an intervention session and see that Shelby has her arms folded across her chest. Nina interprets that gesture as displeasure or disapproval which should not be imitated. However, for the culture that Shelby and Jack share, the folded arms are an indicator of respectful attention. If Nina continues to carefully observe Shelby (e.g., describe what she sees and doesn't see and under what conditions the various responses would be appropriate or optimal), she is more likely see that when training someone from another culture, Shelby is careful not to cross her arms. Part of what this careful observation can teach Nina is that the meaning of observed words, gestures, and contextual arrangements can vary across people with different cultural experiences and identities.

> **Observational Learning Sequence**
> - Describe the sequence of events
> - Predict the desired outcome and whether it was obtained
> - Consider why that response occurred versus a different response
> - Identify potential decision points
> - Discuss the degree of cultural responsiveness
> - Compare to other, standard approaches
> - Identify back up plans
> - Develop a plan for trying out and evaluating the new skill

A highly effective supervisor can teach self-observing and self-reflecting skills by implementing structured instruction on self-observing and post-performance evaluation for self-reflection. First, the supervisor can arrange explicit teaching opportunities to begin to teach the supervisee to engage in responses while thoughtfully attending to their own performance. The supervisor should choose skills that the supervisee can perform fluently, but not so expertly that they can perform the skill "mindlessly." The supervisor can instruct the supervisee to perform the skill at a slightly slower-than-typical pace and simultaneously narrate the steps in the response as they are performed. Once the supervisee can vocally narrate the discrete responses or behavior, the supervisor can teach the supervisee to add a narration of their private events (i.e., "describe what you are doing and what thoughts you are having about your performance"). Over time, the supervisor can introduce decision points and problems to be solved by using more complex tasks, such that the supervisees increase the complexity of their self-observing and narrating skills, including conditionalities and culturally-dependent situations. In other words, once the supervisee can effectively describe the doing and thoughts about the doing, they need to develop the more advanced skills of observing and describing points of discrimination (why did they do X instead of Y?).

After establishing effective self-observing and describing skills, the supervisor can teach the supervisee to engage in post-performance self-reflection. This entails a sort of honest self-evaluation of one's own responding. The supervisor can support this skill set by fading their descriptions and feedback following a performance, and instead prompting the individual to summarize their own performance. For example, the supervisor might say "Okay, so tell me what things you did well and what might need some additional practice." As the supervisee provides their self-evaluation, the supervisor can praise thoughtful and accurate responses and nominate aspects of the performance that the supervisee may have missed.

This process allows the supervisor and supervisee to establish the accuracy of the supervisee's self-reporting skills and shape them, if needed. For example, if the supervisee is overly critical and unable to identify things done well, the supervisor can ask the supervisee to only describe those things done well or done better than last time. Alternatively, if the supervisee is overly confident, or unable to self-detect errors, the supervisor can focus on developing that skill. Throughout this process the supervisor should prompt the supervisee to not only identify aspects of their overt responding, but also of any decisions that were made and to discriminate what controlled those in-the-moment responses and to finally evaluate if their choices were effective. If there were errors, or non-optimal decisions, the supervisor can facilitate a discussion to have the supervisee identify what they might do differently next time.

Once supervisees learn self-observation and self-reflection skills, supervisors can leverage those skills in addressing more complicated topics. For example, Chapters 4 and 5 discuss the need to engage in self-assessment and reflection around issues related to multiculturalism and diversity, and Chapter 9 covers the topics of interpersonal and therapeutic relationships. Exploring biases, perceptions, behavior, and practices related to these topics is certain to be challenging for supervisors and supervisees. Therefore, supervisors may wish to target a supervisee's ability to successfully engage in self-observation and reflection early on in the supervisory relationship so that the supervisor can more effectively address these more complex and difficult areas. This also prepares the supervisee to benefit from the structured self-evaluation tools provided throughout this book, as well as the activities provided in the various appendices.

Despite the supervisor's best efforts, some supervisees may struggle with developing a keen ability to self-observe and reflect on their own performance and make changes to their own behavior. This may be evident to the supervisor when there is a disconnect between the supervisee's response to receiving corrective feedback and future performance of the skill for which feedback was provided; in other words, when the supervisee appears receptive to the feedback but does not, or is unable to, make the needed changes. If a supervisee has difficulty discriminating the presence of errors in their own behavior, no amount of the highest-quality feedback or enthusiasm about receiving that feedback will help in the supervisee being able to tell if they are making an error or not. Therefore, in instances where a supervisee does not implement the corrective feedback provided, it may be necessary for the supervisor to systematically teach self-observing and reflection skills and do so across multiple exemplars. Obviously, deficits related to discriminating one's own performance issues are not the only possible causes for failing to implement feedback. Other contributing factors include things like low-quality feedback and instruction from the supervisor (see Chapter 5 and earlier sections of the current chapter) and lack of motivation on the part of the supervisee (see Chapter 11 on identifying and addressing issues within the supervisory relationship).

Through this process, the supervisee will be able to successfully engage in self-observing and self-reflection, which should lead to sustained, high-quality responding as well as systematic improvements where necessary. Eventually, individuals may become so fluent at self-observing and reflection that they can complete all the steps without interrupting their performance and adjust their responding to situational variables. At this point, the supervisor has likely stopped providing explicit instruction and prompts related to self-observing and reflection. The supervisor should ask the supervisee to independently engage in self-observing and reflection. The supervisor may even suggest that the supervisee reach out to a trusted colleague or peer for the purposes of reviewing and discussing their self-evaluation. Directing the supervisee to engage in periodic check-ins with supervisors and peers may facilitate continued self-improvement for the duration of their career. It is most helpful to have a diverse group of peers and supervisor who are able to see things from both technical and cultural vantage points.

Teaching Self-Management for Long-Term Success

We have provided a discussion of the critical skills of self-observation and reflection. Each skill, by itself, is incredibly useful, and together they are invaluable for effective and continued learning. However, when those two components are joined with goal setting, recording data on one's own performance, and implementing contingencies based on the performance, the result is the powerhouse skill of self-management (Murphy & Ensher, 2001). Self-manage-

> *Self-management allows an individual to take an active role in monitoring and managing their own performance.*

> **Primary Components of Self-Management**
> (Manz & Simms, 1980; Murphy & Ensher, 2001)
>
> 1. Observe own performance (self-monitoring)
> 2. Record (self-monitoring)
> 3. Self-assess
> 4. Set goals
> 5. Implement consequences & other strategies
> 6. Evaluate outcome

ment allows an individual to take an active role in monitoring and managing their own performance. Although the specific steps and their order varies across articles and descriptions, the primary components of self-management include: 1) observing one's own performance (self-monitoring); 2) recording (self-monitoring); 3) self-assessing; 4) goal setting; 5) implementing consequences and other strategies; and 6) evaluating the outcome (Manz & Simms, 1980; Murphy & Ensher, 2001). See Appendix B for a *Self-Management Planning* worksheet.

Self-management is a critical skill that can enhance training and supervision experiences, as well as job satisfaction (Murphy & Ensher, 2001). Furthermore, effective self-management can replace frequent or close-in supervision and training supports when they are removed or significantly thinned as clinicians advance throughout their careers. In early and mid-career, individuals who can successfully engage in self-management strategies are well positioned to make the most of any mentoring or advanced training that they access, as they will enter those experiences having already done much of the leg work for success, and are well positioned to maintain the skills that they have learned.

Supervisors can enhance the effects of supervision and the supervisee's future success by explicitly teaching supervisees to implement self-management strategies and then supporting their use of self-management within supervisory activities. The supervisor can begin by describing self-management and each step of the process. During this initial discussion, the supervisor should provide clear examples of how to apply self-management across a variety of different areas and tasks (e.g., academic tasks, client-related tasks, interpersonal skills, supervision and training activities, self-care, continued professional development). The *Self-Management Planning* worksheet provided in Appendix B can be used to support this initial discussion.

Early on in the supervisory relationship, the supervisor should work with the supervisee to identify an area that would be appropriate for self-management. This should be a task or series of tasks that the supervisee can perform fairly independently, but perhaps still requires prompts to complete or complete accurately. The supervisor and supervisee can then use the *Self-Management Planning* worksheet to map out a self-management plan. Next, the supervisor can set clear expectations for regular check-in and evaluation meetings during which the pair can review the progress and make any adjustments to facilitate improved performance and self-direction. As supervision progresses, the supervisor can continue to ask the supervisee to nominate tasks or projects that would be appropriate for self-management. If the supervisee independently nominates a task, or reports that they have taken it upon themselves to implement self-management strategies, the supervisor should be sure to praise this behavior and clearly indicate that taking responsibility for managing their own tasks and performance is likely to increase their success in the future.

In Chapter 5 and in this chapter, we discussed skills for which self-management strategies could be applied, including all the applied behavior analytic content included in the task list (BACB, 2017) and *Supervisor Training Curriculum Outline 2.0* (BACB, 2018c). We also discussed planning for continued professional development through observing experts and one's own performance and self-observation. There are several other areas of self-management that may benefit the professional development of the supervisee. Self-management is useful in the areas of self-care, organization, and task management (Chapter 8) as well as complex skills such as structured problem solving (Chapter 7) and developing interpersonal skills and therapeutic relationships (Chapter 9).

Accordingly, supervisors should be prepared to teach supervisees how to manage the myriad pressures that could negatively impact their performance and well-being (e.g., work-related stress, poor deadline management, life stressors) by engaging in appropriate self-care (e.g., practice relaxation skills, monitoring access to reinforcers, monitoring negative self-talk). In addition, supervisors should be prepared to practice what they preach and actively manage their own responses to stress and work pressure. Any professional in any field encounters multiple competing contingencies and demands upon their time. These demands and contingencies occur within the work setting (i.e., multiple work tasks with similar deadlines) and across work-life contexts (i.e., personal demands that conflict with work demands). These stressful situations may occur during graduate training, but they are virtually guaranteed to occur throughout the span of a person's career.

Burnout can result from failure to handle stress effectively by monitoring one's own stress level, accessing support from colleagues, and actively engaging in self-care (Dounavi, Fennell, & Early, 2019; Plantiveau, Dounavi & Virues-Ortega, 2018). This effect is particularly pronounced for new professionals who often struggle with the requirements of their first position: effectively managing a caseload (Ervin, 2008), continuing to develop new skills, and managing various personal life milestones that often occur during the decades of one's mid-twenties and early thirties. For example, in addition to professional development activities, the individual may be managing a clinical caseload, training therapists and parents, creating products and materials for the work setting, navigating a personal relationship, addressing the needs of others (e.g., children or aging parents), and managing financial responsibilities and payment of student loans. All of these activities require time, effort, and self-management. New and complex demands may make it difficult to protect time for personal activities critical for self-care (e.g., sleeping seven hours each night, eating well, exercising, engaging in preferred leisure, and community activities) if the supervisee does not actively use self-management strategies. These various work and personal life demands are going to exist for any young professional, but the situation many be exacerbated if the work setting demands are excessive or occur in the midst of organizational dysfunction. The issue of organizational dysfunction is beyond the scope of this book but interested readers are directed to Binder, 2016, Daniels and Bailey, 2014, Gilbert, 2013, Hantula, 2015, Mawhinney, 2009, and Rummler and Brache, 2013 (see References).

Let's consider the example of a supervisor named Xiuying and her supervisee Nadeem with whom she has been working for two months. Xiuying has noticed that Nadeem appears to be more stressed than usual. She thinks this because he has been a few minutes late to their last few meetings, looks tired, and has mentioned that his courses are quite difficult this semester. He has several clients going through intake-assessment procedures, and he has not been able to maintain observance of his spiritual practices. Xiuying decides that this is a great opportunity to teach Nadeem how to implement self-management strategies, which she describes to Nadeem. He is eager to learn how to implement behavior analytic strategies to help him more effectively manage the demands on his time.

To begin supporting the development of a self-management plan, Xiuying asks Nadeem to implement step one (self-monitoring his own performance) and step two (recording) by asking him to track the frequency and/or duration of engagement in activities that they identified as critical for good self-care. Nadeem decides to use existing apps and the calendar on his phone to track the number of hours of sleep, the number and content of meals, minutes spent walking his dog or playing at the dog park, number of pages read in a preferred book for leisure, and number of times he prays and meditates each day for two weeks. Xiuying also asks him to use a simple rating scale that they develop together to indicate his degree of anxious private events and responding in the morning, afternoon, and evening for the data collection period. Once the data are collected, Xiuying instructs Nadeem to reflect (step three, self-assessing) on the data collected relative to how he performed over those weeks, in terms of required work or school tasks and self-care activities. Furthermore, she asks him to come to the next meeting with a few ideas for how to: 1) increase engagement in self-care activities; 2) measure progress toward meeting those goals; and 3) implement some contingencies that could be put in place for meeting or failing to meet the goals. Nadeem finds that he slept an average of five hours per night, ate pretty well, did not walk their dog at all, read a total of three pages of his preferred book, and prayed and meditated four times over the course of the two-week recording period. He settles on some goals to present at the next meeting and identifies that, when he meets his goals, he would like to buy a pair of expensive athletic shoes.

At the next meeting he shares that he would like to set the following goals: 1) get an average of seven hours of sleep per night; 2) walk his dog for at least 30 minutes four times a week; 3) read an average of ten pages of a preferred leisure book each night and; 4) pray and meditate for ten minutes each day. Xiuying praises him for collecting the data and engaging in some self-reflection and evaluation. She notes that his goals are fairly ambitious, and suggest that those should be his terminal goals after achieving smaller goals that will successively move him closer to his final goals. They decide that for the first week his goals should be: 1) increase his sleep to an average of six hours per night for at least five days a week; 2) walk his dog for 15 minutes twice a week; 3) read one to three pages of his preferred book Monday through Friday; and 4) pray or meditate for five minutes each evening. They identify systematic increases to be implemented each week he is successful. She also recommends that Nadeem continue to track his eating habits, as he is already doing well with that and may help to reinforce all his other self-care behavior. They agree that he will contribute a certain amount of money toward his shoe fund each week that he meets a certain percentage of this goals. Xiuying suggests that he might also consider allowing himself to buy a preferred coffee drink at the end of the week, in addition to the monetary contribution to his shoe fund. They agree on weekly check-ins at first, with a plan to fade to monthly after six weeks of success. Xiuying and Nadeem continue to review his performance and make slight adjustments where needed until Nadeem has meet his goals and decides to implement a new self-management plan focused on him learning how to play the guitar, a skill he has longed dreamed of mastering. Each of the steps described in Nadeem's case is important to his successful self-management.

Considering Communities of Practice as Long-Term Supports

In Chapter 4 we discussed Communities of Practice and their importance for advancing the goals of culturally-responsive practices. Communities of

Practice are also relevant to developing expertise in other areas of behavior analysis. Each community contains members of varying skill levels that are dedicated to a common mission and actively supporting one another in learning skills that will advance that mission (Wegner & Snyder, 2000). The most effective supervisor directly teaches supervisees to actively pursue communities of practice that contain experts in their area of practice or area of interest (see Chapter 4 for specific strategies). As we have covered in this chapter, the competent supervisor will teach supervisees the skills required to effectively learn from experts such that they not only increase their skills during supervision, but for the remainder of their career. The need for sustained learning becomes critical when contact with supervisors or mentors is significantly thinned as an individual advances through a career. This is so important that Bailey and Burch suggest that at least for the first few years of employment, novice practitioners choose work settings that contain a sufficient number of experts to facilitate continued growth and mentorship (Bailey & Burch, 2010).

In summary, a high-quality supervisor is mindful to ensure that supervisees develop skills that facilitate effective observation and analysis of expert performance, as well as strong self-observation and evaluation skills. A high-quality supervisor also teaches supervisees strategies for self-management of self-care and technical performance and how to develop or access a community of practice. When these skills come together supervisees have powerful strategies for effective and self-directed learning for acquiring and refining repertoires throughout their career.

Appendix A: Observational Learning Self-Checklist

Instructions: Once you have decided to observe an expert's performance, use this checklist to prepare for and carry out the observation, and then to reflect and debrief following the observation.

Before the Observation
- ☐ Describe the purpose of the observation
- ☐ Describe the desired outcome if the performance is successful
- ☐ Describe anything to which you or your supervisor want to pay special attention

During the Observation
- ☐ Describe what you see
- ☐ Describe what you don't see
- ☐ Describe any questions that arise as you observe the performance

After the Observation
- ☐ Describe if you think the performance was successful (i.e., the desired outcome was achieved) and why or why not
- ☐ Consider why you think the individual engaged in a given response versus a different response
- ☐ Identify and describe any specific decision points during the performance
- ☐ Describe the degree of cultural responsiveness and any modifications you think were made
- ☐ After reflecting, outline any questions you have for the performer
- ☐ Describe how the performance you saw differed from other approaches
- ☐ Plan whether you will incorporate anything from the observation into your repertoire and how you will do it and evaluate yourself

Appendix B: Self-Management Planning

Name: _____

Define the skill or areas to be addressed: _____
_____
_____
_____
_____

Steps for Self-Management Planning

1. Describe how you will observe your own performance.

2. Describe how you will record your performance (direct measures, ratings/self-report). Consider whether you need someone else to help to ensure that you are accurately measuring the desired performance/skill.

3. Describe how you will self-evaluate your performance once you have collected data (what is the desired performance level and how do you compare).

4. Describe your goals. Consider whether you need multiple short-terms goals that will lead to your terminal goal.

5. Describe if there are antecedent strategies you should implement (e.g., prompts, reminders, check-ins). Consider if you need someone to help manage the set up and/delivery of these antecedent strategies.

6. Describe the consequences you will implement for meeting or failing to meet the goals.

7. Consider if you need someone to help manage the set up and/delivery of these consequences.

8. Describe how and when you will evaluate the outcomes.

Chapter 7

Structured Problem Solving Skills

All problems become smaller when you confront them instead of dodging them.
—Admiral William F. Halsey

Problems are inevitable. Therefore, having a strong problem-solving repertoire is useful for both personal and professional situations. Problems can cause stress, anxiety and avoidance because solutions are not readily apparent, not accessible, or only probable in their effectiveness. However, problems can also create the opportunity to learn and grow if one has a framework for examining and solving problems. This chapter focuses on strategies for teaching a supervisee to use a structured approach to problem-solving. The supervisor who focuses on teaching problem-solving skills is programming for the supervisee's future independence and success by teaching them *how* to solve future problems, rather than simply providing a solution to the current problem. Over time, the goal is for the supervisee to approach, rather than avoid, problems with confidence in their ability to analyze the problem, generate potential solutions, and evaluate the success of the chosen option. That is, the supervisee learns that they should not be afraid if they do not have the answers because they have developed the ability to find those answers through the problem-solving process.

Definitions: Problems and Problem-Solving

> *The supervisor who focuses on teaching problem-solving skills is programming for the supervisee's future independence and success by teaching them how to solve future problems, rather than simply providing a solution to the current problem.*

The dictionary defines *problem* as "a question raised for inquiry, consideration, or solution; an intricate unsettled question; or a source of perplexity, distress or vexation" (http://www.merriam-webster.com/dictionary/citation). Skinner (1984) defines a problem as a situation in which the person has no immediate response that is likely to work or "a question for which there is at the moment no answer" (p. 583). Donahoe and Palmer (1994) add that defining something as a problem should also require that a solution is possible. See Skinner (1984), Donahoe and Palmer (1994) and Holth (2008) for more detailed behavior analytic conceptual accounts of problem solving. By this definition, a family has a problem when their child exhibits progressively worsening tantrums. The worsening behavior may result in injury and limit access to public settings. A behavior analyst has a problem when they encounter an ethical dilemma and do not know how to respond to ensure that their behavior comports with the guidelines that protect their client's well-being. They know that the situation could create harm, but they do not know how to respond to resolve the situation and avoid even greater harm. A graduate student has a problem when they have two exams the following day and insufficient time to prepare for both. They must choose which exam to allocate time to knowing that the score on the other will be lower than desired.

Another type of problem occurs when multiple solutions are evident, but it is not immediately clear which solution will produce the most immediate and greatest long-term benefit. An example of this type of problem occurs when a behavior analyst identifies the function of problem behavior and must choose between the various function-based interventions that have empirical support. Each different intervention has a set of strengths and weaknesses. If the chosen intervention does not have a set of strengths and weaknesses that match the client situation, the intervention is less likely to be effective. Another example of this type of problem occurs when a recent graduate and newly certified BCBA has multiple job offers and must choose which one to accept and which ones to be cast aside.

For several reasons, people don't always agree that a given situation is problematic. For example, people may have different tolerance levels for client behaviors (e.g., duration of tantrums, frequency of cancellations of sessions) and staff behaviors (e.g., raised voices during meetings). They may have different values (e.g., co-sleeping is proper or unacceptable, managers should or should not change responsibilities without rationales). Finally, a given situation may not be problematic for all involved. For example, one person in a relationship may wish that communication occurred more frequently and openly while the other person is completely satisfied with the situation. Differences in how a problem is perceived may result from different cultural learning histories or unclear boundaries within an organization or relationship.

Skinner also defines problem solving as "any behavior which, through the manipulation of variables, makes the appearance of a solution more probable." He suggests that problem-solving strategies often involve "constructing discriminative stimuli" (p. 584) or generating stimuli to supplement what is already present and generating a response that is likely to be reinforced, also known as precurrent behavior (Skinner, 1953). Problem solving is the critical behavior to target. It is evoked by a problem, which functions as the motivating operation. Problem solving involves the mediating responses of manipulating, supplementing, and generating stimuli to which an individual can subsequently respond (Axe, Phelan, & Irwin, 2019; Donahoe & Palmer, 2004; Skinner, 1953, 1957, 1968).

> *Skinner defines problem solving as "any behavior which, through the manipulation of variables, makes the appearance of a solution more probable."*

This definition is broad enough to encompass a wide range of behaviors as long as the behavior produces a functional outcome (i.e., a response that might solve the problem and encounter reinforcement). By this definition, it becomes obvious that two common types of responses to problems DO NOT qualify as problem-solving. First, responding impulsively, even when there is minimal chance of reinforcement for the response, is not really problem-solving. Generally, the probability of reinforcement has been overestimated or has not been considered at all. Skinner also mentions trial and error haphazard responding, which can actually worsen the problem rather than solve it. For example, if a behavior analyst quickly implements a behavior intervention strategy and immediately switches to a different one if the results are not satisfactory, it could erode the motivation of the implementer to try subsequent interventions. Finally, inactivity or avoidance of the problem (e.g., waiting and hoping, denying that there is a problem) also generally does not increase the probability of identifying a solution and, thus, does not qualify as problem solving.

Let's take a moment to think about the function of each of these common, but ineffective, responses to problems. The distress experienced when we encounter a problem is aversive, and impulsive responding often produces an immediate alleviation of the discomfort, which is a negative reinforcer. That is, the situation momentarily improves (or we perceive that it improves), and that response is differentially negatively reinforced. For example, one person may interrupt another in a discussion when he or she no longer wants to hear what the other person is saying. The interruption may produce an immediate negative reinforcer (i.e., terminates the other person's speaking), but it may also produce resentment and damage the relationship in the long term. In addition, there may be positive reinforcement associated with having generated a solution, leading the person to fail to see other options or complications associated with the solution. Similarly, the problem may be so overwhelming that it is aversive to even acknowledge that is exists. Even if the problem is acknowledged, the potential solution may be so aversive that the person is reluctant to act. Avoidance is the culprit here because delaying engaging in the appropriate behavior (i.e., naming the problem, taking the effortful or unpleasant action) results in avoidance of the aversive stimulus in the short term, even though the aversive situation may be ultimately unavoidable in the long term.

The supervisor plays a critical role in helping the supervisee overcome any avoidance contingencies that may be preventing them from noticing or reporting problems. The supervisor should consistently prompt the supervisee to monitor for problems so that they can be detected and reported early. LeBlanc has explained this strategy to supervisees as "bring me smoke so that we can prevent or address the fire together." This is intended to illustrate that smoke is as much of a problem as fire and should never be ignored. Buildings have smoke detectors to evoke responses earlier in the situation to avoid the worst outcome. She tells supervisees that if they are "not sure whether it is smoke or not, bring it anyway" so that she can help them recognize the critical features of problems. Barrera & Kramer (2009) talk about this as part of a respectful relationship in creating "allowing" environments that set the occasion for openness in reporting problems.

> *Bring me smoke so that we can prevent or address the fire together.*

The supervisor also needs to respond carefully when a supervisee brings a report of a problem or a precursor to a problem. The supervisor should keep in mind that our learning histories around problems make it inherently hard for most people to bring a problem forward to an authority figure (i.e., the supervisor). Thus, it is important to provide potent reinforcement for reporting. Cultural variables can increase the discomfort if there is an identity differential (e.g., male to female or vice versa, young to older or vice versa). This means the supervisor should praise the detection and report of the problem and model an approach where problems are seen as an opportunity to learn. Edmondson (1999) refers to this phenomenon as psychological safety in the workplace. LeBlanc tries to remember to always respond with something like "Thank you so much for letting me know about this. It was excellent that you noticed this as something that we need to tackle. This sounds like an interesting problem and now we get to solve it together."

> **Check Your Knowledge**
>
> In your own words, write a definition of "problem" and "problem solving." Once you are done, go back through the previous section to compare your definitions to what appears in the text and edit your definitions if needed.

A Structured Approach to Problem-Solving

Multi-step, structured problem solving approaches have been implemented with a broad array of user groups from children to executives in multinational corporations and to tackle problems as diverse as aggression and social skills problems to cultural sensitivity (Arya, Margaryan, & Collis, 2003; Smith, Lochman, & Daunic, 2005). A supervisor who implements a structured problem-solving approach in their own work could use the opportunity to model the process for supervisees. They could clearly describe the steps while going through them, discussing decision points and encouraging active participation by the supervisee in problem solving with a wide range of problems. The supervisor can teach the supervisee that clinical decision-making is problem solving and should be approached in a systematic way. In addition to client services, behavior analysts should take a structured problem solving approach to issues that arise in staff management, and self-management, as well as operational practice management issues such as scheduling services, managing funding source constraints, and deciding how and when to expand services.

Different versions of structured problem-solving include four, five, six, or seven steps but all focus on the same basic repertoire (Glago, Mastropieri, & Scruggs, 2009; Kolb & Stuart, 2005). For the purposes of this chapter, we present five steps that should be followed in systematic progression: 1) detect; 2) define; 3) generate solutions; 4) select solution; and 5) implement and evaluate). These steps and the strategies in each are based on LeBlanc (2020). That means that during structured problem-solving, one should fully engage in each step, in order (i.e., do not jump ahead), and self-monitor the quality of actions at each step. For each step, we also present common errors that might occur and strategies to facilitate higher quality problem solving.

> *During structured problem solving, one should fully engage in each step, in order (i.e., do not jump ahead), and self-monitor the quality of actions at each step.*

Step 1: Detect the Problem. It is far easier to detect a crisis (e.g., escalating problem behavior, an angry phone call from a parent, a staff resignation) than it is to detect the subtle indicators of a problem that has yet to fully manifest. Often the subtle indicators are the lack of behavior when one would expect behavior to occur (e.g., lack of questions when covering a complex topic, minimal positive affect during interactions with a client or supervisee) or the existence of environments that foment problematic behavior (e.g., an aversive and competitive workplace, an environment with very little attention available). The ability to detect these subtle indicators and problem-producing environments can be termed "nuanced noticing" (i.e., the ability to observe small changes in behavior that precede or indicate that problems exist; LeBlanc, 2020). The person who can notice these subtle indicators has an advantage over one who fails to notice because they can prevent problems rather than having to respond to ones that have already occurred. "Nuanced noticing" is equally important across cultural contexts. Different responses may mean different things in different cultures, and the indicators that offense has been given or taken is usually going to be subtle (e.g., change in facial expression) rather that clearly and directly spoken. For example, in one culture, not making eye contact or crossing one's arms can mean there is a problem forming, whereas in another it is a sign of respect for the speaker and concentration on what the speaker is saying.

> *"Nuanced noticing" refers to detecting subtle, small changes in behavior that precede a problem or indicate that a problem exists.*

The supervisor can teach this skill using several strategies. First, the supervisor can describe the subtle indicators they have noticed in past situations, as well as the outcomes that followed those indicators. This allows the supervisee to derive rules about the behaviors that have been described and the probability of a negative outcome if those behaviors remain unaddressed. The supervisor can also highlight the importance of any similar indicators in current situations that arise in supervision. The supervisor can ask the supervisee open-ended questions about what things make them think that a current clinical situation (e.g., a therapeutic relationship with a family) is going well or going poorly. For example, this question might be useful to ask after a supervisee has indicated that they do not have any new data because the family has cancelled recent sessions. The process of answering the question may sensitize the supervisee to the fact that frequent cancellations can sometimes, but not always, be a subtle indicator of dissatisfaction with services or the relationship with the provider. Even if the supervisor and supervisee had no reason to believe that the recent cancellations were related to emerging or present problems, taking the time to engage in the question asking and answering will increase the likelihood that the supervisee will strengthen their subtle noticing skills.

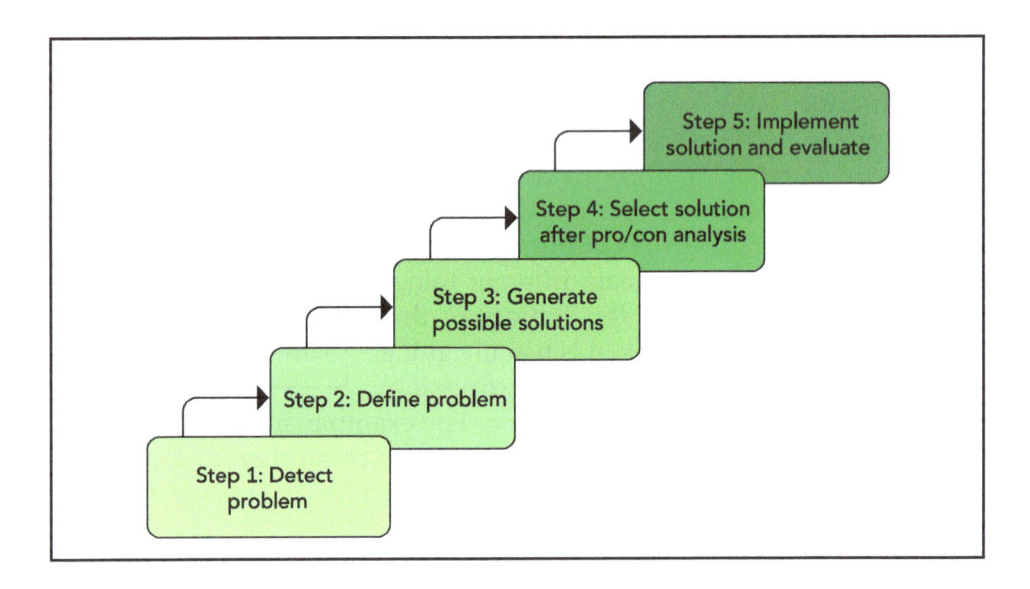

Another strategy to help supervisees recognize subtle indicators of a problem (e.g., the absence of something that should be there) is to use video examples, when possible and appropriate, to facilitate discrimination of subtle environmental conditions and changes in behavior. A supervisor could show video of a low-attention environment and pause before, as well as after, problem behavior occurs (similar to the approach used by Scott, Lerman, & Luck, 2018). The supervisee can then be asked to identify what they observed that could be problematic (i.e., the absence of attention suggests that there could be a motivating operation for attention) and taught to describe similar conditions as problematic (e.g., less frequent communication than usual). As another example, a supervisor could show a video of a parent-clinician interaction where the clinician interrupts or talks over a parent who is asking a question. The supervisor could ask the supervisee if they noticed anything that might decrease the parent's question-asking or talking in session.

Reflection

Pause here and take a few minutes to think of a few instances where you engaged in nuanced noticing that allowed to you to catch a problem before it developed, or just as it was emerging. What were the specific things that you noticed? Now take a few minutes to think about some instances where, in retrospect, you missed some subtle indicators that a problem was brewing or occurring. What were the specific things that you missed? Did missing those things change your ability to better attend to similar nuanced behavior or variables since then?

Step 2: Define the Problem. This step involves identifying the functional determinants of the problem (i.e., why this problem is occurring). One can mistakenly think that the topography is the problem rather than the environmental contingencies that produce and sustain the problem. For example, for a parent, the problem is their child's tantrums and the distress, embarrassment, and restriction of life events that result from the tantrum. This is indeed a problem for the family. However, a behavior analyst might identify that the tantrums occur in public when new and exciting activities and events are present but cannot be accessed (i.e., a tangible function), and this aspect of the environment can be targeted as part of the solution (e.g., non-contingent access to preferred items on outings, differential reinforcement of asking for things that are available). In another example, an RBT may consistently make errors in implementing a teaching program (i.e., the topography). However, the behavior (i.e., procedural error) is preceded by an antecedent and followed by a consequence that sustains that behavior. It may be the case that the original training did not produce competent and fluent performance of the teaching procedure, or that accurate implementation of the program is more effortful and aversive than the error, or that the procedure does not produce the intended effects for the child or produces unintended effects such as increased problem behavior. In a final example, one person may discover that a colleague has said harsh, gossipy, or incorrect things about them to co-workers. Initially, the problem may appear to be that the colleague has incorrect information that should be studiously corrected in a direct exchange. Calm, unemotional reflection suggests that the problem is not incorrect information, but is actually the antecedents and consequences supporting covert gossipy interchanges with colleagues. A direct exchange might actually worsen the behavior by providing attention and coercion-based reinforcers.

Problem solving is enhanced by focus on the antecedents and the consequences (i.e., the causes or functions) rather than just the topography of the problem. Behavior analysts already have a great framework for identifying the function of problem behavior. An experimental functional analysis involves systematically manipulating the hypothesized antecedents and consequences for problem behavior to detect sensitivity to various sources of reinforcement (e.g., attention, escape, access to tangibles; Beavers, Iwata, & Lerman, 2013). In the organizational behavior management literature, staff problems are typically assessed with a pre-intervention descriptive assessment tool (Johnson, Casella, McGee, & Lee, 2014; Wilder, Lipshultz, King, Driscoll & Sigurdsson, 2018). *The Performance Diagnostic Checklist–Human Services* (PDC-HS; Carr, Wilder, Madjaleny, Mathisen, & Strain, 2013) is one such tool that provides a framework for examining the functional determinants of staff performance problems with recommended function-based interventions. The tool examines the potential contributions of: 1) lack of training or poor training; 2) insufficient antecedents to evoke the correct behavior; 3) lack of consequences or competing consequences; and 4) response effort of the task. Performance interventions indicated by the PDC-HS have been more effective than standard, non-indicated interventions at addressing persistent staff performance (Bowe & Sellers, 2018; Carr, et al., 2013; Ditzian, Wilder, King, & Tanz, 2015; Wilder, Lipschultz, & Gehrman, 2018).

> *Problem solving is enhanced by focus on the antecedents and the consequences (i.e., the causes or functions) rather than just the topography of the problem.*

The task of the supervisor is to help their supervisee begin to see a broad range of potential problems in terms of the functional determinants of the problem. Daniels and Bailey (2014) suggest framing questions to examine the influence of the environment on behavior (e.g., What happens to them when they do that?). For example, clients who do not consistently implement behavioral recommendations (i.e., non-adherence) or who cancel sessions with short notice might do so because of lawful and understandable reasons (e.g., extinction is aversive to implement, other activities are more reinforcing than therapy sessions). Identifying and understanding those reasons can lead you to more effective solutions. To teach problem identification, the supervisor

> *The task of the supervisor is to help their supervisee begin to see a broad range of potential problems in terms of the functional determinants of the problem.*

can prompt the supervisee to identify the functional determinants of any problem that they bring to supervision. Ask open-ended questions (e.g., "Why do you think that this parent is inconsistent with this sleep protocol?") and prompt attention to motivating operations (e.g., "Are there any biological motivating operations that may be in play at 2:00 a.m. when the parent is reinforcing the crying by bringing the child to their bed?"). When a supervisee expresses frustration with underperformance of a technician whom they supervise, prompt them to operationalize the underperformance and then use a tool such as the PDC-HS to examine the functional determinants of the underperformance. This process can feel threatening to the supervisee, as it will often identify aspects of their own supervisory behavior that need to change (e.g., provide more frequent or specific feedback). Therefore, the supervisor must make a consistent effort to focus on the reinforcing outcome of fully engaging in this step (i.e., knowing the function tells you what interventions are most likely to prove successful) and avoid statements of blame (e.g., you need to provide better feedback).

Step 3: Generate Potential Solutions. The third step is to generate possible solutions to the problem, particularly ones that directly address the functions identified in Step 2. There are always multiple potential solutions to any problem, with some of the potential solutions destined to produce a better or quicker outcome than others. However, people have a propensity to use a strategy that has worked before or most recently (i.e., it has encountered reinforcement), even if that strategy does not readily apply to the current situation (i.e., overgeneralized use of the strategy).

While it could be advantageous to rely upon a previously effective problem-solving strategy, it is important to pause and reflect on whether other solutions might work just as well or better based on the function of the current problem identified in Step 2. Over-use of a specific strategy (e.g., use of extinction as a treatment, describing the importance of treatment implementation) occurs when the problem-solver is responding to a similarity between the current problem and a prior problem for which the

> *While it could be advantageous to rely upon a previously effective problem-solving strategy, it is important to pause and reflect on whether other solutions might work just as well or better based on the function of the current problem identified in Step 2.*

solution has worked, rather than responding to the critical differences between this problem and the one solved before. For example, extinction may have worked well as an intervention for a young child with an annoying, but not dangerous, topography of problem behavior maintained by attention, whereas the current situation involves an older, stronger child who is dangerously aggressive during task demands. In the second situation, the difficulty of implementation and danger will likely decrease procedural integrity and result in a worse situation rather than an improved one. As another example, additional training may have been highly effective in increasing implementation accuracy with an underperforming technician who had not been adequately trained. However, it is likely to prove ineffective with a technician who was well-trained and is currently underperforming due to competing contingencies outside of the workplace (e.g., financial struggles, substance abuse problems).

The primary activity of Step 3 is often referred to as "brainstorming" and the goal is to emit a high rate of varied behavior (i.e., generate many different potential solutions). Collaboration in a brainstorming activity helps to increase the number and variability of responses and may increase the probability that a meaningful and satisfactory solution will be identified and selected. It is also important to emit the responses without initially evaluating them, as response evaluation often suppresses subsequent responding (i.e., it is punishing to immediately encounter the flaws of your ideas) and suppression means overall fewer possible ideas.

We recommend the following strategies for increasing response variability during a brainstorming session. First, the leader of the brainstorming activity could open the meeting by clearly stating the expectations (e.g., "The purpose of this brainstorming session is to generate as many possible solutions as we can without evaluating or judging them. Nothing is off the table, in terms of ideas, even if they seem too effortful or costly, as those ideas might lead to an effective but more doable solution." Second, it is important to respond in ways that encourage everyone to participate in the brainstorm. For example, the leader of the brainstorming activity should orient to each person as he or she speaks, make affirmative comments, such as "interesting," as opposed to rejecting statements, such as "we tried that" and avoid making faces or checking in with non-speakers when the speaker is giving an idea). Third, the brainstormers can set a goal for the target number of responses (e.g., at least six options) and continue responding until the goal has been met or exceeded. Fourth, the person leading the brainstorming session can set a rule to write down all their other suggestions except the first one that is emitted (i.e., the solution that is at greatest strength and has the shortest latency) until the goal number of responses has been reached (e.g., at least five other possible options before they write down the first one that was emitted). The first option is not eliminated from consideration, but there may be an increased likelihood that the group will generate other good options to consider as well.

> **Strategies to Increase Variability During Brainstorming:**
> 1. State the expectations
> 2. Encourage participation
> 3. Set a goal for the number of options
> 4. Wait until you hit the goal to write down the first one
> 5. Be ambitious with ideas
> 6. Change your environment

A fifth strategy is to prompt people to name an option that they would like to try if there were unlimited resources (e.g., "If we had the resources for X, I think it would solve the problem"). That idea (e.g., around-the-clock staffing to implement environmental enrichment) might end up being impossible to implement, but having that option on the board might stretch the range of acceptable responses so much that other excellent, less resource-heavy options are emitted. It may also be possible to backtrack from the most resource-intensive option to a midpoint that matches your current resources. This strategy of using an idea as a springboard to generate other ideas is great for increasing response volume and variability and can be combined with self-questioning and self-prompting (Axe, et al., 2019; Sautter, LeBlanc, Jay, Goldsmith, & Carr, 2011).

Sixth, remember that environmental stimuli (e.g., the office, the desk, sights, sounds) are associated with doing things a certain way (i.e., stimulus control). Disrupting stimulus control by entering a new environment with new stimuli (e.g., a conference room rather than your office, a coffee shop, outside) may increase variability in responding. Seventh, list things and people in the client's environment (e.g., a sister, a van with three rows of seats) and use them as the stimuli to generate new ideas. And finally, use the hypothesized function of the problem as an intraverbal prompt to increase the likelihood that the solutions that you generate are function-based strategies (e.g., "this technician has not seen the procedure implemented correctly recently, so we need to demonstrate..."). Searching the literature using function-related key words may generate ideas for strategies with empirical support.

A supervisor might use Appendix A: Problem Solving Worksheet to guide a supervisee through a brainstorming activity about the next problem that they bring to supervision. When brainstorming potential solutions, actively try to increase response variability, as most people tend to embrace a small set of regular options (e.g., using functional communication as an intervention strategy for problem behavior). One of the many benefits of a diverse and inclusive environment is that new ideas emerge from a welcoming brainstorming process, leading to more innovative and responsive solutions (Barrera & Kramer, 2009).

Step 4: Select an option based on a pro-con analysis. The fourth step of problem solving is about teaching the supervisee to develop the critical skill of carefully questioning their own ideas and strategies before implementing. Following a brainstorming session, conduct a careful analysis of the strengths and considerations for each option (i.e., a pro-con analysis). If too many ideas were generated to evaluate all of them, examine the ideas to potentially combine some and to choose two or three of the most promising ideas. Consider the pros and cons in both the short-term (e.g., what are the positive benefits to the child, the family, the staff, how effortful is immediate implementation, how likely is the option to work quickly, are there other barriers or resistance to the options) and the long-term (e.g., will this option likely produce sustained positive effects, can the environment support sustained implementation). It is also important to consider various perspectives (when appropriate, consider how the child, the family, the staff, the agency, the community, and/or the discipline would view the options). In conducting the pro-con analysis, one should expect to identify several pros and cons for each potential solution. If few or no pros or cons have been identified, the analysis should continue prior to a selection. The supervisor should guide the supervisee through this process for a wide variety of problems, people, and settings (i.e., multiple exemplar training) and help the supervisee identify a robust set of pros and cons.

There are existing models to assist with structured clinical problem solving for some of the most common problems associated with problem behavior (e.g., measurement, function-based treatment). The models guide the supervisee through a series of questions about the most common barriers to solution implementation (e.g., safety concerns, lack of resources). These models then provide a pro-con analysis that assists the behavior analyst in collaborative decision-making with the ultimate implementer (e.g., parent, teacher). For example, LeBlanc, Raetz, Sellers, & Carr (2016) describe a model for selecting appropriate measures for assessing and treating problem behavior. The model is informed by the research literature on measurement and guides the user through questions about the topography of the behavior, environmental resources, and the importance of temporal dimensions for treatment planning. The answers to the questions in the model lead the user toward the measure(s) that are generally well-suited to the needs and constraints of the situation. The table provides a comprehensive pro-con analysis that allows the user to compare each reasonable option for the specific situation. Similarly, Geiger, Carr, & LeBlanc (2010) provide a decision-making model and pro-con analysis for selecting function-based treatments for escape-maintained problem behavior, and Grow, Carr, & LeBlanc (2009) provide the same information for attention-maintained problem behavior. The supervisor might review these articles with the supervisee, explaining the importance of the collaborative process in making clinical decisions.

Sometimes the analysis of the pros and cons will reveal that additional information is needed before a decision can be made (i.e., I need more data). For example, the PDC-HS might identify that a technician has not had performance-based (i.e., directly observed performing the task) and competency-based (i.e., training continues until a criterion is met rather than for a specific amount of time) training on a specific task. It may also identify that the task may be particularly effortful and unnecessarily complicated. In conducting a pro-con analysis for the solutions of: 1) simplify the task; and 2) conduct additional training, the supervisor may need to gather additional data related to option one before selecting one or both strategies. The supervisor may need to conduct observations, try a few different ways to simplify the task, and evaluate whether the best simplified version produces the same benefits as the more complicated task. In this instance it is appropriate to defer the selection of a particular option until the relevant data have been obtained. After any additional analyses have been conducted, either pick one of the current possible solutions to the problem or brainstorm alternative options. In selecting a potential solution, consider whether one solution more completely addresses the function of the problem, protects consumers and staff, and matches the available resources. If all of the best options have significant drawbacks, avoidance behavior may ensue because selecting an option results in the presentation of a difficult or aversive task. The avoidance behavior may involve statements such as "I need more data" or "I need to think about it more before I make a decision." It may be possible to recruit a trusted colleague or mentor to help make an informed selection with confidence in the selected option.

> *Because you cannot predict exactly how well a strategy will work until you have tried it, you have to trust that if you have carefully engaged in the structured problem solving process and have achieved a reasonable level of confidence about the soundness of your choice, you can and should take action.*

In the absence of a clear plan about what information is needed or how that data would alter the decision, fear that the solution will fail could lead to indecision and persistence of the original problem. Someone who tends to be rigid, anxious, and a perfectionist may struggle at this critical juncture of the problem solving process. Because you cannot predict exactly how well a strategy will work until you have tried it, you have to trust that if you have carefully engaged in the structured problem solving process and have achieved a reasonable level of confidence about the soundness of your choice, you can and should take action. Failure to decide and seeking more data can lead to what is often referred to as "paralysis by analysis" in the business world (Ansoff, 1965).

If the solution does not go as well as expected, a second round of problem solving occurs and a new option is selected. It can also be helpful to include "do nothing" as one of the options because it allows the supervisee to compare the options to the current situation. In the example provided above about the gossipy, critical co-worker, one option is to do and say nothing about what you have heard and other options are: 1) directly engage with the co-worker; and 2) work on the professional relationship with the co-worker so that they are less likely to find it reinforcing to engage in covert attacks. The task becomes deciding which of your options beats doing nothing with the least amount of risk, given that implementing Step 5 will allow you to quickly detect if the selection did not solve the problem.

Step 5: Implement and Evaluate the Solution. This step allows the problem solver to establish parameters for testing the effectiveness of the solution and allows a mechanism for ongoing decisions about the acceptability of the solution. At this juncture, either the brainstorming team or a single, ultimate decision-maker decides under what conditions the solution will be tried, for what period, and how success will be evaluated. In any case, the outcomes and the information learned will be important for the present problem as well as future and/or related problems.

It may be the case that the chosen solution is ineffective at producing the desired outcome. Finding out that your solution did not work does not have to be perceived as a personal failure. There is no requirement that every solution that is implemented be effective. Step 5 in the process involves carefully monitoring for the effects of the solution that was implemented and re-starting the problem-solving process at a prior step (e.g., Step 3, Step 4) if the strategy proves ineffective. We learn as much from the strategies that do not work as we do from the ones that *do* work! In many ways, this should be the most intuitive and natural step in the problem-solving process for any behavior analyst. It is a hallmark of our field that we collect data and evaluate the effects of our efforts rather than assuming that our good intentions have resulted in success (Baer, Wolf, & Risley, 1968).

Finding out that your solution did not work does not have to be perceived as a personal failure. It is a hallmark of our field that we collect data and evaluate the effects of our efforts rather than assuming that our good intentions have resulted in success.

This step is much more straightforward when you think about evaluating the effects of a selected solution on client progress (e.g., did the problem behavior decrease or accuracy on a skill increase when you implemented your intervention?) or on a staff performance issue (e.g., did implementation accuracy increase when your intervention was implemented?). Evaluating the effects of these kinds of solutions is standard practice. However, when the problem is something subtle (e.g., a strained relationship with a family, constant competition between two valued staff members), it may be harder to imagine the data that would allow an evaluation of a solution. Instead of a rate measure or a percentage accuracy measure, a better match might be agreed-upon subjective ratings of whether things seem to be going better and looking for behaviors that correlate with the answer (e.g., more smiles, agreement, and initiation of communication from the family).

The most common downfall of executing this step is avoiding information that suggests the strategy didn't work well. Naturally, people tend to avoid this type of information if it means encountering situations in which success is not achieved. Again, those supervisees who are quite anxious or fearful of mistakes are likely to struggle with this step and require support and encouragement from the supervisor. The supervisee may also struggle with knowing how to evaluate the effects of their solution and the conditions under which they evaluate the effects. For example, if a parent is trained to implement a behavior plan and performs well (i.e., to a high performance and stability criterion) during training, but then does not implement the program outside of the monitored training context (i.e., the RBT or BCBA sees them respond to the situation as they did in baseline), this means that the new program is not effective for the family. The novice clinician may see it as the parent failing to implement the program, but the larger context suggests that the program was likely too effortful, complex, or non-preferred for the parent to implement outside of the demand context of parent training sessions, or that the training was insufficient to produce generalized effects in the non-training context. The parent is unlikely to tell the clinician this unless the clinician supports this disclosure by fostering a strong and non-judgmental therapeutic relationship (see Chapter 9).

The supervisor should encourage the supervisee to view the need for revision and mistakes as valuable and meaningful lessons learned. The supervisor might share a story of a time when they were quite certain that a strategy was going to work, but it failed. The story should also explain how the supervisor recognized that the strategy didn't work, what the next steps were (e.g., try something else, seek consultation), and how future efforts benefitted from the lesson learned. The supervisor must create a punishment-free environment (i.e., the supervisory relationship) making it easy and reinforcing to be honest about mistakes and problems that have been detected. An important part of becoming a better problem solver is being willing to learn not only from your successes, but also from your mistakes. If a supervisor helps the supervisee become comfortable making a few mistakes and learning from them, then he or she will develop more confidence in trying different strategies when the supervisor is no longer available.

Reflection
Think about a time when you were faced with a difficult or complex problem for which you identified a solution that worked. As you think back on that example, do you think you implemented some version of the five steps outlined here? Can you identify specific indicators that the solution you chose was likely to be successful? How about an example of a difficult or complex problem for which your identified solution did not work? Did you implement some version of the five steps outlined here, or did you miss some? How did you know that your selected "solution" did not work? What were your next steps? Did that situation produce changes in how you have approached similar problems since then?

Problem Solving in the Supervisory Process

As a supervisor, you can employ this structured problem-solving process to assist the supervisee in solving the problems they encounter in their behavior analytic endeavors. You can also use this process to address problems that you detect in the supervisee's behavior. For example, you might detect that organization and time management represents an area of relative weakness for a supervisee. The next chapter will walk you through how to address these issues using a problem solving framework. In addition, you might determine that the supervisee's interpersonal skill deficits are creating problems in their relationships with colleagues and co-workers or families and schools. Chapter 9 will walk you through how to address these issues. Finally, you might detect that there are problems that have developed in the relationship that you are building with the supervisee. Chapter 11 will help you use this problem-solving framework to detect, assess, and intervene.

We encourage you to actively teach structured problem solving and systematic decision making to all supervisees across a wide range of situations. You can use the questions in Appendix B as a pre-test assessment as you begin to teach the skills to supervisees. You can also employ these questions as a self-assessment that the supervisee completes as you teach problem solving skills and how to evaluate their own skills. However, some supervisees will struggle more than others despite your best efforts. In these instances, reflection, self-monitoring, and targeted practice in structured problem solving may be beneficial. In addition, you may have noticed that some of your supervisees tend to struggle with problem solving and frequently bring relatively easy problems to supervision meetings (i.e., you may have reinforced bringing problems without teaching problem solving). In these cases, you can use the questions in Appendix B as a diagnostic assessment for those who are struggling with specific content. Finally, this chapter may have sparked the realization that you are prone to impulsive or delayed decision making and you could benefit from your own reflection and practiced use of these skills. In that case, we recommend using the questions in Appendix B as a self-reflection exercise for yourself to determine if you might also benefit from a structured approach to problem solving.

Appendix A: Problem Solving Worksheet

With a collaborator or supervisor, choose a problem and engage in each step of the problem-solving process. Use this form to document your work. Make sure you fully engage in each step and DO NOT jump ahead. Use the questions for each step to assist you with developing an answer.

List the problem-solvers: _____

Step I: Identify the Problem: Provide a specific description and indicate how you knew it was a problem.

Helpful questions:

1. Are there behaviors missing (i.e., not exhibited) that I would expect to see under similar circumstances (e.g., lack of question asking, no or minimal greeting or closure, no or minimal positive facial expressions and body language)?
2. Have there been subtle or obvious changes in typical behavior or performance (e.g., changes in affect, increased cancellations or call outs, increases in variable responding, increases in some aspect of problem behavior, decreases in skill acquisition)?
3. Are there aspects of the environment that might be unpleasant or undesirable?
4. What things about this problem (e.g., clinical programming, staff performance, therapeutic relationship) make you think that it is going well or poorly?
5. Are there aspects of my culture or the other person's culture that might lead me to misinterpret subtle behavior as an indicator of a problem or overlook subtle behavior as an indicator of a problem?

_____
_____
_____
_____
_____
_____
_____
_____

Step II: Define the Problem: Ask yourself questions and make observations that help you get at the cause or functions of the problem. Use functional assessment tools such as the PDC-HS if this is appropriate. List your answers (and any questions besides the ones we have listed below) as numbered items.

Helpful Questions:
1. What exactly does the "problem" look like?
2. For whom is this a "problem" (i.e., who contacts the negative or undesirable outcomes)?
3. Under what conditions does the "problem" occur?
4. What is the typical result of the "problem" occurring?
5. Create a summary statement that defines the core cause or causes of the problem.

_____
_____
_____
_____
_____

Step III: Generate Possible Solutions: Conduct a brainstorming session to generate lots of possible ideas for solutions. Encourage yourself to think creatively and to behave variably. Write down all ideas and do not evaluate them yet.

Helpful Questions:
1. Will a solution to a similar problem from the past work in this situation?
2. If there were no restrictions on time or resources, what things might solve this problem?
3. If we could have a complete re-do of this situation, are there things we would do differently?
4. What possible solutions are related to the likely function of the problem?

_____
_____
_____
_____
_____

Step IV: Evaluate the Options: Write your most promising solutions in the left column and evaluate the pros and cons of each option. Mark each as a **short term (S) and/or long term (L)** pro and con. If one of your solutions is clearly linked to the function from step 2 that is a pro.

Helpful Questions:

1. What are the positive benefits to the critical individuals (e.g., child, family, staff)?
2. What are the risks or possible negative outcomes associated with the solution?
3. How effortful, costly, time-intensive is immediate implementation of the solution?
4. How likely is the option to produce sustained positive effects?
5. How likely is the option to work quickly?
6. What are the barriers to success?
7. Will there be resistance to implementing the solution?
8. Can the environment support sustained implementation of this solution?
9. Does this solution completely address the function of the problem, protect consumers and staff, and match the available resources?
10. What would happen if I did nothing?

	Pros		Cons	
Solution	Short Term	Long Term	Short Term	Long Term

Step V: Evaluate the Effects of your Solution: Develop a plan to evaluate the effects of your solution.

Helpful Questions:
1. Who will implement the solution, how, and for how long?

2. Who will evaluate the solution and when?

3. How will I evaluate the outcomes of the solution (i.e., did it work or not)?

4. What will you measure? How much change must occur to feel like you have solved the problem?

5. Was the solution effective (i.e., did it produce the desired change, in the desired contexts, in the desired timeframe)?

6. Are the positive effects of the solution sustaining?

7. What were the specific outcomes of the solution (both intended and unintended)?

8. Do I need to modify the solution?

9. Do I need to try another solution?

Notes:
_____
_____
_____
_____

Appendix B: Assessing Common Difficulties with Problem Solving

1. Is it difficult to generate more than one potential solution to a problem?

2. Do you behave impulsively in your problem-solving and decision-making activities (e.g., assume you know the full extent of a problem, the cause of a problem, or a good solution to the problem without gathering details or consulting others)?

3. Do you avoid making difficult decisions (e.g., focusing on minor issues instead of major issues, frequently requesting more time to think about things)?

4. Are you insecure about your decisions (e.g., seeking many people's input, seeming pessimistic about accuracy) even when you have made a well-considered and reasonable choice?

5. Are you able to describe the benefits of making a difficult decision and implementing an action plan even if it is effortful or unpleasant?

6. Can you describe what you would do if your initial plan did not work out well?

7. Are you relying on the same strategies that you have used in the past even if the strategies are not appropriate to the context or if the strategies have not worked in the past?

8. Are you able to describe the variables that should be influencing your clinical choices (e.g., safety, ease of implementation, speed of desired result) in a wide range of situations?

Chapter 8

Organizational and Time Management Skills

Productivity is never an accident. It is always the result of a commitment to excellence, intelligent planning, and focused effort.

—Paul Meyer

If you think that organizational and time management (OTM) skills are pivotal skills for the success of a new professional, we agree. A pivotal skill, once acquired, produces beneficial changes across a wide range of other skills as an ancillary effect (Koegel, Koegel, Harrower, & Carter, 1999). For young children, joint attention skills are considered pivotal because once a child shares interests and socially references others, skills such as language and social skills also increase (Jones & Carr, 2004). For elementary school children, reading is a pivotal skill for later success as new information is primarily gained by reading text; conversely, illiteracy is associated with many poor outcomes (Nelson, Benner, & Gonzalez, 2005). For an adult, OTM skills influence many other repertoires in both work (e.g., academic success, clinical effectiveness, productivity) and personal life (e.g., household management, money management) and are pivotal to success as a practicing professional and supervisor (Kaya, Kaya, Pallos, & Küçük, 2012).

> *OTM skills influence many other repertoires in both work (e.g., academic success, clinical effectiveness, productivity) and personal life (e.g., household management, money management) and are pivotal to success as a practicing professional and supervisor (Kaya, et al., 2012).*

Organizational skills refer to planning and prioritizing activities (e.g., tracking multiple projects through lists, choosing between simultaneous demands), goal-setting, and organizing various materials (e.g., organized storage systems, efficient retrieval and use of materials) and aspects of work or personal life. This term subsumes time management skills in some frameworks (Wolf, Lockspeiser, Gong, & Guiton, 2018), with time considered one more thing that should be planned and organized. Other frameworks single out time management as a separate and critical skill (Ervin, 2008; Kaya, et al., 2012). Time management refers to planning the use of available time in line with priorities, personal goals and lifestyles, and professional demands. The ultimate goal of time management is effectiveness and efficiency such that goals are achieved in the minimum time possible through planning and self-monitoring of speed of task completion. The two are considered to be separate but related skills in this chapter.

Repeatedly, OTM skills have been shown to be related to successful transition from high school to higher education (George, Dixon, Stansel, Gelb, & Pheri, 2008; Gibney, Moore, Murphy, & O'Sullivan, 2011) and successful transition into the workforce in various disciplines from nursing (Ervin, 2008) to athletic training (Mazerolle, Walker, & Thrasher, 2015). Effective OTM skills may facilitate professional success, assuming that core content knowledge and skills exist. In the field of nursing, effective caseload management has been studied extensively and described as requiring a combination of organizational, time management, and priority-setting skills (Ervin, 2008; Gran-Moravec & Hughes, 2005). Conversely, poor time management can result in insufficient time allocation for

> *Effective OTM skills may facilitate professional success, assuming that core content knowledge and skills exist.*

personal priorities, increased stress and depression, and impaired decision making and critical thinking (Campbell & Svenson, 1992; Gran-Moravec,

& Hughes, 2005; Häfner, Stock, Pinneker, & Ströhle, 2014; Jex & Elacqua, 1999; Simpson & Courtney, 2002). For undergraduate students and students in training for practice-oriented careers, time management training has produced decreased procrastination, increased efficiency, and lowered perceived stress (Häfner, Stock, & Oberst, 2015; Pagana, 1994; Van Eerde, 2003) even when task demands do not change.

These same effects occur in transition to practice and caseload management skills in behavior analysis. LeBlanc, Sleeper, Mueller, Jenkins, & Harper-Briggs (2020) found that OTM skills were the single best predictor of success or failure in caseload management skills for BCBAs. These skills (e.g., explicit use of strategies, efficiency and effectiveness of task completion, proportion of primary activities off task) were more predictive of success or failure than the size of the caseload, the match between client needs and clinical skills, and geographic or funding constraints. Behavior analysts with strong OTM skills demonstrated an increased capacity to serve their clients and supervise others. That is, those who were successful at caseload management were given larger caseloads to manage, given discretionary opportunities to develop systems, and were more likely to be promoted and earn performance-based pay than those who struggled with OTM skills.

Sellers, LeBlanc, and Valentino (2016) suggest that poor OTM skills are common barriers encountered in supervision. These skills should constitute part of the formal professional training and supervisory experience in behavior analysis to minimize negative impacts on stress level and quality of client services (e.g., late reports, too few programs, delayed or poor clinical decisions; LeBlanc, et al., 2020). The transition to practice as a behavior analyst typically requires refined OTM skills compared to the skills that led to success in prior circumstances (e.g., undergraduate school, graduate school, single life). The effects may also be magnified as supervisory and clinical responsibilities increase if OTM skills are subpar. Given the need for these skills in applied work, supervisors should be prepared to model and teach the supervisee refined OTM skills, and may well discover that doing so enhances his or her own skills.

OTM Skills

This chapter covers four interrelated sets of OTM skills to assess and directly target with supervisees or yourself when needed. Each skill shares some features with the other skills, but makes a unique contribution to overall planning and productivity success for the common task demands of practicing behavior analysts (LeBlanc & Nosik, 2019; LeBlanc, et al., 2020). The OTM skills include: 1) planning and managing tasks and time

(Classens, Van Eerde, Rutte, & Roe, 2007; Wolf, et al., 2018; Kaya, et al., 2012); 2) managing systems for organizing materials and workspace and using technology (Pagana, 1994; White, 2017); 3) designing and conducting effective meetings (LeBlanc & Nosik, 2019; Pagana, 1994); and 4) problem solving, decision-making, and managing your own behavior (Buckner, 1992; Miltenberger, 2016; Wolf, et al., 2018).

Planning and Managing Tasks and Time. Planning is critical for both task *and* time management (Wolf, et al., 2018). Task management involves prioritizing, planning, and completing the steps involved in any work that needs to be undertaken. Time management involves planning what you will do with your time, how long something will take, and exactly when it will occur (Kaya, et al., 2012). These two skill areas intersect because any planned steps in task management activities must then be integrated into the work schedule in terms of how long each step will take and when it will occur.

In a survey of task management skills, Fukuzawa, Joho, and Maeshiro (2015) found that most undergraduate student participants had a reasonable sense of the priority of tasks, but tended to perceive a task as a big chunk rather than a series of small chunks. In addition, creating time estimates was a good indicator of task completion and poor time management was the major contributor to uncompleted or uninitiated tasks. Several practical resources exist to guide task management (Allen, 2015; Allen & Hall, 2019; Tucker, 2018). There is no empirical evidence to suggest that one of these guides is superior to others, but anyone struggling with task management should use one to assist in developing these skills (see resource list).

An important early step in task management is breaking the task into component sub-tasks or chunks (Fukuzawa, et al., 2015). Allen (2015) refers to these as "actionable steps" with phrasing that is brief, specific, immediate, and incorporates an action verb. These next actionable steps involve behaviors that can quickly encounter reinforcement. The steps can then be placed in the order of occurrence with a corresponding list of resources required to complete each (e.g., access to a journal or book, access to an assessment tool). If no specific order is required, the steps might be arranged in order from subjectively least to most difficult or preferred, or vice versa. The list of steps and resource materials can guide development of a general deadline for each step in a simple chart as illustrated in Appendix A. In general, creating checklists and process charts help to sequence and organize tasks (see Tucker, 2018, for a primer on creating checklists for task management).

Once the task steps, materials, and general timelines are developed, time management strategies need to be implemented. The time to completion must be estimated for each task. In addition, the specific time for task completion must be identified. Stress-free success is unlikely if one assumes the task will be done sometime between now and when it is due without specifying when that time will be. However, many people make this mistake because of the history of this strategy proving successful in the past when there were fewer demands on their time and fewer complex tasks to complete. It is better to overestimate time requirements rather than underestimate (i.e., I think the task will take 25 minutes, so I block out 30 minutes on my calendar to complete it). There is no science around how much to overestimate, but any overestimate will help to minimize stress associated with minor interruptions, logistical issues, and mistaken estimates (Pagano, 1994). Estimates for new tasks are likely to be underestimated (i.e., everything takes longer than you think it will, especially the first time you do it).

A task management analysis is provided for the task of completing an assessment and report for a client (see Appendix A). Any BCBA working in human services completes this task for virtually every client a few times a year. The task involves many subtasks (e.g., obtaining the materials, conducting the assessments, scoring the assessments, writing the report, submitting the report for review) that must occur in a certain sequence. Each subtask includes smaller tasks, and the time allocation for each will vary. Some tasks require coordination of efforts with another person, which could result in delays if there is no advanced planning to create a reasonable timeline for each person's schedule. The assessment and report writing task has a firm and important deadline. If the deadline is missed, the client may lose their authorization for services, the company may not be paid for services that are delivered without authorization, and the BCBA may encounter performance management sanctions. Therefore, it is best to start planning the timeline backward from the ultimate deadline and build in a cushion of extra time at each step. The sample task plan in Appendix A illustrates this approach. Without task planning, the behavior analyst might forget a critical step, begin at the wrong step, or be unable to complete all steps before the deadline.

Once the required time estimates and timelines are created, the specific time for task completion must be identified and protected in the schedule. Many people make the mistake of leaving work tasks off of their schedule. That is, they only protect time that is committed to someone else (e.g., meetings, appointments) without protecting committed time for their own task completion. This may result in completing work tasks at home during nonwork hours, missing deadlines, overcommitting, and an overall increased stress level (Häfner, et al., 2014).

Scheduling task-related work allows an accurate estimate of the remaining discretionary time prior to saying "yes" to another task or opportunity. Pagana (1994) lists "learning to say 'no'" as an important time management skill to teach. She describes the importance of determining whether a new opportunity is a good use of time and quickly saying "no" if it is not. Saying "no" in a kind and diplomatic manner is an important skill that the supervisor will likely need to model and shape in the supervisee's repertoire. A new opportunity should not be considered until the schedule is evaluated to determine whether there is sufficient time available to fit in the new task, even if it is a valuable one. If there is not sufficient time available, the new opportunity must be evaluated against the current priorities of the work/school environment. If the new opportunity should be prioritized, the supervisee can be guided through identifying which existing commitments will be sacrificed to accommodate the new event (see the section on pro-con analysis in Chapter 7 for a structured approach to comparing multiple options).

In the absence of a comprehensive scheduling system, some tasks and commitments are going to suffer, potentially in a haphazard manner. The ones that suffer may have been forgotten altogether or else could not be completed on time due to lack of planning rather than due to actively deprioritizing the least important task. It is important to periodically conduct an analysis of the accuracy of your own time estimates for tasks (e.g., it consistently takes less than the estimated time to write a report but longer than the estimated time to manage email). This analysis may be done as part of problem solving as described in Chapter 7 (i.e., detect the problem, identify the determinants of the failure to complete the tasks on time, generate and select a solution, implement and evaluate the solution.

Finally, anyone who wants to become a master of time and task management must "guard prime time" and protect and use planning time (Kelly, 2002; Pagana, 1994). Some tasks are better suited to certain times of day, depending on the individual and their required tasks. For example, LeBlanc finds it easier to write in the morning when she has a higher level of alertness, and very cumbersome to write in the mid-afternoon. She protects her writing time accordingly, and schedules meetings and organizational tasks for the mid-afternoon to make maximum use of all work hours. Ala'i finds that mid-morning is her best time for collaborative meetings that require brainstorming, attentive listening, and flexible thinking, while early mornings and afternoons are better for clinical reviews and late afternoons for organizing

> **Mastering Time and Task Management**
> 1. Assign tasks to the time of day that allows maximal productivity.
> 2. Plan and protect time to plan.

tasks. When possible, each person should assign tasks to a time of day that allows them to maximize productivity (e.g., writing an assessment report in the morning). Second, the planner must protect time in the schedule for planning activities. Time to plan is perhaps the single most important time to protect. Doing so will enhance use of all remaining time to accomplish prioritized tasks. A supervisor should ask the supervisee when they plan their schedule and how much time they are protecting for planning. If the supervisee does not regularly schedule time for planning, the supervisor should explain why it is critical to do so and then support the supervisee in drafting a plan.

Time for planning might be protected on a monthly, weekly, and daily basis. Monthly planning might include an advanced review of the entire month with particular attention to deadlines such as report due dates, expiring authorizations, monthly team meetings, upcoming project management deadlines, and planned time off of work. Those events allow one to work backward in the month to create task plans, protecting sufficient time to complete the necessary tasks in advance of the deadline. LeBlanc likes to schedule her time so that she is able to complete tasks up to one week in advance of the upcoming deadline because this allows her to recover from unexpected problems (e.g., illness, childcare problems, a task being unexpectedly difficult) and still meet the deadline.

Weekly planning involves reviewing all of the events of the upcoming week. The first purpose is to determine if there are any remaining tasks that need to be accomplished (e.g., creating an agenda, double checking the timing of a meeting) (LeBlanc & Nosik, 2019). A second purpose is to identify any adjustments that need to be made (e.g., "I did not finish that task yesterday, so I need to plan for at least 30 additional minutes of worktime on this before Thursday afternoon's deadline"). Sellers schedules time at the end of each week to review completed goals, identify barriers to those she failed to complete and plan for their completion, review upcoming goals, and adjust the coming week's schedule. Finally, daily planning involves fitting in the everyday details (e.g., "I am tightly scheduled so I need to pack a lunch) and adjusting to unexpected events (e.g., reschedule an event so you can take your car in for unexpected repairs). Daily planning may occur in the first fice to ten minutes of the day and at the close of the day for the next day's schedule.

As described in Chapter 4, time and behavior related to time are areas where cultural tensions might arise. Groups have different experiences with the importance of time and how to manage it. People from different cultures understand and respond to time differently (Meyer, 2014). Both the supervisor and the supervisee must understand the expectations of the organization and the community in which practice and supervision take place. Priority is given to the obligation to serve clients according to the needs and the requirements of the organization mission and structure. If the organization's customs and priorities are different than the person's values, adaptations will need to be made to ensure success in that environment.

Consider the case of one employee whose reports are consistently late. At first glance it looks like she "does everything late" and takes a long time to complete the reports. This may or may not be related to her cultural conditioning in relation to time and deadlines. After an open discussion between the supervisor and the employee, it appears there is a difference in understanding about priorities for time management. For example, unscheduled consultations with co-workers who walk by her office when she is working on reports seems to be one of the reasons for delays. She does not feel comfortable closing the door or turning co-workers away and feels the time to informally connect with them is more important than delayed reports. In this case, tardiness on reports is not acceptable to the funding agency and a solution needs to be developed. The two of them consider different options. She may need to move to another location to finish reports, schedule report writing to occur during times of the day with less foot traffic outside her office, or implement a strategy such as placing a sign on the door for schedule periods protected for report writing. At the same time, connecting emotionally with her colleagues is a priority and so time for that also needs to be planned and should not be disregarded. Morning time may be best for report writing, but the task could be moved to a time with less co-worker contact (e.g., before her coworkers arrive). It may not be initially clear whether this type of problems is an OTM skill deficit or a cultural difference in how time is managed. In all cases, conversations and creative solutions will involve honoring strengths and values, planning, and scheduling. Pant and colleagues' (2016) example in Chapter 4 provides an illustration of how employees with different priorities respond to time and efficiency and bring different added value to an organization (Pant, Chamorro-Premuzic, Molensky, Hahn, & Hinds, 2016).

Managing A System for Organization and Using Technology. The second skill involves development and refining of systems for organizing material and technology skills that facilitate efficiency (Coll, Zegwaard, & Hodges, 2002). Individuals who are slow to respond to e-mails, phone calls, and requests from the supervisor (or supervisee) are also likely not responding in a timely manner to other things. If someone cannot quickly access the information they need during supervision meetings (e.g., a requested graph or protocol, the date of a recent session with a client), deficits in these skills are likely the culprit. The supervisor might use the following ideas to teach these valuable skills to their supervisees as well as to improve their own skills.

According to Allen (2015), stress-free productivity is not simply about getting organized with respect to planning tasks and entering them into your calendar. One also needs a comprehensive system for capturing the relevant things that need our attention, specifying the actions associated with those things, and organizing the results. That is, getting organized cannot be a one-time event. Instead, consistent productivity hinges on developing a comprehensive and well-organized method for capturing thoughts, ideas, demands, and turning those into actionable steps that can be planned and executed. Capturing ideas in a permanent written or electronic form introduces a potentially more effective discriminative stimulus and removes the need to repeatedly self-prompt remembering of the task. It is hard to be relaxed, focused, and productive when completing a task if you are constantly reminding yourself not to forget three things that have just occurred to you.

> *Getting organized cannot be a one-time event.*

To combat this, Allen (2015) recommends an activity called the *mind sweep*. He provides a list of common incompletion triggers (e.g., emails that I need to send, personal errands) to evoke writing down specific action items (e.g., send the agenda, email client's mother, pick up the dry-cleaning by 4 pm). During this activity, each response to a trigger is written down, incorporated into a list, and integrated into a project planning tool or time management tool (i.e., calendar). For example, the trigger of "reports to complete" might lead one to respond with the names of three different clients who have reports that must be completed soon. The trigger of "e-mails that I need to send" might lead one to list several recipients and the topic the correspondence that should be sent. See Allen (2015) for a detailed mind sweep activity.

In modern workplaces, email management is a critical technology-based organizational skill. The literature in business and management clearly indicates that there can be negative effects of email. For example, email content and volume along with the perceived demand for an immediate response can create perceived stress and the phenomenon referred to as "information overload" (McMurtry, 2014; Pignata, Lushington, Sloan, & Buchanan, 2015). In addition, some researchers have used the phrase "email addiction." This phrase refers to the effects observed from the intermittent schedule of reinforcement associated with checking email, despite the disruptive effects of email checking on completion of other tasks (Marulanda-Carter & Jackson, 2012).

There are two critical components to an email management system: 1) the filing system; and 2) the strategies used to manage the inbox and sort email into those respective files and ongoing actions. Incoming emails arrive in the inbox of whichever electronic mail system is used (e.g., Microsoft Outlook®, Google Mail®). If the inbox is not regularly reviewed and managed with a goal of getting to "inbox zero," it will quickly become overwhelming and dysfunctional. The filing system usually includes a trash folder and a series of categorized reference folders. Allen (2015) also recommends a pending folder (i.e., you will need to do something about this at some point, but not right now). The number and structure of the reference folders should be based on the user's tasks, clients, or any other category that readily conveys at a glance what is inside. The most important aspect of the organizational system is that email should not be kept in the inbox. Emails should be managed and cleared (see strategies below) so that the inbox includes all of the new things that need your attention and *only* the things that need your attention.

Email management strategies are usually designed to have two desired effects: 1) increase the efficiency and timeliness of email management; and 2) decrease interruptions of work tasks caused by email (Allen, 2015; Marulanda-Carter & Jackson, 2012). Allen (2015) provides a system for triaging email that is well-suited to the first effect. In this context, the term triage refers to quickly scanning and categorizing each email in the inbox according to whether it is valuable and actionable. Items that are not valuable (e.g., a marketing email for a product you don't want) or actionable (e.g., a brief confirmation email that does not need a response) are immediately deleted (i.e., filed to trash). An email that is not currently actionable but might prove useful in the future can be filed to the appropriate reference folder (e.g., company policies). Emails that are actionable require either an immediate brief email response or integration into a task management system. Then the email is filed appropriately (e.g., pending, reference, trash). Marulanda-Carter & Jackson (2012) provide recommendations well-suited to the second desired effect. Email management should be contained to consistently scheduled, protected periods of 30 minutes or less throughout the day. The frequency of email management (e.g., once a day, several times a day) depends on the volume and the criticality of incoming emails. During other times, the email program should be closed, and alerts should be turned off to prevent frequent interruptions of ongoing tasks. Instead, email should be actively managed as an efficient, single-task event. LeBlanc refers to this as "getting your email instead of letting your email get you."

Behavior analysts must use various technology solutions (e.g., email and file storage, videoconference platforms, practice management software) in the course of everyday clinical practice. When these skills are weak, tasks take longer than necessary and important information may not be accessible when needed. Finally, poor skills in this area may lead to inadvertent failure to protect confidentiality and privacy rights (e.g., using a product that is not HIPAA-compliant). In addition to the email filing systems described above, it is important to develop storage systems for all other files as well (e.g., graphs, documents, videos, articles). Whether the files are stored on a single computer or in a cloud-based file sharing system (e.g., Box®, Dropbox®, Cloudshare®, Google drive®), ease and speed of retrieval depends on the quality of the filing system (e.g., naming conventions, subfolder structure) and the skills of the user. If a supervisee is struggling with use of a technology, the supervisor should encourage the supervisee to watch a tutorial, take a course on the use of the tool, or find a less complicated technology solution.

Designing and Conducting Effective Meetings. Supervisees may also be new to the realm of professional meetings. Therefore, it is helpful to review specific expectations related to the supervision meetings and meetings in general (e.g., arrive on time, be prepared, have a well-planned agenda; see LeBlanc & Nosik, 2019; Anderson, 1994 for resources). The supervisor is often the first model for conducting professional meetings, so they should endeavor to meet their own expectations (e.g., be on time, be prepared) in every interaction with the supervisee. When a supervisor cannot meet their own expectations, the supervisor can model taking responsibility for their actions and proactively making corrections. For example, if a supervisor is late in returning edits on a report to their supervisee, they might say: "Thanks for your patience. I apologize for getting this to you a day late. I underestimated how long another task would take, but I have adjusted my time-planning system so this shouldn't happen again."

Supervision and individual performance feedback typically occur in private, individual meetings to protect client confidentiality and supervisee privacy. These meetings and direct observation events should occur regularly to facilitate a strong supervisor–supervisee relationship (Sellers, Valentino, et al., 2016). These interactions have several purposes: setting performance expectations, monitoring performance, shaping professional and technical repertoires, generating ideas, developing and reviewing products, and establishing and maintaining rapport and interpersonal relationships. In a recent report from the Behavior Analyst Certification Board (BACB), the most commonly reported ethical violation alleged against BACB certificants in 2016 and 2017 involved improper or inadequate supervision or delegation of supervision (BACB, 2018b). Thus, behavior analysts might benefit from evaluating their supervision and individual feedback meetings, devoting time to planning these meetings, and teaching their supervisees (i.e., the supervisors of tomorrow) how to plan and lead effective meetings.

Most supervisees will not know how to prepare a supervision agenda until the supervisor teaches them how to do so using a structured approach such as behavioral skills training. In fact, the supervisee may have a history with prior meetings that were not well-organized and effective. The supervisor can teach the supervisee the value of an agenda for organization, time management, prioritization, and communication. Next, the supervisor can point out the important components of an agenda (i.e., prioritized list of things that will be covered with a time estimate for each) and provide a model agenda for the first supervision session as a model (See Appendix B for an agenda for the first supervision meeting). Following the first meeting, the supervisee can rehearse the new skill by creating an agenda 24-hours in advance of the next individual supervision meeting and sending it for feedback (Sellers, Valentino, et al., 2016; Bailey & Burch, 2010). The supervisor can then provide feedback on the agenda (e.g., reprioritizing the items, decreasing the number of items to ensure that each can be covered, altering time estimates). This exercise provides goal-setting, rehearsal, and feedback opportunities for the supervisee on agenda development, prioritization, and time-management, and may improve the outcomes of the supervision meeting (LeBlanc & Nosik, 2019).

> **Teach the Supervisee to Prepare Agendas:**
> 1. Teach the value of the agenda
> 2. Teach the components of the agenda
> 3. Provide a model of an agenda
> 4. Have them create one and provide feedback
> 5. Repeat until proficient

Crafting an effective agenda requires the supervisee to plan in a comprehensive and thoughtful way to prioritize their needs and make the supervision time productive. The supervisor can review the agenda items and add items that they would like to cover. This advanced notice of the agenda also gives the supervisor the opportunity to review materials and gather resources that they might share with the supervisee in the meeting. The supervisor should set specific expectations around note taking, deadlines for completion of products, and systems for managing documentation (e.g., tracking experience and supervision hours). For example, the supervisor may ask the supervisee to send documents before the next supervision meeting (e.g., an agenda, a tracking sheet with accrued hours, a prepared documentation form).

In addition to supervision meetings, a practicing behavior analyst will have many other meetings (LeBlanc & Nosik, 2019). Meetings can offer behavior analysts a platform for generating ideas, detecting and solving problems, assigning tasks, communicating and seeking consultation, generating work products, monitoring performance, shaping a supervisee's professional repertoire, and enhancing interpersonal relationships (Hindle, 1998; Hood, 2013; Sellers, Valentino, et al., 2016). Leach, Rogelberg, Warr, and Burnfield (2009) indicate that five characteristics that impact the perception of a meeting as "good" (i.e., these are present) or "bad" (i.e., these are absent): (a) use of an agenda; (b) keeping of minutes; (c) punctuality; (d) appropriate meeting environment; and (e) having a meeting leader. Meetings are costly to any organization (i.e., hours x number of people x pay per hour) and the costs are not usually built into core process (Lencioni, 2004; Jacobs, 2013). Thus, it is important to use an understanding of human behavior to make them as effective, efficient, and productive as possible. The difference between a productive meeting and an unproductive meeting is in the behavior of those planning, leading, and participating in the meetings.

Planning the meeting is the responsibility of the meeting leader, whereas conducting the meeting requires effective performance of both the leader and the participants (e.g., contributing productively, staying on task). The meeting organizer should identify the purposes of the meeting (see the checklist provided by LeBlanc & Nosik (2019) for the common stated and unstated purposes of meetings). The meeting leader should also identify whether each person is likely to be prepared to accomplish the purposes of the meeting. The next step is developing the full agenda as a planning tool to help participants prepare for the meeting and contribute more effectively. The agenda usually includes a summary of the purpose of the meeting, each task associated with the meeting goal, and a time estimate for completion of each task. LeBlanc & Nosik (2019) provide a template for creating a meeting agenda that allows the notetaker to record comments (see their article). The meeting leader also manages the meeting by opening the meeting on time and managing the time and interpersonal dynamics to stay on track with the agenda (see LeBlanc & Nosik, 2019 for strategies). Finally, the meeting leader should close the meeting with a clearly articulated list of actions items and notes about the discussion that occurred during the meeting.

Explicit Purposes of a Meeting:
1. Supervision and performance management
2. Communication
3. Problem solving
4. Project management and product generation

Implicit Purposes of a Meeting:
1. Setting deadlines
2. Observing interactions
3. Providing feedback
4. Modeling interpersonal skills

The same planning approach can be used for planning case management time or direct observation experiences. For example, a behavior analyst who oversees services provided in a client's home will likely schedule less frequent, longer duration supervision and case management sessions than when services are center-based to minimize the time lost to driving. Thus, the BCBA may need to accomplish 10 to 15 different tasks (e.g., review technician notes, speak with the parents about a recent concern, review the most recent data points and mastered targets, observe implementation of a program, collect IOA data, train the technician on a new program, modify an existing program that is not producing rapid acquisition, show the parent a new data sheet for problem behavior, write the current progress note) during the two- to three-hour on-site visit. Unless the tasks and time allotment are carefully planned, important tasks may be forgotten, the required materials may not be available, or the BCBA may run out of time to complete the tasks required for high quality case management. For example, when planning the tasks, the BCBA is likely to see that productive use of time will be maximized if he or she reviews the prior notes and data prior to observing implementation of the intervention programs. Other tasks may also be best suited to a specific timing in the session, which should be planned in advance. See Appendix C for a sample agenda for a client session.

Problem Solving and Managing Yourself. The content of Chapters 6 (Self-Monitoring) and 7 (Problem Solving) are integrally related to the content of this chapter. First, it is important to consistently self-monitor OTM skills to determine whether: 1) the current skills and systems are adequate; and 2) whether the skills and systems are consistently being used. New demands in personal and professional life require development of new strategies and systems; failure to do so likely results in feeling stressed and overwhelmed. Self-detecting stress or failure to meet commitments can be difficult. It requires self-monitoring, self-reflection, and judgement-free honesty about performance. The questions in Appendix D can serve as: 1) a pre-test assessment for teaching the skills to supervisees; 2) a diagnostic assessment for those struggling with OTM; 3) a supervisee self-assessment; and 4) a self-reflection exercise for supervisors.

> *New demands in personal and professional life require development of new strategies and systems; failure to do so likely results in feeling stressed and overwhelmed.*

It may also be helpful to have a trusted colleague provide an external evaluation of whether stress is evident and whether the current strategies seem to be working. This can be useful for every professional at some point in a career, so the supervisor might be just as likely as the supervisee to need periods of self-reflection and evolution of their OTM strategies. Once an issue with these skills surfaces, increased stress or negative performance feedback is also likely to be evident. The information learned about problem solving becomes critically important. Step 1 of problem solving is detecting that there is an issue, but Step 2 requires a careful analysis of the cause of the problem. The supervisee and the supervisor might together explore the likely culprits (e.g., poor technology use skills, lack of editing, use of a fragile capture device such as human memory) and use the resulting information to design and select an intervention that will solve the problem (i.e., Step 3).

Finally, as has been a theme in the last few chapters, overly rigid OTM skills can produce dysfunction. Different people might use different capture devices and they might each use their own device well. Isolation and conflict may result from an inability or unwillingness to collaborate with people who use different strategies and tools than you do. The supervisor should not endeavor to have their supervisees duplicate all of their strategies, but instead should try to serve as a model for effectiveness and efficiency when one follows general recommended practices. In addition, the supervisor can teach prioritization when common caseload management barriers occur. For example, sometimes a funding source will not provide payment for as much time as it would take to complete a task, making prioritization and efficiency critical. Similarly, regardless of whether the time can be billed, it takes far longer to produce a single perfect product (e.g., the most fantastic parallel play program ever written) than it does to produce a really great program that will still result in skill acquisition. Newly minted BCBAs may mistakenly value a perfect product for one client program without realizing that all other clients and programs end up being neglected as a result of that one program. The wise supervisor helps a supervisee to eschew pursuit of perfection in favor of prioritization, flexibility, excellence, and productivity.

Appendix A: Sample Task Plan for Completing an Assessment Report

Task Analysis for a Reauthorization Report

Task	Subtasks	Resources	Time Estimate	Timeline
Choose assessments and obtain the relevant assessment materials	Review prior assessment (if applicable) to determine if you need to re-administer assessments Review funder requirements for specific assessments used	Prior report Assessment protocols and manuals	1 hour	At least 45 days before report is due to funder
	Determine need for new assessments to be administered Purchase assessment protocols (if applicable)	Background knowledge about assessments Input from supervisor	30–60 mins	At least 40 days before report is due
Contact family	Review assessment process and plan steps Review relevant consent forms Review necessary intake forms (for initial report only, not reauthorization)	Consent forms Intake forms (for initial report only, not reauthoriza tion)	1 hour	At least 30 days before report is due
	Schedule assessment Record services for proper billing as applicable	Scheduling software CPT codes as applicable	15 mins	At least 30 days before report is due

Conduct the assessment	Conduct Parent Interview Conduct observations Conduct any standardized tests or curricular assessments Conduct FBA as needed	Interview form, observation form, assessment protocols and materials	2–4 hours	Might require multiple visits
	Score Assessment	Automated scoring tools	2 hours	ASAP after Assessment sessions
Obtain a report template	Confirm if funder requires a specific template or use organization template	Organization electronic data collection systems/ templates	10 mins	At least 30 days before report is due
Write the report	Goals Treatment History Medical History Other services/ school services Discharge criteria	Assessment results Record review summary	2–3 hours	At least 3 weeks before report is due
	Send draft report to supervisor	HIPAA compliant file share	2 mins	3 weeks before report is due
	Complete all requested edits		15–60 mins	At least 2 weeks before report is due
	Re-submit to Supervisor (if requested)	HIPAA compliant file share		

Meet with family to review it	Update report as appropriate based on review with family		30–60 mins	5–10 days before report is due
Final submission	Add service level recommendations based on review with family, using proper CPT codes as applicable

Ensure HIPAA compliant electronic submission via email or fax

Conduct medical review call as applicable (some funders) | Knowledge of preferred submission info (e.g., fax number, email address).

Access to HIPAA compliant email account to send the report

Access to the report file | Less than 15 mins | At least 2 days before expiration date for the current authori-zation |

Appendix B: Agenda for Initial Supervision Session

Estimated Duration: 1.5 hour

I. Welcome to the Experience! Let's get to know each other (15 to 30 minutes)
   a. Discuss importance of understanding one another, our ways of communicating, our reinforcers and our priorities
   b. My background and experience as a supervisor, my life, interests and guiding values
   c. Your background and experiences, your life, interests and guiding values

IV. Contract Review and Questions (20 to 30 minutes)

V. How to Create an Agenda for Supervision (5 minutes)

VI. Review of how to complete the Collaboration Activity (5 minutes)

VII. Overview of documentation and storage (5 minutes)

VIII. Planning for next contact (5 minutes)
   a. Set the appointment
   b. Assist supervisee with planning to meet the following objectives
   c. Complete the Collaboration Tool to Review Next Time
   d. Reminder to bring documentation and review materials
   e. Send a draft agenda for next week 48 hours in advance – indicate that you would like to add an item to that agenda on the role of feedback with a time estimate of about 5 minutes

Appendix C: Sample Agenda for Client Session

Client Initials: LL
Therapist in session: TS
Date/Time: 2/28/19 10:00–11:00 a.m.

Primary Session Objectives
- Review all session notes, staff questions, and data to inform needed modifications to programs or initiating new programs
- Conduct procedural integrity check on two active programs (focus on those programs for which you have concerns about acquisition or the data)
- Train on any newly-initiated programs
- Re-train as needed
- Mention upcoming professional development opportunities

Agenda
10:00 – 10:15   Arrival and Preparation
- Greet therapist (and parent or caregiver if it is an in-home session) and remind her that you are observing and providing feedback today. Ask if today is a typical day for the client (e.g., not sick, no sleep or medication issues). Ask if she needs anything or has any questions, let her know which programs you want to observe and ask if she would like you to observe any others. Remind her she should run her session as she typically does and that you'll make time for questions during breaks and at the end of the session.
- Review session notes (sign or edit and sign and give feedback), questions from staff, and graphs from past week (assuming that you observe weekly). Make a list of all programs or targets that need to be changed (e.g., moved to maintenance, reintroduced, combined into larger sets). Make any changes that take less than two minutes.
- Organize procedural integrity checks for each of the programs you are observing and prepare data collection for IOA check during the programs.

10:15-10:40 Observe One or Two Programs

- Make sure to smile and be friendly.
- Observe the program implementation and collect data on PI and IOA.
- After at least 10 trials of each program, and at a natural break in programming, calculate PI and IOA. Prepare your thoughts to give feedback: praise for high scores, pick one or two focus points for suggestions or modeling, remember to frame it as a positive suggestion rather than a "don't."
- Ask if there are any questions.

10:40-10:50

- If appropriate, conduct needed generalization probes with the client.
- Leave general notes for the team highlighting any changes, additions, or requests (e.g., probing new targets).
- Thank the therapist (and the parent or caregiver if applicable) and indicate when the next team meeting and observation will take place. Remind the therapist of any upcoming professional development opportunities.

Appendix D: Assessing Organiation & Time Management Issues

1. Do you use a paper or electronic system for scheduling your time? If so, how accurately do you stick to that schedule in any given week?

2. Do you use a paper or electronic to-do list to manage tasks? If so, how frequently do you review it for task completion?

3. Do you use a to-do list system in conjunction with a scheduling system to organize your time and activities?

4. Do you actively take notes and add action items to you to do list during meetings?

5. Do you use written or electronic prompts and reminders for upcoming events and deadlines on your schedule?

6. Do you use a structured system for managing emails and needed follow-up tasks?

7. Are you usually able to quickly access and produce requested electronic or print versions of materials (e.g., reports, notes, data, graphs, programs, emails)?

8. Do you frequently check your watch/phone or schedule to make sure that you will be able to make it to your next commitment?

9. Do you frequently arrive late to meetings or have to leave earlier than scheduled to make your next commitment?

10. Do you seek or provide clarification about tasks?

11. Do you volunteer for more than you are likely to be able to do?

12. Do you effectively break down complex tasks into a series of smaller tasks and actionable steps?

13. Do you accurately estimate how long it will take to accomplish a task? If you underestimated and are not able to complete the task in the assigned time, what do you do?

14. Are you usually able to independently manage tasks involving technology (e.g., no frequent requests for support or excuses about how technology led to a missed deadline) and shared access to files?

Chapter 9

Interpersonal and Therapeutic Relationship Skills

I've learned that people will forget what you said, people will forget what you did, but people will never forget how you made them feel.

—Maya Angelou

In Chapter 8, we suggested that organization and time management are pivotal skills (i.e., skills that facilitate and moderate other repertoires). Interpersonal skills are also pivotal, because the ability to interact effectively with others influences your ultimate success as a practicing behavior analyst and as a supervisor. The motivation underlying the development of interpersonal skills is foundational. That is, care and compassion for the well-being of others propels our practice. The development of genuine interpersonal skills reflects our commitment to support betterment in our supervisees and clients.

These skills are often referred to as "soft skills," as contrasted with "hard" or technical skills which are discipline-specific (Tulgan, 2015; Wentz, 2013). The value of interpersonal skills, as well as technical content knowledge for hiring and job success, has been established in several fields including business and management, information technology, and marketing (Finch, Hamilton, Baldwin, & Zehner, 2013; McMurray, Dutton, McQuaid, & Richard, 2016; Osmani, et al., 2015). A behavior analyst may have amazing technical (i.e., hard) skills (e.g., analyzing the function of a particular problem behavior), but struggle to manage interpersonal relationships and conflict in professional contexts (e.g., collaborating with a multidisciplinary treatment team to develop a plan to address the problem behavior). As Tulgan (2015) noted, someone is more likely to be hired for their technical skills and more likely to be fired for problems related to relationship skills.

Those who are not personable may risk losing career opportunities and, perhaps more importantly, may risk losing the opportunity to influence and collaborate with others (e.g., those they supervise and teach, those on multidisciplinary teams, families, and clients). Bailey and Burch (2010) speak to the importance of interpersonal effectiveness during interactions with clients (e.g., schools, families), colleagues and co-workers, and supervisors and supervisees. That is, many people give up the opportunity to influence others in various situations by virtue of their own interpersonal deficits and lack of interpersonal awareness. Those who refine their interpersonal skills are likely to have greater influence upon others (Carnegie, 1936). Behavior analysts who engage in these core interpersonal skills in a refined way have been referred to as "behavioral artists" (Foxx, 1998, p. 14) and their use of these skills is termed "behavioral artistry" (Callahan, et al., 2019).

> *Those who are not personable may risk losing career opportunities and, perhaps more importantly, may risk losing the opportunity to influence and collaborate with others.*

The Code (BACB, 2014) and the Task List (BACB, 2017) identify the importance of collaborative relationship skills. For example, Code sections 1.05 and 3.04 include items related to the importance of clear and effective communication. Sections 2.0 and 4.0 also speak to the importance of collaboration with the client, family, and other important people in the environment when planning and implementing treatment. These ethics elements suggest that behavior analysts must take into account environmental variables (e.g., family context, preference for treatment) when developing change programs, indicating that a collaborative, rather than expert model, is preferable. Section 4.05 directly refers to the importance of the ongoing collaborative process in professional relationships. The Task List includes items related to collaboration with other professionals (H-9) and with parents on intervention goals and strategies (H-4). A behavior analyst who is socially adept and skilled at compromising, active listening, and demonstrating empathic concern will be more likely to collaborate well with others and build strong relationships with caregivers (LaFrance, Weiss, Kazemi, Gerenser, & Dobres, 2019; Taylor, LeBlanc, & Nosik, 2019).

This chapter outlines the skills that you should focus on in teaching your supervisees to increase their ability to work effectively in various roles (e.g., service provider, colleague, multi-disciplinary team member, supervisor). The first section focuses on core interpersonal skills. The remaining three sections focus on the application of those interpersonal skills in supervisory and workplace relationships, multi-disciplinary collaboration, and therapeutic relationships with families and clients.

CORE INTERPERSONAL SKILLS

There are five important interrelated sets of interpersonal skills and behaviors sets that we will explore: communication, noticing and self-reflection, perspective taking, compromise, and integrity. When one excels at these core skills, the result is a highly likeable person who can exert substantial positive influence on those around them. When a person struggles with even one of these core skills sets, interpersonal difficulties and stress may occur. With deficits across all core areas, people often have persistent difficulties with interpersonal relationships with all but the most tolerant of friends and partners. Sometimes a person will experience difficulties with only one of these skills in times of significant stress (e.g., finals week, transition to a new job, an upcoming wedding). However, with training and guidance, the majority of individuals will steadily acquire increasingly effective interpersonal skills. Some who refine these skills along with their technical skills may function as leaders and models for future generations of effective and caring behavior analysts. Therefore, it is critical that supervisors develop their own skills in these areas and facilitate their supervisees' development of these critical skills.

> **Core Interpersonal Skills**
> 1. Communication
> 2. Noticing and Self-Reflection
> 3. Perspective Taking
> 4. Flexibility and Compromise
> 5. Integrity and Accountability

Communication Skills

The first pivotal repertoire is communication skills, which encompasses spoken communication and listening skills, body language, and written communication skills (Schulz, 2008).[1] Regardless of the means of communication (e.g., live conversation, text, email, public speaking), an effective communicator knows when to initiate their communication, the impact they hope to have on the recipient, which strategies are likely to achieve

---
[1] Referred to as verbal behavior, Skinner (1957).

the desired impact, and which behaviors of the listener indicate whether the intended impact has occurred. These strategies involve many do's (e.g., listen to the speaker, give some indication that you have understood, ask questions rather than give orders) and don'ts (e.g., don't interrupt, don't multitask, don't let negative emotion show on your face or in the tone of your voice during a meeting).

> **An Effective Communicator Knows**
> 1. When to initiate the communication
> 2. The impact they hope to have on the recipient
> 3. Which strategies are likely to achieve the desired impact
> 4. Which behaviors of the listener indicate whether the intended impact has occurred

Effective communication occurs on a continuum. Communication is comfortable and effective under the best of conditions and complex and challenging under conditions of difference or tension (Barrera & Kramer, 2009). That is, effective and skilled communication becomes more critical as increases occur in the difference between communication partners, alignment regarding values and outcomes, and life experiences. The culturally responsive and respectful supervisor understands when to adjust communication strategies based on the context and the response of their interaction partners. In fact, Isaura Barrera and Lucinda Kramer, two recognized experts in diversity and communication, suggest that the process of skilled dialogues among professionals and families in diverse intervention settings is critical to the success and advancement of everyone in those settings (2009; 2017).

> *The culturally responsive and respectful supervisor understands when to adjust communication strategies based on the context and the response of their interaction partners.*

Supervisees can learn to describe the desired effects of an upcoming communication (e.g., with a parent, with a co-worker, in an IEP meeting) and plan and practice specific strategies for that communication. Trainees might initially identify only one or two desired effects (e.g., teach the components of a procedure) when other effects (e.g., conveying support and optimism, ensuring understanding of the purpose of the procedure, observing the response of the parent, assessing parent comfort with the procedure) should also control their communications. The supervisor can model the use of various strategies (e.g., smiling while pausing, asking open-ended questions). The trainee can practice their intended communications in role play while the supervisor provides clear and salient

> **Strategies for Teaching Communication Skills**
>
> 1. Have the supervisee describe the desired effects of an upcoming communication and practice delivering the communication.
> 2. Model different types of communication, especially the use of non-technical language.
> 3. Provide templates and examples for written products.
> 4. Edit the written products using a checklist until a success criterion is met.

responses (e.g., changing body posture, looking away, exhibiting limited affect) that should occasion changes in the trainee's behavior. In this way, the supervisor is applying BST, described in Chapter 5, to teach communication skills. The supervisor is also addressing the need to thoughtfully plan the goals for different interactions and to adjust communication style for different interactions.

For example, a behavior analyst who is explaining the function of problem behavior to a parent should communicate with specific attention to: 1) using language that is fully understandable and avoiding jargon; 2) phrasing the conversation in a way that minimizes the perception of blame; 3) timing the communication appropriately given the ongoing interactions with that parent; and 4) respecting the parents' cultural context and communication style (e.g., greeting phrases, voice tone, use of direct eye contact, smiling, focus of attention). If the BCBA does not pay attention to the parent as listener (i.e., audience control), he or she might use overly technical, jargonistic, culturally offensive, and off-putting communication because this type of language has been differentially reinforced in academic coursework (Critchfield, et al. 2017; Foxx, 1996, 1998; Taylor, et al., 2019). Even if the BCBA makes this mistake, it is important to teach the supervisee that changes in the parents' behavior might indicate that the conversation is not going well. An observant behavior analyst would respond to those behaviors by changing the communication strategy (e.g., "that sounds a little more technical than I meant it to. I really meant that..."). Responsiveness to the parent's behavior and shifting communication styles are like other skills we have discussed that a supervisor can teach using BST.

The supervisor can also teach the supervisee to recognize situations and indicators that suggest that an upcoming conversation with a client, peer, or supervisor is likely to be a difficult one. For example, if the conversation is between two parties who disagree, if the issue is important to both parties, and if the choices made could potentially determine success, the conversation is likely to be a difficult one (LaFrance, et. al, 2019; Taylor, LeBlanc, & Nosik, 2019). If a parent has a history of previously failed behavioral interventions with the supervisee or with another provider, the conversation is likely to be difficult. If emotions are high due to prior conflict or disagreement about events that have occurred or tension related to identity (e.g., racial, cultural), conversations are also likely to be difficult (Stone, Patton, & Heen, 2010). Advanced recognition allows preparation for the conversation using strategies described in the aforementioned Patterson, et al. and Stone, et al. can be very useful resources. The use of simulated conversations to prepare for difficult conversations has proven to be beneficial in fields such as education, medicine, and counseling and clinical psychology (Attoe, Lavelle, Sherwali, Rimes, & Jabur, 2019; Day-Vines, Booker Ammah, Steen, & Arnold, 2018; Wiesbeck, et al., 2017).

The strategies recommended in the studies and textbooks described above focus on what a person can do prior to the conversation (e.g., stay focused, state the desired outcomes, actively listen to others, manage your emotions). For example, one can think about the desired outcomes that are important. Before a hard conversation with a supervisee, the supervisor can make a list reminding themselves of particular outcomes, such as maintaining a good relationship with their supervisee and teaching the supervisee ethical decision-making skills.

Similarly, it is also sometimes helpful to think about the emotional states and motivations of the other person in a meaningful and respectful manner. That is, upon reflection, a supervisor might see that the other person is expressing deep concern and anxiety for themselves and their child. Noticing these emotions can often help the supervisor have a sensitive and compassionate response during distressing situations. For example, in a crucial conversation with a parent of a child with autism, your motivation to encourage the parent to implement a behavior plan may be to achieve a reduction in problem behavior and an increase in quality of life. The parent almost certainly desires both of these outcomes as well. However, the parent may have concerns about the effort involved in implementing the plan for 16 hours a day (i.e., the intervention procedure is not a socially valid one even though the potential outcome might be socially valid; Wolf, 1978). This reflection would possibly change your choice of words and even your choice of strategies (e.g., simplify the protocol and designate specific times for implementation).

Another component of effective communication involves written correspondence. Written communication is somewhat different from oral communication, due to the formality and the lack of immediate feedback to the writer. The most critical writing skills include vocabulary, knowledge of grammar and syntax, and self-editing skills. The most common writing tasks for BCBAs are reports, treatment plans, performance reviews, emails, and summaries of meetings and projects. It is notable that most of these common writing tasks do not share many features with common types of writing assignments in most graduate course assignments. Graduate course assignments are generally written for a professional audience using highly technical language and references from the research literature (e.g., written essay examinations, article summaries, literature reviews, theses and dissertations). Most written products of a practicing behavior analyst are written for funding sources, professionals from other disciplines, business colleagues, and families, and should not include overly technical language or assume a mastery of the literature. In addition, these produces must be written under time constraints. Thus, a supervisor should not count on a supervisee having the skills or experience to create these written products without actively teaching them to do so.

The supervisor can provide templates for each type of written product. The template language should be sensitive to diversity and flexible enough to allow respect for variations (Kornack, Cernius, & Periske, 2019). For example, matters related to family composition (e.g., single parent, same sex parents, extended families), linguistic needs (e.g., multiple languages), cultural adaptions, and special considerations (e.g., diet restrictions, holy days, travel schedules) could all be built into the templates. Initial products should be carefully edited by the supervisor using the word processing software's "track changes" function as a means of shaping the trainee's editing skills. The supervisor may even need to teach the supervisee how to use and respond to track changes, spelling, and grammar tools. In addition to direct copyedits (e.g., typographical errors, punctuation, basic grammar errors), the supervisor can provide written feedback and examples to guide the trainee (e.g., "This is an example of passive voice. You could re-write this sentence as 'the scores indicate significant delay' rather than 'delays are indicated by these scores.'"). Including a rationale with feedback can allow the supervisor to model particular ways of phrasing and presenting information in the context of family culture (e.g., this child is being raised in a two-father home and we don't know if both parents will be involved in parent training, so it is best to say "fathers" throughout the entire document to respect the role that both play in their son's life). A supervisor who embraces the role of teacher and coach will focus on teaching better writing strategies (e.g., use of grammar and syntax tools) rather than fixing documents. The products can be evaluated against a checklist or scoring rubric until the initial submission meets an established success criterion (e.g., two or fewer grammar or punctuation errors, clearly stated goals).

Noticing and Self-Reflection Skills

This skill set refers to the ability to notice your own behavior (i.e., self-monitoring) and that of others (i.e., monitoring) and to reflect on the personal motivations and environmental variables that lead to that behavior (i.e., self-reflection). There can be overlap between the core skill areas. As an example, self-reflection and self-monitoring can overlap with communication skills in that effective communicators self-monitor their own communicative efforts and the effects on the listener as well as their own motivations for communicating (e.g., information sharing, emotional impact, producing insight and understanding). As another example, one can self-monitor written communication skills to evaluate how long it takes to complete a writing task, how often attention drifts from the writing task, whether time of day is correlated with better or worse writing performance, or whether writing is generally perceived as aversive.

Chapter 6 covered the importance of noticing and self-reflection and strategies for teaching these skills, so this current chapter will focus exclusively on the role of this skill in interpersonal relationships. Effective noticing and self-reflection require understanding of what should be noticed and reflected upon. In social situations, many interpersonal responses need to be self-monitored, including frequency of initiations, congruence of facial expressions with spoken language, interrupting, and respectful versus overly brusque language, among others. Even when the response of the social partner seems confusing or unexpected (i.e., "I am not sure why he was offended by that statement"), the person who notices that response and reflects on their own behavior that immediately preceded the unexpected response is more likely to be able to repair the situation. This is equally important in group collaboration where multiple and diverse partners are attempting to support an individual or organization. Here, the ability to self-evaluate interactions with team members is important in successful interdisciplinary efforts (LaFrance et al. 2019). Finally, the supervisee's ability to self-monitor their social problem solving skills will determine the degree to which those skills advance (Barerra & Kramer, 2007).

Perspective-Taking Skills

Perspective-taking has been defined as understanding that what another person perceives (i.e., sees, hears, feels, smells, tastes), thinks, or believes. It means that their beliefs may be different from your own experience, and even from reality, and that those beliefs will guide their future behavior (Sigman & Capps, 1997). This basic skill develops in early childhood and is illustrated by the classic Sally-Anne false-belief task (Baron-Cohen, Leslie, & Frith, 1985) in which a child predicts the search behavior of a puppet that has seen an object hidden in one location but has not seen that it was later moved. To demonstrate perspective-taking, the child indicates that the puppet will search in the original location, behaving based on its own directly-observed information even though it is false.

Perspective-taking serves an integral function in social behaviors such as sharing, turn-taking, effective listening, empathy, and compromising. From a behavior analytic viewpoint, perspective-taking involves: (a) observing the behaviors of another individual in a given situation; (b) predicting the individual's subsequent behavior (e.g., "He's going to be offended if I say that"); and (c) responding in accordance with the private thoughts or emotions another individual might typically experience in that situation (e.g., making consoling remarks such as "Better luck next time," after the observed individual lost a tennis match). Basic kindness toward others is rooted in perspective-taking (e.g., this person would probably appreciate a compliment about their work), as is understanding and forgiveness for another's mistakes (e.g., "I don't think she meant it that way; She says that but probably doesn't fully understand…").

> **Perspective-Taking Involves:**
> a. Observing the behaviors of another individual in a given situation
> b. Predicting the individual's subsequent behavior
> c. Responding in accordance with the private thoughts or emotions another individual might typically experience in that situation

Pat Friman has repeatedly provided excellent examples of the importance of perspective-taking and compassionate understanding in everyday life and the professional experiences of behavior analysts. Friman (2019) describes a personal experience where a woman attending one of his presentations repeatedly interrupted to ask questions that were not directly relevant to his talk.[2] After calmly answering the first few questions, he became frustrated with what he perceived as her "selfish" behavior. He explains that in the moment he failed to appreciate that he did not know her circumstances and was over-controlled by his own current circumstances. He later learned that this single mother of two children with special needs had no access to services and was trying to gain knowledge through any means that she could. He came to realize that the woman's experience, feelings, and perspective led her to behave in way that momentarily annoyed him, but was perfectly reasonable and functional for her.

Friman's fully and thoroughly behavior analytic view of behavior is predicated on perspective-taking and compassion. One should assume that the other person's circumstances are not fully known, but that their behavior is understandable and predictable when seen from their perspective, in the context of their immediate controlling variables. This statement

---
[2]https://www.youtube.com/watch?v=MyClJpztOSs

can apply to less obvious, but no less relevant circumstances than interrupting a public talk. For example, a supervisee may be concerned about a parent who repeatedly brings her child to the center late and make an incorrect assumption about the circumstances based on the family culture or socio-economic level. The supervisor can help the trainee approach the issue as a communication and perspective-taking opportunity and help them to understand the parent's circumstances and values more fully. Assume that there is a reasonable explanation for behavior and be kind to others whenever possible.

> *One should assume that the other person's circumstances are not fully known, but that their behavior is understandable and predictable when seen from their perspective, in the context of their immediate controlling variables.*

Allen and Warzak (2000) encourage behavior analysts to carefully examine the variables that influence the behavior of parents as implementers of treatment. They outline a behavior analytic framework for the variables that determine parental adherence to treatment recommendations (see Table 1). That is, the success of an intervention "is dependent not only upon its effectiveness but also upon its precise delivery… to achieve a satisfactory clinical outcome" (p. 595–596). This behavior analytic framework includes motivating operations, generalization and skill acquisition variables, response effort, and contingencies for adherence and nonadherence, and the anchor is fully from the perspective of the parent. Using this framework, there is no longer any need to complain about parents who do not comply with treatment as the clinician might wish. Instead, the clinician can examine nonadherence from the perspective of the parent and their perceived or real barriers to implementation and make changes to the treatment that address those barriers.

Compromising and Harmonizing Skills

This skill set refers to the ability to recognize and act in situations in which there is conflict about the right course of action. *Compromising* involves making reasonable concessions in a way that is agreeable to everyone. In many cases, it means choosing the best of the known options to which everyone can agree to achieve desired outcomes. In some cases, the selection of an option will be based on knowledge of the evidence base in the context of the resource and environmental constraints of the situation (Geiger, Carr, & LeBlanc, 2010). Engaging in perspective-taking can help one appreciate the potential concerns of the other parties with differing opinions and may make compromise easier, potentially resulting in better treatment adherence (Allen & Warzak, 2000).

Table 9.1
Adherence Variables*

Establishing operations
 Failure to establish intermediate outcomes as reinforcers
 Failure to disestablish competing social approval as reinforcers

Stimulus generalization
 Trained insufficient exemplars
 Trained narrow range of setting stimuli
 Weak rule following

Response acquisition
 Excessive skill complexity
 Weak instructional technology
 Weak instructional environment

Consequent events
 Competing punitive contingencies
 Competing reinforcing contingencies

*Reprinted with permission from Allen & Warzak, The problem of parental nonadherence in clinical behavior analysis: Effective treatment is not enough. *Journal of Applied Behavior Analysis, 33*, 373–391.

Harmonizing is an advanced skill that involves seeing value in multiple options and being willing to collaboratively develop a new option (i.e., flexibility) that allows goals to be met. Harmonizing involves synergy rather than concession, making it a good strategy for maintaining relationships. According to Barrerra and Kramer (2007), skilled harmonizing involves choosing the health of the relationship over being in control or being right. The problem solving process is entered with the idea that a solution will be discovered together. Barrera and Kramer suggest that harmonizing requires the following prerequisite behaviors: 1) inviting and listening to the other person's perspective; 2) trying to make sense out of the person's view of the situation; 3) acknowledging the perspectives; and 4) jointly generating solutions built on appreciation of each person's point of view.

Harmonizing implies a focus on shared overarching goals, broader context, and more far-reaching solutions. In this way, creative solutions are developed and contradictions tend to disappear. Jointly generated solutions may solve the problem and also address the various perspectives, needs, and preferences of each participant. For example, a supervisor may want a supervisee to start telehealth sessions immediately due to an emergency situation and the family's needs. The supervisee has been through training and showed proficiency on the component skills, but still feels uncomfortable with delivering services via telehealth. The supervisor may feel frustrated with the supervisee's anxiety and the supervisee may feel frustrated with the supervisor's insistence. If they listen to each other's positions and brainstorm solutions, they may generate new alternatives such as additional training for the supervisee and shared oversight of the case as it transitions to telehealth. Similarly, a BCBA may think that it is critical for a young child with autism to have at least 30 hours per week of ABA treatment services while the family feels stretched in their work schedule beyond 22 hours of treatment per week. If the BCBA harmonizes with the family, identifying the shared goal of optimal treatment effects, the solution might involve flexibility in the form of: a) a period of fewer hours of service for a few months until work schedules can be changed; b) greater emphasis on parent training so that the parents are able to implement additional hours of valuable intervention within the home and community; and/or c) creative problem-solving with respect to timing of services.

This skill can be particularly difficult for those who place undue importance on being right or in charge of situations. In interpersonal situations, being right should never be the goal: Being effective should be the goal. This involves avoiding the temptation to see things from one vantage point (i.e., there is one right or wrong way to be effective). In fact, those who recognize the positive and negative effects of their social behavior and evaluate the pros and cons of multiple choices simultaneously are more likely to realize the value of flexibility. Those who are inflexible or unwilling to compromise often find themselves losing the opportunity to interact with others who have been hurt, offended, or angered by the inflexibility. For example, clients might seek another service provider, supervisees might seek a different supervisor, and employers might seek another employee if they find the supervisee is unable to compromise or harmonize in situations of importance.

> *In interpersonal situations, being right should never be the goal: Being effective should be the goal.*

Integrity

Acting with integrity involves doing what is right or good, even when it is difficult and even when no one is likely to know of the good you have done. It involves being true to your word (i.e., doing what you say you will do). A supervisor who behaves with integrity is honest, authentic, and behaves in accordance with a strong moral code. Acting with integrity involves behaving *reliably* (e.g., a supervisee can count on you to follow through and to keep your word), behaving *justly* (e.g., a supervisee can rely on fair treatment regardless of gender, sexual orientation, race, ethnicity, or religion), behaving *accountably* (e.g., a supervisee knows that the supervisor

> *Acting with integrity involves behaving…*
> *Reliably*
> *Justly*
> *Accountably*
> *Trustworthily*

will take responsibility for their instructions and training protocols), and behaving *trustworthily* (e.g., the supervisee knows that the supervisor will maintain confidentiality).

The notion of behaving in a trustworthy manner can be extended to the notion of psychological safety (Brown, 2012; Austin, 2019). Supervisors can behave in ways that help supervisees feel comfortable being vulnerable (e.g., revealing that they do not understand, revealing cultural differences). The more different the supervisor and supervisee are from one another, the greater the need for the supervisor to signal safety in response to behaviors that reveal vulnerability.

APPLYING THE CORE SKILLS IN DIFFERENT CONTEXTS

The first four chapters of this book focused heavily on approaching the professional supervision relationship in a positive, constructive manner that is predicated on clear expectations, effective communication, and appropriate positive contingencies to support the supervisee's skill development. We would like to point out how those chapters include coverage of the core skills described above. You may even want to re-read those chapters now that you have read about the core interpersonal skills. Chapter 1 focused on the supervisor as a resource for information and guidance, a provider of positive reinforcement, and a role model for technical and professional behavior of all kinds. The core interpersonal skills described above (e.g., communication skills, integrity, perspective-taking) are critical for building healthy supervisory relationships. Chapter 2 focused on strategies for establishing strong relationships, while Chapter 3 focused primarily on an analysis of how past experiences influence one's supervisory repertoires and relationships. The core skill of self-reflection (on both the beneficial and troublesome influences from your history with behavior analysis and supervision) is the primary focus of the activities in this chapter. These activities are designed to assist the supervisor or future supervisor in constructing their own purposeful and positive approach to supervising and mentoring others. Finally, Chapter 4 addressed cultural issues in supervisory relationships. Interpersonal skills such as communication, noticing, perspective-taking, harmonizing, and authenticity, become especially important the more diverse the supervisory relationship.

The remainder of this chapter focuses on application of the core skill sets described above in other important and commonly occurring professional contexts for practicing behavior analysts (i.e., peer relationships, multi-disciplinary teaming, therapeutic relationships with clients). These are certainly not the only types of professional relationships that behavior analysts will encounter, but these will definitely be repeatedly encountered throughout a career. These contexts also serve to provide examples that, with hope, will be sufficient for communicating the range and relevance of these core skills for successfully training and mentoring a caring, effective, and responsive behavior analyst.

Peer Workplace Relationships

Throughout the course of a career, each person will encounter many workplace relationships requiring the use of all of the core skills described above. Some professional relationships are hierarchical, such that one person is responsible for overseeing the work of others and managing their performance (i.e., a supervisory or managerial relationship). The majority of workplace relationships, however, are peer-based relationships. That is, neither party oversees the work of the other, but the success of the work effort depends upon the ability of the peers to work together effectively using all of the core skills described above. When co-workers (in any type of relationship) struggle with the skills described above, workplace conflict is typically the result (Kazemi & Carter, 2019).

> *The majority of workplace relationships are peer-based relationships. That is, neither party oversees the work of the other, but the success of the work effort depends upon the ability of the peers to work together effectively using all of the core skills described.*

Workplace conflict can be the result of deficits in the core skills described above or failure to recognize the importance of these skills when interacting with peers. That is, it may be easy to identify the value and consequences of behaving disrespectfully to your supervisor, but difficult to identify that there are negative consequences (e.g., strained relationship, avoidance, reputation for poor teaming skills) for behaving disrespectfully to your peers as well. When groups of peers are working together on a project, the skills of compromising and harmonizing, along with communication skills, are critical. The members of the work group are likely to have differing perspectives on the task and the specific qualities of a successful product, meeting the criteria for crucial conversation opportunity. These differences can be advantageous as long as the group members are able to brainstorm respectfully, resolve any conflicts that arise from differences by compromising, harmonize to find third alternatives, or effectively and politely communicate a critical drawback of an idea.

Related skills deficits may also be involved in workplace conflict. For example, timeliness and effective task completion (see Chapter 8) in group projects conveys integrity (i.e., accountability, responsibility, reliability). In contrast, failure to meet group deadlines can place strain on the interpersonal relationships of those in the group and convey a lack of respect and failure to prioritize tasks that are important to others. Thus, someone who struggles with organization and time management may also find that it negatively impacts their workplace relationships. Someone who struggles with perspective-taking may also strain workplace relationships by inadvertently taking advantage of the kindness of co-workers without reciprocating. In addition, those who do not effectively self-monitor their behavior in peer contexts may not notice when their actions are culturally insensitive or harmful to peers of different backgrounds and experiences.

The supervisor can address workplace relationship problems proactively, and if necessary, reactively. First, the supervisor can model treating all people with respect. Some indicators of respect may include using non-hierarchical terms (e.g., colleague, peer, mentor/mentee) rather than hierarchical ones (e.g., boss, manager, senior staff, direct report) and acknowledging performance strengths. It can also involve attention to differences in the way people are acknowledged. For example, a supervisor may notice that others refer to a male Ph.D. as "Dr." and a female Ph.D. by her first name, and advocate for the female to be addressed as "Dr." as well. Second, supervisors can actively monitor peer interactions and social dynamics in the contexts of meetings, group projects, and peer mentoring relationships. Third, supervisors can teach skills for conflict resolution and crucial conversations using published resources (Cloke & Goldsmith, 2011; Patterson, et al, 2012; Stone, et al., 2010). If workplace relationship problems do arise and direct discussion does not readily resolve the issue, the supervisor should identify an available resource for mediation and encourage those who are engaged in the conflict to reflect on the impact of their conflict on others (e.g., distraction from client services, negative impact on workplace culture).

Multi-Disciplinary Collaboration

Behavior analysts who practice in educational, medical, or human services settings may find themselves working in a specific kind of peer relationship—one with professionals from other disciplines within an interdisciplinary or multidisciplinary group. There is some ambiguity about what and how to use terms about collaboration. For our purposes, we use the terms multidisciplinary to refer to collaborations in which each professional retains and uses their disciplinary worldview, practices, and methodology in collaboration with other professionals for the benefit for a particular client and/or mission.

In these collaborations, behavior analysts are likely to work closely with speech-language pathologists, occupational and physical therapists, special educators, physicians, and nutritionists, among others (LaFrance, Weiss, Kazemi, Gerenser, & Dobres, 2019). The core skills described above are necessary to ensure that the BCBA is in a position to: a) enjoy the collaborations and the learning opportunities those collaborations provide: b) collaborate effectively to promote better client outcomes; and c) represent the field of behavior analysis in an ethically responsible way.

Unfortunately, interdisciplinary and multidisciplinary teams are somewhat notorious for being dysfunctional (LaFrance, et al., 2019). This is often the result of poor interpersonal skills (e.g., ineffective communication, unmanaged tensions between team members) and lack of understanding of the other expertise of the other disciplines. Successful collaboration requires shared professional values (Cox, 2012), demonstration of respect for the other disciplines, frequent and effective communication, and consistent perspective-taking with regard to how your behavior might impact the other members of the team who have different theoretical orientations and professional training. One way for a behavior analyst to increase their ability to effectively take the perspective of other disciplines is to become familiar with the similarities and differences in the disciplines with respect to professional training, scopes of practice, and theoretical orientation. LaFrance, et al. (2019) provide an excellent framework and overview of the disciplines with whom behavior analysts most commonly collaborate to assist team members in understanding the limitations of their

> *One way for a behavior analyst to increase their ability to effectively take the perspective of other disciplines is to become familiar with the similarities and differences in the disciplines with respect to professional training, scopes of practice and theoretical orientation.*

own expertise and valuing of the expertise of others. For behavior analysts working in schools, the *Adaptive Schools Seminars* by Thinking Collaborative may prove useful (www.thinkingcollaborative.com) (see resource list for Chapter 9).

The core skills described above related to perspective-taking, empathy, and communication are often explicitly taught as part of the professional training for participation in multidisciplinary teams (Coulehan, et al., 2001; Epstein, Campbell, Cohen-Cole, Whinney, & Smilkstein, 1993; Taylor, et al., 2019). Brodhead (2015) suggests that skilled professional interactions may increase the probability that BCBAs will earn the trust and partnerships of other members of the team, illustrating the importance of honesty and authenticity. With regard to communication, Critchfield, et al., (2017) suggest that behavior analysts' use of highly scientific, discipline-specific terms (i.e., jargon to others) does not effectively match the needs of the listener and may result in the behavior analyst not being understood. Even worse, failure to effectively and actively listen and reflect the other person's point of view can lead to team members or clients feeling devalued or disrespected. On the other hand, effective collaboration can lead to innovative treatment that is superior to that which either discipline could provide in isolation. Howard & Gerenser (in press) describe a fully integrated model for speech-language pathology and behavior analysis which involves shared training, shared values for evidence-based practice, and valuing of the unique expertise of each discipline to influence all aspects of assessment and treatment of clients.

Therapeutic Relationships with Clients and Families

Of all of the types of professional interpersonal relationships behavior analysts might find themselves in, perhaps the most important one is the therapeutic relationship with a client and their family. As of 2016, 69 percent of respondents to a survey conducted by the BACB worked in the practice area of providing services to individuals with autism (n.d.). Success in this arena requires technical behavior analytic skills (e.g., functional behavioral assessment, treatment plan development) and critical interpersonal relationship-building skills. Technical skills are necessary to ensure client outcomes, but they are insufficient without additional skills to develop relationships with clients and their caregivers. Relationships are vital to ensure success; to maintain increased and sustained input and engagement in the treatment process; and to improve clinical outcomes (Taylor, et al., 2019). A behavior analyst's failure to practice essential therapeutic relationship skills may have deleterious effects on treatment. Possible effects include lack of parental participation and implementation of programming, requests for re-assignment or replacement of treatment team personnel, or withdrawal from treatment altogether.

Taylor, et al. (2019) suggest that many academic training programs in behavior analysis may not currently incorporate training in these skills as part of their professional training curriculum, and may not even include relevant assigned readings in this area (Pastrana, et al., 2016). LeBlanc, Taylor, & Marchese (2019) confirmed the accuracy of this suggestion in their survey of practicing behavior analysts about their graduate training and post-graduate professional development experiences in compassionate and therapeutic relationship skills. Most respondents (24 to 28 percent of 225 responses) indicated that they received no explicit didactic training or reading assignments on relationship-building skills in their graduate coursework in behavior analysis. Approximately half indicated that their practical experience supervisor provided guidance and mentoring on these skills. The majority of behavior analysts indicated that it is very or extremely important that professional training programs develop formal training in this area. Thus, training in these critical interpersonal relationship skills falls primarily to supervisors of practical experience and supervisors for the first positions after graduation.

Communication skills are particularly important in therapeutic relationships. The behavior analyst must be able to communicate effectively to parents without using the technical training and verbal precision that was emphasized in graduate coursework. Failure to translate technical concepts into family-friendly terms may lead parents to perceive the behavior analyst as authoritative rather than collaborative (Critchfield, et al., 2017; see Chapter 5 for additional information on developing competencies related to explaining procedures to parents without using technical jargon). A supervisor should create opportunities for supervisees to develop fluency with family-friendly language and examples, and fluency with switching from technical language to family-friendly language.

Effective listening skills are just as important as speaking skills. In therapeutic relationships, the client or their family often has no other outlet to share important and emotional information about their hopes, fears, and burdens. To build successful relationships, behavior analysts must be able to actively and patiently listen. These skills also allow the behavior analyst to gain critical information for collaboration (e.g., which are the most important target behaviors, what are the overall life goals, which interventions are likely to match the family situation). These communications often occur when the client or family member is experiencing an emotional response or responses (e.g., anger, sadness, guilt, fear; Bozosi, 2016; Fiske, 2017; Lutz, Patterson, & Klein, 2012; Post, et al., 2013). If clinicians are ill-prepared to respond to typical parental stress and emotion (Hayes & Watson, 2013), they may respond unskillfully (e.g., blaming parents when treatment integrity is compromised, ceasing treatment) or engage in escape or avoidance behaviors that give the impression of indifference, argumentativeness, or apathy. Cultural differences between families and behavior analysts require special attention to nuances and variations related to emotional responses to events and the expression of those emotional responses. Supervisees may enhance their understanding of and sensitivity to this issue through training that fosters responsivity, sensitivity, and humility about the feelings and expressions of those emotions.

Perspective-taking skills are also critically important to therapeutic relationships, and a recent survey suggests that behavior analysts may struggle with perspective-taking and the related skills of empathy and compassion. Taylor, et al. (2019) surveyed parents of children with autism regarding their impressions of behavior analysts' relationship skills in three domains: Listening and Collaboration, Empathy and Compassion, and "Negative" behaviors that could contribute to problems in the relationship. The results indicated that behavior analysts have deficits in a number of core relationship skills related to perspective-taking (e.g., failure to compromise, not inquiring about satisfaction with services and the relationship, not acknowledging mistakes, and having their own, non-collaborative, agenda about services).

Taylor, et al. (2019) encourage those training and supervising behavior analysts to provide comprehensive training in core competencies related to compassionate and empathetic care similar to that which is provided in other health and human services industries such as medicine, mental health, nursing, and palliative care (Derksen, Bensing, & Lagro-Janssen, 2013; Di Blasi, Harkness, Edzard, Georgiou, & Kleijnen, 2001; Fogarty, Curbow, Wingard, McDonnell, & Somerfield, 1999; Hojat, et al., 2011; Karver, Handelsman, Fields, & Bickman, 2006; Lown, 2016; Riess, 2015; Sinclair, Norris, et al., 2016). These critical skills typically focus on the constructs of empathy and compassion (Goetz & Simon-Thomas, 2017; Sinclair, Beamer, et al., 2016).

Empathy involves the professional perceiving the client's perspective with some understanding of the person's emotional response within that experience (Taylor, et al., 2019). This perspective-taking allows the professional to predict how the client will respond to their actions based on an assessment of how they might feel in that same situation. The professional must understand, the client's contextual situation, perspective, and feelings, and communicate that understanding (Goetz & Simon-Thomas, 2017). For example, a behavior analyst interacting with a parent who is upset about the recent diagnosis of her child must be able to respond to indicators of distress (e.g., sad expression, crying, voice breaking). The clinician can then privately relate that to their experience of loss in the past.

> *Empathy involves the professional perceiving the client's perspective with some understanding of the person's emotional response within that experience (Taylor, et al., 2019).*

The clinician might empathize with the parent by recognizing the parent's pain and sadness, acknowledging and confirming the feelings expressed by the parent, and genuinely appreciating and experiencing the parent's pain. Importantly, the empathetic response does not require that the professional have had the same experience (i.e., having a child or a child with special needs). Instead, the behavior analyst must recognize the distress and emotional fragility of the parent, draw upon similar experiences of loss and distress, and behave accordingly. Comfort and proficiency with developing empathetic responses can be effectively developed through role-playing and discussion (Blell, Ala'i-Rosales, & Rosales-Ruiz, 2010).

Compassion involves empathy plus action aimed at alleviating the person's suffering. Lown et al. (2014) described compassion as recognizing, understanding, and experiencing emotional resonance with the distress or suffering of others coupled with motivation and helpful action. For example, a clinician may empathize with a parent who is sad and frustrated that her son is not making the progress she had hoped for by listening attentively to the parent, taking the parent's perspective, acknowledging and accepting the parent's feelings, and allowing themselves to feel what the parent is feeling in the moment. Compassionate care by the clinician aims to reduce the parent's sadness and frustration over time, perhaps by assisting the parent in reorienting the goals for her child, helping her be more compassionate with herself as parent (Gould, Tarbox, & Coyne, 2017), or by helping the parent to acknowledge and appreciate incremental gains. A clinician rushing to fix the problem, on the other hand, may undermine or invalidate the parent's expression of sadness and frustration, potentially jeopardizing the therapeutic relationship and the parent's trust in the clinician and the treatment.

> *Compassion involves empathy plus action aimed at alleviating the person's suffering.*

Taylor, et al. (2019) propose a curriculum specifically for behavior analysts that focuses on teaching empathy and perspective-taking, communication and listening skills, and compassionate collaboration with caregivers (see tables in Taylor, et al., 2019, and Table 2). Ideally, the skills proposed by Taylor and colleagues would be taught in a course, but they will also require introduction and practice during fieldwork. Appendix A provides a tool to evaluate the use of recommended strategies for building and sustaining therapeutic relationships. A version of this checklist was developed as part of the clinical standards initiative at Trumpet Behavioral Health.

Teaching supervisees to effectively interact with others across the wide variety of therapeutic relationships and contexts is a fundamental area of focus during supervision. Like other skills, an effective supervisor will explicitly teach, practice, monitor, and nurture critical interpersonal skills. However, despite your best efforts, some supervisees will struggle more than others. In these instances, honest and caring feedback from a supervisor, self-reflection, self-monitoring, and additional targeting of interpersonal skills may be required. Unlike the other chapters, Appendix B

Table 2: Proposed Skills Areas and Activities for Teaching Compassionate Care Skills*

Core Skill	Subskills to Teach	Skills to Monitor	Proposed Activity	Evaluation/Measures
Engages in Positive Social Interactions	Smiles and acknowledges parent with eye contact and appropriate greeting. Makes positive comments about child behavior. Makes positive comments about parent behavior. Provides realistic hopeful comments about child's prognosis. Demonstrates general enthusiasm about the direction of the child's program. Asks parent how she/he is doing. Clarifies rules. Asks parent if she/he is happy with how things are going	Flat affect. Overly focuses on negative child outcome. Feedback to parent is negative.	Role play activities with supervisor and colleagues. Observation of video interactions of good and poor exemplars. Trainee tacts correct and incorrect interactions. Trainee practices in vivo and videotapes interactions. Videos are reviewed by supervisor and evaluated for presence of skill. Self-evaluation of skill demonstration in video review.	Supervisor records presence of absence of skills. Frequency measure of positive comments. Social validity measure of parent perception of these skills in trainee. Rating Scale to evaluate others' (e.g. colleague) impression of the skill in trainee.
Demonstrates Empathy	Makes eye contact. Sits up, leans forward, and maintains a positive neutral facial expression. Voice tone is reassuring. Nods head to indicate active listening. Uses vocalizations to indicate on-going interest (e.g., "mm-hmm," "go on"). Asks open-ended questions. Pauses to allow parent to answer. Paraphrases back what parents state.	Distracted by technology, phone, or computer. Interrupts parent. Jumps to solutions too quickly. Shows distress based on parent's distress. Redirects or interrupts parent's emotional response.	Role play activities with supervisor and colleagues. Audio recordings of parent communication are played and trainee tacts parent's emotional content (e.g., sad) and states appropriate empathetic response to parent's emotion and content. Observation of video interactions of good and poor exemplars. Trainee tacts correct and incorrect interactions. Trainee practices in vivo and videotapes interactions. Videos are reviewed by supervisor and evaluated for presence of skill. Self-evaluation of skill demonstration in video review.	Supervisor records presence of absence of skills. Frequency measure of positive comments. Social validity measure of parent perception of these skills. Rating Scale to evaluate others' (e.g. colleague) impression of the skill.

*Reprinted with permission from Taylor, LeBlanc, & Nosik, Compassionate care in behavior analytic treatment: Can outcomes be enhanced by attending to relationships with caregivers?. *Behavior Analysis in Practice, 12,* 654–666.

includes questions for targeted use as a diagnostic assessment for those struggling with interpersonal skills, though you may also find it useful as a self-reflection guide for yourself. You may also want to have another person assess social effectiveness. Often, those with interpersonal skill deficits (e.g., poor perspective-taking, poor communication skills, rigid thinking and interpersonal patters) may lack insight into their own deficits and excesses: thus, an outside perspective is often helpful. You may find these questions useful in examining the scope of your supervisee's needs in this area and determining whether the problematic repertoires are responsive to intervention. Note that those who are unable or unwilling to develop these interpersonal repertoires may need to be carefully counseled out of the profession of applied behavior analysis. In addition, this chapter may have sparked the realization that you would like additional training in therapeutic relationship skills if, like so many others, you did not receive this training in graduate school. In this case, you might consider attending workshops (LeBlanc & Taylor, 2019) or enrolling in courses specifically designed to teach therapeutic relationship skills and compassionate care.

Appendix A: Therapeutic Relationship Self-Evaluation

Acknowledgement: A version of this tool was developed by the first author and collaborators as part of the Clinical Standards Initiative at Trumpet Behavioral Health and is published for use with permission of the organization.

Instructions: Use the first portion of the checklist to reflect back on your efforts to establish the therapeutic relationship with your client and/or their family. Rate each section according to your therapeutic relationship by circling from the 1-to-5 rating scale to indicate your agreement or disagreement with the statement above (past tense in verbs as you should be past the establishment when you complete this). Use the second portion of the checklist to reflect on your recent and ongoing efforts to strengthen and maintain or repair the therapeutic relationship (present tense verbs as you should be actively engaged in these efforts). There is no scoring rubric, but lower scores are generally better and you could track your own progress on scores throughout a relationship with a family or compare your scores with all of the families you serve at one time.

Initial Relationship Establishment

Built initial overall rapport with the client and their family/guardians. (Used active listening, validated emotions, defined common goals, non-judgmental, supportive and sensitive)

1	2	3	4	5
Strongly Agree	Agree	Neither	Disagree	Strongly Disagree

Listened actively and carefully. (Ensured body language was attentive and positive, paraphrased to ensure understanding and convey interest, used reflective language)

1	2	3	4	5
Strongly Agree	Agree	Neither	Disagree	Strongly Disagree

Validated emotions ("I can understand why you'd feel ...")

1	2	3	4	5
Strongly Agree	Agree	Neither	Disagree	Strongly Disagree

Defined common goals. (Sought input about values and priorities, integrated this information into goals and targets for services, ensured understanding and agreement with the purpose and model of services)

1	2	3	4	5
Strongly Agree	Agree	Neither	Disagree	Strongly Disagree

Flexibly allowed the client to discuss issues which are important to them. (Asked open-ended questions about what is important to the family, responded to those issues in a respectful way, took time to allow the family to express hopes, fears, concerns, and tell the stories that they find important)

1	2	3	4	5
Strongly Agree	Agree	Neither	Disagree	Strongly Disagree

Considered any cultural differences and asked family about culturally-important variables. (Asked open-ended questions, ascertained how family is most comfortable communicating, asked about the conditions for respect and inclusion, and the meaning assigned to important events described in other portions of this assessment)

1	2	3	4	5
Strongly Agree	Agree	Neither	Disagree	Strongly Disagree

Helped to establish or re-establish hope for a family's future and their loved one's opportunities for a meaningful life. (Emphasized the strengths of child and family life, helped family learn tools in aiding the client to learn and be as independent as possible, kept long-term goals in mind but put focus, thought, energy, and effort into small-scale and achievable goals)

1	2	3	4	5
Strongly Agree	Agree	Neither	Disagree	Strongly Disagree

Ensured that families understood the rationale for services and that everyone's goals for therapy and outcomes are well-aligned. (Developed goals with family for the child, provided reasons for services that are easily understandable and with non-technical language, provided as much information as possible to clients, and discussed research showing effectiveness of treatment)

1	2	3	4	5
Strongly Agree	Agree	Neither	Disagree	Strongly Disagree

Ensured that families are completely ready for services at the recommended intensity. (Planned sessions with families, spoke openly and honestly about logistics and recommended intensity, discussed possible barriers or challenges)

1	2	3	4	5
Strongly Agree	Agree	Neither	Disagree	Strongly Disagree

Relationship Strengthening, Maintenance, and Repair

Communication is frequent, open, direct and comfortable. (Email, phone and in person communications are readily understood by all parties, there are no unexpected emotionally-laden communications, each party is comfortable and eager to communicate with the other)

1	2	3	4	5
Strongly Agree	Agree	Neither	Disagree	Strongly Disagree

I follow through on the tasks and changes that I have discussed with the family. (I do what I say I will do in a timely fashion; I communicate to the family that I have done it and how it has worked out)

1	2	3	4	5
Strongly Agree	Agree	Neither	Disagree	Strongly Disagree

I emphasize client progress, and provide positive feedback and encouragement for the family. (Describe areas of recent progress and tie that progress to family efforts, welcome bringing forth new ideas and concerns, recognize appropriate aspects of implementation even if there are other areas that need improvement)

1	2	3	4	5
Strongly Agree	Agree	Neither	Disagree	Strongly Disagree

I ask for client input and feedback and I respond graciously and sincerely to that input and feedback. (Every session ask for suggestions, opinions, andideas for programming, listen intently to the suggestions, acknowledge the value of the suggestions, offer suggestions and minor amendments to the suggestions if needed, follow up on the input and feedback)

1	2	3	4	5
Strongly Agree	Agree	Neither	Disagree	Strongly Disagree

I am professional and engaged for interactions with the family. (On time and prepared to use time wisely, professionally dressed, composed, fully engaged with no distractions, emotionally present, and ready for interactions.

1	2	3	4	5
Strongly Agree	Agree	Neither	Disagree	Strongly Disagree

I continually work to establish, re-establish, or reinforce hope for the family's future and their loved one's opportunities for a meaningful life. (Emphasize the strengths of child and family life, help family learn tools in aiding the client to learn and be as independent as possible, keeping long-term goals in mind but putting focus, thought, energy, and effort into small-scale and achievable goals)

1	2	3	4	5
Strongly Agree	Agree	Neither	Disagree	Strongly Disagree

I ensure the family understands the rationale for services and that everyone's goals for therapy and outcomes are well-aligned (Develop goals with family for the child, provide reasons for services that are easily understandable and with non-technical language, provide as much information as possible to clients and discuss research showing effectiveness of treatment, include family as part of treatment, help families learn the tools to help their child)

1	2	3	4	5
Strongly Agree	Agree	Neither	Disagree	Strongly Disagree

I ensure that families are completely ready for services at the recommended intensity (Planning sessions with families, speak openly and honestly about recommended logistics and intensity, discuss possible barriers or challenges)

1	2	3	4	5
Strongly Agree	Agree	Neither	Disagree	Strongly Disagree

I assess the family's wellness and stressors and adjust therapeutic services accordingly. (Frequent check ins, parent stress assessment, assess family's informal social support, information, and community services, involve all members of the family in the intervention, change goals as the family's participation levels change)

1	2	3	4	5
Strongly Agree	Agree	Neither	Disagree	Strongly Disagree

I identify emerging problems in the therapeutic relationship if they occur. (Notice changes in communication style and modify supports to the family, re-evaluate my own opinions or viewpoints on family, take notice of changes of behavior, take notice of parents' concerns or dissatisfaction with team or team stress over family interactions, notice sudden changes in services or commitment in family support)

1	2	3	4	5
Strongly Agree	Agree	Neither	Disagree	Strongly Disagree

I identify and address various factors (e.g. cultural and religious, SES, ethnicity, race, sexuality, and gender roles) *that might impact my relationship with client.* (Language barriers, being culturally sensitive and aware, re-evaluate goals to match family's priorities, gender roles, and assumptions)

1	2	3	4	5
Strongly Agree	Agree	Neither	Disagree	Strongly Disagree

I consistently work to re-establish or repair the therapeutic relationships with the family if we become disconnected or disengaged. (Recognize, respect, and accommodate family's individuality, create a context for family-centered participation, set up expectations and commitment, check-in on the family's commitment to goals and how to achieve them in their current circumstances)

1	2	3	4	5
Strongly Agree	Agree	Neither	Disagree	Strongly Disagree

Appendix B: Assessing Difficulties with Interpersonal Skills and Therepeutic Relationships

When answering these questions, consider if the answers represent behavior that is consistently displayed across a variety of contexts and over a prolonged period of time, or if the behavior is only present in certain contexts or has only recently developed. Behavior that is context-specific likely requires additional assessment of the potential contributing factors or variables. Consider whether behavior that has only recently developed is occurring in the context of a recent life event that may be causing or exacerbating the individual's behavior.

1. Does the supervisee seem to engage in behavior that would lead you to describe them as shy, or do they describe themselves as socially anxious or insecure?

2. Does the supervisee frequently make negative or self-deprecating statements?

3. Does the supervisee have an affect that matches the affective expressions of the people they serve (e.g., generally neutral affect with subtle facial expressions when interacting with highly animated people)? Is this a function of different cultural communication styles or does it represent a discordant relationship, such as apathy or misunderstandings?

4. Does the supervisee have limited perspective-taking skills (e.g., cannot see things from another's point of view, does not predict what effect their behavior will have on others, limited or no empathy or compassion)?

5. Does the supervisee frequently interrupt or argue with others during social interactions?

6. Does the supervisee come across to others as abrupt, condescending, or dismissive in social interactions?

7. Does the supervisee seem to judge the behavior of others more harshly than they judge their own?

8. Does the supervisee seem to engage in "in-group/out-group" behavior, or become involved in cliques?

9. Does the supervisee behave in ways that others may perceive as culturally insensitive, discriminatory, disrespectful of diversity, or generally offensive?

10. Does the supervisee seem to respond to hierarchical relationships (i.e., being managed, managing others) better than peer relationships?

11. Does the supervisee struggle with interactions and communication in group or multi/interdisciplinary team situations?

12. Does the supervisee respond emotionally and defensively (e.g., blame others, deflect responsibility, argue, justify) to feedback or disagreements with others?

13. Is the supervisee inflexible (i.e., particular) in a way that seems overly controlling about a "right way" to do things?

14. Is it difficult to follow the train of thought of the person in conversations due to tangents, excessive detail in stories, or jumping from topic to topic?

15. Is the supervisee able to change their communication patterns for different audiences?

16. Does the supervisee use excessive jargon outside of the academic context?

17. Does the supervisee seem to behave as if they are still in a student role rather than in a professional role (e.g., overly casual dress, language, and demeanor in professional contexts)?

Section Three

Evaluating Supervision and Building Career Resilience

The first two chapters in this section focus on evaluating supervision and solving barriers to effective supervision. Chapter 10 focuses on how to evaluate the effects of supervision on multiple people (e.g., the supervisee, the client of the supervisee). The chapter provides various data-based and interpersonal strategies that can be used in this endeavor. Chapter 11 focuses on problem solving when things are not going well in the supervisory experience using the structured problem-solving approach introduced in Chapter 7. Chapter 11 also provides tools to help you identify emerging problems in supervision and to assess the scope and functional determinants of the problems. Next, Chapter 11 provides multiple examples to illustrate the remaining steps in the problem-solving process (e.g., generating, implementing, and evaluating strategies).

The last two chapters focus on providing strategies for building professional resilience and career longevity. Chapter 12 focuses on the importance of knowing your personal and professional reinforcers and maintaining access to those reinforcers throughout your career. The indicators and causes of stress and burnout are reviewed along with strategies for combatting both. Chapter 13 summarizes the main messages of the book and emphasizes the nature of supervision as a process of learning and growth. The chapter uses the therapeutic technique of "writing a letter to your past self" to illustrate each of the author's progression as a supervisor from less skilled to more skilled and the importance of tolerance for mistakes.

Chapter 10

Evaluating the Effects of Supervision

If you haven't measured something, you really don't know very much about it.
—Karl Pearson

The previous chapters have focused on the importance of effective supervision, healthy supervisory relationships, critical behavior analytic and professional skills, and using a competency-based approach to supervision. The next logical topic is evaluating whether supervisory efforts have produced the desired outcomes in the quality of the relationship and the supervisee's content knowledge and skills. Just as it is standard practice to conduct ongoing, data-based monitoring of behavioral interventions used with clients, supervisors can take the same approach to their work with supervisees. That is, supervisors must engage in continued evaluation of the *outcomes* of their supervisory practices (Sellers, Valentino, & LeBlanc, 2016; Turner, Fischer, & Luiselli, 2016). Although it is important for supervisors to con-

> *The focus of this chapter is on evaluation of whether supervision is actually producing the desired behavior change.*

duct fidelity checks on their supervision practices, the focus of this chapter is on evaluation of whether supervision is actually producing the desired behavior change.

The BACB's *Supervisor Training Curriculum Outline* (2.0) requires that supervisors assess the effects of their supervision activities (BACB, 2018c), as does element 5.07 of the Code (BACB, 2014). Item I-8 under Personnel Supervision Management in the Applications section of the 5th ed. Task List includes the expectation that those sitting for the BACB exam be able to evaluate the effects of supervision (BACB, 2017). Therefore, the supervisor is at least partially responsible for ensuring that they teach their supervisees how to assess the impacts of their own supervisory activities.

Supervision refined through ongoing data collection of outcomes can lead to optimized progress and risk reduction There are risks to clients if the supervisee is not acquiring the necessary behavior analytic repertoires (as discussed in Chapter 5) during supervision. Ineffective training could translate into ineffective clinical programming for clients, resulting in failure to build necessary skills or to decrease problem behavior. More subtly, if the supervisee is not acquiring the skills required to develop and maintain healthy therapeutic relationships (as discussed in Chapter 9) clients may switch providers. Switching providers may result in wasted time and regression in the client's skills and may result in the caregiver's perception that ABA services are ineffective. Such risks extend to future clients *and* future supervisees for whom the individual might be responsible. Finally, the supervisor is at risk of continuing the ineffective supervisory practices with current and future consumers, clients, and supervisees. In summary, the ethical necessity of evaluating the effectiveness of supervision is multi-dimensional and carries significant importance for individual clients, supervisees, and the field.

> *The ethical necessity of evaluating the effectiveness of supervision is multi-dimensional and carries significant importance for individual clients, supervisees, and the field.*

It is not enough to rely on one's own perception that everything is going well. This reliance would be counter to the field's use of direct and repeated measures to evaluate outcomes. As self-evaluators, our perceptions are at risk of being biased. Biases may be especially impactful when the conditions of supervision are culturally diverse, and when goals for supervision are not outlined, understood, and agreed upon at the outset. One benefit of direct measurement is that meaningful measures can be identified through a collaborative process agreed upon by key stakeholders (Fawcett, 1991). In the case of supervision, the stakeholders are the supervisee and the recipients of their services (Sellers, Ala'i-Rosales, & McDonald, 2016).

Evaluating the effects of supervision without objective measures of the impacts on behavior may inadvertently set the occasion for a supervisor to attend to positive outcomes and minimize non-optimal outcomes. Researchers have demonstrated that people are often inaccurate when evaluating their own skills and the skills of others. The Dunning-Kruger effect describes this overconfidence phenomena wherein individuals with less experience tend to overestimate their own skills and underestimate the performance of others (Kruger & Dunning, 1999). This means that novice supervisors may overinflate the positive effects of their supervision. Systematically evaluating the effects of supervisory practices may offset this tendency, or at least give the supervisor a point of comparison.

Given the risks associated with failure to evaluate the effects of supervision, it is critical that supervisors develop structured processes that allow for a meaningful assessment of outcomes. This chapter provides a discussion of how supervisors can develop a planned, comprehensive approach to evaluating the outcomes of their supervisory practices. With the goal of presenting a streamlined discussion with practical recommendations, we have organized the sections by the focus of the evaluation. We begin by discussing strategies for evaluating the effects of supervision on the client. Next, we turn our attention to assessing the effects on the supervisee. We then cover recommendations for evaluating the effects on caregivers and other stakeholders. We provide a section dedicated to looking at the effects of supervisory activities on the supervisor. Finally, we discuss strategies for teaching supervisees to engage in these evaluative activities, thereby preparing them for their own future supervisory roles.

Evaluating Effects Using Data from the Client

During training, supervisors develop a supervisee's skills to ensure that clients receive high-quality services and make appropriate progress while a supervisee oversees the programming. This oversight requires that the supervisor take an active role in all aspects of the client's programming and data review. The most straightforward method of evaluating the effects of supervisory activities on the client is to attend to clinical programming data. A supervisor can ask the broad question *"Is the client making progress?"* A supervisor can also conduct regular checks on more specific progress indicators, such as the number and type of programs for each client, and the rate of mastery of those programs. Within programs, a supervisor should assess the number and type of targets, the rate of fading prompting supports and reinforcement schedules, and the rate of mastery of targets within and across targets.

It is critical that supervisors assess overall progress as well as rate of progress, particularly for young learners. This includes generalization and maintenance data for clients to ensure that the programming provided by the supervisee or novice clinician produces pervasive and lasting change. Regarding behavior reductive programming, the supervisor should be closely monitoring the quality of operational definitions, assessment procedures, selected interventions, and the impact on the target behaviors. A supervisor can also evaluate whether or not the supervisee is addressing programming issues apparent in the data (e.g., stalled progress, reduction in performance level, highly variable performance, increase in behavior targeted for reduction). Evaluating these aspects of client's programming provides a means of assessing the impact of the instruction and clinical guidance provided in supervision on client progress and outcomes.

Another area that a supervisor can assess is the relationship between the client and the supervisee. Admittedly, this is a more amorphous undertaking, but it is no less critical than reviewing the clinical programming data. A supervisor can observe the supervisee interact with clients and attend to the activities and the client's responses. For example, a supervisor should periodically observe the start of a session when the client arrives. During this interaction, a supervisor can watch for signs that there is a healthy therapeutic relationship between the client and the supervisee. Some positive signs include friendly greetings, clear interest in each other, and positive, caring interactions with the client. At the same time, a supervisor can attend to the client to gauge their affect during these interactions. A supervisor might watch the interaction to see if the client's behavior is positive (e.g., smiling, laughing, independently approaching). A supervisor might also conduct regular observations of the supervisee working directly with clients to evaluate similar indicators (e.g., is the client trying to leave the area, is the client engaged during reinforcement delivery, do the supervisee and client engage in interactions with positive affect and affection). Clearly,

Evaluating Effects Using Data from the Client

- Degree of client progress
- Adequacy of operational definitions, and assessment procedures
- Appropriateness of interventions and procedures for targeted behaviors
- Number and appropriateness of programs
- Number and type of targets within programs
- Appropriate and timely fading of supports while maintaining progress
- Rate of mastery within and across targets
- Generalization and maintenance of targets
- Quality of therapeutic relationships

these indicators are not universal; therefore, a supervisor must be familiar with clients to make this observation meaningful. If a client has the skills to communicate, a supervisor should consider asking the client how they feel about their interactions with the supervisee. Assuming that clients are progressing and all other indicators are positive, then it is likely that the supervisor's practices are effective when measured against client outcomes.

Evaluating the Effects Using Data from the Supervisee

It will come as no surprise that a supervisor should also gather data to evaluate the effects of supervision on the supervisee. Moreover, evaluation of the effects for multiple supervisees may provide the supervisor with repeated measures evaluation of their particular approach to supervision. Ongoing evaluation of specific strategies over time can result in supervisors developing a diverse repertoire of approaches to training and supervising. In other words, if a supervisor identifies that a general strategy used successfully with multiple supervisees is not effective for a specific supervisee, the supervisor can adjust their strategy to a different one that may be more effective. In that way, the supervisors' collective skill set increases over time. For example, consider a supervisor who uses successfully uses informal check-ins during meetings to solicit specific feedback from supervisees (i.e., all of her supervisees provide some specific feedback about what she could do differently or better). Now imagine that she has one supervisee who never provides any specific feedback during the informal check-ins. If she was tracking the feedback provided to her during the informal check-ins, she may be able to identify that she needs to take a different approach for the one supervisee. She can then use what she knows about that individual to determine an alternative strategy (e.g., specifically ask for two things the supervisee likes and two things the supervisor could do better, schedule a specific meeting expressly designated for discussing feedback from the supervisee about the supervisor's performance, ask for the supervisee to provide some written feedback).

Supervisory practices should be individualized for each supervisee. The greater the diversity among supervisees and settings, the greater the need for an individualized approach to supervision. An individualized, functional approach is beneficial for several reasons. First, supervisees may be more likely to acquire skills and to produce meaningful change for their clients. Second, functional approaches require collaborative efforts and a focus on shared values and outcomes. Often this collaboration results in innovation and the development of new strategies for both the supervisor and the supervisee. For example, a supervisee may come from a culture that communicates effectively by using stories or narratives. By incorporating narratives into the supervision process, the supervisor may learn to give more contextual detail about implementation, resulting in a form of multiple exemplar training through stories. As another example, a supervisor in a program that offers bilingual services may find it useful to help the supervisee develop written instructions that are translated into both languages. In this way, the supervisee has the terminology and concepts in both languages and the two of them can ensure understanding of the central concepts. This would be especially useful if the supervisee and client's primary language is different from the supervisor.

There are several areas that a supervisor should consider when evaluating the effects of their supervisory practices on the supervisee. First, evaluate the supervisee's performance related to the activities specifically targeted during supervision. Chapter 5 provides a comprehensive framework for taking a competency-based approach to teaching concepts and training skills. The supervisor can use this approach to continually evaluate the effects of supervision on those concepts and skills. For example, a supervisor can track the time from introducing a concept or skill to mastery and skill maintenance and generalization. This approach is similar to how clinicians evaluate the effects of programming on client outcomes. The supervisor can conduct procedural fidelity checks, observations, and reviews of permanent products (e.g. treatment plans, progress reports, protocols). A reasonable amount of time and instruction to achieve mastery and skill maintenance and generalization suggest that the supervisory practices are effective.

The next area to evaluate is the development of skills such as case conceptualization and planning, organization and time management, problem solving, and interpersonal and communication skills. In our experience, these skills are frequently overlooked and can be challenging to address. We provide an in-depth discussion of each of these skills and how to teach them in previous chapters. Chapter 7 covered the importance of teaching supervisees how to take a structured and thoughtful approach to problem solving. We detailed organization and time management skills in Chapter 8. Finally, Chapter 9 provided a discussion of how to address skills related to interpersonal communication and developing positive therapeutic relationships. Each of these chapters provides checklists to use for measuring the impact supervisory practices have had on the supervisee. The checklists can also be used as a tool for the supervisor to engage in structured self-reflection of their own skills.

A third important area to evaluate is the social validity of the supervision. Social validity refers to the degree to which the consumer is satisfied with the interventions or services (Baer, Wolf, & Risley, 1968). Translated to the context of supervision, the direct consumer is the supervisee, so social validity refers to the degree to which the supervisee likes the supervisory activities. As Baer, Wolf, and Risley (1968; 1987) pointed out, one can hardly consider an intervention effective if the recipients find it so unpleasant or unacceptable that they will not participate in it. In a subsequent article, Wolf outlined three aspects of social validity. According to Wolf (1978), we must evaluate the social significance of the goals, the social appropriateness of the procedures, and the social importance of the effects. The social significance of the goals relates to whether the skills we teach in supervision are meaningful to the supervisee and to society, or the field. The social appropriateness of the procedures refers to whether the supervisee considers the supervision procedures acceptable. The social importance of the effects refers to whether the supervisee is satisfied with their resulting skill sets and readiness for practice.

There are several things that supervisors can do to increase the likelihood that supervisees will provide accurate self-reports about the social validity of supervision. First, supervisors should educate supervisees at the outset of the supervisory relationship about various approaches to supervision and the supervisor's specific approach. This would allow the supervisee to consider whether a different approach would be a better match and minimizes their self-report reflecting a "well, this is just how all supervision is done" understanding. Clearly communicating the purpose and value of feedback and establishing frequent and meaningful bi-directional feedback may increase the quality of the supervisee's self-reports. Supervisors should also strive to provide anonymity in the feedback process, which requires there to be at least two supervisees. To facilitate anonymity, individuals can type the feedback, place it in a sealed envelope, and place it in a feedback box or with a third party who can pass it along to the supervisor. Use of free online survey systems also prevent the supervisor from knowing the identity of the respondent. Supervisors can also direct supervisees to the sub-section on how to give feedback to

---

Steps for Increasing Accurate Self-Report of Supervision Satisfaction

1. Describe various supervisory approaches and clearly outline your personal approach to supervision
2. Discuss the purpose and logistics of feedback
3. Create a culture of frequent bi-directional feedback
4. Solicit anonymous feedback whenever possible
5. Teach supervisees how to give feedback

a supervisor (p. 62) in Chapter 6 of the book by Kazemi and colleagues (Kazemi, Rice, & Adzhayn, 2018). Specifically, the authors suggest thinking about what to say ahead of time, asking the supervisor about their rationales, and preparing to generate solutions or next steps.

There are several potential ways to collect social validity data from supervisees. One of the easiest ways is to simply ask, though this should only occur if there is a well-established and trusting supervisory relationship. The level of openness and trust in the relationship will be culturally dependent and may be affected by the power differential in the supervisory relationship. The supervisor should be aware of this differential and explore ways to help the supervisee feel comfortable expressing their perspective. Some of the most common power differentials occur with the intersections of gender, race, sexuality, religious, and class differences (Fiorenza, 1992). For example, a female supervisee may feel less comfortable asking or answering questions from a male supervisor. A first generation college student from a background of poverty may not have the skills to explain what is bothering her about feedback. A supervisee of a non-dominant religion may feel uncomfortable asking for breaks to perform religious obligations. In each case, as the supervisor understands how power differentials might affect openness, he or she has the responsibility to facilitate productive communication and a trusting relationship that allows for assessment of social validity for each component of the supervision process.

A supervisor can conduct regular informal check-ins with supervisees. These check-ins may occur during protected time at the end of some supervision meetings or during a specific meeting. Appendix A includes questions a supervisor can pose during these check-ins. In fact, these questions could be reviewed in an early supervision meeting (e.g., the third one in the relationship) and the questions can be provided for advanced preparation. It is important to take notes and to let the supervisee know that you will do so to assist in your evaluation of the effectiveness of your supervisory practices. Alternatively, if taking notes during the meeting is not possible or helpful (e.g., you forgot note-taking materials, this supervisee is particularly anxious), take notes immediately after the meeting, documenting the feedback provided and your next steps. To begin, a supervisor might ask: "I just wanted to check-in and ask you—how do you think supervision is going?" It is important to phrase this as an open-ended question to facilitate a thoughtful and robust answer. Follow up questions can be posed to gather detailed information.

The function of the questions is to gather information about enjoyment of the supervisory practices and supervisee perceptions of the effectiveness of those practices. The purpose is *not* to explain why the practices were used. Following the supervisee's answers, a supervisor should thank them for the thoughtful and informative feedback just as the supervisor would expect the supervisee to do when they have received feedback. If some of the feedback was constructive, a supervisor might address them at the end of the meeting. For straightforward suggestions or requests (e.g., minimize public praise, more frequent observations), a supervisor might acknowledge the request and indicate how they will work to meet those needs. If the feedback requires thought and planning, a supervisor can let the supervisee know that they will come up with an action plan and then the supervisor *must* follow through. A supervisor should keep notes from these feedback meetings and review them for themes. Track whether the feedback is novel each time, or if the supervisee is repeatedly bringing up the same or similar issues. In this manner, a supervisor can evaluate if most of the feedback is useful and if they have addressed identified needs or issues.

Another option for gathering social validity data from a supervisee is to use a survey. A survey allows the supervisor to create the questions in advance, adjust the content as the supervisory relationship progresses, and use the same questions with a variety of supervisees. Turner and colleagues (2016) provided the *Supervision Monitoring and Evaluation Form* as supplemental material to the article to support supervisors gathering feedback from their supervisees (reprinted as Appendix B with permission from the authors). A supervisor can include a rating scale, as well as open ended, short-answer questions. A supervisor could elect to use a validated tool created for assessing the supervisory relationship in clinical settings, such as the *Supervisory Relationship Questionnaire* (SRQ) (Schweitzer & Witham, 2018).

Using a survey may increase the level of detail provided by the supervisee, may reduce some of the anxious thoughts and responding about giving in-person feedback, and may increase how honestly the supervisee answers. If a supervisor has two or more supervisees, they should consider making the survey anonymous by using an on-line survey platform or other system that would conceal the identity of the respondent. Providing anonymity may further increase the honesty of the supervisee's feedback. Just as with the data collected from information check-ins and interviews, once the supervisor gathers the survey data, they should review those data to identify themes and make plans to address any relevant issues.

Evaluating the Effects Using Data from Caregivers and Others

Other sources of valuable information about the effects of supervisory practices include caregivers, other professionals serving the client (e.g., teachers, SLPs, OTs), and supervisees of the supervisee (e.g., RBTs, line-technicians), if applicable. A supervisor can observe interactions to see what effects are evident with these individuals. For example, do the individuals seem engaged? Do they ask questions, volunteer ideas, and smile? The topics of interpersonal skills and therapeutic relationships are covered in Chapter 9 and include resources for a supervisor to use to evaluate the effects of their supervisory practices.

In addition to observing interactions, a supervisor can use the information from Chapter 9 to develop questions that can periodically be posed to relevant stakeholders. To gather information about the effects of the supervisory practice on the supervisee's behavior, a supervisor should formulate questions about whether the supervisee is implementing the strategies covered in supervision (e.g., problem solving, effective training, rapport building), as well as questions about social validity (e.g., do they like working with the supervisee, do they feel like a valued collaborator, would they recommend the supervisee to people they know?).

Evaluating the Effects Using Data from the Supervisor

Whereas the bulk of the data for evaluating the effectiveness of a supervisor's practices come from the supervisee, the client, and other stakeholders, we would be remiss not to suggest that the supervisor assess the effects on their own behavior. To do this, a supervisor can evaluate their own responses to supervision (e.g., positive or negative thoughts, excitement or dread prior to supervision meetings, confidence or insecurity). Supervisors can also look at their own supervisory processes (e.g., setting clear expectations, providing frequent high-quality feedback, modeling, creating practice opportunities). A supervisor should periodically reflect on how those practices have changed over time and in response to issues they have identified in working with past or current supervisees, or that supervisees or others have brought to their attention. Newer supervisors will have a higher frequency of making changes to their practices in response to their evaluations, while more established supervisors may adapt their practices less frequently.

No matter how long a supervisor has been providing supervision, their practices should evolve and improve because of their continued evaluations and the feedback provided to them. That is perhaps the most important message of this chapter. As behavior analysts, we have an ethical and disciplinary obligation to measure the effects of our supervisory practices. In addition, we have a responsibility to respond to those measures in a way that increases the success of our supervisees, their clients, the clients' stakeholders, and ourselves.

Appendix A: General "Check-In Questions"

- How are things going for you?
- Tell me what's been happening with (your courses, your other cases, your colleagues/peers/fellow students or clinicians, your family).
- I know that you love to (fill in the blank with the individual's hobby; e.g., cook, garden, read, see movies). Tell me about what you have been up to with that. Are you finding time to (fill in)?

Conversation Starters for Soliciting Feedback

- I wanted to a take few moments to check in and see how things are going for you. How's your stress level related to the tasks I have been assigning in supervision?
- Remember how I mentioned that I was going to periodically check in to see how our supervisory relationship is going? Well, I'd like to take some time to do that now, if that's all right with you. So, what are your thoughts about how supervision has been going? What is working well, and what things could be improved?
- Because we have covered everything on our agenda, let's spend some time discussing how supervision is going. Because I value your feedback, I am going to take some notes to make sure that I address the feedback you give me and the ideas we come up with today.
- I know that we are pretty good at providing each other with feedback in our meetings and observations, but it's also important for us to take time to specifically check in about how things are going. What feedback do you have for me about the supervision I am providing for you? In other words, what are some things I am doing that are working well? What are some things I need to try to do more or less of?
- As we have discussed before, it is really important for me to continually evaluate the effects of the supervision I provide, and one of the impost important ways to do that is for me to hear how you think supervision is going. What are your thoughts about my supervisory practices?

Follow-Up Questions

- What do you think is going particularly well?
- What do you like best about the supervision processes or activities?

- What could I do to better support you, as your supervisor?
- What things am I missing or not covering in enough depth?
- What things do you think have been particularly effective and how can you tell?
- What things do you think have been less effective and how can you tell?
- What are some activities or practices you would more or less of and why?

Follow-Up Statements

- Thank you for providing me with such great feedback, I really appreciate your thoughts and ideas.
- Your feedback is so valuable to me and will help me continue behaving in accordance with my value of providing effective supervision.
- I know that providing feedback to a supervisor can be awkward, so thanks for your feedback today.
- Your feedback is so helpful at helping me identify what to do more of and what I might need to adjust. Thanks for helping me on my continued journey of learning!

Appendix B: Supervision Monitoring and Evaluation Form
(Turner, Fischer & Luiselli 2016, used with permission)

Trainee:
Supervisor:
Placement Site:
Evaluation Period:

Supervision Arrangement

Measures	YES	NO or NOT ALWAYS: Explain
Supervision sessions occur as scheduled		
Supervision sessions start and end on time		
Supervision sessions are free of distractions		
Supervision sessions can be re-scheduled as warranted		
I am able to correspond with my supervisor between supervision sessions		

Supervisor Behavior

Measures	Rarely		Sometimes		Always
Supervisor is approachable					
Supervisor is attentive to my current abilities and training needs					
Supervisor gives me behavior-specific positive feedback about my strengths					
Supervisor gives me behavior-specific corrective feedback about my weaknesses					
Supervisor gives clear performance expectations and evaluation procedures					
Supervisor models professional behavior (clinical decision-making, ethics, confidentiality)					
Supervisor models technical skills					
Supervisor requires me to practice (e.g., role play) when learning new skills					

Measures	Rarely		Sometimes		Always
Supervisor delivers feedback in a variety of modalities (e.g., verbal, written, graphic)					
Supervisor reviews my written work					
Supervisor facilitates my critical thinking					
Supervisor shows support and positive regard					
Supervisor listens well					
Supervisor shows energy and enthusiasm					
Supervisor is able to shift focus during sessions as warranted					
Supervisor is prepared for supervision sessions					
Supervisor advises about my professional development					
Supervisor suggests and/or assigns up to date readings and other materials					

Supervision Content

Measures	Rarely		Sometimes		Always
Supervision addresses the BACB Task List and ethical and professional guidelines of the field					
Supervision is a collaborative experience					
Supervision informs me about evidence-based practices					
Supervision addresses objectives in my individualized training plan					
Supervision builds and enhances my clinical skills (e.g., case conceptualization)					
Supervision expands my knowledge base					
Supervision considers matters of diversity and inclusion					
Supervision is conducted within the boundaries of confidentiality					

Supervision advises helpfully about my clinical interactions with clients, constituents, and other service providers					
Supervision fortifies my professional development					
Supervision enhances my ability to make clinical decisions and solve problems					

Please complete this form and review it with your supervisor during your next scheduled session. Use the space below to note any additional comments or discussion points.

Trainee Signature:	Date:
Supervisor Signature:	Date:

Chapter 11

Identifying and Resolving Problems in the Supervisory Relationship

Avoidance has never been a great tactic in solving any problem. For most situations in life, not addressing what's going on only makes matters worse.

—Luvvie Ajayi

We hope the prior chapters have taught you about building a strong supervisory relationship (Chapters 1 through 4), delivering high-quality, structured, well-rounded supervision (Chapters 5 through 9), and evaluating the effects of your supervisory practices (Chapter 10). Several of these chapters provide checklists to help you assess your supervisee's skills or your own skills in that particular domain. However, we would be remiss if we did not acknowledge that even the best laid plans do not always unfold as intended, and even the most skilled and thoughtful supervisor is likely to encounter at least one supervisory relationship that feels markedly different than others. And by different we mean more uncomfortable, less successful—in a word, worse. For a novice supervisor, the difference might be obvious, significant, and distressing. In contrast, for the experienced supervisor the difference might be less drastic, but still detectable as different from other supervisory relationships.

Some of the common causes of a strained or damaged supervisory relationship include issues with quality of the supervision (e.g., overly harsh feedback, unclear performance expectations, lack of follow through). Sometimes difficulties in the supervisory relationship stem from one or both individuals behaving in a manner that offends or hurts the other person. These issues often are a result of personal histories or biases, disconnects in communication styles, and cultural differences.

> *Even the best laid plans do not always unfold as intended, and even the most skilled and thoughtful supervisor is likely to encounter at least one supervisory relationship that feels markedly different than others.*

Presented with a difficult or problematic supervisory relationship, supervisors may take one of many ineffective approaches, such as erroneously thinking the problem will somehow fix itself or go away over time. At times, supervisors may even feel the supervisee, rather than the supervisor, should adjust their behavior. None of those approaches are likely to be successful. In fact, they are likely to worsen the immediate problem and produce future problems under similar conditions. Furthermore, the supervisor who avoids addressing these issues misses the opportunity to expand their own skills and to model proactive, structured, and compassionate problem solving. When there are issues within the relationship, it is best for everyone's growth and development to take a structured approach to identifying and addressing the barriers and contributing variables.

This chapter discusses the importance of continually evaluating the health of the relationship to identify and address barriers that may arise. These infrequent, albeit inevitable, difficult supervisory relationships can become learning opportunities. We begin by describing strategies for how to detect if there are emerging or existing issues with the supervisory relationship. It may be the case that issues are related to deficits or excesses on the part of the supervisee, the supervisor, or both. Supervisors can revisit relevant chapters for questions aimed at identifying performance barriers and for strategies to address related performance issues. Because some difficulties may be the result of a damaged relationship, this chapter promotes engaging in self-reflection and evaluating the role of perception, biases, and power dynamics in the supervisory relationship. Finally, if the relationship remains stressed and ineffective even after a thoughtful and structured approach to identifying and addressing the problems, the relationship may need to end. For those rare cases, we outline some considerations for ending the relationship in a compassionate and positive manner.

DETECTING ISSUES: LOOKING FOR SMOKE

It is risky to assume that supervisory practices are effective without evaluating the outcomes (Chapter 9). It is equally risky to assume that a supervisory relationship is healthy without assessing how things are going. It may be possible for you to detect that something is off in the relationship. Sometimes a relationship that is satisfactory to you may be uncomfortable or even aversive to the supervisee. Detecting this disconnect in perceptions requires careful, active, on-going evaluation.

Whereas an issue might come to light on its own, a skilled supervisor is always assessing the health of the supervisory relationship. The information gathered from your evaluation of the effects of supervisory practice (Chapter 9) might provide insight into the strength of the supervisory relationship or help to identify problems. As described in Chapter 5, early detection of a problem increases the likelihood of a successful outcome. Therefore, a supervisor should always be looking for smoke that might indicate an emerging or existing issue. This on-going assessment may strengthen the relationship and allow detection of emerging issues that can be addressed immediately and directly before they become bigger and more difficult to successfully address (Sellers, LeBlanc, & Valentino, 2016).

Detecting Indicators in the Supervisee's Behavior

Engaging in an on-going evaluation involves talking about how things are going with the supervisee and attending to their behavior. A supervisor can do this by including check-ins with the supervisee at each meeting to ask questions like: "How are you feeling about our supervision?" "Is the approach I take to providing you feedback helpful?" or "What else can I do to ensure that you feel supported?" Chapter 9 and the article by Sellers and colleagues (2016) provide other sample questions. As discussed in Chapters 2 and 3, these questions and ensuing conversations must be genuine and compassionate. If the supervisor asks these types of questions without actively listening to the answer or making meaningful change in response to answers, the supervisee might come to view the supervisor in a negative light, or even find them untrustworthy.

The supervisee may independently and directly tell the supervisor about their concerns. Bringing up specific concerns may be an indicator that the supervisory relationship is relatively healthy, especially when there are power differentials created by cultural identity. The supervisor's willingness to discuss concerns may be an indicator that the supervisor has created a noncoercive environment. In such a situation, the supervisor should take the opportunity to thank the supervisee for the critical and helpful feedback, apologize if needed, and articulate a plan to address the concerns. For example, the supervisor might say something like: "Thank you. I appreciate that you are providing me with direct feedback. That's exactly the kind of feedback I need to help me improve as a supervisor." The supervisee may, alternatively, indicate that things are fine and give examples of what is going well and why. If there is correspondence between what they are saying and how they are behaving (e.g., engaged and present), then things are probably going well. If their answers seem strained or do not match their behavior (e.g., they indicate that everything is fine, but they are disengaged and frequently late or absent), then there is cause for concern and additional evaluation.

> **Indicators of Problems in a Supervisory Relationship**
> - Unfavorable affect (disengaged, unhappy, apathetic, fearful, sullen)
> - Avoidance, tardiness, absenteeism
>
> **Indicators of Health in a Supervisory Relationship**
> - Favorable affect (engaged, happy, laughter, approach, interest)
> - Both parties can describe tangible examples of supervisory satisfaction

Regardless of whether the feedback is solicited or unsolicited, positive or corrective, the supervisor should express sincere appreciation. The supervisor might say "Wow, thanks so much for providing me with that feedback," "Thank you for sharing your perspective," or "I am so glad that you pointed that out." It is critical that the experience of giving feedback to the supervisor is positive and productive for the supervisee to reinforce the behavior and increase future feedback delivery. The supervisor should also consider asking follow-up questions for two reasons. First, follow-up questions establish questioning and answering as interverbal chains that can increase the likelihood of a robust conversation in that moment and in the future. Second, follow-up questions may garner more insight into effective and ineffective supervisory practices. Some examples of follow-up questions are: "That's a really interesting point. Can you please tell me more about why you think X is/is not effective for you?" "Can you tell me what you are thinking to yourself when that happens?" "If we could fix one thing right now, what would it be and how would changing it help you?" A productive conversation can then lead to action planning to address any identified needs and discussing the importance of self-management and evaluating the effects of supervisory practices (see Chapters 6 and 9).

In addition to soliciting feedback, the supervisor should track the supervisee's behavior including affect, level of engagement, requests for additional feedback, and timeliness for supervisory meetings. Positive affect, engagement, and prioritization of supervision are indicators of a healthy supervisory relationship. Negative or pervasive neutral affect, disengagement, changes in affect during meetings, avoiding feedback, or chronic lateness and cancelling meetings are indictors that there are issues in the supervisory relationship.

See Appendix A for a checklist of indicators to detect emerging problems and to determine the scope of an issue. The skilled supervisor is attentive to the supervisee's feedback and other behavioral indicators. An important part of the assessment process is appreciation for personal context. That is, behavior means different things to different people. For example, one person may have learned that it is always appropriate to acquiesce to authority, regardless of personal preference. This may translate into smiling and head nodding even though there is disagreement. In this case, it becomes important to ask for examples and to give explicit instructions ("It's important that you share with me at least two concerns with what I am proposing"), so the person feels comfortable discussing concerns. Conversely, a person may appear combative (e.g., raised voice, furrowed eyebrows, rapid speech). These actions might indicate anger and dissatisfaction or might be intended to convey strong motivation and commitment to solving issues. It is helpful to expressly acknowledge the difference in communication styles, as well as acknowledge the commitment to the relationship.

The resources in Chapter 4 should help with clarifying some of these issues that might be due to cultural differences. It is also helpful to find "cultural informants" and trusted colleagues with experience working across cultures. Having conversations with these colleagues about how culture and diversity impact supervisory relationships in frustrating and beautiful ways will provide you with insight and strategy. Understanding indicators of problems in a supervisory relationship is always more difficult across cultures and will require careful observation, study, and consultation, as well as constant effort.

Detecting Indicators of Problems in the Supervisory Relationship in Your Own Behavior

A supervisor's interactions with a supervisee are always informed by the supervisor's own biases, perceptions, and prejudices that can damage the relationship. This may result in relationship conflict that may be the result of viewpoints held by the supervisee and supervisor, or a mismatch between one or more core values (Lau & Cobb, 2010; Sellers, LeBlanc, et al., 2016). The supervisor should monitor for indicators of problems within the supervisory relationship in their own covert and overt behavior. Paying attention to our own reactions to the supervisee and their patterns of behavior may provide insight into difficulties in the relationship. Working with a supervisee who struggles to master content or who can be frustrating may lead to the supervisor responding negatively.

Overt indicators of a problem might include a supervisor cancelling supervision meetings, providing higher ratios of corrective to supportive feedback and praise, providing low-quality feedback, multi-tasking during supervision meetings, or failing to follow through on tasks for the supervisee. The supervisor might also detect covert behavior such as dreading upcoming meetings, feeling irritated by the supervisee, feeling awkward around the supervisee, or thinking that the supervisee's behaviors are due to race, religion, gender identity or personal characteristic (e.g., laziness).

Finally, when one person (i.e., supervisor) has all the power, it can be easy to be dismissive of the other person's unhappiness or concerns. Dismissiveness involves rejecting or overlooking things that are deemed unworthy of one's attention. A dismissive supervisor might notice that the supervisee seems unhappy, or even be told that directly by the supervisee, but perceive that the supervisee is overly sensitive, or that experiencing some level of stress and discontent is just "part of the experience" and fail to take any action to address the issue. As such, "dismissiveness" is probably one of the most important indicators for a supervisor to monitor in their own behavior. Be watchful for this response and use this as a barometer for when to initiate active problem solving.

EVALUATING AND ADDRESSING CONTRIBUTORS TO THE ISSUE

When a potential issue with the supervisory relationship is detected, it should be examined and assessed using a structured problem solving approach as outlined in Chapter 7. In that chapter we offered five steps for taking a structured approach to addressing problems: 1) detect; 2) define; 3) generate solutions; 4) select solution; and 5) implement and evaluate. The information in the preceding "Detecting Issues—Looking for Smoke" section addresses Step 1 in the problem solving process. The current section addresses Step 2, guiding you through how to define the problem in functional terms by identifying the scope of the problem and the contributing factors to the problem. The section on addressing the issue encompasses Steps 3, 4, and 5 and provides some case examples. Supervisors may find it helpful to use the problem solving worksheet (Appendix A) and helpful questions (Appendix B) at the end of Chapter 7, in conjunction with the resources in this chapter's appendices as they work to evaluate and address a problem in the supervisory relationship.

Begin by assessing the scope of the issue (i.e., acute and specific; pervasive and long-standing), as doing so will help drive your action plan. Appendix B will help you determine the scope and focus of the issue. To determine the scope, a supervisor should ask: "Is the performance issue severe and/or has the issue recently and suddenly developed or significantly worsened, or is there a pattern where the issue arises with intensity and then subsides?" Answering yes to this question may suggest that one or more significant personal events, changes in life or work circumstances, or mental health issues may be impacting performance. For example, a supervisee might be ill, caring for an ill child or parent, experiencing difficulties in a personal relationship, or struggling with finances. It may be difficult to determine if life circumstances are impacting performance without discussing the issue with the supervisee.

If the supervisee volunteers information, or you suspect that these variables may be contributing to the issue, prepare for a compassionate discussion about the concerns with the supervisee. Frame the discussion as an opportunity to access supports to address the issue. Seek your own supports from your human resources or student support service personnel to guide you with this discussion. It may be appropriate for these support personnel to have the discussion with the supervisee without you present or you may be able to have the discussion together. The goal is to create a context in which the supervisee feels comfortable sharing personal information.

If the supervisee indicates that life events (e.g., financial difficulties, personal relationships, bereavement, illness, depression) are a concern, the supervisor can direct the supervisee to relevant resources, such as the Employee Assistance Plan (EAP) or federal student aid programs. The supervisor might also help the supervisee follow through on a self-management or self-care plan. Supervisors might also need to develop a plan of accommodations for the supervisee (e.g., additional time to complete tasks, pausing pursuit of accrual of experience hours). If there are self-reporting requirements that apply to the supervisee (e.g., the supervisee is a BCaBA and obligated to self-report a mental health condition that impacts their ability to work to the BACB), the supervisor should offer assistance with the process if the supervisee desires. Most issues related to life circumstances will involve a negotiation. For example, if a supervisee is working two jobs and supporting their family, quitting the extra job and getting more rest may not be an option. Values may differ in terms of what can and cannot be compromised. In such cases, it is critical to listen without judgment and with genuine compassionate curiosity. If the supervisee is also an employee or a student, work with your Human Resources personnel or relevant University Student Services to ensure that you are acting in accordance with any applicable laws and organizational policies.

In contrast, answering "yes" to the question: "Is the performance issue mild to moderate and has the performance issue, or indicators of the performance issue, been consistently present for some time?" indicates that the issue has been developing for some time. In this case, the supervisor should evaluate the contributing factors and determine which behaviors of the supervisor (yes, it could be you!) or supervisee are impacting success. You can use the questions in Appendix B to assess whether problems are unique to one supervisory relationship or are pervasive across multiple supervisory relationships. If the scope is narrow (i.e., unique to one relationship), then you should complete the remaining sections to evaluate the specific contributing factors. If the scope is broader (i.e., present in multiple relationships), the supervisor should focus on the self-evaluation section and make needed changes. If problems persist after the supervisor's behavior has changed, it is worthwhile to evaluate the supervisee's contributions to the relationship. You can revisit the questions about scope any time during the completion of other sections.

Supervisor Self-Evaluation

Appendices C and D are designed to help a supervisor with self-reflection to examine their own role in impacting the supervisee's success and the health of the relationship. In Chapter 6 of *Crucial Conversations* (Patterson, Grenny, McMillan, & Switzler, 2012), the authors provide several excellent questions to facilitate honest self-reflection. The authors suggest asking oneself what emotions and thoughts they are experiencing, what story they are creating based on those emotions and thoughts, and what evidence they have to support the story they created (Patterson et al., 2012, p. 112). The authors specifically suggest asking "Am I pretending not to notice my role in the problem?" (p. 123) to facilitate taking accountability. The authors also recommend reflecting on identifying the goal for the conversation and if one's behavior is in line with achieving that goal (pp. 125–126). Self-reflection might be difficult and uncomfortable, but a skilled and committed supervisor recognizes the benefits of identifying their own role in emerging problems. The supervisor is best positioned to understand and change their own behavior, which may prove to be the most useful solution to the problem. The supervisor holds the primary *responsibility* for the health of the relationship, including problem solving resolutions that help the supervisee develop and gain skills as a professional.

Self-Reflection on Supervisory Practices. Because supervisory practices have such an important effect on supervisee performance and the supervisory relationship, the supervisor should reflect on the quality of their supervisory practices. Chapters 1, 2, and 3 provide information to help a supervisor determine if they have followed core practices (e.g., clarifying the nature of the supervisory relationship, establishing a committed relationship). Next, the supervisor should review their practices around supervision meetings and observations. Supervision should be driven by a structured, competency-based curriculum and planned assessment and instructional activities as discussed in Chapters 5 and 6. Skills should always be taught using BST (e.g., provide a description and rationale, model, practice with feedback, reach a pre-determined mastery criterion; see Chapter 6 for more information). Supervisors should conduct effective meetings using an agenda and they should teach the supervisee to do the same (see Chapter 8). Supervisors should also evaluate the effects of their supervisory practices, adjusting and refining practices as needed (see Chapter 10).

Self-evaluation is a difficult activity. Fortunately, it is a skill and can be learned and refined, as we discussed in Chapter 6. A committed and effective supervisor understands the need for self-evaluation and is willing to take a hard look at their own practices. Appendix C includes a list of questions and several activities to facilitate an evaluation of supervisory practices and how those practices may impact performance issues of a supervisee. We recommend that the supervisor schedule time to carefully read and think about these questions in a distraction-free setting. Once the supervisor has reflected on a question or area of performance, it can be helpful to collect data in supervision meetings and observations, rather than relying only on memory. If (or we should say *when*) the supervisor identifies areas for self-improvement, we recommend creating a systematic plan to address those areas and evaluate the effects of the plan. The supervisor could then move on to further assess the supervisee's potential contributions to the issue. Recommendations for addressing any identified issues can be found throughout the related chapters in this book, as well as in the many referenced resources.

Self-Reflection on Supervisor's History and Biases. The supervisor should reflect on their own history with supervision, their values regarding supervision, and the impact of these on the current supervisory relationship. We covered these topics in depth in Chapters 1 and 2, and we provided specific activities to facilitate evaluating these areas. This self-reflection might reveal inadvertent imitation of the actions of a previous supervisor (e.g., giving harsh feedback). The supervisor might recall their experience in receiving that feedback and elect to take a different approach (e.g., softening feedback delivery, identifying missing prerequisite skills, praising performance).

As stated in the section on detecting indicators, the supervisory relationship is informed and impacted by the supervisor's own biases, perceptions, prejudices, and values. Therefore, the supervisor should engage in honest self-reflection on their own biases, perceptions, prejudices, and values, as well as the impact of the power differential on the supervisory relationship. See Appendix D for guidance in engaging in thoughtful self-reflection. In addition, reviewing the content and activities in Chapters 3 and 4 can facilitate exploring past experiences and perspectives and identifying any cultural or gender biases that are in effect.

After a thorough self-evaluation and efforts to change your own behavior, you may see a positive change in the supervisee's behavior and in the quality of the supervisory relationship. If that happens, congratulate yourself and discuss the self-reflection process with your supervisee. Remember that one critical goal of supervision is training the supervisee to be an effective future supervisor. Exposing them to your processes for assessment, self-reflection, and plan development allows them to see the "behind the scenes" activities required for effective supervision.

Sometimes, the supervisor successfully addresses their contributions to the difficulties in the relationship, but the supervisee continues to behave in problematic ways. This pattern suggests that supervisee-related factors are contributing to the problem. The supervisee may have skill deficits or perceptions and beliefs that are impacting the relationship. This may require redoubling your efforts as described in Chapters 5 through 9 and it may also require a direct conversation with the supervisee. We discuss strategies for doing so in the next section.

ADDRESSING ISSUES

Once you have evaluated and assessed contributors to the problem, the next step is to have an open and compassionate conversation to begin to address the issue(s). There are several available resources for supervisors to develop skills related to difficult conversations. Specifically, we direct supervisors to the books *Crucial Conversations* (Patterson, et al., 2012) and *Difficult Conversations* (Stone, Patton, & Heen, 2010). There are general components to this type of conversation: 1) opening the conversation; 2) describing or exploring the issue; 3) describing or exploring related barriers and contributing factors; 4) describing or developing a plan of action; and 5) recommitting to actively working on developing a positive supervisory relationship. You may need to adjust each component, depending on the nature of the problem.

The supervisor might start the conversation by saying something like: "I want to take some time to talk to you about our supervisory relationship,

> **Skills Related to Difficult Converations**
>
> 1. Opening the conversation
> 2. Describing or exploring the issue
> 3. Describing or exploring related barriers and contributing factors
> 4. Describing or developing a plan of action
> 5. Recommitting to actively working on developing a positive supervisory relationship

as I have been feeling like we have been struggling a little bit." The supervisor can describe the issue and what is concerning them. They may also ask questions to facilitate the exploration of the issue with the supervisee. The supervisor could ask the supervisee for their impressions of the situation. The supervisor could ask whether the supervisee has any ideas about potential barriers or contributing factors. If it is clear that the supervisor's behavior contributed to the issue, the supervisor can apologize for their actions. The next step in the conversation is collaboration on solution identification and selection. Finally, the supervisor can end the conversation by expressing that they value the supervisee and want them to be successful. The supervisor can invite the supervisee to join them in actively committing to strengthening the supervisory relationship.

Because this conversation is crucial, and likely uncomfortable for both individuals, it is important that the supervisor identify a clear purpose ahead of time. The supervisor should know exactly what outcome they want to achieve from the conversation. The supervision should use a structured approach to direct the conversation toward that desired outcome. The conversation should occur in a location that makes the supervisee feel comfortable and during a time that will facilitate shared brainstorming and resolution. If the supervisor's own perceptions or behavior was the primary contributing factor to the damage, the purpose or desired outcome of the conversation is to repair the damage. Specifically, the supervisor can describe how they detected the problems, their self-reflection, their self-management plan and their perceived outcomes.

We have included three case examples to illustrate some of the issues that might arise and how a supervisor might go about evaluating and addressing those issues. These examples illustrate how to explore an issue in a conversation so that each party can accept responsibility for their behavior and develop a plan to address the issue.

Case Example 1—Multitasking while Supervising

Rachel, a supervisor, has not really been looking forward to supervision meetings with Sam. This feeling has been increasing over the past few weeks. Upon reflecting on Sam's behavior in supervision meetings, they realize that Sam has not been as engaged in conversations and has not been asking as many questions as heyhas in the past. Rachel continues to self-reflect and think about how they and Sam have behaved in their past supervision meetings. As Rachel replays their own behavior in the past few meetings, they wonder if their tendency to "multi-task" (e.g., checking and responding to email, looking over documents) in response to time sensitive tasks has become a problem. They recall multiple instances over the past few supervision meetings where they were checking emails, replying to text messages, and scanning over documents while also discussing Sam's clients and items for the Task List. Rachel decides to track their own engagement in non-supervisory tasks and the number of questions and comments from Sam during the next two supervision meetings. These data confirm the suspicion that the increase in Rachel's multi-tasking is negatively impacting the relationship. Rachel creates a self-management plan to minimize distractions and continues to collect data for three more supervisor meetings. The data indicate that their distracted behavior has decreased, Sam's engagement has increased, and Rachel now looks forward to supervision meetings again.

Rachel decides to have a conversation with Sam about this process. They open the conversation by asking: "Sam, how do you think our meetings have been going?" Sam shares that he looks forward to the meetings and thinks they have been going well. Rachel then says: "I am so glad to hear that. I actually want to talk about an issue that may have been developing and what I did to address it, and I'd love to hear your thoughts." Rachel then goes on to describe what had taken place and facilitates a conversation about continually evaluating the supervisory relationship and using self-management strategies. They end the conversation by agreeing that they will discuss strategies to engage in self-evaluation in an upcoming meeting. They commit to checking in with each other at the first signs of any issues. This example illustrates a supervisor watching out for "smoke" indicating that an issue may be developing, taking a structured approach to evaluating and addressing the emerging issue, and using the situation as a teaching opportunity for their supervisee.

Case Example 2—A Supervisor's Harsh Feedback

Elaine notices that her supervisee Miko has gone from being engaged and inquisitive to being withdrawn during meetings. As Elaine reflects on these changes, she asks herself questions about her own supervisory experiences. She remembers her own past supervisor who provided direct, almost harsh, feedback. She recalls feeling like she could not do anything right and she dreaded giving answers to questions. Elaine also remembers that in early conversations, Miko shared that she had a college softball coach who frequently berated her about her errors and that she eventually quit the team. Elaine reviews her supervision notes for Miko for the past several months and notices that they have been stuck on a few difficult concepts. Miko has been struggling to master these concepts and Elaine has provided very direct and repeated feedback.

Elaine opens the conversation by stating "I really appreciate your efforts with your clients and our work together during supervision. In the spirit of that collaborative approach to our supervisory relationship, I have something I'd like to talk about." After opening the conversation Elaine describes the situation: "I've noticed that in our recent meetings I find myself dominating the conversation with feedback and you seem to be asking fewer questions. I miss your questions because they show your eagerness and inquisitiveness." She then moves to exploring contributing factors by saying: "I have thought back on my own supervisory experiences and our early conversations. I am wondering if I have been too direct with some of my corrective feedback and if I have missed opportunities to point out your many successes and accomplishments. What are your thoughts about this?" Miko then feels comfortable enough to share that she feels like she is not making progress and is disappointing Elaine. Elaine responds: " I am so sorry that I have been overly focused on these difficult concepts and skills. I am noticing the great things you are doing, but I haven't been saying that to you. I am so glad that we talked about this and that you feel comfortable enough to share that feedback with me."

Elaine and Miko then move into a collaborative conversation that involves them reviewing the training strategies used to identify if they need to make any changes and Elaine committing to actively focus on pointing out more of Miko's strengths and interspersing challenging content with some easier tasks. At the same time, Miko commits to soliciting positive feedback when she feels overwhelmed with corrective feedback. This example illustrates a situation wherein a supervisor resolved an issue by engaging in self-reflection had an open conversation with the supervisee, and both individuals agreed to make changes in their own behavior.

Case Example 3—A Supervisee's Immaturity

Jennifer is a new to the clinician role at a large clinic where she has worked for three years as a direct-line therapist. Her performance evaluations over that period were always positive. Jennifer has an energetic, fun personality that preschool-aged clients love. In her new role she is supervised by Tanisha. Tanisha is impressed with Jennifer's clinical understanding and skills with clients. However, she is concerned with Jennifer's overall professionalism and maturity. Tanisha has noticed that Jennifer is too informal in her interactions with her team and with parents. Tanisha has addressed this issue with Jennifer in the past and has described the importance of building rapport while still behaving as a professional. They have even role-played scenarios to practice friendly, professional behavior. Tanisha notices that she is increasingly frustrated with Jennifer's behavior and has snapped at her a few times, for which Tanisha immediately apologized. It seems that Jennifer is now avoiding interactions with Tanisha.

Sensing developing issues in the supervisory relationship, Tanisha begins documenting her concerns and engages in self-reflection. She reviews their meetings and considers her potential contribution to the issue, asking herself "Did I fail to set clear expectations or model unprofessional behavior (e.g., snapping when frustrated)?" Tanisha carefully reflects on her past behavior with Jennifer recalling that she has modeled formal and professional behavior in their supervision meetings and during Tanisha's interactions with caregivers and other staff that Jennifer has observed. She also remembers several conversations and role-play activities focusing on professional behavior and communication. Tanisha concludes that she is not likely the source of the issue. Tanisha suspects that Jennifer's level of maturity is contributing to the issue and resolves to address this with Jennifer before any more damage to their supervisory relationship can occur.

Tanisha opens the conversation: "Jennifer, you have worked here a long time, your clinical work is wonderful, and I know that you value the work we do here. That's why it's important for me to discuss a concern I have." Tanisha describes the issue to Jennifer. "Despite us talking about the importance of being professional in your interactions with staff and parents, you continue to be very informal in your interactions. I feel stumped because in thinking back over things, I know you value your work, and I am pretty sure that I have clearly communicated my expectations. We have talked about this on occasion in supervision meetings. It has gotten to the point that I am concerned that your informal relationships are going to impact your ability to manage your teams and have parents take you seriously. Do you have thoughts on why you continue to struggle with this?"

Jennifer indicates that she wants to connect with staff and parents and doesn't want to come off as stuffy or like a know-it-all. Tanisha decides to take a more direct route, since her previous strategies have not been successful. She says: "It seems like you might be at a point in your career where you have really developed your clinical skills, but still see yourself as a therapist and may be scared to take on more of a leadership role. I think if you can't make this shift, your team and clients might suffer. How does that feedback sit with you?" Jennifer takes a few minutes to think and then responds: "You know, I think I needed to hear that. I really don't see myself as a clinician; I worry that people will know that I feel like I don't know what I am talking about. I know I am ready for the next stage in my career, I am just struggling with how to make that shift, especially since I used to be on teams as a therapist with some of my staff."

Tanisha and Jennifer then develop a plan for Jennifer to reflect on her professional goals and the types of behaviors related to professional interactions. Tanisha commits to identifying opportunities for Jennifer to observe other clinicians running team and parent meetings. They both agree that Jennifer might benefit from taking on new tasks that will require professionalism (e.g., interviewing applicants, training new therapists). Tanisha takes the opportunity to apologize for snapping at Jennifer recently. They agree to check in about these strategies in their next meeting. This example illustrates a supervisor detecting a persistent performance issue that was threatening the supervisory relationship, reflecting on contributing factors, and addressing the issue.

Ending the Supervisory Relationship

Some issues can be detected and repaired while others cannot be repaired. We encourage supervisors to engage in reasonable efforts to repair situations or address performance problems whenever possible. We hope the structured, functional approach to problem solving proves helpful. However, some cannot be resolved in a timely manner or repaired to the satisfaction of one or both parties. Perhaps the supervisor lacks the skills or experience necessary to ensure the success of their supervisee and cannot address their deficits quickly enough to benefit this supervisee. Perhaps the supervisee needs support beyond the resources available to the supervisor. The decision to terminate the supervisory relationship should not be made lightly. The decision should be made primarily to benefit the supervisee. The lessons that the supervisor learns through the termination process will, hopefully, benefit future supervisees.

As indicated in Chapter 1, the conditions under which the supervisory relationship might be terminated should be clearly outlined in the supervision contract and discussed in meetings during the beginning of the relationship. The supervisor and supervisee should have had several discussions about the challenges in the relationship before the topic of termination ever arises. Those discussions should have included specific behavioral pinpoints for improvement and specific action plans and follow-through. Therefore, the conversation to transition the supervisee to another supervisor should not come as a surprise. Turner and colleagues offer helpful guidance on ending a supervisory relationship (Turner, Fischer, & Luiselli, 2016). The conversation should focus on review of the conditions and procedures in the contract and the steps both parties have taken to identify and address the issues.

The supervisor can facilitate the supervisee's learning by acknowledging any gains that the supervisee has made, their strengths, and their efforts to address the issue. The supervisor can also restate their commitment to the supervisee's continued success. The pair can then work together to identify a reasonable plan. The supervisor can demonstrate their support by offering to assist in identifying one or more possible supervisors. This assistance is a critical action if the relationship is terminating due to an irreconcilable mismatch or a deficit in the supervisor's current skills or abilities. The pair should then develop a list of tasks (e.g., introduction to potential supervisors, updating a skill assessment, completing required paperwork) and a timeline that minimizes disruption to clinical services and progress toward certification or promotion. It may also be instructive for the pair to review any applicable ethics requirements from the BACB by reviewing relevant ethics codes and supervision standards (BACB, 2014; BACB, 2018c). Overall, the goal of the termination process is acknowledging the difficulties that led to the termination, understanding your own development needs, and preparing this supervisee for a successful future.

CONCLUSION

Healthy supervisory relationships require effort and skills. There will be situations in which our supervisory skills do not meet the needs of the supervisee or in which issues in the supervisee skill set become evident. Supervisee deficits in pivotal professional skills (e.g., time management, interpersonal skills) can create stress in the relationship. Supervisor behaviors (e.g., providing harsh feedback, unclear expectations, poor time management or too many supervisees can contribute to problems, as can different cultural contexts, conflicting communication styles, or incompatible values. Early detection of problems often simplifies the problem solving process. Once problems are identified, there is usually a path to resolving the challenges and to helping both parties grow as professionals.

Appendix A
Looking for Smoke: Detecting Indicators of Issues in the Supervisory Relationship

Use the checklist to detect indictors of emerging issues in the supervisory relationship, either due to your behavior or your supervisee's behavior. This list is not exhaustive. In considering these indicators, remember that everyone has off days. These behaviors and characteristics are not necessarily problematic in and of themselves; therefore, only check an item if it is consistently problematic or represents an acute and severe problem. Use the "Notes" section to include relevant contextual information. Reflect on the following questions: What specific behavior make you think this indicator is present? What does this behavior mean to you? What does this behavior mean to the supervisee? What are the risks associated with this indicator or issue?

Indicators	Supervisee or Self	Notes
☐ Anxious	supervisee self	
☐ Blames others	supervisee self	
☐ Cancels meetings	supervisee self	
☐ Complains or overly critical	supervisee self	
☐ Condescending	supervisee self	
☐ Defensive	supervisee self	
☐ Delayed response to communication	supervisee self	
☐ Disinterested	supervisee self	
☐ Dismissive	supervisee self	
☐ Disorganized	supervisee self	
☐ Disrespectful	supervisee self	
☐ Dominates conversations or interactions	supervisee self	

IDENTIFYING AND RESOLVING PROBLEMS • 229

Indicators	Supervisee or Self	Notes
☐ Impulsive	supervisee self	
☐ Inflexible/overly rigid in thinking or behavior	supervisee self	
☐ Insensitive/rude Late for meetings	supervisee self	
☐ Misses deadlines/requests extensions	supervisee self	
☐ Overly emotional (e.g., argumentative, tearful)	supervisee self	
☐ Passive in conversations or interactions	supervisee self	
☐ Poor follow through	supervisee self	
☐ Poor quality work	supervisee self	
☐ Reserved or sullen	supervisee self	
☐ Self-critical	supervisee self	
☐ Socially awkward	supervisee self	
☐ Uncommunicative (e.g., avoidant)	supervisee self	

Upon completion, engage in self-reflection and work to identify the function of the problematic behavior (e.g., escape, access to supervisor attention) and barriers to the desired behavior (e.g., skill deficits in time management, damaged supervisory relationship, life events).

Appendix B: Considerations to Determine Scope and Focus of the Issue

Use this list to help determine the scope and focus of the performance problem and consider possible barriers.

If the issue represents a recent and sudden change in the supervisee's behavior, consider:
- A recent interaction that could have damaged the relationship
- A potential life event or emerging physical or mental health concern

If the issue represents a long-standing pattern of behavior by the supervisee, consider:
- Frequency of high-quality feedback with follow-through from supervisor
- Deficits in supervisee's repertoire and history
- Cultural differences in the expression and/or value of the behavior patterns/context

If the issue occurs only with you (not with other supervisors, colleagues, peers), consider:
- Possible damaged supervisory relationship
- Specific power struggles or misunderstanding, differences related to authority and communication

If this issue occurs across multiple contexts, supervisors, or co-workers, consider:
- Deficits in supervisee's repertoire and history (specific skill deficits, past experiences)
- If supervisee is from non-dominant cultural group, there may be differences in acceptable patterns of behavior and/or prejudice intolerance

If the issue is present only with this supervisee, consider:
- Deficits in supervisee's repertoire and history (specific skill deficits, past experiences)
- Possible damaged supervisory relationship

If the issue is present in other past or current supervisees, consider:
- Deficits in *your* supervisory repertoire
- Cultural differences in acceptable patterns of behavior and/or prejudice intolerance

Appendix C: Self-Reflection on Supervisory Practices

Questions to Consider

- Have you clarified the nature of the supervisory relationship?
- Do you use a structured agenda for your meetings with this supervisee?
- Do you regularly (i.e., at least every other week) check in with your supervisee about how they are doing in general (e.g., how they are feeling, how school is going, interests outside of work)?
- Do you use a structured approach to identifying knowledge content and skills to address?
- Do you use behavioral skills training to teach skills (e.g., provide instructions, model, practice with feedback, reach a predetermined mastery criterion)?
- Do you provide frequent high-quality supportive and corrective feedback (e.g., multiple times in each supervision meeting/observation)?
- Is your ratio of positive to corrective/directive feedback at least 5:1?
- Do you document your feedback and follow-through to ensure that it was implemented and the desired performance change occurred?
- Have you solicited feedback about your supervisory practices from this supervisee and/or other supervisees?
- Have you ever received specific feedback about your supervision practices?
- Have you ever had a more experienced colleague or mentor observe and evaluate your supervisory practices?
- Do you regularly engage in professional development activities (e.g., attend trainings or workshops, read practice or research articles or books) related to supervision?
- Do you engage in activities that help you understand the diversity, cultural frameworks, and experiences of the people you are supervising?
- Have you ever had a more experienced colleague or mentor observe and evaluate your practices in relation to culture or diversity?

Self-Reflection Activities

1. Using your answers to the above questions, make a list of your general supervisory practices, behavior, and style. Go back through that list and expand on the things that you do (or don't do) that might be related to the supervisee's performance issue. For example, if your supervisee is being very argumentative in meetings with you, reflect on and describe your communication style. Are you argumentative? Do you praise others when they are argumentative? Are you passive? Do you back down or give in when someone argues with you? Do you end the conversation or argue back? If you identify that your supervisee is disorganized, reflect on your organizational skills. Are you prompt? Can you quickly find information or materials when you or others need them? Do you manage your time and tasks effectively? Ask self-evaluative questions to determine the scope of the issue and your specific role in it.

2. Reflect on your past supervisors and list things they did that were particularly effective and enjoyable. Review that list and check each behavior that you currently engage in with your supervisees on a regular basis. Are there things on the list that you only sometimes do, or do not do at all? Plan to incorporate those behaviors or strategies into your current supervisory practice and observe the responses of your supervisees.

3. Reflect on your past supervisors and list things they did that were ineffective or unpleasant. Review that list and check each behavior that you currently engage in with your supervisees on a regular basis. Think about how those behaviors impacted you and how they might be impacting your supervisee.

Appendix D:
Self-Reflection on Personal History and Biases

Reflect on your culture, background, and personal beliefs. How would you describe your general culture or personal beliefs to someone else? What are your most important personal beliefs? How do those inform how you perceive and interact with others? Do you have frequent interactions with individuals from cultures, backgrounds, geographic areas that differ from your own? What have your learned about cultural responsiveness? What can you do to increase the comfort of cross-cultural interactions?

Think about the influence of your culture on your supervision practices in general. In what positive ways does your culture inform your supervisory practices? In what negative ways? How about with supervisees? How about with a particular supervisee with whom you have had issues? How do you manage each of the common supervisory "hot spots" listed in Chapter 4?

Think about the influence a supervisee's culture may have on your interactions. Do you know about your supervisees' cultures and cultural practices? Do you ever find yourself thinking in terms of labels? Do you consider these labels desirable (e.g., hard-working, intelligent, friendly, calm, easy-going?) or undesirable (e.g., controlling, lazy, disorganized, rigid, argumentative)? Do you associate these with particular groups based on culture, religion, ethnicity, gender/sexuality, age, etc.? If so, list those labels and all the people who you think demonstrate them. Reflect on what these lists mean. Are they fair assumptions? Are the individuals different from you in terms of lifestyles or culture? Are there times and places where some of these behaviors are meritorious and times when you think they are not desirable? It may be helpful to review the list with a colleague or friend from a different culture or who has made different lifestyle choices.

Chapter 12

Planning for a Sustained Career and Lifelong Growth

There is no passion to be found playing small—in settling for a life that is less than the one you are capable of living.

—Nelson Mandela

Early in our careers we are often consumed with the tasks that allow us to enter our chosen profession. In the field of behavior analysis, these tasks likely include completion of graduate school, supervised fieldwork experience, and the certification exam to practice as a certified behavior analyst. At some point early in your career, accomplishing these tasks might have felt like reaching the finish line of a marathon. In reality, completing these milestones marks the beginning of your career of practicing independently, supervising others, and growing as a professional.

Having invested so much time, energy, and money into preparation for your career, of course you want to sustain and enjoy that career for decades to come! That is our wish for you too. However, a long and fulfilling career in any profession requires planning, self-monitoring, and thoughtful decision-making at critical choice points over the course of years and decades. Three threats to that sustained, enjoyable career are related to: 1) difficulties in transitioning to the workforce; 2) the loss of professional reinforcers; and 3) and the phenomenon referred to as "burnout." The remainder of this chapter focuses on how to neutralize, or at least miminimize, these threats to career longevity.

TRANSITIONING INTO YOUR CAREER

Most theories of career development use the concept of stages to describe progress through the career span. For example, common theories described five stages of a career, beginning with exploration and establishment, followed by career advancement, subsequently followed by maintenance, and eventually withdrawal (Super, 1980). New behavior analysts are moving from exploration into establishment of their career as they transition from graduate school to initial employment. The constraints of the job and the newness of the professional repertoires mean that early career success depends on a willingness to continue to learn, an environment to support continued learning, and resilience against common bumps in the professional road. There will be no need to seek new challenges, as virtually every daily professional experience is a new challenge at this stage. Three aspects of clinical work that can make the transition from graduate school to employment difficult are: 1) a shift in the complexity, scope, and timelines related to required tasks; 2) an increase in the complexity of interpersonal relationships; and 3) the addition of significant supervisory duties.

> *There will be no need to seek new challenges, as virtually every daily professional experience is a new challenge at this stage.*

Work-task demands increase dramatically after graduate school, while contingencies become more delayed and academically-oriented deadlines disappear. The duties associated with caseload management (e.g., scheduling, training staff and caregivers, assessment and treatment planning, report writing) occur many times a day for many different clients, stakeholders, and staff. These duties require a well-planned balance of effort and time allocation if the transition to the workforce is going to be successful (Ervin, 2008; Mazerolle, Walker, & Thrasher, 2015).

> **Transition to Employment Challenges**
>
> 1. Increased complexity and scope of tasks
> 2. Increased complexity in inter personal relationships
> 3. Addition of supervisory duties

Each of the work tasks must be planned, carried out, and evaluated independently. In addition, a BCBA encounters a greater number and diversity of problems in ongoing practice than were encountered during graduate training and fieldwork experiences. Deficits in the skills reviewed in Chapter 7 (problem solving) and Chapter 8 (organization and time management) are frequent culprits for underperformance and increased stress right after graduate school.

Second, many BCBAs provide services to families who are often experiencing significant stress and worry. The new practitioner must often navigate these relationships with little or no support from more senior staff. Newly minted behavior analysts providing clinical services are likely to be responsible for collaborating with and training individuals who are older and have more life experience than them. New practitioners, or anyone who is insecure about their professional skill sets may struggle to develop effective, collaborative relationships with families (see Chapter 9). Failure to do so may result in conflicts and stressful professional relationships that could erode job satisfaction and result in adverse consequences for families.

Third, the transition to caseload management introduces the responsibility of supervising others who are new to the field (e.g., RBTs). This responsibility may require creation of training and supervision systems, training large numbers of individuals quickly, and providing corrective feedback. All of these tasks and activities may be new and challenging for a new practitioner as they transition from supervisee to supervisor, particularly if they receive little support and/or have a large number of supervisees. New practitioners may also find themselves responsible for direct-line staff who have many more years of experience working in the field, but who may have deficits or developed problematic work behavior. Failure to take a systematic approach to staff training, performance monitoring, and management can increase stressors, negatively impact client progress, and leave the new practitioner questioning their abilities.

If the skill sets described in Chapters 7 through 9 have been established throughout graduate training and supervised fieldwork experiences, the new challenges are more likely to be perceived as exciting learning opportunities rather than overwhelming failures. Thus, the first recommendation for career sustainability is to hone your skills in problem solving (Chapter 7), organizing and planning your time and tasks (Chapter 8), and building stronger relationships with co-workers, colleagues, and families (Chapter 9). The resources reviewed in this book will help you strengthen your own skill sets as well as the skills of those you supervise. The second recommendation is to take an active approach to maintaining and continuing to grow these skills. Specifically, we encourage you to find a mentor, coach, or peer to support your continued improvement.

Another recommendation for making a smooth transition to practice is to develop strong professional peer relationships through a community of practice. In Chapter 4 we discussed communities of practice and their importance for advancing the goals of culturally responsive practices. Communities of practice are also relevant to developing expertise in other areas of behavior analysis. In this case, the mission should include a commitment to professional excellence as it relates to case management responsibilities. Each community contains members of varying skill levels who are dedicated to a common mission and actively supporting one another in learning and advancing that mission (Wenger & Snyder, 2000). Developing the skills to learn from experts (see Chapter 6) remains useful for the remainder of a career. Accessing these supports can help you increase success and assist in addressing the challenges and difficult times that will undoubtedly come. Bailey and Burch (2010) have suggested that for at least the first few years of employment, novice practitioners choose work settings where there are experts to provide continued support.

As your career advances, the support of mentors will become more situational. Bailey and Burch suggest that over the span of a professional career, one needs trusted colleagues (Bailey & Burch, 2016) to serve as counsel for situational guidance and feedback. Trusted colleagues are met and developed through work experiences, trainings and conferences, and professional collaborations. Once a relationship has been established and areas of expertise are understood, senior behavior analysts will serve as peer mentors to one another. They call upon these mentors for assistance with solving new problems or ethically challenging dilemmas, for providing outside review of professional activities, and for guidance about career directions and opportunities.

KNOW YOUR VALUES AND REINFORCERS AND MAINTAIN ACCESS TO THEM

Your ability to articulate your values, reinforcers, and professional mission will be invaluable in guiding your decision-making throughout your career. Return to your mentor tree to revisit your overarching values and professional mission. Remind yourself of what attracted you to this field and why you valued the opportunity to practice behavior analysis. Perhaps you found it reinforcing to interact with clients and families and reveled in the positive changes that you could help them make in their lives. Perhaps the intellectual and scientific aspects of our field excited your inner geek. Because graduate

> *Your ability to articulate your values, reinforcers, and professional mission will be invaluable in guiding your decision making throughout your career.*

coursework and fieldwork experience is often planned out for the supervisee, the intial employment experience may be the first opportunity to think about personal and professional reinforcers. To make a successful transition into the workplace and sustain that success over the decades of a career, give yourself time to identify your core values and top reinforcers. Have a discussion with colleagues, supervisiors, mentors, or former professors about how they identify their values and reinforcers, and how they make decisions in accordance with their values and strategies they use to maintain frequent access to reinforcers.

Many students enjoy the intellectual learning community encountered in graduate training while simultaneously grumbling about the academic demands. External deadlines and contingencies for reading the literature (e.g., exams, papers) disappear after graduate school, often resulting in decreased contact with the literature. A young professional becomes responsible for their own continuing professional development, whether or not there is an ongoing relationship with a supervisor or mentor to facilitate these activities. One either chooses to read, attend conferences, and seek out additional training or not. One either chooses to seek out colleagues for intellectual discussions or not. If these activities decrease, the young professional may feel like the enjoyable learning experiences are behind them. However, because each professional is responsible for their own continued learning experiences, these experiences can be reintroduced as soon as they are detected as valued and missing. See Carr and Briggs (2010) for recommendations for staying in touch with the literature, and Becerra, Sellers, and Contreras (2020) for recommendations for making the most of conference experiences. If attending conferences functions as a professional reinforcer but access is difficult due to distance or lack of funds, consider attending a conference that has a live-streaming option for remote attendance.

Setting goals can evoke desired behavior and allow measurement of progress toward an important outcome. For example, it is reasonable to set a goal to read one new article per week or to scan the newly distributed table of contents (TOC) of favored journals to find a few articles to read in the next month. Almost every journal webpage has an icon that can be used to set up electronic delivery of the TOC. Because every BCBA has access to multiple behavior analytic journals and a search engine as part of an organizational subscription of the BACB, at least some of the literature is available to you at no extra cost beyond a few clicks in your portal account. Once those goals are set, you can use the organization and time management skills learned in Chapter 8 to plan time to read the selected articles and to measure how many you read within the target time frame. This is another opportunity to enagage with your community of practice. Articles can be shared and discussed with co-workers and colleagues in other settings with whom you share a common mission for continued learning and improvement. A community of practice can also assist with contingency management by holding its members accountable for the desired behaviors (e.g., reading journal articles) and celebrating accomplishments.

Values are related to your reinforcers and they drive behavior toward a goal, especially when immediate reinforcers are scarce. For example, you are more likely to set a goal to read new journal articles if you value being a science-informed practitioner and being a life-long learner. You are more likely to set and achieve goals for exercise and healthy eating habits if you value physical wellness and enjoy (at least a little bit) being active and eating fruits and vegetables. You are more likely to set a goal of having healthy stimulus control patterns for your work if you can explicitly state that you value evening and weekend time with your spouse and children. Knowing your values, which likely focus on helping others, can also help you monitor how often you say "yes" to help prevent you from overextending yourself and failing to honor commitments.

Knowing your values can help you make decisions when faced with choices that place you in a position inconsistent with your values. A clinician with a caseload of ten clients and three supervisees pursuing fieldwork experience hours could be asked by their employer to take on another supervisee. That supervisee is brand new and is working remotely with a rural population that is different from the population of clients the clinician is used to. The clinician likely has multiple values associated with being a team player and others associated with providing high quality clinial and supervisory services. The first value of being a team player who likes to help others could lead to a quick "yes" response that could jeopardize the second value. The clinician might have reasonable concerns that taking on the additional supervisee will negatively impact clients, the other supervisees, and the quality of the supervision provided to the new supervisee. The clinician might also recognize there may be cultural learning required for effectively serving rural families. If the clinician identifies that that honoring the first value will compromise the second value, the realization might prompt an honest discussion with their employer about their concerns.

Knowing your values and setting goals to behave in accordance with them is predicated on knowing your own reinforcers. Do you love collaborating with other clinicians? Do you love working with very young clients who make rapid progress with skill acquisition? Perhaps you love nothing more than working with adults and making critical progress toward their independence. Maybe you find serving linguistically diverse populations important and satisfying. Maybe you enjoy building and refining systems and training others. Maybe your most potent reinforcer is working in multidisciplinary teams in school settings and being a positive emissary for the field of behavior analysis. Activity A provides ideas for assessing your own preferences. Preferences change over time, so the activity of identifying values, reinforcers, and personal mission should be repeated periodically throughout your career.

Professional advancement opportunities (e.g., new positions, new organizations, new projects) often involve exchanging mastered tasks for ones that are new and, by definition, not yet mastered. This experience can be exciting and often is accompanied by social recognition and monetary incentives. As you navigate your career, knowing what reinforces your work-related behavior will increase the likelihood that you will accept positions and opportunities that will provide access to those reinforcers rather than remove them. For example, many behavior analysts entered the field to access the reinforcers associated with interacting with clients and families and designing the programming for their services. The opportunity to supervise and mentor others may or may not serve as a reinforcer. Supervising others may, in fact, be only enjoyed under certain conditions. Perhaps the supervision provided to technicians who implement programming is enjoyable while the supervision of fieldwork experience is not enjoyable. Both of these types of supervision will likely be required at some points in the career of a behavior analyst. Someone who knows that they do not prefer supervising aspiring behavior analysts might make different choices about whether or not to apply for promotions for positions that focus heavily on this activity. For example, the job duties associated with a training position might allow continued access to reinforcers while offering a new professional challenge. However, in this case, a senior behavior analyst position would likely involve trading the most valued reinforcers (e.g., contact with your own clients and families) for non-preferred activities (e.g., managing others, supervising aspiring certificants).

If collaborating with other behavior analysts is near the top of your list of preferred activities, but you have also chosen to work in a context with little to no contact with other behavior analysts (e.g., a small or new company, a rural area), then you might have to seek a different work context or find other ways to access those collaborative activites. One way to collaborate with other behavior analysts is to become involved in your state or regional professional association. These organizations often rely heavily on volunteer efforts of members of the organizations either as committee members or as elected officers. You might also create a community of practice from other geographic areas or other organizations and meet once a month live or via video-conference. Small groups of colleagues, whether near or far, can allow you to access reinforcers such as clinical problem solving, program development, contact with the published literature, discussions about ethical dilemmas, and social contact (Ellis & Glenn, 1995).

Finally, keep in mind that a long career may need to include a pivot or multiple pivots to periodically introduce new reinforcers and exciting challenges. The change may involve a sabbatical to learn new skills, a new work project like writing a book on supervision, a change of practice area, or an entire career change within the same field. In each instance, the change should be one that is likely to produce exciting new demands while retaining the critical reinforcers that are valued (e.g., positive impact on lives of others, solving complex problems).

LeBlanc has periodically changed the focus of her clinical work from autism and intellectual disabilities to dementia care to building clinical oversight systems. See LeBlanc, Heinicke, & Baker (2012) for strategies for expanding your consumer base if this option appeals. She also created clinical decision-making models as a challenge to bring her decision-making skills from the level of automatic responding to carefully planned and described rule-based rubrics. The task of creating the decision-making models was far more difficult and intellectually stimulating at that point in her career than the task of making individual decisions. She left academia to pursue new reinforcers and challenges associated with directing a large human service agency.

Similarly, Sellers changed clinical focus several times in her career of working with individuals with autism and intellectual disabilities (adults, young children, social skills, severe problem behavior). She also transitioned from clinical work to academia and then to work in the field of certification regulation and ethics. Ala'i started out in early intervention services, but quickly found her way to colleage teaching. That university positon has allowed her to continue early intervention work as well as expand to other areas of applied behavior analysis. The university has allowed her to engage in her passions (e.g., collaboration with other disciplines, serving vulnerable populations, mentoring students in applied behavior analysis) and to be in constant contact with opportunities related to her values (e.g., public service, social justice).

PREVENTING AND ADDRESSING BURNOUT

The term "burnout" has been used for at least four decades to refer to a commonly observed phenomenon in many human services (e.g., nursing, psychology; Maslach, Shaufeli, & Leiter, 2001). The phenomenon involves a negative response to the workplace and the stressors associated with the workplace. The workplace stressors could include conflicts with clients, co-workers, and supervisors; conflicts between work demands and personal preferences; and chronicly excessive workplace demands (Maslach & Goldberg, 1998; Plantiveau, Dounavi, & Virués-Ortega, 2018). The most common conceptualization of burnout includes three core dimensions: 1) overwhelming exhaustion and depletion of emotional and physical resources; 2) feelings of cynicism and detachment from the job that lead to callousness and detachment with clients and coworkers; and 3) a sense of ineffectiveness and lack of accomplishment (Maslach, 1998). One commonly used psychometrically-sound scale, the *Maslach Burnout Inventory* (MBI) developed by Maslach & Jackson (1981), is available for purchase by individuals or organizations at MindGarden (https://www.mindgarden.com/314-mbi-human-services-survey). Note there are multiple versions of the tool, including one for human services. In addition, a generic, free self-assessment tool for burnout is available online at Mindtools (https://www.mindtools.com/pages/article/newTCS_08.htm).

Burnout seems to be most pronounced in new professionals (Maslach, et al., 2001; Plantiveau, et al., 2018), perhaps for many of the reasons described in the earlier section of this chapter on transitioning to the workforce (e.g., feeling unprepared, losing reinforcers, loss of mentors). Plantiveau, et al. found that over 60 percent of surveyed behavior analysts scored in the moderate to high range on each of the three dimensions of burnout. In contrast, Dounavi, Fennell, & Early (2019) found lower percentages with just over one-third of participants experiencing high levels on each dimension of burnout. Perhaps unsurprisingly, burnout seems to be more common for those who work with the most challenging and aggressive clients with special needs (Howard, Rose, & Levenson, 2009; Rose, Mills, Silva, & Thompson, 2013). Burnout also seems to be more common in those who feel disconnected from a professional community, with behavior analysts suggesting that social support at work, professional support from colleagues, and strong supervisor relationships may be protective against burnout (Dounavi, et al., 2019; Plantiveau, et al., 2018).

All of these findings suggest that behavior analysts—particularly new ones—and the staff they supervise are at risk for burnout and that the information provided throughout this book is critical to prevention of burnout. That is, young professionals who learn effective skills for interpersonal relationships, effective problem solving strategies, and effective organization and time management strategies in addition to concepts, principles, and procedures, are likely to be better prepared for the challenges of the workforce that might otherwise lead to burnout. Additionally, every behavior analyst who becomes an effective supervisor focused on supervision as a relationship is more likely to serve as a buffer for burnout for those they supervise. Those who struggle with core professional skills or who become disconnected from their professional reinforcers and support community may be at risk of abandoning behavior analysis as a career. If a person has a true passion for behavior analysis and a life of service, but withdraws from the field due to burnout, the loss is a painful one for both the field and the person who leaves the field.

> *Those who struggle with core professional skills or who become disconnected from their professional reinforcers and support community may be at risk of abandoning behavior analysis as a career.*

Another common term, "self-care," is used in conjunction with preventing and treating professional and personal distress associated with imbalances between personal and professional life (i.e., lack of "work-life balance") and burnout (Burke, Dye & Hughey, 2016). Self-care refers to activities undertaken to enhance health, prevent disease, limit illness, and restore health (Australian Self-Medication Industry, 2009; Moryaga, Devries, & Wardle, 2015). These activities include psychological and emotional self-care, spiritual self-care, healthy eating, getting sufficient sleep, and exercising, among others. These self-care activities are often beneficial to the individual in both the personal and the professional context and are promoted for those in helping professions, including physicians, nurses, and counselors by multiple professional organizations including the World Health Organization (Moryaga, et al., 2015; WHO, 2009).

A particular form of self-care termed "mindfulness" or "mindfulness-based stress reduction" has been used effectively to reduce stress, workplace anger, and various other symptoms of distress associated with burnout (McKay, Wood, & Brantley, 2007). It is noteworthy that many of these studies have been conducted with students in training, new professionals, or those who are training new professionals (Moryaga, et al, 2015; Shirey, 2007). These findings may suggest that poor self-care practices developed during professional training can carry over into the early years of one's career. Mindfulness practices such as meditation, self-reflection, and acceptance are designed to enhance ongoing awareness of sensory experiences, thoughts, feelings, somatic sensations, and behaviors to manage stress and release strong emotions often encountered in helping professions (Proulx, 2003; Shapiro, Brown, & Biegel, 2007; Shirey, 2007; Thomas, 2003). Finally, mindfulness practices also incorporate the principle of personal responsibility (McKay, Rogers, & McKay, 2003), such that the person practicing mindfulness accepts that they are responsible for their behavior, thoughts, and emotions. These practices have also appeared in behavior analytic approaches to psychotherapy in the form of Acceptance and Committtment Therapy. In this model, acceptance refers to experiencing the thoughts and emotions, and recognizing that attempts to avoid thoughts and emotions is the primary source of personal distress, as opposed to the behavior of others (Hayes, 2019). Along with personal responsibility comes the opportunity to develop coping, stress management, time management, and interpersonal strategies to improve stressful situations and your responses to those situations. This approach has been used to decrease burnout in substance abuse counselors (Hayes, et al., 2004) and government workers (Lloyd, Bond, & Flaxman, 2013),

Many of the activities associated with mindfulness and self-care are directly related to identifying and accessing your own personal reinforcers on a regular basis. As with professional reinforcers, the individual is the best source of information about their own personal reinforcers and access to those reinforcers lies squarely within their own responsibility. For example, one mindfulness strategy involves sitting quietly to attend to your own thoughts and replacing negative thoughts with healthier, more functional ones (Taylor, LeBlanc, & Nosik, 2018). The thought "I don't know how to connect to this difficult family" could be replaced with the thought "I care about this family and I am going to talk about my struggle with a colleague who may have good ideas for me." Another common strategy involves attending to the surrounding environment (e.g., the trees, sky, and chirping birds on your walk) and is referred to as "being present" (Brown & Ryan, 2003). This strategy is typically only practiced in an environment that is reinforcing. You are less likely to accept and mindfully attend to the environment sitting next to an open trash can, because that environment is unpleasant. That is, attending to your environment and experiences is not the only critical part of acceptance and mindfulness. If you are in an unpleasant environment, this may only make things worse. Another important part of mindfulness and self-care practices is maintaining contact with your reinforcers and attending to the reinforcing aspects of the experience. Increasingly, there are behavior analytic community training opportunities related to mindfulness practices for the human service professions online and as live events.

Although it may seem unlikely that a person would struggle to identify or access their own reinforcers, people who are struggling with burnout and stress may have difficulty doing so. For example, someone who is chronically sleep-deprived may forget how enjoyable it is to feel well-rested and clear-headed after a great night of sleep. It may be necessary to specifically attend to the fact that a nap is a preferred event that is enjoyable while you do it, preferably in a hammock, and enhances the enjoyment of the activies that follow it. Use Activity B as a self-reflection tool to help you identify personal life reinforcers and health-related practices that may have inadvertently been eliminated from the priority list. Notice that small moment-to-moment reinforcers are often the easiest to access once you remember that these bring you joy and that they are available with relatively little effort. Once you create your list, the skills learned from

Chapter 8 on organization and time management skills will be useful in working these activities back into your daily experience.

SUMMARY AND RECOMMENDED STRATEGIES FOR SUSTAINED CAREER ENGAGEMENT AND ENJOYMENT

A long and fulfilling career in any human services profession requires planning, self-monitoring, self-care, and thoughtful decision-making over the course of years and decades. The three greatest threats to that sustained, enjoyable career come early in the career (i.e., transitioning to the workforce, burnout), or throughout the career (i.e., loss of professional reinforcers, job boredom). Although the explicit purpose of this book is to explore strategies for enhancing supervison and mentoring relationships, you may also have noticed that the content of this book is designed to combat those threats. The list on the next two pges distills many of the recommended practices from this chapter and others that may help you to program for career resilience or to take action to reinvigorate your career enjoyment. Practice long and prosper!

> **Recommended Practices for Career Resilience and Enjoyment**
>
> 1. Engage in self-care for a healthier, more stress-free life.
>   a. Eat well, sleep well, exercise vigorously and take care of your personal relationships.
>   b. Notice your own stress level and examine your behavior as a contributor to or treatment for the stress. Practice mindfulness and savor your reinforcers.
>   c. Manage your time and stress.
>
> 2. Know your professional reinforcers and maintain access to them.
>   a. Create contingencies to support your continued engagement with the published literature and intellectually stimulating events such as conferences.
>   b. Select a work environment and a position that provides access to at least some of your professional reinforcers.
>   c. Carefully consider advancement opportunities in terms of whether the opportunity provides access to your professional reinforcers or removes them.
>   d. If you are from a non-dominant culture, find allies to support your enagement in all aspects of your workplace.
>   e. If you are from a non-dominant culture, protect the opportunity to engage in your cultural practices by communicating your needs for accommodations or advocating for more generally inclusive practices.
>   f. Periodically reassess your skills and professional reinforcers.
>   i. Make a pivot to re-energize your professional life. Seek a new opportunity that takes advantage of or builds on your prior experiences and skills.
>   ii. Take a sabbatical, working vacation, or explore a new experience in the field to build new skills.
>   iii. Prepare in advance for a career shift to serving a new population or developing new competencies.
>   iv. Get involved in professional organizations and communities.

3. Prevent or Address Burnout
    a. Monitor for burnout (e.g., emotional exhaustion; cynicism, detachment and callousness; and feeling of ineffectiveness).
        i. When stress and demands are high and access to reinforcers is limited, reflect on how your behavior and your environment contribute to the outcome. Change your own behavior or choose a different work environment without losing the reinforcers associated with the field.
    b. Seek the support of your supervisor or professional community if you have one. If you don't have one, seek a mentor or community of practice.

Activity A
Identifying Your Preferred Work Activities

Use this activity to help you identify preferred work activities, plan to access them, and try to identify other similar activities that may also be reinforcing.

1. Perceived Preferences: Make a list of the things that you think you love to do at work.

2. Choices: Make a list of the things that you consistently choose to do at work. These should be things that you choose to do if all your tasks were completed, or things you would freely volunteer to do. In other words, how would you choose to allocate your time at work if you could? Don't' work too much about the things that you *have* to do at work, unless those are also things that you also choose to do.

3. Compare: Look at the lists from step 1 and 2. How much overlap is there? Are you an accurate reporter of the things you like to do in the professional setting? Refine your list of preferred work activities as many times as needed.

4. Reflect: Once you have a good list of work activities you identify as preferred, spend some time thinking and writing about the features of those activities that make them preferred (problem solving, creating new things, spending time with others, spending time alone, contacting the literature).

5. Plan: Review your list and indicate how often you get to engage in your preferred activities (daily, weekly, monthly). Is it possible to ensure that you access at least some of the activities daily or weekly? Review your list and your calendar and see if you can add in more time doing the things that you love. For example, if you love collaborating with other clinicians, but only get to do that intermittently (i.e., when a problem arises), consider if you can find one hour once a month to calendar for planned collaboration time.

6. Expand: Now go back to each preferred activity and come up with at three other activities that are similar, in terms of reinforcing properties. For example, if you included clinical problem solving you might identify: 1) problem solving ethical dilemmas; 2) conducting systems diagnostics; and 3) strategic business planning as three other similar activities that you might be able to engage in to increase access to reinforcement in the work setting.

Activity B
Identifying Your Personal Reinforcers

Use this activity to help you identify your personal reinforcers, evaluate how frequently you are accessing them, and planning how to increase access to them. There are some activities listed to get you thinking and some empty spaces to add in more. Use the "Current Frequency of Access" column to indicate how often you access these activities (e.g., daily, weekly, almost never, never) and then use the "Plans for Accessing or Increasing Access" column to set goals for adding these activities into your schedule, or increasing how frequently they appear. For example, if you love to work out, but find that you are only working out sporadically, you could plan to schedule workout times with a friend, take a call that fits your schedule, or get an app that allows you to work out at home and has a built-in system for sending reminders and tracking progress.

Activity	Current Frequency	Plans for Accessing or Increasing Access
cooking		
crocheting/knitting		
eating your favorite treat		
gardening		
going for a walk or hike		
going out to eat		
going to a museum		
hanging out with family/friends		
hanging out with pet (cat, dog, horse, potbelly pig)		
learning to do something new/taking a class		
listening to music		
painting		

playing a musical instrument		
playing board games		
playing video games		
reading a book		
riding a bike		
taking a bath		
visiting a bookstore		
volunteering		
walking the dog		
watching a movie		
working out		

Chapter 13

Be Kind to Yourself: Failures and Sucesses are Teachers

Every new experience brings its own maturity and a greater clarity of vision.
—Indira Gandhi

Throughout this book, we suggest that the supervisory experience is best viewed as a relationship. Healthy relationships are characterized by intention, action, progress, and respect. The ripple effects of a supervisory relationship are large and important. Both the supervisor and the supervisee may be changed as a result. This book provides a guide for the supervisor in beginning, nurturing, and expanding healthy supervisory and mentoring relationships. In doing so, supervisees and mentees will hopefully learn how to positively affect the lives of their clients and their own future supervisees and mentees.

Each chapter of this book focuses on core lessons with supporting illustrations and resources to build and maintain strong supervisory relationships:

- Supervision is best viewed as a collaborative relationship.
- Supervision quality and effectiveness will affect an individual's overall development.
- Supervision quality and effectiveness will affect clients and caregivers.
- Supervision quality and effectiveness will affect the development of our field.
- Supervisory practices will be a result of many influences over time.
- Reflecting on your past and current influences will shape your supervisory practices.
- Diversity brings opportunities for growth and progress in a supervisory relationship.
- Culture should be explicitly considered and embraced within the supervisory relationship.
- For both technical and professional skills, effective supervision is competency-based.
- In our field, supervision begins with building competency in BACB Task List skills.
- Learning how to learn from experts and how to effectively self-manage promotes growth.
- Knowing what you know and don't know is important.
- The highly effective supervisor problem solves and teaches this skill to their supervisees.
- Organization and time management are strong predictors of career success and should be explicitly taught to supervisees.
- Care and compassion for the wellbeing of others drives high quality supervision and services for clients and families.
- Positive influence and collaborative outcomes increase with strong interpersonal skills.
- Supervision that is guided by monitoring and evaluation will be more effective.
- Supervision is a never-ending learning-oriented process, full of challenges and growth.

We offer these lessons and insights from decades spent supervising others. Many of the lessons were, in fact, lessons learned the hard way. That is, at some point(s) we failed to do these things or did them poorly and people suffered as a result. Each of us was a new supervisor at one point and none of us is an optimal supervisor yet. As we discussed early in the preface of the book, being an effective supervisor and mentor to young professionals is akin to yoga or a martial art. You never achieve perfect balance or perfect mastery. You will never be a perfect supervisor. The joy and fulfillment provided by guiding and teaching others comes from the fact that the experience changes you and helps you grow.

The view backward showed you all the twists and turns your life had taken, all the contingencies and chances, the random elements of good luck and bad luck that made up one person's existence.
—William Boyd

The final lessons offered in this book are ones that we found extremely valuable in the process of working together as supportive colleagues: a) be kind to yourself about your past mistakes; and b) take pride in your past successes. We each offer our own stories of professional development to illustrate a commitment to self-reflection, ethical self-care, and responsible action. These stories take the form of a letter of caring advice to our past selves. Our "mature" selves reflect on our accomplishments, errors, and growth along the way. Although this book is not of the science fiction genre, we ask you to suspend disbelief a bit and read these letters as if our past selves could actually open them for counsel and support in a time of need (i.e., open this at your low point). In fact, the process of writing these letters and this book has done far more for our current selves than any of these letters could do for our past selves.

Dear young Shahla,

I am writing you at the point that you have started to train, supervise and mentor people who can make important changes in the lives of others. For many decades I have been watching you develop. It's good that you like to analyze your experiences. This will help you reflect, not only on supervisory processes and outcomes, but also about meaning. Meaning is important: it is what makes life matter—both to you and to those you serve across your lifespan.

You started this journey at the dining room table with mom and dad, listening to them talk about community activism and watching them participate in movements to create change in in the world. Early on, as is the case with community activism, you learned that it is a collaborative endeavor. You also came to understand that a life should have a mission. Your mission turned into a continuation of your parents' dream—helping build an inclusive world that cares for the well-being of everyone—regardless of income, social status or identity. You were lucky to figure this out early on and will be blessed with a sense of purpose through the years.

As you went through formal training and supervision, the majority of your supervisors were excellent models. You tended, and still tend, to be attracted and work better with supervisors who focus on principles, general guidelines, and allowing space (within ethical boundaries) for you to figure out how to better perform in a given context. You also need to be able to move quickly once you have mastered something and be given new problems as soon as possible. It has taken a while for you to understand your best learning environments. It is also hard for you to be able to communicate when you are uncomfortable with supervision. Unfortunately, both you and some of your supervisors have suffered as a result. Relationships are bi-directional. Keep learning to listen and to talk through differences. Understanding that people have different experiences and values will help you learn about how to create inclusive environments. You will learn a lot building collaborations. Over time, this will become one of your central areas of focus.

The more responsibility you are given, the more you realize that an intervention is only as effective, kind, and meaningful as the supporting supervisory systems and institutional structures. This is a hard lesson. Systems and structures can be hard to change. You like solving problems, but problems can become heavy and overwhelming. There are a few things that might help you with the heaviness:

1) As a supervisor, you are a model for hope, competence, and persistence. When you find you can't be those things, be a good model for taking a break and regrouping until you can jump back in and be part of the solution, not part of the problems.

2) Well chosen, simple solutions can leverage incredible change in systems—don't feel the solutions have to match the complexity

of troubled educational or healthcare systems. Strive to develop simple and doable procedures that are transformative.

3) Keep your purpose up front and center. Systematically teach, supervise, and mentor in the context of the outcomes you and your colleagues cherish; meaningful and valued changes in the lives of the people you serve. In doing so, you and your colleagues will keep learning new ways to do it better.

Sweet Shahla, you are young and optimistic. There will be periods when you become jaded. Both you and the people around you will suffer great loss and pain. People you care for and serve will be hurt in unimaginable ways. Humans will behave badly. At this point in your career, you respond to things in black and white and are disappointed in yourself and others. This is part of life's journey. These situations will teach you compassion and allow you to build wisdom. Suffering offers precious learning opportunities, but they won't feel like it. Take time to pray, meditate, and find communities that focus on brave and loving actions to solve personal and societal problems. What happens in your personal life, your professional life, and on our planet will affect you in different ways. Part of what I want to ask is that you not give up. Strive to learn from it all and build a coherent life that is based on a belief in love.

While it is important to be responsible, I want to ask you to not always be so serious. Enjoy the ride. Amidst the hard times are so many beautiful people and adventures. Remember to live with joy. And, as one of your dearest teachers will remind you, remember to pass all that learning on. That is one of the best things about supervision and mentoring. It is a chance to pass on our collective skills, wisdom, and joy.

With deep affection and love,

An older, hopefully gentler, and wiser, Shahla

Dear young Linda,

I write this letter from the vantage point of decades of experience that you will soon have. If you are reading this letter, it means that you reached a point in your career where you have struggled or failed, and you feel like you have let someone down. It is very likely that the people whom you feel you have let down are your students or supervisees and… yourself. I offer you these words of support and comfort with hope that they will assist you in picking yourself up, dusting yourself off, offering sincere apologies, and getting right back at the valuable mission you have chosen to accept.

First, remember that your boundless energy and enthusiasm for almost everything is a great strength. Your curiosity and willingness to try what others might consider impossible will be a hallmark of your career and of your life. This same quality often leads you to commit to too many things. In the words of Nemo's father, "you think you can do these things, but you can't." Well actually, you can! You are going to be amazed at what you accomplish in the span of 30 or more years. However, your self-created workload and the corresponding stress sometimes get the better of you. The bad news is that stressed, impulsive, grouchy Linda sometimes breaks free of the chain and is unkind to those around her, communicating a spoken or unspoken message of disappointment or frustration. The somewhat better news is that you will have many opportunities to practice making wiser choices and to improve your apologies. Remember to apologize to yourself as well as others and to allow yourself to make mistakes. That insatiable curiosity and enthusiasm will serve you well as you learn from your mistakes and become a better supervisor. Realizing that imperfect can be a synonym for your own "special brand of awesome" is going to allow you to appreciate the community of people around you. It will also set you up to write a book on supervision one day, as if you knew the good stuff all along.

Second, take pride in your commitment to your professional mission and relish the opportunities that you have to inspire others to do the same. You choose positions that involve teaching and supervising because you want to share your mission of improving the lives of those who are vulnerable. Others may not realize how much you wanted to be the one directly serving clients rather than experiencing only vicarious reinforcement of client success. Sometimes you came across as bossy or impossible to please, but you still managed to convey that you care deeply about your profession and "your people." Over the years, you accept a broader mission of preparing others to develop their own values and pursue their own professional goals. You learn the value of strengthening others by teaching them how to learn and succeed, instead of just teaching them the specifics of the day. Your first several students experience the brunt of your fear that the teaching and supervising might not be worth having given up direct clinical work. Take heart, because these people are going to make you tremendously proud, at least in part because you inspired them to do so. Be grateful for them and thank them for being in your professional life. Remember that you are building your professional extended family. Treat them as if you want to be connected to them forever!

Third, and perhaps most importantly, breathe and let things be okay without you. Early on, you experience supervision as a torment of answers that you might not have or questions that the supervisee might not know to ask. As a result, you tend to give direct answers, solve problems for people, and worry too much about mistakes that might happen if you are not there to prevent them or fix them. You are going to recognize how capable and willing to learn people are, just as your early supervisors recognized those same qualities in you. Focus on teaching others to solve their own problems and help them become their own best heroes and self-managers.

There is a chance that you still cannot take a compliment, so I will keep this brief… it is worth it and you turn out pretty darn good, kid. They all do.

Most sincerely,

Your wiser, happier, future self

Dear back-in-the-day Tyra,

I have this opportunity to write to you from this current place; a place strengthened by over twenty-five years of experience working in rich and diverse contexts with some of the smartest and most skilled individuals in our field. I have this opportunity to reach back across the years to fortify, encourage, and soothe you. You have generally not sought out advice, sometimes to your detriment, so I have no reason to believe that my words would provide comfort or prove instructive. I will keep this brief as I find myself, uncharacteristically, without words.

It's ok to take the long way, the bumpy way, the way made more difficult with vines and downed trees that crisscross your path. Your crooked path to where you end up does not make you less prepared or less skilled than others, it gives you perspective, rich experiences, and loads of learning. Your strengths will always be your persistence and your ability to find beauty in the smallest thing. Spoiler alert—you make a lot of mistakes along the way, and sometimes you hurt people. Remember to find the beauty and growth in each mistake. Remember to find the grace to fix the hurt and to honor that person by not hurting others in the same way moving forward. Gravitate to people who, like the rain and sun, will nourish you. Some will be your mentors, most will be your students and supervisees. It takes you a number of years to realize and articulate your truth, your highest value, and that is that you wish more than anything to simply be able to make each interaction, each situation you encounter, slightly better when you leave than when you got there. This is not a goal, so you will never reach it, but it will help you move forward, especially when things are difficult.

Cheers,

An older, much more tired, but still wildly distracted by a perfect cherry blossom or fallen crimson leaf, future self

CONCLUSION

Each of us has had different winding paths, and each has made a difference in the lives of the many people that we have mentored and supervised and who have mentored and supervised us. Our lessons to our younger selves are meant to provide you with examples to strengthen your path forward and help you create your own commitment to self-reflection, ethical self-care, and responsible action. To that end, we offer you one last activity. We ask that you write a letter to your future selves.

To prepare a letter to your future self, it will be helpful to review the lessons of this book in a very specific way. First, go through Chapters 4 through 10 and make a list of the main points of each chapter that apply to your intended areas of practice. Next, look at your mentor tree activity and consider your influencers. Note what was important about each of these people and qualities they have that you would like to develop in yourself as a supervisor. After that, interview a few older, more experienced people whom you admire. Try to select people from within and outside of your field. Explore with them the lessons that they have learned over the course of their professional and personal lives. Focus on areas highlighted throughout the book. Finally, compose your letter to your future self, taking into consideration the lessons given throughout our book. Combine this information with careful consideration of your strengths, areas for growth, and your life's purpose and mission. It is our hope that this exercise offers you a way to integrate the lessons we have offered here and to focus your direction and goals as a supervisor.

We wish you well on your supervisory journey. We hope that we have helped make it more effective and enjoyable.

Walking, I am listening to a deeper way. Suddenly all my ancestors are behind me. Be still, they say. Watch and listen. You are the result of the love of thousands.

—Linda K. Hogan
Writer in Residence for the Chickasaw Nation

References

Ala'i-Rosales, S., Ferris, K. & Fabrizio, M. (February, 2014). *Forming culturally responsive parent-provider relationships in behavior analytic practices.* Organization for Autism Research and Learning. Seattle, Washington.

Allen, K. A., & Warzak, W. J. (2000). The problem of parental nonadherence in clinical behavior analysis: Effective treatment is not enough. *Journal of Applied Behavior Analysis, 33*, 373–391. doi: 10.1901/jaba.2000.33-373

Allen, D. A. (2015). *Getting things done: The art of stress-free productivity (Revised).* London, UK: Penguin Publishing.

Allen, D. A., & Hall, B. (2019). *the getting things done workbook: 10 moves to stress-free productivity.* Platkus.

Algiraigri, A. H. (2014). Ten tips for receiving feedback effectively in clinical practice. *Medical Education Online, 19*(1), 25141. doi:10.3402/meo.v19.25141

Aljadeff-Abergel, E., Peterson, S. M., Wiskirchen, R. R., Hagen, K. K., & Cole, M. L. (2017). Evaluating the temporal location of feedback: Providing feedback following performance vs. prior to performance. *Journal of Organizational Behavior Management, 37*(2), 171–195.

Anderson, D. C., Crowell, C. R., Hantula, D. A., & Siroky, L. M. (1988). Task clarification and individual performance posting for improving cleaning in a student-managed university bar. *Journal of Organizational Behavior Management, 9*, 73–90. doi:10.1300/J075v09n02_06

Angell, A. M., Frank, G., & Solomon, O. (2016). Latino families' experiences with autism services: Disparities, capabilities, and occupational justice. *OTJR: Occupation, Participation and Health, 36*(4), 195–203.

Anderson, K. (1994). *Making meetings work: How to plan and conduct effective meetings.* West Des Moines, IA: American Media

Ansoff, H. I. (1965). *Corporate strategy: An analytic approach to business policy for growth and expansion.* New York: McGraw-Hill.

Arya, K., Margaryan, A., & Collis, B. (2003). Culturally sensitive problem solving activities for multinational corporations. *TechTrends, 47*, 40–49.

Attoe, C., Lavelle, M., Sherwali, S., Rimes, K., Jabur, Z. (2019). Student interprofessional mental health simulation (SIMHS): Evaluating the impact on medical and nursing students, and clinical psychology trainees. *The Journal of Mental Health Training, Education, and Practice, 15* (1), 46–58. doi:10.1108/JMHTEP-06-2018-0037

Augilar, A. (2015). California Partnership to End Violence https://www.cpedv.org/post/intersectionality-privilege-oppression-and-tactics-abuse). accessed March 10, 2020.

Austin, J. (2019). *What have you tried or seen others do to effectively build psychological safety?* Retrieved November 11, 2019 from https://reachingresults.com/psychological-safety/.

Australian Self-Medication Industry (2009). *Self care in Australia: a roadmap toward greater personal responsibility in managing health.* Prepared by the Australian Self-Medication Industry. Retrieved on September 12, 2012 from http://www.asmi com.au/self-care/What-Is-Self-Care.aspx

Axe, J. B., Phelan, S. H., & Irwin, C. L. (2019). Empirical evaluations of Skinner's problem solving analysis. *The Analysis of Verbal Behavior, 35*(1), 39–56. doi.org/10.1007/s40616-018-0103-4.

Baer, D. M., Wolf, M. M., & Risley, T. R. (1968). Some current dimensions of applied behavior analysis. *Journal of Applied Behavior Analysis, 1,* 91–97. doi: 10.1901/jaba.1968.1–91

Baer, D. M., Wolf, M. M., & Risley, T. R. (1987). Some still-current dimensions of applied behavior analysis. *Journal of Applied Behavior Analysis, 20,* 313–327.

Bailey, J. & Burch, M. (2010). *25 essential skills & strategies for the professional behavior analyst.* New York, NY: Routledge.

Bailey, J., Burch, M. (2016). *Ethics for behavior analysts.* New York: Routledge, https://doi.org/10.4324/9781315669212

Bandura, A. B. (1997). *Self-efficacy: The exercise of control.* New York: W. H. Freeman.

Barnes-Holmes, D. (2018). A commentary on the student-supervisor relationship: A shared journey of discovery. *Behavior Analysis in Practice, 11,* 174–176.

Baron-Cohen, S., Leslie, A. M., & Frith, U. (1985). Does the child with autism have a theory of mind? *Cognition, 21,* 37–46. https://doi.org/10.1016/0010-0277(85)90022-8

Barrera, I., & Kramer, L. (2009). *Using skilled dialogue to transform challenging interactions: Honoring identity, voice, & connection.* Baltimore, MD: Paul H. Brookes.

Barrera, I., & Kramer, L. (2017). *Skilled dialogue: Authentic communication and collaboration across diverse perspectives.* Balboa Press.

Bassey, M. O. (2016). Culturally responsive teaching: Implications for educational justice. *Education Sciences, 6*(4), 35.

Beaulieu, L., Addington, J., & Almeida, D. (2019). Behavior analysts' training and practices regarding cultural diversity: The case for culturally competent care. *Behavior Analysis in Practice, 12*(3), 557–575.

Beavers, G., Iwata, B. A., & Lerman, D. C. (2013). Thirty years of research on the functional analysis of problem behavior. *Journal of Applied Behavior Analysis, 46,* 1–21. doi.org/10.1002/jaba.30

Becerra, L. A., Sellers, T. P. & Contreras, B. P. (2020). Maximizing the conference experience: Tips to effectively navigate academic conferences early in professional careers. *Behavior Analysis in Practice, 13:* 479–491. https://doi.org/10.1007/s40617-019-00406-w

Beene, N. (2019). Letter to the Editor: One perspective on diversity in ABA. *Behavior Analysis in Practice, 12*(4), 899–901.

Behavior Analyst Certification Board. (2014*). Professional and ethical compliance code for behavior analysts.* Littleton, CO: Author.

Behavior Analyst Certification Board. (2017). *BCBA/BCaBA task list (5th ed.).* Littleton, CO: Author.

Behavior Analyst Certification Board. (2018a). *US employment demand for behavior analysts: 2010–2017.* Littleton, CO: Author.

Behavior Analyst Certification Board. (2018b). *A summary of ethics violations and code-enforcement activities: 2016–2017.* Littleton, CO: Author. Retrieved from: www.bacb.com/wp-content/uploads/180606_CodeEnforcementSummary.pdf

Behavior Analyst Certification Board. (2018c). *Supervision training curriculum outline (2.0)* Littleton, CO: Author.

Behavior Analyst Certification Board. (2018d). *RBT ethics code.* Littleton, CO: Author.

Behavior Analyst Certification Board. (2019). *US employment demand for behavior analysts: 2010–2017.* Littleton, CO: Author.

Behavior Analyst Certification Board. (2020). *BCBA fieldwork requirement.* Littleton, CO: Author.

Behavior Analyst Certification Board. (2020, June 08). *Supervision and training.* https://www.bacb.com/supervision-and-training/

Behavior Analyst Certification Board. (n.d). *BACB certificant data.* Retrieved from https://www.bacb.com/BACB-certificant-data

Belisle, J., Rowsey, K. E., & Dixon, M. R. (2016). The use on in situ behavioral skills training to improve staff implementation of the PEAK relational training system. *Journal of Organizational Behavior Management, 36,* 71–79. doi:10.1080/01608061,2016,1152210

Bertone, M. P., Meessen, B., Clarysse, G., Hercot, D., Kelley, A., Kafando, Y., Lange, I.,Pfaffmann, J., Ridde, V., Sieleunou, I., & Witter, S. (2013). Assessing communities of practice in health policy: A conceptual framework as a first step towards empirical research. *Health Research Policy and Systems, 11,* 39. https://doi.org/10.1186/1478-4505-11-39.

Betancourt, J. R., Green, A. R., & Carrillo, J. E. (2002). *Cultural competence in health care: Merging frameworks and practical approaches* (Vol. 576). New York, NY: Commonwealth Fund, Quality of Care for Underserved Populations.

Binder, C. (2016). Integrating organizational-cultural values with performance management. *Journal of Organizational Behavior Management, 36*(2–3), 185–201.

Blank, R., & Slipp, S. (1994). The white male: An endangered species? *Management Review, 83*(9), 27–33.

Blell, Z., Ala'i-Rosales. S., & Rosales-Ruiz, J. (2010). The effects of a supportive communication training workshop on the verbal behavior of behavior analysts. *Behavior and Social Issues, 19,* 144–166.

Bowe, M., & Sellers, T. P. (2018). Evaluating the Performance Diagnostic Checklist–Human Services to assess incorrect error-correction procedures by preschool paraprofessionals. *Journal of Applied Behavior Analysis, 51,* 166–176. https//doi.org: 10.1002/jaba.428

Bozosi, J. (2016). Applying grief theory to autism treatment. *Behavior Analysis Quarterly, 2*(1), 12–18.

Britton, L. N., & Cicoria, M. J. (2019). *Remote fieldwork supervision for BCBA® trainees.* Academic Press.

Brodhead, M. T. (2015). Maintaining professional relationships in an interdisciplinary setting: Strategies for navigating nonbehavioral treatment recommendations for individuals with autism. *Behavior Analysis in Practice, 8,* 70–78. doi: 10.1007/s40617-015-0042-7

Brodhead, M. T., Cox, D. J., & Quigley, S. P. (2018). *Practical ethics for effective treatment of autism spectrum disorder.* Academic Press.

Brown, B. (2012). *Daring greatly: How the courage to be vulnerable transforms the way we live, love, parent, and lead.* Penguin Group.

Brown, K. W., & Ryan, R. M. (2003). The benefits of being present: Mindfulness and its role in psychological well-being. *Journal of Personality and Social Psychology, 84,* 822–848. doi:10.1037/0022-3514.84.4.822

Buckner, M. O. (1992). New professionals in private practice. *The Counseling Psychologist, 20* (1), 10–16.

Burke, M. G., Dye, L., & Hughey, A. W. (2016). Teaching mindfulness for the self-care and well-being of student affairs professionals. *College Student Affairs Journal, 34* (3), 93–107.

Callahan, K., Foxx, R. M., Swierczynski, A., Aerts, X., Mehta, S., McComb, M. E., Nichols, S.M., Segal, G., Donald, A., Sharma, R. (2019). Behavioral artistry: Examining the relationship between the interpersonal skills and effective practice repertoires of applied behavior analysis practitioners. *Journal of Autism and Developmental Disorders, 49,* 3557–3570. https://doi.org/10.1007/s10803-019-04082-1.

Campbell, R. L., Svenson, L. W. (1992). Perceived level of stress among university undergraduate students in Edmonton, Canada. *Perceptual and Motor Skills 75*(2), 552–554.

Carnegie, D. (1936). *How to win friends and influence people.* Simon and Schuster.

Carr, J. E., & Briggs, A. M. (2010). Strategies for making regular contact with the scholarly literature. *Behavior Analysis in Practice, 3,* 13–18.

Carr, J. E., Wilder, D. A., Majdalany, L., Mathisen, D., & Strain, L. A. (2013). An assessment based solution to a human-service employee performance problem. *Behavior Analysis in Practice, 6,* 16–32.

Catania, A. C. (2012). *Learning* (5th ed.). Cornwall-on-Hudson, NY: Sloan Publishing.

Cihon, T. M., & Mattaini, M. A. (2019). Emerging cultural and behavioral systems science. *Perspectives on Behavior Science, 42*(4), 699–711.

Clark, H. B., Wood, R., Kuehnel, T., Flanagan, S., Mosk, M., & Northup, J. T. (1985). Preliminary validation and training of supervisory interactional skills. *Journal of Organizational Behavior Management, 7,* 95–115.

Claessens, B. J. C., Van Eerde, W., Rutte, C. G., & Roe, R. A. (2007). A review of the time management literature. *Personnel Review, 36,* 255–275.

Cloke, K. & Goldsmith, J. (2011). *Resolving conflicts at work: Ten strategies for everyone on the job.* San Francisco, CA: Josey Bass.

Coll, R. K., Zegwaard, K., & Hodges, D. (2002). Science and technology stakeholders' ranking of graduate competencies part 2: Students perspective. *Asia Pacific Journal of Cooperative Education, 3,* 19–28.

Conners, B., Johnson, A., Duarte, J., Murriky, R., & Marks, K. (2019). Future directions of training and fieldwork in diversity issues in applied behavior analysis. *Behavior Analysis in Practice, 12,* 1–10.

Cooper J. O., Heron T. E., Heward, W. L. (2020). *Applied behavior analysis* (3rd ed.). Upper Saddle River, NJ: Pearson.

Coulehan, J. L., Platt, F. W., Egener, B., Frankel, R., Lin, C. T., Lown, B., & Salazar, W. H. (2001)."Let me see if I have this right...": Words that help build empathy. *Annals of Internal medicine, 135*(3), 221–227.

Cox, D. J. (2012). From interdisciplinary to integrated care of the child with autism: The essential role for a code of ethics. *Journal of Autism and Developmental Disorders*, 42(12), 2729–2738. https://doi.org/10.1007/s10803-012-1530-z.

Critchfield, T. S., Doepke, K. J., Epting, L. K., Becirevic, A., Reed, D. D., Fienup, D., & Eccot, C. L. (2017). Normative emotional responses to behavior analysts or how not to use words to win friends and influence people. *Behavior Analysis in Practice*, 10, 97–106. https://doi.org/10.1007/s40617-016-0161-9

Cross, T. L. (1989). Towards a culturally competent system of care: A monograph on effective services for minority children who are severely emotionally disturbed.

Curry, S. M., Gravina, N. E., Sleiman, A. A., & Richard, E. (2019). The effects of engaging in rapport-building behaviors on productivity and discretionary effort. *Journal of Organizational Behavior Management*, 39(3–4), 213–226.

Daniels, A. C., & Bailey, J. S. (2014). *Performance management: Changing behavior that drives organizational effectiveness.* Atlanta, GA: Aubrey Daniels International, Inc.

Danso, R. (2018). Cultural competence and cultural humility: A critical reflection on key cultural diversity concepts. *Journal of Social Work*, 18(4), 410–430.

Day-Vines, N. L., Booker Ammah, B., Steen, S., Arnold, K. M. (2018). Getting comfortable with discomfort: Preparing counselor trainees to broach racial, ethnic, and cultural factors with clients during counseling. *International Journal for the Advancement of Counselling*, 40(2), 89–104. doi:10.1007/s10447-017-9308-9

Derksen, F., Bensing, J., & Lagro-Janssen, A. (2013). Effectiveness of empathy in general practice: A systematic review. *British Journal of General Practice*, 63(606), 76–84. https://doi.org/10.3399/bjgp13X660814

DiAngelo, R. (2011). White Fragility. *International Journal of Critical Pedagogy*, 3 (3), 54–70.

Di Blasi, Z., Harkness, E., Edzard, E., Georgiou, A., & Kleijnen, J. (2001). Influence of context effects of health outcomes: A systematic review. *The Lancet*, 357, 757–762.

Dishon-Berkovits, M., & Koslowsky, M. (2002). Determinants of employee punctuality. *The Journal of Social Psychology*, 142(6), 723–739.

Ditzian, K., Wilder, D. A., King, A., & Tanz, J. (2015). An evaluation of the Performance Diagnostic Checklist–Human Services to assess an employee performance problem in a center-based autism treatment facility. *Journal of Applied Behavior Analysis*, 48, 199–203. doi:10.1002/jaba.171

Donahoe, J. W., & Palmer, D. C. (2004). *Learning and complex behavior.* Boston: Allyn & Bacon.

Dounavi, K., Fennell, B., & Early, E. (2019). Supervision for certification in the field of applied behavior analysis: Characteristics and relationships with job satisfaction, burnout, work demands, and support. *International Journal of Environmental Research and Public Health*, 16(12), 2098. doi: 10.3390/ijerph16122098

Dreyfus, S. E., & Dreyfus, H. L. (1980). *A five-stage model of the mental activities involved in directed skill acquisition.* (No. ORC-80-2). California University Berkeley Operations Research Center.

Dreyfus, S. E. (2004). The five-stage model of adult skill acquisition. *Bulletin of Science, Technology & Society*, 24(3), 177–181. https://doi.org/10.1177/0270467604264992

Dunst, C. J., Trivette, C. M., & Hamby, C. W. (2010). Meta-analysis of the effectiveness of four adult learning methods and strategies. *International Journal of Continuing Education and Lifelong Learning*, 3, 91–112.

Eby, L. T., Rhodes, J. E., & Allen, T. D. (2007). Definition and evolution of mentoring. In T. D. Allen & L. T. Eby (Eds.), *The Blackwell handbook of mentoring: A multiple perspectives approach* (pp. 7–20). Malden: Blackwell Publishing.

Edmondson, A. (1999). Psychological safety and learning behavior in work teams. *Administrative Science Quarterly*, 44, 350–383. doi: 10.2307/2666999

Ehrlich, R.J., Nosik, M.R., Carr, J.E., & Wine, B. (2020). Teaching employees how to receive feedback: A preliminary investigation. *Journal of Organizational Behavior Management.* Advanced online publication. https://doi.org/10.1080/01608061.2020.1746470

Ellis, J. E., & Glenn, S. S. (1995). Behavior analytic repertoires: Where will they come from and how can they be maintained? *The Behavior Analyst*, 18(2), 285–292.

Epstein, R., Campbell, T. L., Cohen-Cole, S. A., Whinney, I. R., & Smilkstein, G. (1993). Perspectives on patient-doctor communication. *The Journal of Family Practice*, 37, 377–388.

Ervin, N. E. (2008). Caseload management skills for improved efficiency. *The Journal of Continuing Education in Nursing*, 39(3), 127–132.

Expert. 2020. In *Merriam-Webster.com.* Retrieved April 14, 2020, from https://www.merriam-webster.com/dictionary/expert

Fawcett, S. B. (1991). Some values guiding community research and action. *Journal of Applied Behavior Analysis, 24*(4), 621–636.
Fiorenza, E. S. (1992). *But she said: Feminist practices of biblical interpretation*. Beacon Press.
Finch, D. J., Hamilton, L. K., Baldwin, R., Zehner, M. (2013). An exploratory study of factors affecting undergraduate employability. *Education & Training, 55*(7), 681–704. doi:10.1108/ET-07-2012-0077
Fisher-Borne, M., Cain, J.M., & Martin, S. L. (2015). From mastery to accountability: Cultural humility as an alternative to cultural competence. *Social Work Education, 34* (2), 165–181.
Fiske, K. E. (2017). *Autism and the family: Understanding and supporting parents and siblings.* New York, NY: Norton.
Fogarty, L. A., Curbow, B. A., Wingard, J. R., McDonnell, K., & Somerfield, M. R. (1999). Can 40 seconds of compassion reduce patient anxiety? *Journal of Clinical Oncology, 17*(1), 371–371.
Fong, E. H., & Tanaka, S. (2013). Multicultural alliance of behavior analysis standards for cultural competence in behavior analysis. *International Journal of Behavioral Consultation and Therapy, 8*(2), 17.
Fong, E. H., Catagnus, R. M., Brodhead, M. T., Quigley, S., & Field, S. (2016). Developing the cultural awareness skills of behavior analysts. *Behavior Analysis in Practice, 9*, 84–94. doi:10.1007/s40617-016-0111-6
Fong, E. H., Ficklin, S., & Lee, H. Y. (2017). Increasing cultural understanding and diversity in applied behavior analysis. *Behavior Analysis: Research and Practice, 17*(2), 103–113. doi:10.1037/bar0000076
Foxx, R. M. (1996). Translating the covenant: The behavior analyst as ambassador and translator. *The Behavior* Analyst, 19, 147–161.
Foxx, R. M. (1998). Twenty-five years of applied behavior analysis: Lessons learned. *Discriminanten, 4*, 13–31.
Fukuzawa, R., Joho, H., Maeshiro, T. (2015). Practice and experience of task management of university students: Case of University of Tsukuba, Japan. *Education for Information, 31*(3), 109–124. doi: 10.3233/EFI-150953
Garden, R.E. (2016). Creating a verbal community for describing emotional responses within a contingency lens: The effects of a brief training workshop, thesis; Denton, Texas. (digital.library.unt.edu/ark:/67531/metadc955041/: accessed February 11, 2019), University of North Texas Libraries, Digital Library, digital.library.unt.edu
Garza, K. L., McGee, H. M., Schenk, Y. A., & Wiskirchen, R. R. (2018). Some tools for carrying out a proposed process for supervising experience hours for aspiring Board Certified Behavor Analysts®. *Behavior Analysis in Practice, 11*, 62–70.
Geiger, K. A., Carr, J. E., & LeBlanc, L. A. (2010). Function-based treatments for escape-maintained problem behavior: A treatment selection model for practicing behavior analysts. *Behavior Analysis in Practice, 3*, 22–32.
George, D., Dixon, S., Stansal, E., Gelb, S. L., & Pheri, T. (2008). Time diary and questionnaire assessment of factors associated with academic and personal success among university undergraduates. *Journal of American College Health, 56*, 706–715.
Gianoumis, S., Seiverling, L., & Sturmey, P. (2012). The effects of behavioral skills training on correct teacher implementation of natural language paradigm teaching skills and child behavior. *Behavioral Interventions, 27*, 57–74. doi: 10.1002/bin.1334
Gibney, A., Moore, N., Murphy, F., O'Sullivan, S. (2011). The first semester of university life; 'Will I be able to manage it at all?' *Higher Education, 62*, 351–366. doi: 10.1007/s10734-010-9392-9
Gilbert, T. F. (2013). *Human competence: Engineering worthy performance*. Hoboken, NJ: John Wiley & Sons.
Gilligan, K.T., Luiselli, J.K., & Pace, G.M. (2007). Training paraprofessional staff to implement discrete trial instruction: Evaluation of a practical performance feedback intervention. *The Behavior Therapist, 30*, 63–66. doi: 10.1177/1088357612465120
Glago, K., Mastropieri, M. A., & Scruggs, T. E. (2009). Improving problem solving of elementary students with mild disabilities. *Remedial and Special Education, 30*, 372–380.
Global Autism Project Skills Corp (2020, June 08). *Skills corps: FAQs*. https://www.globalautismproject.org/skillcorps-faqs/
Goetz, J. L., & Simon-Thomas, E. (2017). The landscape of compassion: Definitions and scientific approaches. *The Oxford handbook of compassion science*, 3–16.
Gould, E., Tarbox, J., & Coyne, L. (2017). Evaluating the effects of acceptance and commitment training on the overt behavior of parents of children with autism. *Journal of Contextual Behavioral Science, 7*(1), 81–88. https://doi.org/10.1016/j.jcbs.2017.06.003
Gran-Moravec, M. B., & Hughes, C. M. (2005). Nursing time allocation and other considerations for staffing. *Nursing & Health Sciences 7*(2), 126–133.

Gravina, N. E., & Siers, B. P. (2011). Square pegs and round holes: Ruminations on the relationship between performance appraisal and performance management. *Journal of Organizational Behavior Management*, 31, 277–287. doi:10.1080/01608061.2011.619418

Gravina, N., Villacorta, J., Albert, K., Clark, R., Curry, S., & Wilder, D. (2018). A literature review of organizational behavior management interventions in human service settings from 1990 to 2016. *Journal of Organizational Behavior Management*, 38(23), 191–224. doi:10.1080/01608061.2018.1454872

Grow, L. L., Carr, J. E., & LeBlanc, L. A. (2009). Treatments for attention-maintained problem behavior: Empirical support and clinical recommendations. *Journal of Evidence-Based Practices for Schools*, 10, 70–92.

Häfner, A., Stock, A., Pinneker, L., & Ströhle, S. (2014). Stress prevention through a time management training intervention: An experimental study. *Educational Psychology*, 34, 403–416.

Häfner, A., Stock, A., & Oberst, V. (2015). Decreasing students' stress through time management training: An intervention study. *European Journal of Psychology of Education*, 30, 81–94. doi: 10.1007/s10212-014-0229-2

Hall, E. T., & Hall, T. (1959). *The silent language* (Vol. 948). Anchor books.

Hall, L. J., Grundon, G. S., Pope, C., & Romero, A. B. (2010). Training paraprofessionals to use behavioral strategies when educating learners with autism spectrum disorder across environments. *Behavioral Interventions*, 25, 37–51. doi:10.3109/17518423.2011.620577

Hantula, D. A. (2015). Job satisfaction: The management tool and leadership responsibility. *Journal of Organizational Behavior Management*, 35(1–2), 81–94.

Hardeman, R. R., Medina, E. M., & Kozhimannil, K. B. (2016). Structural racism and supporting black lives-the role of health professionals. *The New England journal of medicine*, 375(22), 2113–2115.

Hayes, S. C. (2019). *A Liberated Mind*. Penguin Random House.

Hayes, S. C., Bissett, R., Roget, N., Padilla, M., Kohlenberg, B. S., Fisher, G., Masuda, A., Pistorello, J., Rye, A. K., Berry, K., & Niccolls, R. (2004). The Impact of Acceptance and Commitment Training and Multicultural Training on the stigmatizing attitudes and professional burnout of substance abuse counselors, *Behavior Therapy*, 35, 821–836. http://dx.doi.org/10.1016/S0005-7894(04)80022-4

Hayes, S. A., & Watson, S. L. (2013). The impact of parenting stress: A meta-analysis of studies comparing the experience of parenting stress in parents of children with and without autism spectrum disorder. *Journal of Autism and Developmental Disorders*, 43(3), 629–642.

Henley, A. J., & DiGennaro Reed, F. D. (2015). Should you order the feedback sandwich? Efficacy of feedback sequence and timing. *Journal of Organizational Behavior Management*, 35, 321–335. doi:10.1080/01608061.2015.1093057

Henrich, J., Heine, S. J., & Norenzayan, A. (2010). The weirdest people in the world? *Behavioral and Brain Sciences*, 33(2–3), 61–83.

Hindle, T. (1998). *Managing meetings*. London, UK: DK.

Hoffman, D. E. & Tarzian, A. J. (2001). The girl who cried pain: A bias against women in the treatment of pain. *Journal of Law, Medicine & Ethics*, 29(10), 13–27.

Hojat, M., Louis, D., Markham, F., Wender, R., Rabinowitz, C., & Gonnella, J. (2011). Physician's empathy and clinical outcomes for diabetic patients. *Academic Medicine*, 86, 359–364. doi:10.1097/ACM.0b013e3182086fe1

Holth, P. (2008). What is a problem? Theoretical conceptions and methodological approaches to the study of problem solving. *European Journal of Behavior Analysis*, 9(2), 157–172.

Hood, J. H. (2013). *The "How To" Book of Meetings: Conducting Effective Meetings*. Adelaide, South Australia: Word Craft Global Pty, Limited.

Hook, J. N., Davis, D. E., Owen, J., Worthington Jr, E. L., & Utsey, S. O. (2013). Cultural humility: Measuring openness to culturally diverse clients. *Journal of Counseling Psychology*, 60(3), 353.

Howard, R., Rose, J., & Levenson, V. (2009). The psychological impact of violence on staff working with adults with intellectual disabilities. *Journal of Applied Research in Intellectual Disabilities*, 22, 538–548.

Howard, J. S., & Sparkman, C. (2019). Behavioral objectives that guide effective intervention. In J. E. Gerenser and M. A. Koenig (Eds), *ABA for SLPs: Interprofessional collaboration for autism support teams* (pp. 305–330). Baltimore, MD: Paul Brookes Publishing.

It's NOT mentor vs. sponsor –It's mentor THEN sponsor. Mentor Loop. Retrieved June, 08, 2020 from https://mentorloop.com/not-mentor-vs-sponsor-it-is-mentor-then-sponsor/

Jacobs, S. (2013). *The behavior breakthrough: Leading your organization to a new competitive advantage*. Greenleaf Book Group.

Jerome, J., Kaplan, H., & Sturmey, P. (2014). The effects of in-service training alone and in service training with feedback on data collection accuracy for direct-care staff working with individuals with intellectual disabilities. *Research in Developmental Disabilities, 35,* 529–536. doi: 10.1016/j.ridd.2013.11.009

Jex, S. M., & Elacqua, T. C. (1999). Time management as a moderator of relations between stressors and employee strain. *Work and Stress, 13,* 182–191.

Johnston, J. M., (2016). Necessity and opportunity: The 1-year master's ABA program at Auburn University. *The Behavior Analyst, 39,* 135–142. doi: 10.1007/s40614-016-0057-6

Johnston, J. M., & Shook, G. L. (2001). A national certification program for behavior analysts. *Behavioral Interventions, 16*(2), 77–85.

Johnson, D. A., Casella, S. E., McGee, H., & Lee, S. C. (2014). The use and validation of preintervention diagnostic tools in organizational behavior management. *Journal of Organizational Behavior Management, 34,* 104–121. doi.org/10.1080/01608061.2014.914009

Johnston, J. M., Mellichamp, F. H., Shook, G. L., & Carr, J. E. (2014). Determining BACB examination content and standards. *Behavior Analysis in Practice, 7,* 3–9.

Jones, E. A., & Carr, E. G. (2004). Joint attention in children with autism: Theory and intervention. *Focus on Autism and Other Developmental Disabilities, 19,* 13–26.

Karver, M. S., Handelsman, J. B., Fields, S., & Bickman, L. (2006). Meta-analysis of therapeutic relationship variables in youth and family therapy: The evidence for different relationship variables in the child and adolescent treatment outcome literature. *Clinical Psychology Review, 26,* 50–65. doi: 10.1016/j.cpr.2005.09.001

Kaya H. A., Kaya N. A., Pallos, A. O., & Küçük, L. (2012). Assessing time-management skills in terms of age, gender, and anxiety levels: A study on nursing and midwifery students in Turkey. *Nurse Education in Practice, 12,* 284–288.

Kazemi, E., & Carter, C. (2019). *Conflict resolution skills for behavior analysts.* Workshop presented at the Behavior Analyst Leadership Council, September 2019, Shelton, CT.

Kazemi, E., Rice, B., & Adzhyan, P. (2018). *Fieldwork and supervision for behavior analysts: A handbook.* Springer Publishing Company.

Keating, A. (2002). Forging El Mundo Zurdo: Changing ourselves, changing the world. In Anzaldúa, G. and Keating A.(eds.), *This bridge we call home: Radical visions for transformation.* New York: Routledge.

Kelly, W. E. (2002). Harnessing the river of time: A theoretical framework of time use efficiency with suggestions for counselors. *Journal of Employment Counseling, 39*(1), 12–21.

Kim, N., & Whitehead, D. (Eds.). (2009). Elisabeth Schüssler Fiorenza and feminist theologies/studies in religion. *Journal of Feminist Studies in Religion, 25*(1), 1–18.

Koegel, L. K., Koegel, R. L., Harrower, J. K., & Carter, C. M. (1999). Pivotal response intervention: An overview of the approach. *Journal of the Association of Persons with Severe Handicaps, 24,* 174–185.

Kolb, S. M., & Stuart, S. K. (2005). Active problem solving: A model for empowerment. *Teaching Exceptional Children, 38*(2), 14–20.

Kornack, J., Cernius, A., & Persicke, A. (2019). The diversity is in the details: Unintentional language discrimination in the practice of applied behavior analysis. *Behavior Analysis in Practice, 12,* 879–886.

Kruger, J., & Dunning, D. (1999). Unskilled and unaware of it: How difficulties in recognizing one's own incompetence lead to inflated self-assessments. *Journal of Personality and Social Psychology, 77*(6), 1121–1134.

Kruse, K. (2014, August 12). *How to receive feedback and criticism* [Blog post]. Retrieved from https://www.forbes.com/sites/kevinkruse/2014/08/12/how-to-receive-feedback-and-criticism/#78cb6e5e7c3f

LaFrance, D. L., Weiss, M. J., Kazemi, E., Gerenser, J., & Dobres, J. (2019). Multidisciplinary teaming: Enhancing collaboration through increased understanding. *Behavior Analysis in Practice, 12,* 709–726.

Lau, R. S. & Cobb, A. T. (2010). Understanding the connections between relationship conflict and performance: The intervening roles of trust and exchange. *Journal of Organizational Behavior Management, 31,* 898–917. doi:10.1002/job.674

Leach, D. J., Rogelberg, S. J., Warr, P. B., & Burnfield, J. L. (2009). Perceived meeting characteristics: The role of design characteristics. *Journal of Business Psychology, 24,* 65–76. doi:10.1007/s10869-009-9092-6

LeBlanc, L. A. (2015). Reflections on my early mentors and their influences on my career. *The Behavior Analyst, 38,* 237–245.

LeBlanc, L. A., (2020). *Nobody's perfect.* Retrieved on April 3, 2020 from https://www.aubreydaniels.com/media-center/nobodys-perfect

LeBlanc, L. A., Heinicke, M. R., & Baker, J. C. (2012). Expanding the consumer base for behavior-analytic services: Meeting the needs of consumers in the 21st century. *Behavior Analysis in Practice, 5,* 4–14.

LeBlanc, L. A. & Luiselli, J. K. (2016). Refining supervisory practices in the field of behavior analysis: Introduction to the special section on supervision. *Behavior Analysis in Practice, 9,* 271–273.

LeBlanc, L. A., & Nosik, M. R. (2019). Planning and leading effective meetings. *Behavior Analysis in Practice, 12,* 696–708.

LeBlanc, L. A., Raetz, P. B., Sellers, T. P., Carr, J. E. (2016). A proposed model for selecting measurement procedures for the assessment and treatment of problem behavior. *Behavior Analysis in Practice, 9,* 77–83.

LeBlanc, L. A., Sleeper, J. D., Mueller, J. R., Jenkins, S. R., & Harper-Briggs, A. M. (2020). Assessing barriers to effective caseload management by practicing behavior analysts. *Journal of Organizational Behavior Management, 39*(3–4), 317–336.

LeBlanc, L. A., Taylor, B. A., & Marchese N. V. (2019). The training experiences of behavior analysts: Compassionate care and therapeutic relationships with caregivers. *Behavior Analysis in Practice, 13,* 387–393. https://doi.org/10.1007/s40617-019-00368-z

Leland, W., & Stockwell, A. (2019). A self-assessment tool for cultivating affirming practices with transgender and gender-nonconforming (TGNC) clients, supervisees, students, and colleagues. *Behavior Analysis in Practice, 12,* 1–10.

Lencioni, P. (2004). *Death by meeting.* San Francisco CA: Jossey-Bass.

Lewis, A. (2010). Silence in the context of 'child voice'. *Children & Society, 24*(1), 14–23.

Lewis, R. D. (2006). *When cultures collide: Leading across cultures* (3rd Ed.). Boston: Nicholas Brealey International.

Lloyd, J., Bond, F. W. & Flaxman, P. (2013). The value of psychological flexibility: Examining psychological mechanisms underpinning a cognitive behavioural therapy intervention for burnout. *Work and Stress, 27*(2), pp. 181–199. doi: 10.1080/02678373.2013.782157

Lown, B. A., McIntosh, S., McGuinn, K., Aschenbrener, C., DeWitt, B. B., Chou, C., et al. (2014). Triple C conference framework tables. Retrieved from http://www.theschwartzcenter.org/media/Triple-CConference-Framework-Tables_FINAL.pdf

Lown, B. A. (2016). A social neuroscience-informed model for teaching and practicing compassion in health care. *Medical Education, 50,* 332–342. doi: 10.1111/medu.12926

Lutz, W., Patterson, B., & Klein, J. (2012). Coping with autism: A journey toward adaptation. *Journal of Pediatric Nursing, 27,* 206–213. doi: 10.1016/j.pedn.2011.03.013

Lynch, E. W., & Hanson, M. J. (2011). *Developing cross-cultural competence: A guide for working with children and their families* (4th ed.) Baltimore: Paul H. Brookes.

Mager, R. F. (1997). *Making instruction work: Or skill bloomers: A step-by-step guide to designing and developing instruction that works* (2nd ed.). The Center for Effective Performance, Inc.

Manz, C. C. & Simms, H. P. (1980). Self-management as a substitute for leadership: A social learning theory perspective. *Academy of Management Review, 5,* 361–367.

Marulanda-Carter, L. & Jackson, T. W. (2012). Effects of e-mail addiction and interruptions on employees. *Journal of Systems and Information Technology, 14* (1), 82–94.

Maslach C. (1998). A multidimensional theory of burnout. In C. L. Cooper (Ed), *Theories of Organizational Stress* (pp. 68–85). Oxford University Press.

Maslach, C., & Goldberg, J. (1998). Prevention of burnout: New perspectives. *Applied and Preventive Psychology, 7*(1), 63–74.

Maslach, C., & Jackson, S. E. (1981). The measurement of experienced burnout. *Journal of Organizational Behavior, 2,* 99–113.

Maslach, C., Schaufeli, W. B., & Leiter, M. P. (2001). Job burnout. *Annual Review of Psychology, 52,* 397–422. doi: 10.1146/annurev.psych.52.1.397

Mawhinney, T. C. (2009). Identifying and extinguishing dysfunctional and deadly organizational practices. *Journal of Organizational Behavior Management, 29*(3–4), 231–256.

Mazerolle, S. M., Walker, S. E., & Thrasher, A. B. (2015). Exploring the transition to practice for the newly credentialed athletic trainer: A programmatic view. *Journal of Athletic Training, 50,* 1042–1053. doi: 10.4085/1062-6050-50.9.02

McGimsey, J. F., Greene, B. F., & Lutzker, J. R. (1995). Competence in aspects of behavioral treatment and consultation: Implications for service delivery and graduate training. *Journal of Applied Behavior Analysis, 28,* 301–15.

McKay, M., Rogers, P.D., & McKay, J. (2003). *When anger hurts: Quieting the storm within* (2nd ed.). New York: Barnes & Noble Books.

McKay, M., Wood, J. C., & Brantley, J. (2007). *Dialectical behavior therapy skills workbook: practical dbt exercises for learning mindfulness, interpersonal effectiveness, emotion regulation, & distress tolerance.* New Harbinger Publications.

McMurray, S., Dutton, M., McQuaid, R., & Richard, A. (2016). Employer demands from business graduates. *Education & Training, 58* (1), 112–132. doi: 10.1108/ET-02-2014-0017

McMurtry, K. (2014). Managing email overload in the workplace. *Performance Improvement, 53*(7) 31–37. doi: 10.1002/pfi.21424

Meyer, E. (2014). *The Culture Map: Breaking Through the Invisible Boundaries of Global Business.* Perseus Books, Philadelphia, PA.

Miles, N. I., & Wilder, D. A. (2009). The effects of behavioral skills training on caregiver implementation of guided compliance. *Journal of Applied Behavior Analysis, 42,* 405–410. doi: 10.1901/jaba.2009.42-405

Miller, K. L., Re Cruz, A., & Ala'i-Rosales, S. (2019). Inherent tensions and possibilities: Behavior analysis and cultural responsiveness. *Behavior and Social Issues, 28*(1), 16–36.

Miltenberger, R. G. (2016). *Behavior modification: Principles and procedures.* Cengage.

Mirsky, J. (2013). Getting to know the piece of fluff in our ears: Expanding practitioners' cultural self-awareness. *Social Work Education, 32*(5), 626–638. doi: 10.1080/02615479.2012.701279

Mitroff, I. I., & Denton, E. A. (1999). A study of spirituality in the workplace. *Sloan Management Review, 40*(4), 83–84.

Mohtady, H. A., Könings, K. D., & van Merriënboer, J. J. G. (2016). What makes informal mentorship in the medical realm effective? *Mentoring & Tutoring: Partnership in Learning, 24,* 306–317. doi: 10.1080/13611267.2016.1252111

Moryaga, M. G., Devries, S., & Wardle, E. A. (2015). The practice of self-care among counseling students. *Journal on Educational Psychology, 8l* (3), 21–28.

Murphy, S. E., & Ensher, E. A. (2001). The role of mentoring support and self-management strategies on reported career outcomes. *Journal of Career Development, 27*(4), 229–246.

Muzio, E., Fisher, D. J., Thomas, E. R., & Peters, V. (2007). Soft Skills Quantification (SSQ) Foi Project Manager Competencies. *Project Management Journal, 38*(2), 30–38.

Nelson, J. R., Benner, G. J., & Gonzalez, J. (2005). An investigation of the effects of prereading intervention on the early literacy skills of children at risk of emotional disturbance and reading problems. *Journal of Emotional and Behavioral Disorders, 13,* 3–12.

Nigro-Bruzzi, D., & Sturmey, P. (2010). The effects of behavioral skills training on mand training by staff and unprompted vocal mands by children. *Journal of Applied Behavior Analysis, 43,* 757–761. doi: 10.1901/jaba.2010.43-757

Osmani, M., Weerakkody, V., Hindi, N. M., Al-Esmail, R., Eldabi, T., Kapoor, K., & Irani, Z. (2015). Identifying the trends and impact of graduate attributes on employability: A literature review. *Tertiary Education and Management, 21*(4), 367–379. doi:http://dx.doi.org/10.1080/13583883.2015.1114139

Pagana, K. D. (1994). Teaching Students Time Management Strategies. *Journal of Nursing Education, 33*(8), 381–383.

Pant, B., Chamorro-Premuzic, T., Molinsky, A., Hahn, M., & Hinds, P. (2016). Different cultures see deadlines differently. *Harvard Business Review.* Retrieved May, 08, 2020 from https://hbr.org/2016/05/different-cultures-see-deadlines-differently

Park, J. A., Johnson, D. A., Moon, K., & Lee, J. (2019). The Interaction Effects of Frequency and Specificity of Feedback on Work Performance. *Journal of Organizational Behavior Management, 39*(3–4), 164–178.

Parnell, A. M., Lorah, E. R., Karnes, A., & Schaefer-Whitby, P. (2017). Effectiveness of job aids and post-performance review on staff implementation of discrete trial instruction. *Journal of Organizational Behavior Management, 37,* 207–220. doi: 10.1080/01608061.2017.1309333

Parsons, M. B., Rollyson, J. H., & Reid, D. H. (2012). Evidence based staff training. *Behavior Analysis in Practice, 5,* 2–11. doi: 10.1007/BF03391819

Pastrana, S., Frewing, T., Grow, L., Nosik, M., Turner, M., & Carr, J. (2016). Frequently assigned readings in behavior analysis graduate training programs. *Behavior Analysis in Practice, 3,* 1–7. https://doi.org/10.1007/s40617-016-0137-9

Patterson, K., Grenny, J., McMillan, R., & Switzler A. (2012). *Crucial conversations: Tools for talking when stakes are high.* McGraw Hill.

Peck, C. A., Killen, C. C., & Baumgart, D. (2010). Increasing implementation of special education instructions in mainstream preschools: Direct and generalized effects of non-directive consultation. *Journal of Applied Behavior Analysis, 22,* 197–210.

Pew Research Center, Washington, D.C. (May 4, 2016). 5 Facts About Prayer. Retrieved March, 11, 2020 from https://www.pewresearch.org/fact-tank/2016/05/04/5-facts-about-prayer/

Pignata, S., Lushington, K., Sloan, J. & Buchanan, F. (2015). Employees' perceptions of email communication, volume and management strategies in an Australian University. *Journal of Higher Education Policy and Management; 37*(2), 59–171.

Plantiveau, C., Dounavi, K., & Virués-Ortega, J. (2018). High levels of burnout among early career board-certified behavior analysts with low collegial support in the work environment. *European Journal of Behavior Analysis, 19*(2), 195–207. doi: 10.1080/15021149.2018.1438339

Post, S. G., Pomeroy, J., Keirns, C. C., Cover, V. I., Dorn, M. L., Boroson, L., Boroson, F., Coulehan, A., Coulehan, J., Covell, K., Kubasek, K., Luchsinger, E., Nichols, S., Parles, J., Schreiber, L., Tetenbaum, S. P., & Wals, R. A. (2013). Brief report: Stony Brook guidelines on the ethics of the care of people with autism and their families. *Journal of Autism and Developmental Disorders, 43*, 1473–1476. doi: 10.1007/s10803-012-1680-z

Proulx, K. (2003). Integrating mindfulness-based stress reduction. *Holistic Nursing Practice, 17*, 201–208.

Reid, D. H., Parsons, M. B., & Green, C. W. (2012). *The supervisor's guidebook: Evidence based strategies for promoting work quality and enjoyment among human service staff*. Morganton, NC: Habilitative Management Consultants.

Riehl, C. J. (2000). The principal's role in creating inclusive schools for diverse students: A review of normative, empirical, and critical literature on the practice of educational administration. *Review of Educational Research, 70*(1), 55–81.

Riess, H. (2015). The impact of clinical empathy on patients and clinicians: understanding empathy's side effects. *AJOB Neuroscience, 6*(3), 51–53. doi:10.1080/21507740.2015.1052591

Rosales, R., Stone, K., & Rehfeldt, R. A. (2009). The effects of behavioral skills training on implementation of the Picture Exchange Communication system. *Journal of Applied Behavior Analysis, 42*, 541–549. doi: 10.1901/jaba.2009.42-541

Roscoe, E. M., & Fisher, W. W. (2008). Evaluation of an efficient method for training staff to implement stimulus preference assessments. *Journal of Applied Behavior Analysis, 41*, 249–254. doi: 10.1901/jaba.2008.41-249

Rose, J., Mills, S., Silva, D., & Thompson, L. (2013). Client characteristics, organizational variables and burnout in care staff: The mediating role of fear of assault. *Research in Developmental Disabilities, 34*, 940–947.

Rosenberg, N. E., & Schwartz, I. S. (2019). Guidance or compliance: What makes an ethical behavior analyst?. *Behavior Analysis in Practice, 12*, 473–482.

Roysircar, G. (2004). Cultural self-awareness assessment: Practice examples from psychology training. *Professional Psychology: Research and Practice, 35*(6), 658–666. doi: 10.1037/0735-7028.35.6.658

Rummler, G. A., & Brache, A. P. (2013). *Improving performance: How to manage the white space on the organization chart* (3rd ed.). John Wiley & Sons.

Salter, T., & Gannon, J. M. (2015). Exploring shared and distinctive aspects of coaching and mentoring approaches through six disciplines. *European Journal of Training and Development, 39*, 373–392.

Sarokoff, R. A., & Sturmey, P. (2004). The effects of behavioral skills training on staff implementation of discrete-trial teaching. *Journal of Applied Behavior Analysis, 37*, 535–538. doi:10.1901/jaba.2004.37-535

Sasson, J. R., Alvero, A. M., & Austin, J. (2006). Effects of process and human performance improvement strategies. *Journal of Organizational Behavior Management, 26*, 43–78. doi:10.1300/J075v26n03_02

Sautter, R. A., LeBlanc, L. A., Jay, A. A., Goldsmith, T. R., & Carr, J. E. (2011). The role of problem solving in complex intraverbal repertoires. *Journal of Applied Behavior Analysis, 44*, 227–244. doi: 10.1901/jaba.2011.44-227

Schulz, B. (2008). The importance of soft skills: Education beyond academic knowledge. *Journal of Language and Communication, 2*, 146–154. doi: 10.1016/0006-3207(93)90452-7

Schweitzer, R. D., & Witham, M. (2018). The supervisory alliance: Comparison of measures and implications for a supervision toolkit. *Counselling and Psychotherapy Research, 18*, 71–78.

Schwiebert, V. L., Deck, M. D., Bradshaw, M. L., Scott, P., & Harper, M. (1999). Women as mentors. *Journal of Humanistic Counseling, Education and Development, 37*, 241–253.

Scott, J., Lerman, D. C., & Luck, K. (2018). Computer-based training to detect antecedents and consequences of problem behavior. *Journal of Applied Behavior Analysis, 51*, 784–801.

Sellers, T. P., Ala'i-Rosales, S., & MacDonald, R. P. (2016). Taking full responsibility: The ethics of supervision in behavior analytic practice. *Behavior Analysis in Practice, 9*, 299–308.

Sellers, T. P., LeBlanc, L. A. & Valentino, A. V. (2016). Recommendations for detecting and addressing barriers to successful supervision. *Behavior Analysis in Practice, 9*, 309–319. doi: 10.1007/s40617-016-0142-z

Sellers, T. P., Valentino, A. L., & LeBlanc, L. A. (2016). Recommended practices for individual supervision of aspiring behavior analysts. *Behavior Analysis in Practice, 9*, 274–286. doi:10.1007/s40617-016-0110-7

Shapiro, S. L., Brown, K. W., & Biegel, G. M. (2007). Teaching self-care to caregivers: Effects of mindfulness based stress reduction on the mental health of therapists in training. *Training and Education in Professional Psychology, 1*(2), 105–115. doi:10.1037/1931-3918.1.2.105

Shirey, M. (2007). An evidence-based solution for minimizing stress and anger in nursing students. *Journal of Nursing Education, 46*(12), 568–571.

Sigman, M., & Capps, L. (1997). *Children with autism: A developmental perspective* (Vol. 34). Harvard University Press.

Simpson, E., & Courtney, M., (2002). Critical thinking in nursing education: Literature review. *International Journal of Nursing Practice 8*(2), 89–98.

Sinclair, S., Beamer, K., Hack, T. F., McClement, S., Bouchal, S. R., Chochinov, H., & Hagen, N. A. (2016). Sympathy, empathy, and compassion: a grounded theory study of palliative care patients' understandings, experiences, and preferences. *Palliative Medicine, 31*(5), 437–447. doi:10.1177/0269216316663499

Sinclair, S., Norris, J. M., McConnell, S. J., Chochinov, H. M., Hack, T. F., Hagen, N. A., et al. (2016) Compassion: A scoping review of the healthcare literature. *BMC Palliative Care, 15*(6), 6. doi: 10.1186/s12904-016-0080-0

Skinner, B. F. (1953). *Science and Human Behavior*. Macmillan.

Skinner, B. F. (1957). *Verbal Behavior*. Englewood Cliffs, NJ: Prentice Hall.

Skinner, B. F. (1968). *The technology of teaching*. New York: Appleton-Century-Crofts

Skinner, B. F. (1984). An operant analysis of problem solving. *Behavior and Brain Sciences, 7*, 583–613.

Smith, S. W., Lochman, J. E., & Daunic, A. P. (2005). Managing aggression using cognitive-behavioral interventions: State of the practice and future. *Behavioral Disorders, 30*, 227–240.

Stokes, T. F., & Osnes, P. G. (2016). An operant pursuit of generalization. Republished article. *Behavior Therapy, 47*(5), 720–732.

Stone, D., Patton, B., Heen, S., (2010). *Difficult conversations: How to discuss what matters most*. Penguin.

Sugai, G., O'Keeffe, B. V., & Fallon, L. M. (2012). A contextual consideration of culture and school-wide positive behavior support. *Journal of Positive Behavior Interventions, 14*(4), 197–208.

Sundberg, D. (2015). *An empirical analysis of the sandwich method of feedback* (Unpublished master's thesis). Florida Institute of Technology, Melbourne FL.

Sundberg, D. M., Zoder-Martell, K. A., & Cox, S. (2019). Why WIBA? *Behavior Analysis in Practice, 12*(4), 810–815.

Super, D. E. (1980). A life-span, life-space approach to career development. *Journal of Vocational Behavior, 16*, 282–298.

Tagg, R. & Biagi, S. (2020). *Self-assessment of the Fifth Edition BACB Task List*. Author.

Taylor, B. A. & LeBlanc, L. A., (2019). *Providing compassionate care and building therapeutic relationships*. California Association for Behavior Analysis Online Webinar (Friday, December 6, 2019).

Taylor, B. A., LeBlanc, L. A., & Nosik, M. R. (2019). Compassionate care in behavior analytic treatment: Can outcomes be enhanced by attending to relationships with caregivers?. *Behavior Analysis in Practice, 12*, 654–666.

The Daily BA. (2019, February 04). Pat Friman - *I didn't know her circumstances* [Video]. YouTube. https://www.youtube.com/watch?v=MyClIpztOSs

Theisen, B., Bird, Z., & Zeigler, J. (2015). *Train ABA supervision curriculum-BCBA independent fieldwork*. CreateSpace Independent Publishing Platform.

Thomas, S.P. (2003). Anger: The mismanaged emotion. *Dermatology Nursing, 15*, 351–357.

Tucker, D. (2018). *Task management: Checklist and self-discipline for personal success*. Author.

Tulgan, B. (2015). *Bridging the soft skills gap: How to teach the missing basics to today's young talent*. Hoboken, NJ: Wiley.

Turner, L. B., Fischer, A. J., & Luiselli, J. K. (2016). Towards a competency-based, ethical, and socially valid approach to the supervision of applied behavior analytics. *Behavior Analysis in Practice, 9*, 287–298. doi: 10.1007/s40617-016-0121-4

Van Eerde, W. (2003). Procrastination at work and time management training. *Journal of Psychology, 137*, 421–434.

Verburg, R. M., & Andriessen, J. H. E. (2006). The assessment of communities of practice. *Knowledge Process Management, 13*, 13–25. doi:10.1002/kpm.241

Wang, Y., Kang, S., Ramirez, J., & Tarbox, J. (2019). Multilingual diversity in the field of applied behavior analysis and autism: A brief review and discussion of future directions. *Behavior Analysis in Practice, 12*, 795–804.

Ward-Horner, J., & Sturmey, P. (2012). Component analysis of behavior skills training in functional analysis. *Behavioral Interventions, 27*(2), 75–92.

Weinkauf, S., Zueg, N., Anderson, C. & Ala'i-Rosales, S. (2011). Evaluating the effectiveness of a comprehensive staff training package for behavioral interventions for children with autism. *Research in Autism Spectrum Disorders, 5*, 864–871.

Wenger, E. C., & Snyder, W. M. (2000). Communities of practice: The organizational frontier. *Harvard Business Review, 78*(1), 139–146.

Wentz, F. H. (2013). *10 things employers expect their employees to know: A soft skills workbook*. Author.

Westby, C., Burda, A., & Mehta, Z. (2003). Asking the right questions in the right ways: Strategies for ethnographic interviewing. *The ASHA Leader, 8*(8), 4–17.

White, B. J. (2017). A Leadership and professional development teaching and learning model for undergraduate management programs. *Journal of Higher Education Theory and Practice, 17*(4), 57–74.

White, L. T., Valk, R., & Dialmy, A. (2011). What is the meaning of "on time"? The sociocultural nature of punctuality. *Journal of Cross-Cultural Psychology, 42*(3), 482–493.

Wiesbeck, A. B., Bauer, J., Gartmeier, M., Kiessling, C., Möller, G.,E., Karsten, G.,… Prenzel, M. (2017). Simulated conversations for assessing professional conversation competence in teacher-parent and physician-patient conversations. *Journal for Educational Research Online, 9*(3), 82–101. Retrieved from https://search.proquest.com/docview/1994337681?accountid=166077

Wilder, D. A., Lipschultz, J. L., King, A., Driscoll, S., & Sigurdsson, S. (2018). An analysis of the commonality and type of preintervention assessment procedures in the Journal of Organizational Behavior Management (2000–2015). *Journal of Organizational Behavior Management, 38*, 5–17. doi: 10.1080/01608061.2017.1325822

Wilder, D. A., Lipschultz, J., & Gehrman, C. (2018). An evaluation of the Performance Diagnostic Checklist—Human Services (PDC–HS) across domains. *Behavior Analysis in Practice, 11*, 129–138. doi: 10.1007/s40617-018-0243-y

Wine, B., Lewis, K., Newcomb, E. T., Camblin, J. G., Chen, T., Liesfeld, J. E., ... & Newcomb, B. B. (2019). The effects of temporal placement of feedback on performance with and without goals. *Journal of Organizational Behavior Management, 39*(3–4), 308–316.

Wlodkowski, R. J., & Ginsberg, M. B. (1995). *Diversity & motivation: Culturally responsive teaching*. Jossey-Bass Higher and Adult Education Series. Jossey-Bass Education Series, Jossey-Bass Social and Behavioral Science Series. Jossey-Bass Inc., 350 Sansome St., San Francisco, CA 94104.

Wolf, M. M. (1978). Social validity: The case for subjective measurement or how applied behavior analysis is finding its heart. *Journal of Applied Behavior Analysis, 11*, 203–214.

Wolf, S. J., Lockspeiser, T. M., Gong, J., & Guiton, G. (2018). Identification of foundational non-clinical attributes necessary for successful transition to residency: A modified Delphi study with experienced medical educators. *BMC Medical Education, 18*, 150. doi: 10.1186/s12909-018-1247-6

World Bank Group. (2016). Global monitoring report 2015/2016: Development goals in an era of demographic change.

World Health Organization (2009). Self-care in the context of primary health care. *Report of the Regional Consultation, 7*(9), 1–72.

Wright, P. I. (2019). Cultural humility in the practice of applied behavior analysis. *Behavior Analysis in Practice, 12*, 805–809.

Zarcone, J., Brodhead, M., & Tarbox, J. (2019). Beyond a call to action: An introduction to the special issue on diversity and equity in the practice of behavior analysis. *Behavior Analysis in Practice, 12*, 741–742.

APPENDIX I

BACB/BCaBA Task List (5th ed.)

Introduction

The *BCBA/BCaBA Task List* includes the knowledge and skills that that serve as the foundation for the BCBA and BCaBA examinations.

Structure

The BCBA/BCaBA Task List is organized in two major sections, *Foundations*, which includes basic skills and underlying principles and knowledge, and *Applications*, which includes more practice-oriented skills.

Section 1: Foundations
A. Philosophical Underpinnings
B. Concepts and Principles
C. Measurement, Data Display, and Interpretation
D. Experimental Design

Section 2: Applications
E. Ethics (*Professional and Ethical Compliance Code for Behavior Analysts*)
F. Behavior Assessment
G. Behavior-Change Procedures
H. Selecting and Implementing Interventions
I. Personnel Supervision and Management

	Section I: Foundations
Task #	**A. Philosophical Underpinnings**
A-1	Identify the goals of behavior analysis as a science (i.e., description, prediction, control).
A-2	Explain the philosophical assumptions underlying the science of behavior analysis (e.g., selectionism, determinism, empiricism, parsimony, pragmatism).
A-3	Describe and explain behavior from the perspective of radical behaviorism.
A-4	Distinguish among behaviorism, the experimental analysis of behavior, applied behavior analysis, and professional practice guided by the science of behavior analysis.
A-5	Describe and define the dimensions of applied behavior analysis (Baer, Wolf, & Risley, 1968).
Task #	**B. Concepts and Principles**
B-1	Define and provide examples of behavior, response, and response class.
B-2	Define and provide examples of stimulus and stimulus class
B-3	Define and provide examples of respondent and operant conditioning.
B-4	Define and provide examples of positive and negative reinforcement contingencies.
B-5	Define and provide examples of schedules of reinforcement.
B-6	Define and provide examples of positive and negative punishment contingencies.
B-7	Define and provide examples of automatic and socially mediated contingencies.
B-8	Define and provide examples of unconditioned, conditioned and generalized reinforcers and punishers.
B-9	Define and provide examples of operant extinction
B-10	Define and provide examples of stimulus control.
B-11	Define and provide examples of discrimination, generalization and maintenance.

© 2017 by the Behavior Analyst Certification Board,® Inc. ("BACB®") all rights reserved. Reprinted here with the permission of the BACB. Unauthorized reproduction, dissemination or distribution in any medium is strictly prohibited. **BACB**: BCBA/BCaBA Task List (5th ed,)

B-12	Define and provide examples of motivating operations.
B-13	Define and provide examples of rule-governed and contingency-shaped behavior.
B-14	Define and provide examples of the verbal operants
B-15	Define and provide examples of derived stimulus relations.

Task #	C. Measurement, Data Display, and Interpretation
C-1	Establish operational definitions of behavior.
C-2	Distinguish among direct, indirect, and product measures of behavior.
C-3	Measure occurrence (e.g. count, frequency rate percentage).
C-4	Measure temporal dimensions of behavior (e.g., duration, latency, interresponse time).
C-5	Measure form and strength of behavior (e.g., topography, magnitude).
C-6	Measure trials to criterion.
C-7	Design and implement sampling procedures (i.e., interval recording, time sampling).
C-8	Evaluate the validity and reliability of measurement procedures.
C-9	Select a measurement system to obtain representative data given the dimensions of behavior and the logistics of observing recording.
C-10	Graph data to communicate relevant quantitative relations (e.g., equal-interval graphs, bar graphs, cumulative records).
C-11	Interpret graphed data.

Task #	D. Experimental Design
D-1	Distinguish between dependent and independent variables.
D-2	Distinguish between internal and external validity.
D-3	Identify the defining features of single-subject experimental designs (e.g., individuals serve as their own controls, repeated measures, prediction, verification, replication).
D-4	Describe the advantages of single-subject experimental designs compared to group designs.

D-5	Use single-subject experimental designs (e.g., reversal, multiple baseline, multielement, changing criterion).
D-6	Describe rationales for conducting comparative, component, and parametric analyses.

Section Two: Applications

Task #	E. Ethics
E-1	Responsible conduct of behavior analysts.
E-2	Behavior analysts' responsibility to clients.
E-3	Assessing behavior.
E-4	Behavior analysts and the behavior-change program.
E-5	Behavior analysts as supervisors.
E-6	Behavior analysts' ethical responsibility to the profession of behavior analysis.
E-7	Behavior analysts' ethical responsibility to colleagues.
E-8	Public statements.
E-9	Behavior analysts and research.
E-10	Behavior analysts' ethical responsibility to the BACB.

Task #	F. Behavior Assessment
F-1	Review records and available data (e.g., educational medical, historical) at the outset of the case.
F-2	Determine the need for behavior-analytic services.
F-3	Identify and prioritize socially significant behavior-change goals.
F-4	Conduct assessments of relevant skill strengths and deficits.
F-5	Conduct preference assessments.
F-6	Describe the common functions of problem behavior.
F-7	Conduct a descriptive assessment of problem behavior.
F-8	Conduct a functional analysis of problem behavior.
F-9	Interpret functional assessment data.

© 2017 by the Behavior Analyst Certification Board,® Inc. ("BACB®") all rights reserved. Reprinted here with the permission of the BACB. Unauthorized reproduction, dissemination or distribution in any medium is strictly prohibited.

BACB: BCBA/BCaBA Task List (5th ed,)

Task #	G. Behavior Change Procedures
G-1	Use positive and negative reinforcement procedures to strengthen behavior.
G-2	Use interventions based on motivating operations and discriminative stimuli.
G-3	Establish and use conditioned reinforcers.
G-4	Use stimulus and response prompts and fading (e.g., errorless, most-to-least, least-to-most, prompt delay, stimulus fading).
G-5	Use modeling and imitation training.
G-6	Use instructions and rules.
G-7	Use shaping.
G-8	Use chaining.
G-9	Use discrete-trial, free-operant and naturalistic teaching arrangements.
G-10	Teach simple and conditional discriminations.
G-11	Use Skinner's analysis to teach verbal behavior.
G-12	Use equivalence-based instruction.
G-13	Use the high-probability instructional sequence.
G-14	Use reinforcement procedures to weaken behavior (e.g., DRA, FCT, DRO, DRL, NCR).
G-15	Use extinction.
G-16	Use positive and negative punishment (e.g., time-out, response cost, overcorrection).
G-17	Use token economies.
G-18	Use group contingencies.
G-19	Use contingency contracting.
G-20	Use self-management strategies.
G-21	Use procedures to promote stimulus and response generalization.
G-22	Use procedures to promote maintenance.

Task #	H. Selecting and Implementing Interventions
H-1	State intervention goals in observable and measurable terms.
H-2	Identify potential interventions based on assessment results and the best available scientific evidence.
H-3	Recommend intervention goals and strategies based on such factors as client preferences, supporting environments, risks, constraints, and social validity.
H-4	When a target behavior is to be decreased, select an acceptable alternative behavior to be established or increased.
H-5	Plan for possible unwanted effects when using reinforcement, extinction, and punishment procedures.
H-6	Monitor client progress and treatment integrity.
H-7	Make data-based decisions about the effectiveness of the intervention and the need for treatment revision.
H-8	Make data-based decisions about the need for ongoing services.
H-9	Collaborate with others who support and/or provide services to clients.

Task #	I. Personnel Supervision and Management
I-1	State the reasons for using behavior-analytic supervision and the potential risks of ineffective supervision (e.g., poor client outcomes, poor supervisee performance).
I-2	Establish clear performance expectations for the supervisor and supervisee.
I-3	Select supervision goals based on an assessment of the supervisee's skills.
I-4	Train personnel to competently perform assessment and intervention procedures.
I-5	Use performance monitoring, feedback, and reinforcement systems.

© 2017 by the Behavior Analyst Certification Board,® Inc. ("BACB®") all rights reserved. Reprinted here with the permission of the BACB. Unauthorized reproduction, dissemination or distribution in any medium is strictly prohibited.

BACB: BCBA/BCaBA Task List (5th ed,)

I-6	Use a functional assessment approach (e.g., performance diagnostics) to identify variables affecting personnel performance.
I-7	Use function-based strategies to improve personnel performance
I-8	Evaluate the effect of supervision (e.g., on client outcomes, on supervisee repertoires).

Appendix II

BACB Supervisor Training Outline 2.0

Table of Contents

Overview   298
Supervision of Ongoing Services   299
Supervision of Trainees   304
Selected Supervisor Resources   307

OVERVIEW

This curriculum outline is comprised of learning objectives, tasks, and considerations that are important for creating an effective supervisory relationship. Supervisors oversee the work of (a) individuals acquiring fieldwork (i.e., experience[1]) for BCBA or BCaBA certification (trainees) and (b) current BCaBA or RBT certificants who are required to have ongoing supervision (supervisees) are required to complete an 8-hour supervision training based on this curriculum before providing any supervision. Supervisors, supervisees, and trainees should confirm the date the supervisor completed the training prior to initiating the supervisor relationship.

Requirements for Training Providers

All Authorized Continuing Education (ACE) Providers and Verified Course Sequences (VCS) are eligible to offer supervision training based on this curriculum outline. The cumulative duration of training must be at least 8 hours (but may be offered in units as brief as 1 hour. The training activities mush include opportunities for trainees to demonstrate verbal or practical competence of the curricular areas below. Training may be conducted in person or online. The training may be completed up to 180 days prior to the learner's[2] original BACB certification date, or, for qualifying non-certified BT supervisors and non-certified VCS instructors, as soon as they meet the other supervision eligibility requirements.

Requirements for Documentation

ACE Providers must provide the learner with a one-page document showing that the learner completed the full training (see the ACE Handbook for documentation requirements). If the training is completed as part of a VCS, the course syllabus and the learner's unofficial transcript, showing a passing grade, will be required. The training provided must include a link to the BACB Supervisor Training Curriculum Outline (2.0), as well as the following text in all online and print materials for their training program:

> "This training program is based on the BACB Supervisor Training Curriculum Outline (2.0) but is offered independent of the BACB."

---

[1] The term *fieldwork* will be used throughout this document to refer to the supervised practical experience required for obtaining BCBA or BCaBA certification.

[2] We are using the term *learner* in this document to refer to those who are taking the supervision training.

The learner must upload the documentation described above into their BACB Account. Once the documentation has been approved and they meet all other relevant supervision eligibility requirements, they may begin providing instruction.

SUPERVISION OF ONGOING SERVICES

The section below applies to supervision of the ongoing delivery of behavior-analytic services and, thus, is particularly relevant ot the supervision of BCaBAs and RBTs.

1) **The supervisor should be able to state the purpose of supervision to the supervisee or trainee.**
   a) Provide high-quality services that result in client improvement
      i) Create context for clear communication
      ii) Ensure procedural fidelity of service delivery
   b) Develop and maintain behavior-analytic, professional, and ethical repertoires of the supervisee (as relevant)
      i) RBT Task List and RBT Ethics Code
      ii) BCBA/BCaBA Task List and Professional Ethical and Compliance Code for Behavior Analysts
   c) Teach conceptual skills using applied case exemplars
      i) Philosophical underpinnings of behavior analysis
      ii) Concepts and principles of behavior analysis
   d) Develop problem-solving skills
      i) Responding to novel behavior and insufficient progress of clients
      ii) Addressing questions from clients/caregivers
      iii) Maximizing learning opportunities for clients
   e) Monitor and evaluate decision-making skills
      i) Professionalism decisions
      ii) Ethical decisions
      iii) Treatment decisions
   f) Model assistance-seeking skills
      i) Identifying problems
      ii) Providing opportunities for feedback
      iii) Seeking assistance from appropriate parties
   g) Improve and maintain beneficial repertoires of the supervisee or trainee
      i) Progress monitoring
      ii) Opportunities for advancement

h) Model effective supervision practices
      i) Professional behaviors
      ii) Ethical behaviors
      iii) Training behaviors

2) **The supervisor should be able to describe the strategies and potential outcomes of ineffective supervision.**
   a) Identify low-quality client services
      i) Insufficient client progress
      ii) Potential for harm to clients
   b) Identify poor performance
      i) Inadequate practice repertoires
      ii) Inadequate professional repertoires
   c) Monitor indicators of potentially unethical behavior
      i) Inability to identify ethical issues
      ii) Inability to problem solve and make decisions in novel or unfamiliar settings
   d) Evaluate modeling of effective supervision practices
      i) Missed training opportunities
      ii) Production of ineffective supervisors
   e) Reduce the risks associated with high-volume work hours
      i) Lower likelihood of compliance with supervisor recommendations
      ii) Costs of attrition

3) **The supervisor should be able to prepare for the supervisory relationship with the supervisee or trainee.**
   a) Determine feasible supervision capacity based on available time and resources for the following activities:
      i) Maintenance of effective services
      ii) Available institutional/organizational resources
      iii) Identification of billable vs. non-billable time, if relevant
      iv) Access to supervision sites (e.g., travel time required)
      v) Preparation of content for supervision
      vi) Timely responding to correspondence (e.g., calls, texts, emails)
   b) Verify and review BACB certification maintenance requirements
      i) Supervision requirements
      ii) Competency assessment requirements (RBT)
      iii) Continuing education requirements (BCaBA)
   c) Verify certification status
      i) Use the BACB registry to check status of certification
   d) Create a secure record system to document the supervisory relationship with the following information;

i) Supervision contracts and forms
   ii) Supervision and work logs
   iii) Background checks
   iv) Supervision performance evaluations
   v) Required documentation for a BACB audit
4) **The supervisor should be able to establish a plan for structured supervision contents and evaluation of competence for supervisees and trainees.**
   a) Review the nature of supervision and include the following:
      i) Set performance expectations
      ii) Observe, implement behavioral skills training, and deliver performance feedback
      iii) Model technical, professional, and ethical behavior
      iv) Guide strategies for developing behavioral case conceptualization, problem-solving, and decision-making repertoires (e.g., consider motivating operations, discriminative stimuli, functions of behavior)
      v) Review written materials (e.g., behavioral programs, data sheets, reports)
      vi) Oversee and evaluate the effects of behavioral service delivery
      vii) Provide ongoing evaluation of the effects of supervision
   b) Review frequency, type, and structure of supervision sessions and consider the following:
      i) Schedule
      ii) Location
      iii) Individual vs. group supervision
      iv) Meeting agendas
      v) Multiple supervisors
   c) Review expectations for behavior while feedback is being delivered, including the following:
      i) Engagement in active listening (eye contact, posture) and engagement (question asking, paraphrasing) strategies
      ii) Taking notes during feedback meetings
      iii) Restatement of feedback to check for understanding
      iv) Requests for clarification, examples, or models as needed
      v) Acknowledgement of responsibility for errors (take responsibility)
   d) Review expectations for behavior after feedback ha been received, including the following:
      i) Acknowledgement of the feedback received
      ii) Goal setting for behavior-change goals

iii) Progress monitoring plan
e) Set appropriate boundaries
   i) Response-time expectations
   ii) Multiple relationships
   iii) Preferred means of communication (e.g., face-to-face, phone, text, email)
f) Review supervisee or trainee performance evaluation processes
   i) Frequency
   ii) Type (e.g., written correspondence, meetings)
   iii) Formal and informal reviews
   iv) Areas of performance (e.g., professionalism, organization, time management, program implementation, ethics)
g) Review supervisor performance evaluation processes
   i) Frequency
   ii) Type (e.g., written correspondence, meetings
   iii) Formal and informal reviews
   iv) Areas of performance (e.g., professionalism, organization, time management, program implementation, ethics)
h) Identify the conditions under which a supervisory relationship may end
   i) Identification of a new supervisor
   ii) Continued failure to meet learning goals

5) **The supervisor should be able to create committed and positive relationships with supervisees or trainees.**
   a) Use positive body language when interacting
      i) Eye contact
      ii) Posture
      iii) Affirmative movements
   b) Communicate regularly
      i) Follow-up
      ii) Regular check-ins
      iii) Timely responses to questions and concerns
   c) Review and provide timely feedback on documents, including:
      i) Data sheets and graphs
      ii) Written protocols and reports
      iii) Treatment notes
      iv) Behavior plans
      v) Professional correspondence
      vi) Training materials
      vii) Portfolios
   d) Provide undivided attention during supervision

i) Engage in active listening strategies
ii) Take notes
iii) Remove distractions (e.g., phone and email notification)

6) **The supervisor should be able to use behavioral skills training to improve supervisee or trainee performance.**
   a) Deliver clear, succinct, and detained instructions
      i) Describe rationale for why the target skills are to be trained
      ii) Provide vocal and written descriptions of the target skills
      iii) Use clear, concise, and simple instructions when describing the skills
      iv) require active participation from the learner
   b) Model the required skills across all relevant contexts
      i) Incorporate role play, in vivo, and video modeling
      ii) Rehearse immediately after the skills is demonstrated
      iii) Practice the skill in relevant settings
   d) Deliver effective feedback to shape performance
      i) Provide contingent, descriptive feedback immediately after skills rehearsal
      ii) Correct errors using empathy statements and descriptive information on how to improve
      iii) Provide vocal, written, modeled, video, and graphic feedback
      iv) Deliver feedback individually and to a group
      v) Deliver feedback using formal and informal methods
      vi) Incorporate self-monitoring
   e) Repeat behavioral skills training steps until skills reaches mastery
      i) Set a pre-determined mastery criterion for the skill
      ii) Measure procedural fidelity with the skill
      iii) Assess application and generalization of skill to new targets, clients, and settings
      iv) Schedule follow-up competency checks
   f) Train across skill areas that are relevant
      i) Measurement, data displays, and interpretation
      ii) Assessment and treatment procedures
      iii) Professionalism
   g) Describe the detrimental effects of withholding feedback
      i) Poor quality control
      ii) Development of an apathetic relationship
   h) Describe the detrimental effects of performing skills independently prior to demonstrating competency
      i) Increase likelihood of harm to the client
      ii) Develop a history of incorrect responding

i) Describe the detrimental effects of avoiding practice opportunities for weak or absent skills within repertoires
   i) Lack of commitment to supervisee's or trainee's training
   ii) Failure to improve client services

SUPERVISION OF TRAINEES

In addition to the section above, supervisors have addidtional responsibilities when supervising trainees pursuing BCBA or BCaBA certification; these responsibilities are described below:

1) **The supervisor should be able to comply with relevant BACB fieldwork requirements when supervising a trainee pursuing BCBA or BCaBA certification.**
   a) Review the requirements for those pursuing BCBA or BCaBA certification that are specific to the trainee, including:
      i) Degree requirements
      ii) Coursework requirements
      iii) Fieldwork requirements
      iv) Maintenance requirements
   b) Develop review, and sign a supervision contract prior to beginning supervision
      i) Write a comprehensive supervision contract
      ii) Review the supervision contract
      iii) Clarify and agree to scope of supervision
      iv) Review the conditions under which a supervisor may refuse to sign forms
      v) Provide copies of signed contracts to all parties
   c) Document the supervisory relationship
      i) Fieldwork verification forms
      ii) Supplemental documentation systems
      iii) Professional portfolios
      iv) Filing system
   d) Collaborate to establish training objectives aligned with the BCBA/BCaBA Task List
      i) Knowledge-based evaluations
      ii) Performance-based evaluations
   f) Identiy training opportunities designe to develop and improve trainiee skills sets that align with the BCBA/BCaBA Task List and fieldwork requirements
      i) Appropriate vs. inappropriate fieldwork activities
      ii) Restricted vs. unrestricted fieldwork activities

- g) Pfovide a variety of fieldwork opportunities that are tied to the BCBA/BCaBA Task List
    - i) Establish pre-determined mastery criterion
    - ii) Incorporate behavioral skills training
    - iii) Identify trainee and supervisor responsibilities for progression through the task list
- h) Create assignments designed to improve and extend the trainee skill set that align with the BCBA/BCaBA Task List
    - i) Assign type (e.g., written, oral, video)
    - ii) Assign hour allocation
    - iii) Set deadlines
    - iv) Document evidence of completion
- i) Model and teach professionalism
    - i) Time management (e.g., measure planned activities vs. actual activities, adherence to deadlines)
    - ii) Organization (e.g., measure client programming, meeting preparation)
    - iii) Prioritization (e.g., measure appropriate allocation of time towards task based on criticality)
    - iv) Social skills (e.g., evaluate posture, adaptation to audience)
    - v) Interpersonal skills
- j) Regularly monitor the supervision experience for effectiveness
    - i) Review the supervision contract and goals periodically to determine satisfaction with the trainee experience (e.g., evaluate frequency and structure of meetings, goals, areas of deficiency)
    - ii) Review supervisor competencies
        1. Identify self-selected goals for supervision
        2. Self-rate supervisory activities
        3. Use supervisor peer-overlap of supervision activities for the purpose of obtaining peer feedback when possible
- k) End the supervisory relationship appropriately
    - i) Compete the accrual of supervised fieldwork hour
    - ii) Plan for fading supervisor-trainee contact
    - iii) Plan for continued mentorship

2) **The supervisor should be able to evaluate the effectiveness of supervision of the trainee.**
   - a) Assess baseline skills
     - i) Conduct interviews
     - ii) Conduct observations

       iii) Consult with previous supervisors, given consent from supervisee or trainee
       iv) Review writing samples and portfolios
       v) Review the BCBA/BCaBA Task List
- b) Schedule observations with clients
  - i) Conduct in-vivo observations
  - ii) Conduct live video observations
  - iii) Conduct recorded video observations
- c) Evaluate supervision based on client performance where appropriate
  - i) Objective measures of client behavior addressed by services (e.g., graphic display of client performance)
  - ii) Interviews and direct observations of client and caregiver satisfaction with services (e.g., social validity/satisfaction questionnaires)
- d) Evaluate supervision based on supervisee or trainee performance
  - i) Objective measures of direct observation of supervisee or trainee behavior addressed in training and supervision
  - ii) Interviews and direct observations of supervise satisfaction with training and supervision
- e) Evaluate professionalism using objective or subjective measures as appropriate
  - i) Attire
  - ii) Social interactions
  - iii) Attendance
  - iv) Time management
  - v) Organization (e.g., measure client programming, meeting preparation)
  - vi) Flexibility (e.g., evaluate problem-solving and responsiveness to changes in tasks)
- f) Evaluate the fidelity of implementation of specific interventions
  - i) Objective measures
  - ii) Self-monitoring
  - iii) Peer monitoring
  - iv) Supervisor monitoring
- g) Describe the potential outcomes of ineffective supervision practices, including the following:
  - i) Limits the supervisor's ability to replicate effects of effective supervision with subsequent supervisees or trainees
  - ii) Disorganized supervisory fieldwork that it time and cost prohibitive

iii) Discourages effective supervisors form supervising
iv) Models ineffective supervisory practices to the supervisee who may later become a supervisor
v) Increases potential risks of harm to current and future clients and supervisees or trainees

3) **The supervisor should be able to incorporate ethics and professional development into supervision of trainees.**
   a) Identify relevant ethical requirements and remain in compliance with them
      i) Professional and Ethical Compliance Code for Behavior Analysts
      ii) BACB code-enforcement systems
      iii) Licensure laws
      iv) Other policies (e.g., funding and institutional requirements)
   b) Analyze and solve ethical dilemmas
      i) Engage in problem-solving activities
      ii) Seek assistance when necessary (e.g., colleagues, supervisors, mentors)
   c) Identify and develop new areas of defined competency to ensure ethical supervision
      i) Review literature related to new competency areas
      ii) Engage with professional groups in new areas of practice
      iii) Pursue training and supervision in new areas
      iv) Identify necessary requirements for new areas of practice
   d) Pursue professional development opportunities for supervisors
      i) Create a continuous learning community to enhance behavior-analytic skills (e.g., study groups and journal clubs)
      ii) Read the literature (e.g., supervision, ethics, practice)
      iii) Attend professional development activities (e.g., conventions, workshops, webinars)
      iv) Engage in peer review
      v) Seek mentorship
      vi) Consult with colleagues
      vii) Participate in professional networks
      viii) Develop self-care strategies to maintain healthy and stable work environments

SELECTED SUPERVISION RESOURCES

DiGennaro Reed, F. D., & Henley, A. J. (2015). A survey of staff training and performance management practices: The good, the bad, and the ugly. *Behavior Analysis in Practice, 8*, 16-20. doi:10.1007/s40617-015-0044-5

Dubuque, E. M., & Dubuque, M. L. (2018). Guidelines for the establishment of a university-based practical training system. *Behavior Analysis in Practice, 11*, 51–61. doi:101007/s40617-016-0154-8

Garza, K. L., McGee, H. M., Schenk, T. A, & Wiskirchen, R. R. (2017). Some tools for carrying out a proposed process for supervising experience hours for aspiring Board Certified Behavior Analysts®. *Behavior Analysis in Practice, 11*, 62–70. doi:101007/s40617-017-0186-8.

Hartley, B., K., Courtney, W. T., Rosswurm, M., & LaMarca, V. J. (2016). The apprentice: An innovative approach to met the Behavior Analysis (sic) Certification Board's supervision standards. *Behavior Analysis in Practice, 9*, 329–338. doi:101007/s40617-016-0136-x

LeBlanc, L. A., Heinicke, M. R., & Baker, J. C. (2012). Expanding the consumer base for behavior analytic services: Meeting the needs of consumers in the 21st century. *Behavior Analysis in Practice, 5*, 4–14. doi:101007/BF03391813

LeBlanc, L. A., & Luiselli, J. K. (2016). Refining supervisory practices in the field of behavior analysis: Introduction to the special section on supervision. *Behavior Analysis in Practice, 9*, 271–273. doi:101007/s40617-016-0156-6

Sellers, T. P., Alai-Rosales, S., & MacDonald, R. P. (2016). Taking full responsibility: The ethids of supervision in behavior analytic practice. *Behavior Analysis in Practice, 9*, 299–308. doi:101007/s40617-016-0144-x

Sellers, T. P., LeBlanc, L. A., & Valentino, A. L. (2016) Recommendations for detecting and addressing barriers to successful supervision. *Behavior Analysis in Practice, 9*, 309–319. doi:101007/s40617-016-0142-z

Sellers, T. P., Valentino, A. L., & LeBlanc, L. A. (2016) Recommended practices for individual supervision of aspiring behavior analysts. *Behavior Analysis in Practice, 9*, 274–286. doi:101007/s40617-016-0110-7

Turner, L. B., Fischer, A. J., & Luiselli, J. K. (2016) Towards a competency-based, ethical, and socially valid approach to the supervision of applied behavior analytic trainees. *Behavior Analysis in Practice, 9*, 287–298. doi:101007/s40617-016-0121-4

Valentino, A. L., LeBlanc, L. A., & Sellers, T. P (2016) The benefits of group supervision and a recommended structure for implementation. *Behavior Analysis in Practice, 9*, 320–338. doi:101007/s40617-016-0138-8

Appendix III

BCBA®/BCaBA® 5th Edition Task List

Self-Assessment

BCBA® / BCaBA® 5th Edition Task List
Self-Assessment

Supervisee:

Supervisor:

Date of Self-Assessment:

Certificate Sought: BCaBA®   BCBA®

Section 1: Foundations
The Foundations section includes basic skills and underlying principles and knowledge

		I have been **exposed** to the concept.	I can **define** the concept.	I can give **examples and nonexamples** of the concept.	I can **demonstrate** the concept with one client/in one environment.	I can **demonstrate** the concept with multiple clients/in many environments.	I can **teach or instruct** this concept.
A	**Philosophical Underpinnings**						
A-1	Identify the goals of behavior analysis as a science (i.e., description, prediction, control)						
A-2	Explain the philosophical assumptions underlying the science of behavior analysis (e.g., selectionism, determinism, empiricism, parsimony, pragmatism)						
A-3	Describe and explain behavior from the perspective of radical behaviorism						
A-4	Distinguish among behaviorism, the experimental analysis of behavior, applied behavior analysis, and professional practice guided by the science of behavior analysis						
A-5	Describe and define the dimensions of applied behavior analysis (Baer, Wolf, & Risley, 1968)						

B	**Concepts and Principles**						
B-1	Define and provide examples of behavior, response, and response class						
B-2	Define and provide examples of stimulus and stimulus class						
B-3	Define and provide examples of respondent and operant conditioning						
B-4	Define and provide examples of positive and negative reinforcement contingencies						
B-5	Define and provide examples of schedules of reinforcement						
B-6	Define and provide examples of positive and negative punishment contingencies						
B-7	Define and provide examples of automatic and socially mediated contingencies						

Created and shared by Becca Marie Tagg, PsyD, MSCP, NCSP, BCBA-D and Shannon Lee Biagi, MS, BCBA (May, 2020). Reprinted with permission from Tagg and Biagi in LeBlanc, Sellers, and Ala'i (2020).

B-8	Define and provide examples of unconditioned, conditioned, and generalized reinforcers and punishers						
B-9	Define and provide examples of operant extinction						
B-10	Define and provide examples of stimulus control						
B-11	Define and provide examples of discrimination, generalization, and maintenance						
B-12	Define and provide examples of motivating operations						
B-13	Define and provide examples of rule-governed and contingency-shaped behavior						
B-14	Define and provide examples of the verbal operants						
B-15	Define and provide examples of derived stimulus relations						

C	Measurement, Data Display, and Interpretation						
C-1	Establish operational definitions of behavior						
C-2	Distinguish among direct, indirect, and product measures of behavior						
C-3	Measure occurrence (e.g., frequency, rate, percentage)						
C-4	Measure temporal dimensions of behavior (e.g., duration, latency, interresponse time)						
C-5	Measure form and strength of behavior (e.g., topography, magnitude)						
C-6	Measure trials to criterion						
C-7	Design and implement sampling procedures (i.e., interval recording, time sampling)						
C-8	Evaluate the validity and reliability of measurement procedures						
C-9	Select a measurement system to obtain representative data given the dimensions of behavior and the logistics of observing and recording						
C-10	Graph data to communicate relevant quantitative relations (e.g., equal-interval graphs, bar graphs, cumulative records)						
C-11	Interpret graphed data						

D	Experimental Design						
D-1	Distinguish between dependent and independent variables						
D-2	Distinguish between internal and external validity						

Created and shared by Becca Marie Tagg, PsyD, MSCP, NCSP, BCBA-D and Shannon Lee Biagi, MS, BCBA (May, 2020). Reprinted with permission from Tagg and Biagi in LeBlanc, Sellers, and Ala'i (2020).

D-3	Identify the defining features of single-subject experimental designs (e.g., individuals serve as their own controls, repeated measures, prediction, verification, replication)						
D-4	Describe the advantages of single-subject experimental designs compared to group designs						
D-5	Use single-subject experimental designs (e.g., reversal, multiple baseline, multielement, changing criterion)						
D-6	Describe rationales for conducting comparative, component, and parametric analyses.						

Analysis of Self-Assessment Section 1 - Foundations

Based on review of this self-assessment, three areas where I am pleased with my progress AND how I made progress are listed below

Based on review of this self-assessment, three areas I'd like to strengthen AND a plan for strengthening those areas are listed below.

Created and shared by Becca Marie Tagg, PsyD, MSCP, NCSP, BCBA-D and Shannon Lee Biagi, MS, BCBA (**May**, 2020). Reprinted with permission from Tagg and Biagi in LeBlanc, Sellers, and Ala'i (2020).

BCBA® / BCaBA® 5th Edition Task List
Self-Assessment

Supervisee:

Supervisor:

Date of Self-Assessment:

Certificate Sought: BCaBA®   BCBA®

Section 2: Applications
The Applications section includes more practice-oriented skills

Ethics: To behave in accordance with the *Professional and Ethical Compliance Code for Behavior Analysts*

E		I have been **exposed** to the concept.	I can **define** the concept.	I can give **examples and nonexamples** of the concept.	I can **demonstrate** the concept with one client/in one environment.	I can **demonstrate** the concept with **multiple** clients/in many environments.	I can **teach or instruct** this concept.
Ethics						
E-1	Responsible conduct of behavior analysts						
E-2	Behavior analysts' responsibility to clients						
E-3	Assessing behavior						
E-4	Behavior analysts and the behavior-change program						
E-5	Behavior analysts as supervisors						
E-6	Behavior analysts' ethical responsibility to the profession of behavior analysis						
E-7	Behavior analysts' ethical responsibility to colleagues						
E-8	Public Statements						
E-9	Behavior analysts and research						
E-10	Behavior analysts' ethical responsibility to the BACB						

F							
Behavior Assessment						
F-1	Review records and available data (e.g., educational, medical, historical) at the outset of the case						
F-2	Determine the need for behavior-analytic services						
F-3	Identify and prioritize socially significant behavior-change goals						
F-4	Conduct assessments of relevant skill strengths and deficits						

Created and shared by Becca Marie Tagg, PsyD, MSCP, NCSP, BCBA-D and Shannon Lee Biagi, MS, BCBA (May, 2020). Reprinted with permission from Tagg and Biagi in LeBlanc, Sellers, and Ala'i (2020).

F-5	Conduct preference assessments					
F-6	Describe the common functions of problem behavior					
F-7	Conduct a descriptive assessment of problem behavior					
F-8	Conduct a functional analysis of problem behavior					
F-9	Interpret functional assessment data					

G	Behavior-Change Procedures					
G-1	Use positive and negative reinforcement procedures to strengthen behavior					
G-2	Use interventions based on motivating operations and discriminative stimuli					
G-3	Establish and use conditioned reinforcers					
G-4	Use stimulus and response prompts and fading (e.g., errorless, most-to-least, least-to-most, prompt delay, stimulus fading)					
G-5	Use modeling and imitation training					
G-6	Use instructions and rules					
G-7	Use shaping					
G-8	Use chaining					
G-9	Use discrete-trial, free-operant, and naturalistic teaching arrangements.					
G-10	Teach simple and conditional discriminations					
G-11	Use Skinner's analysis to teach verbal behavior					
G-12	Use equivalence-based instruction					
G-13	Use the high-probability instructional sequence					
G-14	Use reinforcement procedures to weaken behavior (e.g., DRA, FCT, DRO, DRL, NCR)					
G-15	Use extinction					
G-16	Use positive and negative punishment (e.g., time-out, response cost, overcorrection)					
G-17	Use token economies					
G-18	Use group contingencies					
G-19	Use contingency contracting					
G-20	Use self-management strategies					
G-21	Use procedures to promote stimulus and response generalization					
G-22	Use procedures to promote maintenance					

H	Selecting and Implementing Interventions					
H-1	State intervention goals in observable and measurable terms					

Created and shared by Becca Marie Tagg, PsyD, MSCP, NCSP, BCBA-D and Shannon Lee Biagi, MS, BCBA (May, 2020). Reprinted with permission from Tagg and Biagi in LeBlanc, Sellers, and Ala'i (2020).

H-2	Identify potential interventions based on assessment results and the best available scientific evidence						
H-3	Recommend intervention goals and strategies based on such factors as client preferences, supporting environments, risks, constraints, and social validity						
H-4	When a target behavior is to be decreased, select an acceptable alternative behavior to be established or increased						
H-5	Plan for possible unwanted effects when using reinforcement, extinction, and punishment procedures						
H-6	Monitor client progress and treatment integrity						
H-7	Make data-based decisions about the effectiveness of the intervention and the need for treatment revision						
H-8	Make data-based decisions about the need for ongoing services						
H-9	Collaborate with others who support and/or provide services to clients						

I		**Personnel Supervision and Management**					
I-1	State the reasons for using behavior-analytic supervision and the potential risks of ineffective supervision (e.g., poor client outcomes, poor supervisee performance)						
I-2	Establish clear performance expectations for the supervisor and supervisee						
I-3	Select supervision goals based on an assessment of the supervisee's skills						
I-4	Train personnel to competently perform assessment and intervention procedures						
I-5	Use performance monitoring, feedback, and reinforcement systems						
I-6	Use a functional assessment approach (e.g., performance diagnostics) to identify variables affecting personnel performance						
I-7	Use function-based strategies to improve personnel performance						
I-8	Evaluate the effects of supervision (e.g., on client outcomes, on supervisee repertoires)						

Created and shared by Becca Marie Tagg, PsyD, MSCP, NCSP, BCBA-D and Shannon Lee Biagi, MS, BCBA (May, 2020). Reprinted with permission from Tagg and Biagi in LeBlanc, Sellers, and Ala'i (2020).

Analysis of Self-Assessment Section 2 - Application

Based on review of this self-assessment, three areas where I am pleased with my progress AND how I made progress are listed below.

1.

2.

3.

Based on review of this self-assessment, three areas I'd like to strengthen AND a plan for strengthening those areas are listed below.

1.

2.

3.

Created and shared by Becca Marie Tagg, PsyD, MSCP, NCSP, BCBA-D and Shannon Lee Biagi, MS, BCBA (May, 2020). Reprinted with permission from Tagg and Biagi in LeBlanc, Sellers, and Ala'i (2020).

Appendix IV

Additional Resources

Chapter 2

Blake-Beard, S. (2019). Mentoring: creating mutually empowering relationships. [Video]. Standford. https://womensleadership.stanford.edu/mentoring-creating-mutually-empowering-relationships

College of Education & Human Development. (2020). Introduction to reflective supervision/consultation using RIOS framework. University of Minnesota. http://ceed.umn.edu/online-courses/introduction-to-reflective-supervision-consultation-using-the-rios-framework/

Eby, L. T., Allen, T. D., Evans, S. C., Ng, T., & Dubois, D. (2008). Does Mentoring Matter? A Multidisciplinary Meta-Analysis Comparing Mentored and Non-Mentored Individuals. *Journal of vocational behavior*, 72(2), 254–267. https://doi.org/10.1016/j.jvb.2007.04.005

Hantula, D. (2017). Effective supervision and ethics. [Presentation]. Association for Behavior Analysis International. https://www.abainternational.org/Shopping/Item-Listing.aspx?intItmKey=25662

Head Start. (2019). Reflective Supervision. Retrieved from https://eclkc.ohs.acf.hhs.gov/family-engagement/developing-relationships-families/reflective-supervision

https://business.ku.edu/mentoring-resources KU School of Business: Mentoring resources.

LeBlanc, L. A. (2018). *The behavior analyst as a supervisor: creating advanced supervision and mentoring repertoires*. Association for Behavior Analysis International.

https://www.abainternational.org/portal/secure-pages/2018-autism-conference/leblanc-workshop.aspx

https://mentorloop.com/resources/

Oregon Health & Science University. (n.d.) *Getting Started.* School of medicine mentoring. (https://www.ohsu.edu/school-of-medicine/mentoring/getting-started

Reinecke, D. & Davis, C. (2019). Best practices in BCBA supervision. [Presentation]. Association for Behavior Analysis International. https://www.abainternational.org/Shopping/Item-Listing.aspx?intItmKey=27508

Scottish Social Services Council. (n.d.). Supervision. http://www.stepintoleadership.info/supervision.html

Social Care Institute for Excellence. (2017). Effective supervision in a variety of settings. https://www.scie.org.uk/publications/guides/guide50/foundationsofeffectivesupervision/

Stone, D., Patton, B., Heen, S., & Fisher, R. (1999). *Difficult conversations: how to discuss what matters most.* Penguin.

Sulzer-Azaroff, B. (2015). Joy and fulfillment as a female behavior analyst. *The Behavior Analyst, 38,* 275–282.

The Pennsylvania Child Welfare Resource Center. (n.d.). *Supervisor training series.* Best practice guidelines for reflective supervision. http://www.pacwrc.pitt.edu/Curriculum/521%20SupervisorTrainingSeries-Module3–TheMiddleWorkPhase/Hndts/HO32_BstPrctcGdlnsRflctvSprvsn.pdf

Thomas D. (2001). The truth about mentoring minorities: race matters. *Harvard Business Review,* 79(4), 98–112.

Zero to Three. (2016). Three building blocks of reflective supervision. https://www.zerotothree.org/resources/412–three-building-blocks-of-reflective-supervision

Chapter 3

Barnes-Holmes, Y., McHugh, L., & Barnes-Holmes, D. (2004). Perspective-taking and Theory of Mind: A relational frame account. *The Behavior Analyst Today,* 5(1), 15–25. http://dx.doi.org/10.1037/h0100133

Bennett-Levy, J. Turner, F., Beaty, T., Smith, M., Paterson, B., & Farmer, S. (2001). The value of self-practice of cognitive therapy techniques and self-reflection in the training of cognitive therapists. *Behavioural and Cognitive Psychotherapy, 29,* 2–3–220. DOI: https://libproxy.library.unt.edu:2147/10.1017/S1352465801002077

Chick, N. (n.d.). *Metacognition: thinking about one's thinking.* Center for Teaching, Vanderbilt University. Retrieved from https://cft.vanderbilt.edu/guides-sub-pages/metacognition/

Cross, T., Bazron, B., Dennis, K. and Isacs, M. (1989) *Towards a culturally competent system of care.* Georgetown University, Washington DC.

da Silva Ferreira, T.A., Simões, A.S., Ferreira, A.R. & Santana dos Santos, B. O. (2020). What are Values in Clinical Behavior Analysis?. *Perspectives on Behavior Science, 43,* 177–188. https://doi.org/10.1007/s40614-019-00219-w

Katz, D., Monette, G., Gaskovski, P., & Eastwood, J. (2017). The creation of the client reflexivity scale: A measure of minute fluctuations in self-awareness and exploration. *Psychotherapy Research, 27*(6), 724–736. DOI: 10.1080/10503307.2016.1158432

Dong, S., Campbell, A., & Vance, S. (2017). Examining the facilitating role of mindfulness on professional identity development among counselors-in-training: A qualitative approach. *The Professional Counselor, 7*(4), 305–317. DOI: http://libproxy.library.unt.edu:2126/10.15241/sd.7.4.305

Fong, E. H., Catagnus, R. M., Brodhead, M. T., Quigley, S., & Field, S. (2016). Developing the Cultural Awareness Skills of Behavior Analysts. *Behavior analysis in practice, 9*(1), 84–94. https://doi.org/10.1007/s40617-016-0111-6

Hayes, S. (n.d.). My ACT tool kit. Steven C. Hayes, PHD. Retrieved from https://stevenchayes.com/my-act-toolkit/

Kane, T. & Greenberg, M. (Ongoing project). Best foot forward: video observation toolkit. *Center for Education Policy Research- Harvard University.* Retrieved from https://cepr.harvard.edu/video-observation-toolkit

Lo, H. (2010). My racial identity development and supervision: a self-reflection. *Journal of Training and Education in Professional Psychology, 4,* 26–28. DOI: 10.1037/a0017856

Marx, R. (2019). Soliciting and utilizing mid-semester feedback. Vanderbilt University Center for Teaching. Retrieved from https://cft.vanderbilt.edu/guides-sub-pages/student-feedback/

Plumb, J. C., Stewart, I., Dahl, J., & Lundgren, T. (2009). In search of meaning: values in modern clinical behavior analysis. *The Behavior analyst, 32*(1), 85–103. https://doi.org/10.1007/BF03392177

Rennie, D.L. (2000). Aspects of the client's conscious control of the psychotherapeutic process. *Journal of Psychotherapy Integration, 10,* 151–167. https://doi.org/10.1023/A:1009496116174

Shafer, L. (2015). Pause and reflect. *Harvard Graduate School of Education.* Retrieved from https://www.gse.harvard.edu/news/uk/15/10/pause-and-reflect

Tamer, M. (2014). The value of self reflection. *Harvard Graduate School of Education*. Retrieved from https://www.gse.harvard.edu/news/uk/14/10/value-self-reflection

Tsai, M., Kohlenberg, R. J., Kanter, R. J., Kohlenberg, B., Follette, W. C., & Callaghan, G. M. (2009). *A guide to functional analytic psychotherapy: awareness, courage, love, and behaviorism*. Springer US. 10.1007/978–0–387–09787–9

Wright, T., Nankin, I., Boonstra, K., & Blair, E. (2019). Changing through relationships and reflection: An exploratory investigation of pre-service teachers' perceptions of young children experiencing homelessness. *Early Childhood Education Journal, 47*(3), 297–308. doi:http://libproxy.library.unt.edu:2126/10.1007/s10643–018–0921–y

Chapter 4

Bailey, V. (n.d.) Creating an Inclusive Campus for Trans and Nonbinary Community Members. Podcast retrieved from https://www.kaltura.com/index.php/extwidget/preview/partner_id/1449362/uiconf_id/14292362/entry_id/1_bg9gzfye/embed/dynamic

Crenshaw, K. (1989). Demarginalizing the Intersection of Race and Sex: A Black Feminist Critique of Antidiscrimination Doctrine, Feminist Theory and Antiracist Politics. University of Chicago Legal Forum, 8, 139–167. Available at: https://chicagounbound.uchicago.edu/cgi/viewcontent.cgi?article=1052&context=uclf

Crenshaw, K. (Ted). (2016). The Urgency of Intersectionality. *TEDWomen2016*. Video Retrieved from https://www.ted.com/talks/kimberle_crenshaw_the_urgency_of_intersectionality/up-next

Cross, T., Bazron, B., Dennis, K., & Isaacs, M. (1989). *Towards a culturally competent system of care: A monograph on effective services for minority children who are severely emotionally disturbed* (Vol. 1). Washington, DC: Georgetown University Child Development Center. Available at: https://spu.edu/~/media/academics/school-of-education/Cultural%20Diversity/Towards%20a%20Culturally%20Competent%20System%20of%20Care%20Abridged.ashx

Diversity. Princeton University. Retrieved April, 2020, from https://mediacentral.princeton.edu/esearch/search?keyword=diversity

Diversity & Inclusion. Office of Personnel Management, Retrieved April, 2020, from https://www.opm.gov/policy-data-oversight/diversity-and-inclusion/reference-materials/

Diversity and Inclusion. Department of Labor, Retrieved April, 2020, from https://www.dol.gov/odep/topics/diversityandinclusion.htm

Diversity and Opportunity. US Department of Education. Retrieved April, 2020, from https://www.ed.gov/diversity-opportunity

Epler, M. (Ted). (2017). 3 ways to be a better ally in the workplace. *TED Salon: Brightline Initiative.* Video Retrieved from https://www.ted.com/talks/melinda_epler_3_ways_to_be_a_better_ally_in_the_workplace/up-next

Everett, T. (Ted). (2019). Valuing Neurodiversity. *TEDxYouth@FAIHS.* Video Retrieved from https://www.ted.com/talks/traci_everett_valuing_neuro-diversity/up-next

Gilbert, J., Goode, T. D., & Dunne, C. (2007). *Curricula Enhancement Module.* National Center for Cultural Competence, Georgetown University Child Development Center. [PDF document]. Retrieved from https://nccc.georgetown.edu/curricula/documents/awareness.pdf

Global & Cultural Effectiveness. The SHRM Store. Retrieved April, 2020, from https://store.shrm.org/education/elearning/global-and-cultural-effectiveness

Hanson, M. & Lynch, E. (2013). *Understanding Families: Supportive Approaches to Diversity, Disability, and Risk* (2nd ed.) Baltimore: Paul H. Brookes.

Knopf, H. & Swick, K. J. (2008). Using our understanding of families to strengthen family involvement. *Early Childhood Education, 35,* 419–427. DOI:10.1007/s10643-007-0198-z

Religious Discrimination. US Equal Employment Opportunity Commission. Retrieved April, 2020, from https://www.eeoc.gov/laws/types/religion.cfm

Resources. Robin DiAngelo, PhD: Critical Racial & Social Justice Education. Retrieved April, 2020, from https://robindiangelo.com/resources/

Resources by Title. Georgetown University National Center for Cultural Competence. Retrieved April, 2020, from https://nccc.georgetown.edu/resources/title.php

Scott, S. (2017). *An Inclusive United States: Religious Inclusion in the Federal Workplace- National Institutes of Health: Office of Equity, Diversity, and Inclusion*. National Institutes of Health, Retrieved April, 2020 from https://www.edi.nih.gov/blog/communities/inclusive-united-states-religious-inclusion-federal-workplace

Spradley, J. P. (1979). *The ethnographic interview*. Harcourt Brace Jovanovich College Publishers.

Tervalon, M. & Murray-Garcia, J. (1998). Cultural humility versus cultural competence: a critical distinction in defining physician training outcomes in multicultural education. *Journal of Health Care for the Poor and Underserved, 9*(2), 117–125. DOI:10.1353/hpu.2010.0233

Toolkits. Community Tool Box. Retrieved April, 2020 from ctb.ku.edu/en/toolkits.

Chapter 5

ABA Ethics Hotline. (n.d.). *Core ethical principles*. Retrieved from https://www.abaethicshotline.com/core-ethical-principles/

BACB (n.d.). Supervision and training. Retrieved from https://www.bacb.com/supervision-and-training/

Cihon, T. M., Cihon, J. H., & Bedient, G. M. (2016). Establishing a common vocabulary of key concepts for the effective implementation of applied behavior analysis. *International Electronic Journal of Elementary Education, 9*(2), 337–348.

Ellis, J. & Glenn, S. S. (1995). Behavior-analytic repertoires: where will they come from and how can they be maintained? *The Behavior Analyst, 2*, 285–292.

Gilbert, T. F. (1967). Praxeonomy: a systemic approach to identifying training needs. *Management of Personnel Quarterly*, Fall, 20–33.

Gilbert, T. F. (1978). *Human competence*. New York: McGraw-Hill.

Goldiamond, I. (1974/2002). *Total institutions and therapeutic goals*. pp. 115–121.

Horner, R. H., Sprague, J. R., & Wilcox, B. (1982). Constructing general case programs for community activities. In B. Wilcox & G. T. Bellamy (Eds.), *Design of high school programs for severely handicapped students* (pp. 61–98). Baltimore: Paul H. Brookes.

Lindsley, O. R. (1991). From technical jargon to plain English for application. *Journal of Applied Behavior Analysis, 24*, 449–458.

Mager, R. F. (1997). *Preparing Instructional objectives, Third Edition*. Center for Effective Performance. Atlanta, GA.

Marzullo-Kerth, D., Reeve, S. A., Reeve, K. F., & Townsend, D. B. (2011). Using multiple-exemplar training to teach a generalized repertoire of sharing to children with autism. *Journal of applied behavior analysis, 44*(2), 279–294. https://doi.org/10.1901/jaba.2011.44-279

Shook, G. L., Ala'i-Rosales, S., & Glenn, S. S. (2002). Training and certifying behavior analysts. *Behavior Modification, 26*, 27–48.

Shook, G. L., Johnston, J. M., & Mellichamp, F. H. (2004). Determining essential content for applied behavior analyst practitioners. *The Behavior Analyst, 27*(1), 67–94. https://doi.org/10.1007/BF03392093

Stokes, T. F. & Baer, D. M. (1977). An implicit technology of generalization. *Journal of Applied Behavior Analysis, 10*, 349–367.

Tiemann, P. W., & Markle, S. M. (1990). *Analyzing instructional content: A guide to instruction and evaluation*. Champaign, IL: Stipes Pub.

Valentino, A. V., LeBlanc, L. A., & Sellers, T. P. (2016). The Benefits of Group Supervision and a Recommended Structure for Implementation. *Behavior Analysis in Practice, 9*, 320–328.

Weiss, M. J., & Shook, G. L. (2010). Resources on training requirements for applied behavior analysts: The Behavior Analyst Certification Board and the autism special interest group consumer guidelines. *European Journal of Behavior Analysis, 11*, 217–222. doi:10.1080/15021149.2010.11434345

Wolf, M. M., Kirigin, K. A., Fixen, D. L., Blasé, K. A., & Braukmann, C. J. (1995). The teaching-family model: a case study in data-based program development and refinement (and dragon wrestling). *Journal of Organizational Behavior Management, 15*, 11–68.

Chapter 6

Benner, P. (2004). Using the Dreyfus model of skill acquisition to describe and interpret skill acquisition and clinical judgement in nursing practice and education. *Bulletin of Science, Technology, & Society, 24*(3), 188–199.

Field, A. (2014). Understanding the Dreyfus model of skill acquisition to improve ultrasound training for obstetrics and gynecology trainees. *Ultrasound, 22*, 118–122.

Gerwirtz, J. L. (1971). Conditional responding as a paradigm for observational, imitative learning and vicarious-reinforcement. *Advances in Child Development and Behavior, 6*, 273–304.

Goldiamond, I. (Dec 19, 2016). Episode 1, "where do we go from here" YouTube]. Retrieved from https://www.youtube.com/watch?v=FttewBR19Sc&list=PLEO3a-NCxrrDzBhiDm5iZFhl16OV0N2rO0p&index=1

Hepner, F. S. (1989). Effects of guided design with and without teacher support on the accuracy in formulating nursing care plans and clinical problem solving by student nurses. (Doctoral dissertation, University of Georgia, 1989). *Dissertation Abstracts International, 50*, 2336.

Kalliath, T., & Brough, P. (2008). Work-life balance: A review of the meaning of the balance construct. *Journal of Management and Organization, 14*(3), 323–327. Retrieved from https://libproxy.library.unt.edu/login?url=https://libproxy.library.unt.edu:2165/docview/233254631?accountid=7113

Karsten, A. M., Axe, J. B., & Mann, C. C. (2015). Review and discussion of strategies to address low trainer-to-staff ratios. *Behavioral Interventions, 30*, 295–313.

Pierce, T., & Miller, S. P. (1994). Using peer coaching in preservice practica. *Teacher Education and Special Education, 17*, 215–223.

Roll-Pettersson, L. & Ala'i-Rosales, S. (2009). Using blended and guided technologies in a university course for scientist-practitioners. *Journal of Intellectual Disabilities, 13*(2), 113–142. doi: 10.1177/1744629509340179

Schwartz, A., & Goldiamond, I. (1975). *Social casework: A behavioral approach.* New York: Columbia University Press.

Skinner, B. F. (1976). *Self-management of behavior*. [YouTube]. Retrieved from https://www.youtube.com/watch?v=XCajvO6CVzE

Sundaresan, S. (2014). Work-life balance- implications for working women. International *Journal of Sustainable Development, 7*, 93–101.

The Behavioral Observations Podcast. (2019). Work/ life balance: session 86 with Kirsten Lancaster and Jonathan Tarbox. [Podcast]. Retrieved from https://behavioralobservations.com/work-life-balance-session-86–with-kristen-lancaster-and-jonathan-tarbox/

Touchette, P., MacDonald, R., & Langer, S. (1985). A scatter plot for identifying stimulus control of problem behavior. *Journal of Applied Behavior Analysis, 18*, 343–351.

Trivette, C. M., Dunst, C. J., Hamby, D. W., O'Herin, C. E. (2009). Characteristics and consequences of adult learning methods and strategies. *Research Brief, 3*, 2009.

Chapter 7

Axe, J. B., Phelan, S. H., & Irwin, C. L. (2018). Empirical evaluations of skinner's analysis of problem solving. *The Analysis of Verbal Behavior*, 35, 39–56. https://doi.org/10.1007/s40616–018–0103–4

Binder C. (1996). Behavioral fluency: Evolution of a new paradigm. *The Behavior analyst, 19*(2), 163–197. https://doi.org/10.1007/BF03393163

Branch, A., Hastings, R. P., Beverley, M. & Hughes, J. C. (2018). Increasing support staff fluency with the content of behaviour support plans: an application of precision teaching. *Journal of Intellectual & Developmental Disability, 43*(2), 213–222.

Goldiamond, I. (1984). Training parent trainers and ethicists in nonlinear analysis of behavior. In R. F. Dangel & R. A. Polster (Eds.), *Parent training: Foundations of research and practice*. (p. 504–546). New York: Guilford.

Goodhue, R.J., Liu, S.C. & Cihon, T.M. (2019). Incorporating the Portable Operant Research and Teaching Laboratory into Undergraduate Introduction to Behavior Analysis Courses. *Journal of Behavioral Education*, 28, 517–541. https://libproxy.library.unt.edu:2147/10.1007/s10864–019–09323–y

Guõmundsdóttir, K., Sigurõardóttir, Z. G., & Ala'i-Rosales, S. (2017). Evaluation of caregiver training via telecommunication for rural Icelandic children with autism. *Behavioral Development Bulletin*, 22, 215–229.

Johnson, K. R., & Layng, T. V. (1996). On terms and procedures: Fluency. *The Behavior analyst, 19*(2), 281–288. https://doi.org/10.1007/BF03393170

Kieta, A.R., Cihon, T.M. & Abdel-Jalil, A. (2019). Problem Solving from a Behavioral Perspective: Implications for Behavior Analysts and Educators. *Journal of Behavioral Education,* 28, 275–300 (2019). https://libproxy.library.unt.edu:2147/10.1007/s10864-018-9296-9

Lindsley O. R. (1996). Is fluency free-operant response-response chaining?. *The Behavior analyst,* 19(2), 211–224. https://doi.org/10.1007/BF03393165

O'Keeffe, B. V., Slocum, T. A., & Magnusson, R. (2011). The effects of a fluency training package on paraprofessionals' presentation of a reading intervention. *The Journal of Special Education,* 47, 14–27. https://doi.org/10.1177/0022466911404072

Robbins, J. K. (2011). Problem solving, reasoning, and analytical thinking in a classroom environment. *The Behavior Analyst Today,* 12(1), 40–47.

Skinner, B. F. (1984). An operant analysis of problem solving. *Behavioral and Brain Sciences,* 7(4), 583–591.

Vasconcellos, A. D. S., Viranyi, Z., Range, F., Ades, C., Scheidegger, J. K., Mostl, E., & Kotrschal, K. (2016). Training Reduces Stress in Human-Socialised Wolves to the Same Degree as in Dogs. *PLoS ONE,* 11(9), e0162389. Retrieved from https://libproxy.library.unt.edu:7175/apps/doc/A470941624/OVIC?u=txshracd2679&sid=OVIC&xid=57a7b7fe

Whimbey, A., Lochhead, J., & Narode, R. (2013). *Problem solving and comprehension* (7th ed.). New York, NY: Routledge.

Zand, D. E. (1972). Trust and managerial problem solving. *Administrative Science Quarterly,* 17(2), 229–239. *DOI: 10.2307/2393957*

Chapter 8

College Advising Support Team. (2017, July). UC Santa Cruz. Retrieved from https://advising.ucsc.edu/success/online/time-management.html

Eighty Percent Solutions Corporation. (2011). *Freedom* (5.0.5). [mobile app]. App Store. https://freedom.to

Farrell, M. (2017).Time Management. *Journal of Library Administration,* 57:2, 215–222, DOI: 10.1080/01930826.2017.1281666

Google LLC. (2020). Google Calendar: Time Planning (2.142.0). [mobile app]. App Store. https://calendar.google.com/calendar/r?pli=1

Guise, S. (2013). *Mini Habits: Smaller Habits, Bigger Results*. CreateSpace Publishing.

Thomack, B. (2012). Time Management for Today's Workplace Deands. *Workplace Health & Safety,* 60(5), 201–203. https://doi.org/10.1177/216507991206000503

Learnhigher. (n.d.). Time management. Retrieved from http://www.learnhigher.ac.uk/learning-at-university/time-management/

Mind Tools Content Team. (n.d.) S.M.A.R.T. *Goals: How to Make Your Goals Achievable*. Mind tools. https://www.mindtools.com/pages/article/smart-goals.htm

Moronz-Alpert, Y. (n.d.) *5 tricks for an efficient morning at work.* Real Simple. http://www.wisnik.com/wp-content/uploads/2014/09/Real-Simple_TM_2014.pdf

Owl Purdue. (2019, April). Writing Motivation: After You Start. Retrieved from https://www.youtube.com/watch?v=HKidIpOdG64

Purdue University. (n.d.) *Why and How to Create a Useful Outline.* Purdue Online Writing Lab. https://owl.purdue.edu/owl/general_writing/the_writing_process/developing_an_outline/how_to_outline.html

Purdue University Global. (2018, April). *Time Management Tips for Busy College Students.* https://www.purdueglobal.edu/blog/student-life/time-management-busy-college-students/

Princeton University (2016). *Principles of Effective Time Management for Balance, Well-being, and Success.* The McGraw Center for Teaching & Learning. https://mcgraw.princeton.edu/sites/mcgraw/files/media/effective-time-management.pdf

RescueTime, Inc. (2018). RescueTime (1.3). [mobile app]. App Store. https://www.rescuetime.com/plans

Silvia, P. J. (2018). *How to Write a Lot: a Practical Guide to Productive Academic Writing* (2nd Ed.). APA LifeTools.

University of Birmingham. (n.d.) *Group Working.* https://www.birmingham.ac.uk/schools/metallurgy-materials/about/cases/group-work/index.aspx

Chapter 9

Abbott, E. A. (1885). *Flatland.* Boston, MA: Roberts Brothers.

Alvey, S. & Barclay, K. (2007). The characteristics of dyadic trust in executive coaching. Journal of Leadership Studies, 1, 18–27. DOI: **https://doi.org/10.1002/jls.20004**

Angelou, M. (1995). A brave and startling truth. Retrieved from https://lakeharriet.mpls.k12.mn.us/uploads/brave_and_startling_truth.pdf

Barsade, S. (2002). The Ripple Effect: Emotional Contagion and Its Influence on Group Behavior. *Administrative Science Quarterly,47*(4), 644–675. doi:10.2307/3094912

Bradford, D. L. & Robin, C. S. (2004). Leadership excellence and the "soft" skills: authenticity, influence, and performance. Stanford Business School. Retrieved from https://www.gsb.stanford.edu/faculty-research/working-papers/leadership-excellence-soft-skills-authenticity-influence-performance

Cary, M. (2018). In medicine, the "soft" skills are essential. HCP Live. Retrieved from https://www.mdmag.com/medical-news/in-medicine-the-soft-skills-are-essential

Conrad, C. A. & Leigh, W. A. (1999). Soft skills: bridge or barrier to employment? *Focus*, 27, 5–6.

Deming, D. J. (2017). The value of soft skills in the labor market. The National Bureau of Economic Research. Retrieved from https://www.nber.org/reporter/2017number4/deming.html

Gavin, M. (2020). 3 ways to create value in a negotiation. Harvard Business School Online. Retrieved from https://online.hbs.edu/blog/post/negotiation-tactics-how-to-add-value

Goleman, D. (2011). Emotional intelligence. [YouTube]. Retrieved from https://www.youtube.com/watch?v=wJhfKYzKc0s

Ianiro, P., Lehmann-Willenbrock, N., & Kauffeld, S. (2015). Coaches and Clients in Action: A Sequential Analysis of Interpersonal Coach and Client Behavior. *Journal of Business and Psychology*, 30(3), 435–456. https://doi.org/10.1007/s10869-014-9374-5

Landry, L. (2019). 8 communication skills every leader needs. Harvard Business School Online. Retrieved from https://online.hbs.edu/blog/post/leadership-communication

Stewart, John (Ed.) (1999) *Bridges Not Walls: A Book About Interpersonal Communication*.7th Ed. New York: McGraw-Hill

Stone, D., Patton, B. & Heen, S. (1999). *Difficult conversations: how to discuss what matters most.* Penguin Books: Cambridge, Massachusetts.

Tulgan, B. (2015). *Bridging the soft skills gap: How to teach the missing basics to today's young talent*. Jossey-Bass: Hoboken, NJ.

Chapter 10

Ala'i-Rosales, S., & Zeug, N. (2010). Three important things to consider when starting intervention for a child diagnosed with autism. *Behavior analysis in practice*, 3(2), 54–55. https://doi.org/10.1007/BF03391766

Besner, A., Ala'i-Rosales, S., Rosales-Ruiz, J., Broome, J., Newcomer, A., Suchomel, N., Jones, A., Ewing, S., & Zeug, N. (2007, May). An analysis of learn units in a parent training program. Symposium Presentation at the Association for Behavior Analysis Annual Convention in San Diego, CA.

Cortazzi, M., Jin, L, Wall, D. & Cavendish, S. (2001). Sharing learning though narrative communication. *International Journal of Language and Communication Disorders*, 36, pp. 252–257. DOI: http://dx.doi.org/10.3109/1368282-0109177893

Dowd, T., Czyz, J. D., O'Kane, S. E., & Elofson, A. (1994). *Effective skills for childcare workers: A training manual from Boys Town*. Boys Town, NE: Boys Town Press.

Foster, S. L., & Mash, E. J. (1999). Assessing social validity in clinical treatment research: Issues and procedures. *Journal of Consulting and Clinical Psychology*, 67(3), 308–319. https://doi.org/10.1037/0022-006X.67.3.308

Geiger, K. B., LeBlanc, L. A., Hubik, K., Jenkins, S. R., & Carr, J. E. (2018). Live training versus e-learning to teach implementation of listener response programs. *Journal of Applied Behavior Analysis*, 51(2), 220–235. https://doi.org/10.1002/jaba.444.

Green, D. R., Ferguson, J. L., Cihon, J. H., Torres, N., Leaf, N., Leaf, R., McEachin, J., Rudrud E., Schulze, K., & Leaf, J. B. (2019). The teaching interaction procedure as a staff training tool. *Behavior Analysis in Practice*, 1–13.

Greer, D. R., & McDonough, S. H. (1999). Is the learn unit a fundamental measure of pedagogy. *The Behavior Analyst*, 22, 5–16.

Harchik, A. E., Sherman, J. A., Sheldon, J. B., & Strouse, M. C. (1992). Ongoing consultation as a method of improving performance of staff members in a group home. *Journal of Applied Behavior Analysis*, 25(3), 599–610.

McLaughlin, D. M., & Carr, E. G. (2005). Quality of rapport as a setting event for problem behavior assessment and intervention. *Journal of Positive Behavior Interventions*, 7(2), 68–91.

Minkin, N., Braukmann, C. J., Minkin, B. L., Timbers, G. D., Timbers, B. J., Fixsen, D. L., Phillips, E. L. & Wolf, M. M. (1976). The social validation and training of conversational skills. *Journal of Applied Behavior Analysis*, 9, 127–139. https://doi.org/10.1901/jaba.1976.9-127.

Rispoli, M., Burke, M. D., Hatton, H., Ninci, J., Zaini, S., & Sanchez, L. (2015). Training Head Start Teachers to Conduct Trial-Based Functional Analysis of Challenging Behavior. *Journal of Positive Behavior Interventions*, 17(4), 235–244. https://doi.org/10.1177/1098300715577428

Schwartz I. S. (1991). The study of consumer behavior and social validity: An essential partnership for applied behavior analysis. *Journal of applied behavior analysis*, 24(2), 241–244. https://doi.org/10.1901/jaba.1991.24-241

Schwartz, I. S., & Baer, D. M. (1991). Social validity assessments: is current practice state of the art?. *Journal of Applied Behavior Analysis*, 24(2), 189–204. https://doi.org/10.1901/jaba.1991.24-189

Turner, L. B., Fischer, A. J., & Luiselli, J. K. (2016). Towards a Competency-Based, Ethical, and Socially Valid Approach to the Supervision of Applied Behavior Analytic Trainees. *Behavior Analysis Practice 9*, 287–298. https://doi.org/10.1007/s40617-016-0121-4

Chapter 11

Babcock, L. & Laschever, S. (2009). Ask for it: how women can use the power of negotiations to get what they really want. Bantam: New York, NY.

Beheshti, N. (2018). How a daily self-reflection practice improves leadership performance. Forbes. Retrieved from https://www.forbes.com/sites/nazbeheshti/2018/09/28/how-a-daily-self-reflection-practice-improves-leadership-performance/#185875055aad

Cohen, A. (2019). 3 steps to having difficult- but necessary- conversations. [TedTalk]. Retrieved from https://www.ted.com/talks/adar_cohen_3_ways_to_lead_tough_unavoidable_conversations/up-next

Daniels, A. C. (1999). Bring out the best in people: how to apply the astonishing power of positive reinforcement. McGraw-Hill: New York, NY.

Engagement at Harvard. (n.d.). Engagement toolkit for managers and leaders. Harvard University. Retrieved from https://hr.harvard.edu/files/humanresources/files/engagement_toolkit_leaders_managers.pdf

Head Start. (2019). Reflective supervision. U.S. Department of Health and Human Services. Retrieved from https://eclkc.ohs.acf.hhs.gov/family-engagement/developing-relationships-families/reflective-supervision

Herbst, S. (2016). Conversations that drive performance: empowering employees with behavior science. bSci21.org. [Webinar]. Retrieved from https://bsci21.org/courses/conversations-that-drive-performance-empowering-employees-with-behavior-science-1-bacb-ceu/

van Seggelen-Damen, I. & van Dam, K. (2016). Self-reflection as a mediator between self-efficacy and well-being. *Journal of Managerial Psychology, 31*(1), 18–33. doi:http://libproxy.library.unt.edu:2126/10.1108/JMP-01-2013-0022

Keyser, J. (2013). Self-reflection for self-awareness. Association for Talent Development. Retrieved from https://www.td.org/insights/self-reflection-for-self-awareness

Kim, E., & Kim, C. (2013). Comparative effects of empathic verbal responses: Reflection versus validation. *Journal of Counseling Psychology*, 60(3), 439–444. https://libproxy.library.unt.edu:2147/10.1037/a0032786

Reflection Toolkit. (2019). Reflecting for self-awareness. The University of Edinburgh. Retrieved from https://www.ed.ac.uk/reflection/reflectors-toolkit/self-awareness

Robbins, S. (2013). Difficult Conversations. Massachusetts Institute of Technology. Retrieved from https://alum.mit.edu/sites/default/files/2017–05/Communication%20–%20Difficult%20conversations%20v2.pdf

Seppälä, E. (2017). 11 keys to mastering difficult conversations. Psychology Today. Retrieved at https://www.psychologytoday.com/us/blog/feeling-it/201707/11–keys-mastering-difficult-conversations

SixFlex. (n.d.). Supervising dynamically: using ACT in BCBA supervision. [Webinar]. Retrieved from https://www.sixflextraining.com/act-for-bcba-supervisors

Wright, P. I. (2019). Cultural Humility in the Practice of Applied Behavior Analysis. *Behavior Analysis in Practice* 12, 805–809. https://libproxy.library.unt.edu:2147/10.1007/s40617–019–00343–8

Chapter 12

AppliedBehaviorAnalysisEdu.org. (2020). How to avoid burnout in a field known for high turnover. Retrieved from https://www.appliedbehavioranalysisedu.org/how-to-avoid-burnout-in-a-field-known-for-high-turnover/

Belker., L. B., McCormick, J., & Topchik, G. S. (2012). The first-time manager. HarperCollins Publishing: New York, NY.

Donovan, C. (2019–2020). Fried. The burnout podcast. [Podcast].

Druskis, M. (2019). Battling BCBA burnout. bSci21.org. Retrieved from https://bsci21.org/battling-bcba-burnout/

Giannicola, R. (2019). How to manager people older than you. [Youtube]. Retrieved from https://www.youtube.com/watch?time_continue=322&v=ltE-jKsSZC-Y&feature=emb_logo

Gould, E. (2018). Adding ACT to your toolkit as a behavior analysts. Praxis. Retrieved from https://www.praxiscet.com/blog/adding-act-your-toolkit-behavior-analyst/

Kelly, A. (2019). Dr. Tyra Sellers on supervision & stopping to smell the roses. Behaviorbabe. [Podcast]. Retrieved from https://anchor.fm/behaviorbabe/episodes/Dr--Tyra-Sellers-on-Supervision--Stopping-to-Smell-the-Roses-e4m6h4

Kelly, A. (2020). Shane spiker on self care and saying no. Behaviorbabe. [Podcast]. Retrieved from https://anchor.fm/behaviorbabe/episodes/Shane-Spiker-on-Self-Care-and-Saying-No-e2v0pk

https://www.mindtools.com/pages/article/newTCS_08.htm. Burnout self test: Checking yourself for burnout.

Murray, S. (2020). The executive education courses teaching how to beat burnout. The Financial Times Limited. Retrieved from https://www-ft-com.ezp-prod1.hul.harvard.edu/content/914e1cfa-8173–11ea-b6e9–a94cffd1d9bf

Pillay, S. (2015). How to protect your employees from burnout. Fast Company. Retrieved from https://www.fastcompany.com/3047192/how-to-protect-your-employees-from-burnout

Provenzano, A. (2016). How to prevent burnout. Center for Primary Care at Harvard Medical Center. [Podcast]. Retrieved from https://primarycare.hms.harvard.edu/multimedia/how-prevent-burnout

RAND. (2017). Burnout, American style. Harvard Medical School. Retrieved from https://hms.harvard.edu/news/burnout-american-style

Sidman, M. (1989). Coercion and its fallout. Authors Cooperative: Boston, MA.

Sundberg, D. (2016). The high cost of stress in the ABA workplace. bSci21.org. Retrieved from https://bsci21.org/the-high-cost-of-stress-in-the-aba-workplace/

Ting, D. Y. (2019). Emerging solutions for administrative burden and provider burnout. Harvard Medical School. Retrieved from https://executiveeducation.hms.harvard.edu/industry-insights/emerging-solutions-administrative-burden-provider-burnout

Wei, M. (2018). Self-care for the caregiver. Harvard Health Publishing. Retrieved from https://www.health.harvard.edu/blog/self-care-for-the-caregiver-2018101715003

Chapter 13

"An Ode to the Giants to Which We Stand Upon Their Shoulders"

Association for Behavior Analysts International. (n.d.). Barbara C. Etzel. ABAI. Retrieved from https://www.abainternational.org/constituents/bios/barbaraetzel.aspx

Cataldo, M. F. (2013). A tribute to Don Baer. *Journal of Applied Behavior Analysis, 35*(3), 319–321. https://doi.org/10.1901/jaba.2002.35–319

Cicoria, M. (2019). In memoriam: Chuck Merbitz. Behavioral Observations Podcast. [Podcast]. Retrieved from https://behavioralobservations.com/in-memoriam-chuck-merbitz/

Favell, J. E. (2013). In memoriam: Ellen P. Reese 1926–1997. *Journal of Applied Behavior Analysis, 30*(4), 723–724. https://doi.org/10.1901/jaba.1997.30–723

Ghezzi, P. M. (2013). In memoriam: Sidney W. Bijou. *Journal of Applied Behavior Analysis, 43*, 175–179. https://doi.org/10.1901/jaba.2010.43–175

Johnson, C., Iversen, I., Kenyon, P., Holth, P., & de Souza, D. G. (2020). Murray Sidman: a life of giving. *Journal of Applied Behavior Analysis*. Advance online publication. **https://doi.org/10.1002/jaba.718**

Palmer, D. (2000). In memoriam: Ullin Place: 1924–2000. *The Behavior Analyst, 23*, 95–98.

Risley, T. (2013). Montrose M. Wolf (1935–2004). *Journal of Applied Behavior Analysis, 38*(2), 279–287. https://doi.org/10.1901/jaba.2005.165-04

Sherman, J. A. (2013). Todd R. Risley: friend, colleague, visionary. *Journal of Applied Behavior Analysis, 41*, 7–10. https://doi.org/10.1901/jaba.2008.41-7

Soreth, M. E., Dickson, C. A., & Terry, C. M. (2017). In memoriam: Maria del Rosario Ruiz (1959–2017). *The Behavior Analyst, 40*, 553–557.

Women in Academia Report. (2012). In memoriam: Betty Hart, 1927–2012. *WIAReport*. Retrieved from https://www.wiareport.com/2012/10/in-memoriam-betty-hart-1927-2012/

...and to all of the other influential powerhouses who bestowed upon us the legacy to facilitate meaningful differences for others. Thank you.

Name Index

A
Addington, J., 44
Adzhyan, P., 17, 87, 204
Ajayi, L., 212
Ala'i, S., 35
Ala'i-Rosales, S., 43, 58, 74, 77, 81, 183, 198
Algiraigri, A. H., 88
Aljadeff-Abergel, E., 21
Allen, D. A., 143, 148, 149
Allen, K. A., 173
Allen, T. D., 29
Almeida, D., 44
Alvero, A. M., 85
Anderson, D. C., 76
Anderson, K., 150
Andriessen, J.H.E., 62
Angell, A. M., 77
Angelou, M., 164
Ansoff, H. I., 130
Arnold, K. M., 169
Arya, K., 120
Attoe, C., 169
Augilar, A., 49
Austin, J., 85, 176
Axe, J. B., 118, 127

B
Baer, D. M., 56, 131, 202, 203
Bailey, J. S., 18, 19, 21, 67, 74, 75, 86, 90, 100, 110, 112, 124, 151, 165, 237
Baker, J. C., 31, 241
Baldwin, R., 164
Bandura, A. B., 103, 104
Barnes-Holmes, D., 3
Baron-Cohen, S., 171
Barrera, I., 50, 51, 55, 119, 128, 167, 171, 174
Bassey, M. O., 46
Baumgart, D., 15
Beamer, K., 182
Beaulieu, L., 44
Beavers, G., 124
Becerra, L. A., 238
Beene, N., 44
Behavior Analyst Certification Board, 4, 6, 17, 19, 43, 45, 46, 47, 57, 69, 70, 71, 74, 75, 81, 83, 86, 90, 96, 97, 109, 150, 165, 198, 218, 227
Belisle, J., 84
Benner, G. J., 141
Bensing, J., 182
Bertone, M. P., 62
Betancourt, J. R., 45
Biagi, S., 82
Bickman, L., 182
Biegel, G. M., 243
Binder, C., 56, 110
Bird, Z., 76

317

Blank, R., 53
Blell, Z., 183
Bond, F. W., 244
Booker Ammah, B., 169
Bowe, M., 124
Boyd, W., 252
Bozosi, J., 181
Brache, A. P., 75, 110
Bradshaw, M. L., 6
Brantley, J., 243
Briggs, A. M., 37, 238
Britton, L. N., 76
Brodhead, M. T., 44, 45, 90, 179
Brown, B., 176
Brown, K. W., 243
Brown, K. W., 244
Buchanan, F., 148
Buckner, M. O., 143
Burch, M., 18, 19, 67, 74, 75, 90, 112, 151, 165, 237
Burda, A., 55
Burke, M. G., 243
Burnfield, J. L., 152
Buzan, T., 96

C
Cain, J.M., 46
Callahan, K., 165
Campbell, R. L., 141
Campbell, T. L., 179
Capps, L., 171
Carnegie, D., 165
Carr, E. G., 140
Carr, J. E., 37, 70, 89, 124, 127, 128, 129, 173, 238
Carrillo, J. E., 45
Carter, C., 177
Carter, C. M., 140
Casella, S. E., 124
Catagnus, R. M., 45
Catania, A. C., 97
Cernius, A., 45, 170
Chamorro-Premuzic, T., 51
Cicoria, M. J., 76
Cihon, T. M., 44
Claessens, B. J. C., 143
Clark, H. B., 5, 15
Cloke, K., 178
Cobb, A. T., 216
Cohen-Cole, S. A., 179
Cole, M. L., 21

Coll, R. K., 147
Collis, B., 120
Conners, B., 44, 76, 77
Contreras, B. P., 238
Cooper J. O., 78
Coulehan, J. L., 179
Courtney, M., 142
Cox, D. J., 90
Cox, S., 45, 179
Coyne, L., 183
Critchfield, T. S., 168, 180, 181
Cross, T. L.. 45, 47
Crowell, C. R., 76
Curbow, B. A., 182
Curry, S. M., 20

D
Daniels, A. C., 21, 86, 100, 110, 124
Danso, R., 45
Daunic, A. P., 120
Davis, D. E., 46
Day-Vines, N. L., 169
Deck, M. D., 6
Denton, E. A., 53
Derksen, F., 182
Devries, S., 243
Di Blasi, Z., 182
Dialmy, A., 51
DiAngelo, R., 49
DiGennaro Reed, F. D., 21
Dishon-Berkovits, M., 52
Ditzian, K., 124
Dixon, M. R., 84
Dixon, S., 141
Dobres, J., 165, 168
Donahoe, J. W., 117, 118
Dounavi, K., 109, 242
Dreyfus, H. L., 98, 99
Dreyfus, S. E., 98, 99
Driscoll, S., 124
Duarte, J., 44, 76
Dunning, D., 98, 199
Dunst, C. J., 15
Dutton, M., 164
Dye, L., 243

E
Early, E., 109, 242
Eby, L. T., 29, 33
Edmondson, A., 120
Edzard, E., 182

Ehrlich, R. J., 89
Elacqua, T. C., 142
Ellis, J. E., 241
Ensher, E. A., 107, 108
Epstein, R., 179
Ervin, N. E., 109, 141, 235

F
Fabrizio, M., 58
Fallon, L. M., 44
Fawcett, S. B., 198
Fennell, B., 109, 242
Ferris, K., 58
Ficklin, S., 45
Field, S., 45
Fields, S., 182
Finch, D. J., 164
Fiorenza, E. S., 204
Fischer, A. J., 81, 197, 209, 226
Fisher-Borne, M., 46
Fisher, D. J., 67
Fisher, W. W., 84
Fiske, K. E., 181
Flaxman, P., 244
Fogarty, L. A., 182
Fong, E. H., 45, 54, 77
Foxx, R. M., 165, 168
Frank, G., 77
Friman, P. C., 172
Frith, U., 171
Fukuzawa, R., 143

G
Gannon, J. M., 6
Garden, R. E., 56
Garza, K. L., 70, 73, 75, 81, 82, 84, 88, 89
Gehrman, C., 124
Geiger, K. A., 129, 173
Gelb, S. L., 141
George, D., 141
Georgiou, A., 182
Gerenser, J., 165, 168
Ghandi, I., 250
Gianoumis, S., 84
Gibney, A., 141
Gilbert, T. F., 110
Gilligan, K. T., 84
Ginsberg, M. B., 46
Glago, K., 121
Glenn, S. S., 241
Goetz, J. L., 182

Goldberg, J., 242
Goldsmith, J., 178
Goldsmith, T. R., 127
Gong, J., 141
Gonzalez, J., 141
Gould, E., 183
Gran-Moravec, M. B., 141
Gravina, N. E., 20, 86, 89
Green, A. R., 45
Green, C. W., 4, 69
Greene, B. F., 85
Grenny, J., 219
Grow, L. L., 129
Grundon, G. S., 84
Guiton, G., 141

H
Häfner, A., 142, 144
Hagen, K. K., 21
Hahn, M., 51
Hall, B., 143
Hall, E. T., 51
Hall, L. J., 84
Hall, T., 51
Halsey, W. F., 116
Hamby, C. W., 15
Hamilton, L. K., 164
Handelsman, J. B., 182
Hanson, M. J., 50, 51, 58
Hantula, D. A., 76, 110
Hardeman, R. R., 55
Harkness, E., 182
Harper-Briggs, A. M., 142
Harper, M., 6
Harrower, J. K., 140
Hayes, S. C., 181, 243, 244
Heen, S., 169, 221
Heine, S. J., 47
Heinicke, M. R., 31, 241
Henley, A. J., 21
Henrich, J., 47
Heron T. E., 78
Heward, W. L., 78
Hindle, T., 152
Hinds, P., 51
Hodges, D., 147
Hoffman, D. E., 55
Hogan, L. K., 258
Hojat, M., 182
Holth, P., 117
Hood, J. H., 152

Hook, J. N., 46, 56
Howard, J. S., 180
Howard, R., 242
Hughes, C. M., 141, 142
Hughey, A. W., 243

I
Irwin, C. L., 118
Iwata, B. A., 124

J
Jabur, Z., 169
Jackson, S. E., 242
Jackson, T. W., 148, 149
Jacobs, S., 152
Jay, A. A., 127
Jenkins, S. R., 142
Jerome, J., 84
Jex, S. M., 142
Johnson, A., 44, 76
Johnson, D. A., 21, 124
Johnston, J. M., 70
Joho, H., 143
Jones, E. A., 140

K
Kang, S., 45
Kaplan, H., 84
Karnes, A., 85
Karver, M. S., 182
Kaya, H. A., 141, 143
Kaya, N. A., 141
Kazemi, E., 17, 18, 87, 89, 165, 168, 177, 204
Keating, A., 42
Kelly, W. E., 145
Kierkegaard, S., 28
Killen, C. C., 15
Kim, N., 49
King, A., 124
Kleijnen, J., 182
Klein, J., 181
Koegel, L. K., 140
Koegel, R. L., 140
Kolb, S. M., 121
Könings, K. D., 14
Kornack, J., 45, 56, 170
Koslowsky, M., 52
Kozhimannil, K. B., 55
Kramer, L., 50, 51, 55, 119, 128, 167, 171, 174
Kruger, J., 98, 199
Kruse, K., 88
Küçük, L., 141

L
LaFrance, D. L., 165, 168, 171, 179
Lagro-Janssen, A., 182
Lau, R. S., 216
Lavelle, M., 169
Leach, D. J., 152
LeBlanc, L. A., 3, 4, 8, 18, 31, 34, 35, 37, 70, 75, 88, 120, 121, 127, 128, 129, 142, 143, 145, 146, 149, 150, 151, 152, 165, 173, 180, 185, 197, 214, 216, 241, 244
Lee, H. Y., 45
Lee, J., 21
Lee, S. C., 124
Leiter, M. P., 241
Leland, W., 56
Lencioni, P., 152
Lerman, D. C., 123, 124
Leslie, A. M., 171
Levenson, V., 242
Lewis, A., 51, 58
Lewis, R. D., 51, 58
Lipschultz, J. L., 124
Lloyd, J., 244
Lochman, J. E., 120
Lockspeiser, T. M., 141
Lorah, E. R., 85
Lown, B. A., 182, 183
Luck, K., 123
Luiselli, J. K., 3, 81, 84, 197, 209, 226
Lushington, K., 148
Lutz, H., 181
Lutzker, J. R., 85
Lynch, E. W., 50, 51, 58

M
MacDonald, R. P., 74, 198
Maeshiro, T., 143
Mager, R. F., 72, 76, 79, 80, 87
Majdalany, L., 89, 124
Mandela, N., 234
Manz, C. C., 108
Marchese, N. V., 180
Margaryan, A., 120
Marks, K., 44, 76
Martin, S. L., 46
Marulanda-Carter, L., 148, 149
Maslach, C., 241, 242
Mastropieri, M. A., 121
Mathisen, D., 89, 124
Mattaini, M. A., 44
Mawhinney, T. C., 110

Mazerolle, S. M., 141, 235
McCarthy, J., 100
McDonnell, K., 182
McGee, H. M., 70, 124
McGimsey, J. F., 85
McKay, J., 243
McKay, M., 243
McMillan, R., 219
McMurray, S., 164
McMurtry, K., 148
McQuaid, R., 164
Medina, E. M., 55
Mehta, Z., 55
Mellichamp, F. H., 70
Meyer, E., 146
Meyer, P., 140
Miles, N. I., 84
Miller, K. L., 43, 54, 58, 77
Mills, S., 242
Miltenberger, R. G., 143
Mirsky, J., 58
Mitroff, I. I., 53
Mohtady, H. A., 14
Molinsky, A., 51
Moon, K., 21
Moore, N., 141
Moryaga, M. G., 243
Mueller, J. R., 142
Murphy, F., 141
Murphy, S. E., 107, 108
Murriky, R., 44, 76
Muzio, E., 67

N
Narayana Murthy, N. R., 69
Nelson, J. R., 141
Nigro-Bruzzi, D., 84, 86
Norenzayan, A. 47
Norris, J. M., 182
Nosik, M. R., 37, 89, 142, 143, 146, 150, 151, 152, 165, 244

O
O'Keeffe, B. V., 44
O'Sullivan, S., 141
Oberst, V., 142
Oppenheimer, E., 14
Osmani, M., 164
Osnes, P. G., 81
Owen, J., 46

P
Pace, G.M., 84
Pagana, K. D., 142, 143, 144, 145
Pallos, A. O., 141
Palmer, D. C., 117, 118
Pant, B., 51, 52, 54, 147
Park, J. A., 21
Parnell, A. M., 85
Parsons, M. B., 4, 69, 83, 84, 85, 87, 88, 89
Pastrana, S., 180
Patterson, B., 181
Patterson, K., 178, 219, 221
Patton, B., 169, 221
Pearson, K., 197
Peck, C. A., 15
Persicke, A., 45, 170
Peters, V., 67
Peterson, S. M., 21
Phelan, S. H., 118
Pheri, T., 141
Pignata, S., 148
Pinneker, L., 142
Plantiveau, C., 109, 242
Pope, C., 84
Post, S. G., 181
Proulx, K., 243

Q
Quigley, S. P., 45, 90

R
Raetz, P. B., 128
Ramirez, J., 45
Re Cruz, A., 43, 58, 77
Rehfeldt, R. A., 86
Reid, D. H., 4, 5, 22, 69, 83
Rhodes, J. E., 29
Rice, B., 17, 87, 204
Richard, A., 164
Richard, E., 20
Riehl, C. J., 45
Riess, H., 182
Rimes, K., 169
Risley, T. R., 56, 131, 202, 203
Roe, R. A., 143
Rogelberg, S. J., 152
Rogers, P. D., 243
Rollyson, J. H., 83
Romero, A. B., 84
Rosales-Ruiz, J., 183

Rosales, R., 86
Roscoe, E. M., 84
Rose, J., 242
Rose, J., 242
Rosenberg, N. E., 75
Rowsey, K. E., 84
Roysircar, G., 58
Rummler, G. A., 75, 110
Rutte, C. G., 143
Ryan, R. M., 244

S
Salter, T., 6
Sarokoff, R.A., 84
Sasson, J. R., 85
Sautter, R. A., 127
Schaefer-Whitby, P., 85
Schaufeli, W. B., 241
Schenk, Y. A., 70
Schulz, B., 166
Schwartz, I. S., 75
Schweitzer, R. D., 205
Schwiebert, V. L., 6
Scott, J., 123
Scott, P., 6
Scruggs, T. E., 121
Seiverling, L., 84
Sellers, T. P., 4, 20, 22, 36, 70, 74, 82, 88, 124, 128, 142, 150, 151, 152, 197, 198, 214, 216, 238, 241
Shapiro, S. L., 243
Sherwali, S., 169
Shirey, M., 243
Shook, G. L., 70
Siers, B. P., 89
Sigman, M., 171
Sigurdsson, S., 124
Silva, D., 242
Simms, H. P., 108
Simon-Thomas, E., 182
Simpson, E., 142
Sinclair, S., 182
Siroky, L. M., 76
Skinner, B. F., 78, 101, 117, 118, 166
Sleeper, J. D., 142
Sleiman, A. A., 20
Slipp, S., 53
Sloan, J., 148
Smilkstein, G., 179
Smith, S. W., 120
Snyder, W. M., 56, 112, 237

Solomon, O., 77
Somerfield, M. R., 182
Sparkman, C., 180
Stansal, E., 141
Steen, S., 169
Stock, A., 142
Stockwell, A., 56
Stokes, T. F., 81
Stone, D., 169, 178, 221
Stone, K., 86
Strain, L. A., 89, 124
Ströhle, S., 142
Stuart, S. K., 121
Sturmey, P., 84, 86
Sugai, G., 44, 54
Sundberg, D. M., 45, 49
Sundberg, D., 21
Super, D. E., 235
Svenson, L. W., 141
Switzler A., 219

T
Tagg, R., 82
Tanaka, S. 45
Tanz, J., 124
Tarbox, J., 44, 45, 183
Tarzian, A. J., 55
Taylor, B. A., 37, 165, 168, 179, 182, 183, 184, 185, 244
Theisen, B., 76
Thomas, E. R., 67
Thomas, S. P., 243
Thompson, L., 242
Thrasher, A. B., 141, 235
Trivette, C. M., 15
Tucker, D., 143
Tulgan, B., 164, 165
Turner, L. B., 81, 82, 197, 205, 209, 226

U
Utsey, S. O., 46

V
Valentino, A. V., 4, 20, 22, 70, 82, 88, 142, 150, 151, 152, 197, 214
Valk, R., 51
Van Eerde, W., 142, 143
van Merriënboer, J. J. G., 14
Verburg, R. M., 62
Virués-Ortega, J., 109, 242
W

Walker, S. E., 141, 235
Wang, Y., 45
Ward-Horner, J., 86
Wardle, E. A., 243
Warr, P. B., 152
Warzak, W. J., 173
Watson, S. L., 181
Weinkauf, S. M., 81
Weiss, M. J., 165, 168
Wenger, E. C., 56, 112, 237
Wentz, F. H., 67, 164
Westby, C., 55
Whinney, I. R., 179
White, B. J., 143
White, L. T., 51, 52
Whitehead, D., 49
Whittaker, J., 35
Wiesbeck, A. B., 169
Wilder, D. A., 84, 124

Wine, B., 21, 89
Wingard, J. R., 182
Wiskirchen, R. R., 21, 70
Witham, M., 205
Wlodkowski, R. J., 46
Wolf, M. M., 56, 131, 169, 202, 203
Wolf, S. J., 141, 143
Wood, J. C., 243
Worthington Jr, E. L., 46
Wright, P. I., 46, 77

Z

Zarcone, J., 44
Zegwaard, K., 147
Zehner, M., 164
Zeigler, J., 76
Zeug, N., 81
Zoder-Martell, K. A., 45

Subject Index

A

Accountability, 7, 9, 31, 166, 175–176, 178, 219, 239

Agenda, 15, 17, 25, 94, 101, 146, 148, 150–153, 158–159, 182, 207, 220, 231

Agreement, 16, 22, 94, 101, 111, 118, 131, 140, 187
   Disagreement, 56, 169, 186, 194, 216

Assessment
   Competency, 199, 220
   Initial, 17, 72, 81–82, 110, 124, 133, 153, 182, 185
   On-going, 82–83, 89, 144, 146, 180, 214, 235
   Performance, 4, 68, 72, 85, 106, 143, 200, 227
   Community of practice, 47, 56–57, 62
   Functional behavior assessment, 72, 73, 135
   Preference, 47, 78–79, 92
   Sample, 155–156, 186–194, 242
   Social validity, 204, 216

Assumptions, 20, 47–50, 74, 97, 99, 144, 170–173, 214, 233

Authority 47–51, 59, 99, 101, 120, 216, 230

B

Behavioral skills training, (BST) 71, 83–84, 86, 88, 93, 103, 151, 168, 220, 231

Bias, 47, 50, 80, 106, 198, 213, 216, 220–221, 233

C

Career planning, 8, 11, 20, 31–36, 38–39, 43, 97, 107–109, 112, 142, 153, 165, 177, 195, 225–226, 234–246

Caseload, 6, 72, 109–110, 141–142, 154, 235–236, 239,

Code, 6, 19, 45, 46, 48, 71, 72, 74, 75, 81, 83, 86, 90, 96, 97, 165, 198, 227

Collaboration, 1, 9, 11, 14–18, 21–24, 43–44, 52–54, 126–128, 145, 154–158, 165–166, 171, 174, 178–183, 198, 201, 210, 222, 236–237, 240–241, 248, 251, 253

Commitment, 9, 16, 19–22, 26, 52–56, 77, 140, 145, 153, 162–164, 192, 216, 222–227, 237–239, 252–257

Communication skills, 4, 51, 55, 166, 171, 176, 181, 185, 202

Community of practice, 35, 46, 56, 62, 63, 112, 146, 237–239, 243, 247, 255

Compassion (compassionate), 37, 55, 86, 164, 169, 172, 180, 182–185, 193, 214, 218, 221, 251, 254

Competence, 2, 9–10, 37, 42, 45–46, 54–57, 69–73, 76–82, 85, 90–92, 97–99, 112, 123, 181–182, 246, 251, 253

325

Competency-based, 83, 89, 197, 202, 220, 251
Compromise 165–166, 172–173, 175, 177, 181–182, 218, 239
Contract, 17, 73, 91, 158, 226
Culture, 2, 18, 42–44, 46–59, 62–65, 77–78, 82, 90, 96, 99, 104– 107, 120–121, 134, 146–147, 168– 173, 176–178, 181, 187, 192– 194, 198, 201, 203–204, 213, 216, 221, 227, 230–231, 233, 246, 251
CulturalCompetency, 55, 57
  Humility, 46, 56, 77
  Identity, 20, 44, 49, 50, 214
  Learning history, 33, 39, 43, 46–48, 118, 239
  Responsiveness, 43, 45, 47, 50, 54– 57, 62– 65, 77, 82, 84, 86–87, 102, 111, 113, 167, 237
Curriculum, 70– 72, 74–76, 83, 89, 109, 180, 183, 198, 220

D
Demonstration, 75–76, 79–81, 83– 86, 88, 91, 97, 127, 142, 165, 171, 179, 184, 199, 227, 233
Dilemma ,74, 89–90, 117, 241, 248
Diversity, 19, 31, 42–48, 54–56, 59, 63–64, 77, 106, 167, 170, 194, 201, 210, 216, 231, 236, 251

E
Email, 17, 25, 145, 148–150, 157, 162, 166, 169, 189, 223
Emotions, 20, 52–53, 95, 124, 147, 167, 169, 171–172, 181–190, 194, 219, 229, 242–243, 247
Empathy, 23, 42, 165, 172, 179, 182–184
Ethics, 4, 18, 27–29, 35, 43, 46, 57, 59, 70–75, 84, 89–90, 96, 117, 150, 169, 179, 198, 206, 209–210, 227, 237, 241, 248, 252, 261, 257
Expectations, 1, 16–23, 35–36, 50, 52–53, 88, 109, 126–127, 146, 150–151, 176, 192, 198, 209, 213, 225, 227
Expert (experts), 29, 31–32, 63, 67, 69, 78, 90, 96, 97, 98, 99, 100–103, 105, 109, 112, 113, 165, 167, 179, 180, 237, 251

F
Feedback
  Corrective, 21, 30, 35, 50, 79, 86, 88–89, 106–107, 209, 224, 236

  Diagnostic, 230–231
  Performance, 87, 89, 150, 154
    Positive, 36, 189, 209, 224
    Supportive, 20, 24– 26, 35, 63, 87–88, 183, 207–208, 214–215, 217
  Job duties, 5, 8, 18–19, 21–22, 55, 76–77, 83, 84, 94–95, 98, 103, 125, 151–152, 158–160, 169–170, 184, 190, 194, 201, 204–206, 210, 213, 216, 220–227, 237
  Bi-directional, 15– 17, 27, 203
Flexibility, 10, 52, 90, 145, 154, 166, 170, 174–175, 187, 194, 229

G
Generalization, 81, 83, 89, 98, 125, 132, 160, 173–174, 199–200, 202

H
Harmonizing, 43, 51, 173–177
Hierarchy, 43–44, 52, 59, 72, 177–178, 194

I
Identity, 20, 44–46, 48–50, 55, 58, 62, 65, 120, 169, 203, 205, 214, 217, 253
Imitating, 29, 33, 39
Imitation, 2, 35, 97, 105, 179, 220
Influences, 2, 6–8, 14, 29, 30, 31, 32, 33, 34, 35, 37, 39, 55, 100, 124, 141, 164, 165, 166, 173, 176, 180, 233, 251,
Influencer, 28–30, 33–34, 37–39, 257
Instruction, 30, 50–51, 69, 71–75, 79, 81, 84– 86, 90, 105, 107, 113, 174–175, 186, 200, 202, 216, 220, 231
Integrity, 80, 93, 126, 159, 166, 175–176, 178, 181
Interpersonal skills, 4–8, 17–18, 29, 32, 51, 68, 83, 90, 106–109, 133, 150–152, 164– 166, 171–185, 193–195, 202, 206, 227, 235, 242, 244, 251

J
Job model, 75–76

L
Love, 36, 207, 239, 248–249, 254, 258

M
Manager 6, 27, 36, 118, 177–178, 256
Mastery
  Evaluation, 70, 75, 81, 83, 85–86, 88, 91, 98, 170, 199–200, 252

Criteria, 72, 76, 78–80, 84, 220, 231
Meeting, 5, 8–9, 16–18, 20, 52–54, 65, 73, 77, 109–111, 115, 118, 126, 133, 143–147, 150–152, 160–169, 177–178, 201–207, 214–217, 220–232
Mentee, 6, 8, 34, 36, 39, 54, 178, 250
Mentor, 1–3, 5–8, 11–13, 28–40, 45, 50, 54–57, 61, 98, 108, 112, 129, 176–178, 181, 231, 236–238, 240–247, 252–257
Mentor tree, 31–36, 38–39, 237, 257
Mentorship, 7, 29, 36–37, 112
Mind sweep, 148
Miscommunication, 36
Multi-disciplinary, 165–166, 177–179, 194

N

Noticing, 119, 121–122, 166, 169–171, 176, 192, 219, 224–225, 244, 246
Narration (narratives), 98–99, 103, 105, 201–202
Nuanced noticing,

O

Objectives, 72, 158, 159, 210
Observance (spiritual), 110
Observational learning, 29, 86, 101, 103, 105, 113, 226,
Observing, 8, 32, 36, 56, 67, 83, 98, 101–109, 112, 114, 152–153, 159, 167, 172, 206, 225,
Observation, 48, 52, 54, 78, 82, 89, 97, 102, 105, 121, 123, 129, 148, 150, 153, 156, 160, 184, 200–202, 205, 207, 216, 220, 231–232, 241
Organization, 15, 18–19, 29, 37, 46, 54, 56–57, 62–64, 68–69, 71, 73, 75, 83, 86, 99, 110, 118, 124, 145–147, 149, 152, 156, 171, 186, 240, 242–243, 246
Organizational skills, 90, 133, 140–141, 148, 164, 178, 202, 232, 236, 238, 245, 251
Organizational time management (OTM), 140–142, 147, 153–154

P

Peer workplace relationships, 177–178
Performance
    Assessment, 72, 76, 78, 81–82, 134, 200, 219–220, 224, 230–232
    Management, 4, 6, 7, 9, 21–22, 26, 30, 69, 79, 123–125, 131, 142, 144, 177–178, 201–202, 213, 218, 226
    Monitoring, 5, 71, 83–89, 97–103, 105–109, 112–114, 150, 152–153, 169, 171, 199, 209, 236
Performance Diagnostic Checklist-Human Services, 89, 124
Perspective
    Taking, 50, 61, 166, 171–174, 176–179, 182–183, 185, 193, 257
    Others (different), 19–20, 35–36, 51, 53, 87, 128, 174, 204, 215, 221
Privilege, 49, 54, 60
Pro-con analysis
Problem solving, 4, 10–15, 30, 34, 47–49, 54, 67, 73–75, 83, 90, 105, 109, 116–147, 151–154, 171, 174–175, 178, 192, 195, 202, 206, 211, 214–219, 221–222, 226–230, 236, 240–242, 248, 252–256

R

Rationale, 26, 43, 74, 83–84, 89, 100, 118, 170, 188, 191, 204, 220
Rehearsal, 26, 85–86, 151
Religion (religious), 43– 46, 48–49, 53, 55, 58, 60, 65, 77, 96, 175, 192, 204, 217, 233
Roles, 5–8, 13, 17, 36, 166, 192, 199,

S

Scope, 17, 54, 71, 73, 76, 79–81, 90, 110, 179, 185, 195, 216–219, 230, 232, 235
Self-care, 40, 108–112, 218, 243–246
Self-evaluation, 77, 97, 98, 104–114, 133, 153, 171–172, 184, 186, 198, 219–224, 232
Self-management, 67, 96–98, 107–114, 120, 153–154, 215, 218, 222–223, 232, 246, 251, 256
Self-observation (observing), 8, 32, 36, 56, 67, 83, 98, 101–109, 112, 114, 152–153, 159, 167, 172, 206, 225
Self-reflection, 11, 18, 22–24, 29–39, 42–47, 50–51, 54–60, 63–67, 75–79, 82, 100, 102–107, 110–113, 123–126, 132–133, 153–154, 164, 166, 169–171, 178, 180, 183–188, 202–203, 206, 213, 219–226–233, 244–248, 251–252, 257
Self-reporting, 82, 106, 114, 203, 218
Skill hierarchies, 72
Soft skills, 67, 164
Solutions, 8, 49, 74, 75, 116–117, 121, 125–131, 135–136, 147, 149, 174, 184, 204, 217, 253
Spiritual, 53, 110, 243
Sponsor, 1, 6–8, 12–13, 33–34

Supervised fieldwork experience, 67, 76, 97, 234, 236, 238, 240
Supervisor, 1–158, 164–184, 196–247, 250–258
Supervisory
　Activities, 1, 12, 16, 22, 30, 58, 60–65, 76, 108, 198, 199, 207, 225, 232,
　Practices, 43, 62, 77, 197–199, 201–207, 212, 214–215, 219–220, 231–233, 251,
　Relationship, 1, 10–24, 28, 36, 42–47, 49–50, 53, 60, 71, 74, 82, 88, 106–108, 132, 166, 176–177, 197, 203–207, 212–231, 250–251

T

Task list, 69–71, 73–76, 83, 90, 109, 165, 198, 210, 223, 251

Task management,143–145, 149
Therapeutic, 15, 18, 37, 68, 79, 83–84, 90, 102, 106, 109, 122, 132, 134, 164, 166, 177, 180–183, 185–186, 191–192, 196, 198, 200, 202, 206
Time management, 5, 68, 73, 83, 133, 140–164, 178, 227, 229, 232, 236, 244–246, 251
Transactional, 9–10

V

Values, 4–8, 14–16, 20, 23, 29–42, 47–52, 56–64, 71, 84, 99–102, 118, 147, 154, 158, 164, 173, 174, 175, 177, 179–180, 187, 190, 201, 203, 207–208, 216, 220–227, 230, 237–241, 253, 256–257